820 PEC 3 WKS   £11.99

Also by the same authors

Literary Terms and Criticism (third edition)
Practical Criticism
The Student's Guide to Writing
How to Study a Shakespeare Play (second edition)

Also by John Peck

Dickens: David Copperfield and Hard Times (New Casebook)
Eliot: Middlemarch (New Casebook)
How to Study a Novel (second edition)
How to Study a Poet (second edition)
Maritime Fiction
War, the Army and Victorian Literature

Also by Martin Coyle

Shakespeare: Hamlet (New Casebook)
Shakespeare: The Merchant of Venice (New Casebook)

All published by Palgrave

A *Brief History* of
English
Literature

John Peck and Martin Coyle

palgrave

First published 2002 by
PALGRAVE
Houndmills, Basingstoke, Hampshire RG21 6XS and
175 Fifth Avenue, New York, N.Y. 10010
Companies and representatives throughout the world

PALGRAVE is the new global academic imprint of
St. Martin's Press LLC Scholarly and Reference Division and
Palgrave Publishers Ltd (formerly Macmillan Press Ltd).

ISBN 0–333–79176–2 hardback
ISBN 0–333–79177–0 paperback

This book is printed on paper suitable for recycling and made from fully managed and sustained forest sources.

A catalogue record for this book is available from the British Library.

Library of Congress Cataloging-in-Publication Data

Peck, John, 1947–
   A brief history of English literature / John Peck and Martin Coyle.
       p. cm.
   Includes bibliographical references and index.
   ISBN 0–333–79176–2 (cloth) – ISBN 0–333–79177–0 (pbk.)
       1. English literature–History and criticism. I. Coyle, Martin. II. Title.
   PR83 .P43 2002   820.9–dc21   2001055701

10   9   8   7   6   5   4   3   2   1
11   10   09   08   07   06   05   04   03   02

Printed in Great Britain by Mackays of Chatham

Contents

Preface

In planning this brief history of English literature, we had three principal objectives in mind. First, and most importantly, we wanted to write an account that a reader with a degree of stamina might wish to read as a whole. It is sometimes the case that histories of literature, aiming for encyclopaedic inclusiveness, overwhelm the reader with detail; almost inevitably, it becomes impossible to see the shape or direction of the material being discussed. What we have sought to present is a clear narrative, with a strong backbone of argument. Not every reader, of course, will want to read the entire book, but we hope that a sense of clarity, design and focus will be apparent to a reader dipping into any of the individual chapters.

Our second objective was to produce a history of literature in which poems, plays, novels and other forms of writing are seen as functioning in history. There was a time when literary critics regarded history as merely a background against which works of literature operated. In the case of a writer such as Dickens, for example, it was as if there was a reality of Victorian London and Dickens's works were seen as reflecting that tangible world. In recent years, however, literary critics have begun to emphasise a rather different view of how literary texts play a role in the society that produced them, and how they intervene in their culture, rather than just passively reflecting values and ideas. Some histories of literature still continue to provide the reader with an outline of events that never really connects with the discussion of the literary works produced in a period or with the texts themselves. We have sought to offer a more dynamic analysis of the interactions between texts and the era of their production.

In adopting this approach, we have been influenced by ways of thinking that characterise literary studies in universities at the present time. This leads us on to the third objective that we had in mind

in writing this book. It is sometimes the case that histories of literature, as works of assessment and reflection, embody the critical views
of an earlier generation of scholars; they contain a great deal of
extremely useful information, but in terms of their informing
assumptions they look to the past rather than to the present. In the
pages that follow we have endeavoured to provide an account that
reflects current thinking in the subject. It may be, therefore, that students of literature, at school, college or university, will find this book
rather more directly relevant than some more traditional histories of
literature. But we also hope that general readers will have their interest caught by the critical ideas that inform the volume.

A sense of what one hoped to achieve in a book is, of course,
always qualified by an awareness of the shortcomings of the finished
product. The major problem we had to face in every chapter was a
practical one: this is a *brief* history of English literature. Many authors
who might have been included were not included, simply because
there was no room for them. But that is not the full explanation. At
an early stage in thinking about the book, we decided that it was
going to prove a lot more useful to provide a reasonably full account
of a few writers in a period rather than offering long lists of names,
or, at the best, a couple of sentences about dozens of writers. The
authors discussed are those that most people would expect to feature
in a history of English literature, but also some of the lesser-known
figures students are likely to encounter on a degree course. By the end
of a chapter in this book we might have failed to mention the particular writer a reader wants to know about, but the chapter should
have provided a framework of understanding for other authors writing at that time.

We can probably be forgiven for our failure to discuss a large number of writers; our omission of certain writers, however, may seem to
some unforgivable. This takes us on to the ideological problems
involved in writing a history of English literature. We have endeavoured to write a balanced account, but the account we have produced inevitably reflects our individual preferences, our cultural
backgrounds and the structures of the system in which we work.
There might have been a time when historians of literature felt they
were offering a true and complete story, but today we are all aware of

the difficulties involved in such a project. These difficulties are apparent in the three words 'history', 'English' and 'literature'.

'History' might be regarded as a narrative that we impose on the past; if, as in the pages that follow, an attempt is made to construct a clear and coherent narrative, then the story that is being told is, inevitably, far too simple and often untrue. By 'English' we mean, for the purposes of this book, works written in Britain rather than works written in English; 'English' is, therefore, stretched to include works written in Scotland, Wales and Ireland (as well as a number of texts from America and the Commonwealth that have been influential in Britain). The inclusion of Irish authors might suggest colonial arrogance in subsuming the works of another nation into Britain's cultural heritage, but that leads us on to a more general problem. There was a time when historians of literature offered a kind of celebration of Englishness; at its best this was nostalgic and amiable, but at its worst it could be insular and arrogant, fuelled by an assumption that everyone shared a common inheritance and that everyone would share a common view of that inheritance. In writing about English literature today, however, we cannot avoid being aware of the many minefields involved in writing about concepts such as England, Englishness and the English tradition.

'Literature' is possibly an even more difficult term, and it is certainly in respect of literature that the practical and ideological difficulties confronted in writing this book have overlapped most. For many years, 'literature' has implied a certain canon of books; these are the books that people considered worthy of study, whereas there are others that they ignored or dismissed. As times change, the canon of approved texts changes; in recent years, for example, literary critics have started to pay far more attention to women writers who have up until now remained unread and even unpublished. In writing this book we have endeavoured to embrace such currents of change without losing sight of or displacing the traditional canon of authors. These are the writers that continue to be the most frequently taught in schools, colleges and universities; they are also the writers that students are expected to know about and that more radical accounts of literary history define themselves against.

Some will judge our approach to be too conventional – a case could be made, for example, for paying more attention to popular forms of literature, such as crime fiction and children's books, as well as scientific, historical and political texts, and far more attention to authors from Scotland, Wales, Ireland and the Commonwealth – but in order to complete the compact and useful book we set out to produce we have had to strike a balance between an infinite variety of texts and possible approaches. We are aware, then, of the problems that lie at the very heart of the conception and execution of this book. At the same time, because a sense of these issues has been at the front of our minds while we have been writing, we would like to believe that this has energised the narrative we have constructed and the choices we have made. In brief, we hope that this book, both in terms of the range of authors considered and in the way that these authors are discussed, will strike the reader as a fresh and stimulating new history of English literature.

John Peck and Martin Coyle
Cardiff University

Acknowledgements

The authors and publisher wish to thank the following for permission to use copyright material:

Anvil Press Poetry, for the extract from 'Warming Her Pearls' from *Selling Manhattan* by Carol Anne Duffy (Anvil Press Poetry, 1987); reproduced by permission of Anvil Press Poetry.

Faber & Faber Ltd, for the extract from 'Cuba' from *Why Brownlee Left* by Paul Muldoon; reproduced by permission of Faber & Faber Ltd.

Farrar, Straus and Giroux, LLC, for the extract from 'Cuba' from *Collected Poems: 1968–1998* by Paul Muldoon, copyright © Paul Muldoon 2001; reproduced by permission of Farrar, Straus and Giroux, LLC.

Every effort has been made to trace all the copyright-holders, but if any have been inadvertently overlooked the publisher will be pleased to make the necessary arrangements at the first opportunity.

1 Old English Literature

Beowulf

Sometime between the year 700 and the year 900 the epic poem *Beowulf* was composed. It tells the story of Beowulf, a warrior prince from Geatland in Sweden, who goes to Denmark and kills the monster Grendel that has been attacking the great hall of Heorot, built by Hrothgar, the Danish king. Grendel's mother, a water-monster, takes revenge by carrying off one of the king's noblemen, but Beowulf dives into the underwater lair in which she lives and kills her too. Returning home, in due course Beowulf becomes king of the Geats. The poem then moves forward about fifty years. Beowulf's kingdom is ravaged by a fire-breathing dragon that burns the royal hall. Beowulf, aided by a young warrior, Wiglaf, manages to kill the dragon, but is fatally wounded in the course of the fight. He pronounces Wiglaf his successor. The poem ends with Beowulf's burial and a premonition that the kingdom will be overthrown.

When we read a Shakespeare play, a poem by Wordsworth, a novel by Dickens or most other works of literature, we usually know something about the author, something about the period in which the text was written, and, perhaps most importantly, a good deal about the conventions of the genre that the writer has chosen to employ. It is such knowledge that helps us arrive at conclusions about the meaning and significance of a literary text. In the case of *Beowulf* and other Old English texts, however, we have relatively little information to work from. We know nothing about the author of *Beowulf*, or who transcribed the poem (which exists in just one fire-damaged manuscript copy). Nor do we know the exact date of its composition. There are, too, other problems we face: not only is the text historically remote from us, involving ideas that seem to

1

bear little resemblance to our own ways of thinking, but it is written in a form of English (sometimes called Anglo-Saxon) that displays little similarity to English today:

> Ða com of more   under misthleoþum
> Grendel gongan.   Godes yrre bær.
> Mynte se manscaða   manna cynnes
> sumne besyrwan   in sele þam hean.
>
> [Then from the moor under the misty slopes
> Grendel came advancing. God's anger he bore.
> The evil ravager intended to ensnare one
> Of the race of men in that lofty hall.]
> (*Beowulf*, ll. 710–23)

Not surprisingly, most readers are initially going to feel at a loss in trying to establish any kind of hold on *Beowulf*, even if they encounter it in a modern translation.

As is often the case with a literary text, however, a good deal can actually be determined from a summary alone. Structurally, *Beowulf* is built around three fights. Each of these involves a battle between those who live in the royal hall and a monster; the monsters, it is clear, are dangerous, unpredictable and incomprehensible forces that threaten the security and well-being of those in power and the way of life they represent. When we have established this much, we have detected a pattern that is specific to the Anglo-Saxon period, but which also echoes down through the whole history of English literature. Time and time again, literary texts deal with an idea, or perhaps just an ideal, of order. There is a sense of a well-run state or a settled social order, and, for the individual, a feeling of existing within a secure framework; this might be the comfort provided by religious faith, the certainty associated with marriage and economic security, or perhaps just the happiness associated with being in love. In *Beowulf*, a sense of security is linked with the presence of the great hall as a place of refuge and shared values; it is a place for feasting and celebrations, providing warmth and protection against whatever might be encountered in the darkness outside. Over and over again, however, literary texts focus on threats to such a feeling of security and confidence. There might be an external threat, such as a monster or a foreign enemy, or an enemy within, such as the rebellious noblemen in Shakespeare's history plays who challenge the authority of the king. But the threat might be more insidious; for example, in a number of eighteenth-century works, there is a sense of chaos overtaking society, and the collapse of established standards of behaviour. Or there might be, as is the case in nineteenth- and twentieth-century texts, a feeling that the world is moving so fast and changing so much that all steady points of reference have been lost. In short, we can say that the most common pattern in literature is one which sets the desire for order and coherence against an awareness of the inevitability of disorder, confusion and chaos.

This recurrent pattern is, as might be expected, felt and expressed in different ways as time passes, the world changes, and people face fresh problems. In the four or five hundred years before the Norman Conquest of 1066, England was a sparsely populated country that had experienced successive waves of invasion. The invaders included, between the late fourth and seventh centuries, different groups of Germanic peoples whose descendants came to be known as Anglo-Saxons. The history of this period is documented by the historian Bede (673–735), a monk whose Latin work *Historia Ecclesiastica Gentis Anglorum* (*Ecclesiastical History of the English People*), completed in 731, provides us with much information about the era. Thanks to Bede and a number of other sources, we know a surprising amount about the government, administration and legal system of Anglo-Saxon England. The impression is of sophisticated mechanisms of social organisation, primarily associated with the king. But the monasteries were also important in this period, in particular as centres of learning; the texts in Old English that survive from Anglo-Saxon England were all probably transcribed during the tenth century by monks, who were both establishing and preserving a native literary culture. Government, administration, a legal system and a literary culture: all these things suggest a regulated, well-ordered and peaceful society. But this is only half of the story.

In 55 BC Julius Caesar landed in Ancient Britain. Colonisation and Christianity followed as Britain became part of the Roman empire. In 407, however, the Roman legions were withdrawn to protect Rome. Meanwhile, Picts invaded Roman Britain from the north. The British king Vortigern, like Hrothgar in Beowulf, sent for help, but the Jutes who came soon seized Kent. Other pagan Germanic tribes, the Angles and the Saxons, followed, driving the Celtic inhabitants into Wales, Cornwall and Scotland. The result was that a number of Anglo-Saxon kingdoms emerged, and, almost inevitably, this led to military conflicts and shifts in power. During the sixth century, it is important to note, a process of re-Christianization began, but in 793 a further period of disruption was initiated, with Viking incursions that led, amongst other things, to the sacking of monasteries.

What becomes apparent from this brief summary is that in this period we are dealing with what is essentially a warrior society, a tribal community with people clustering together in forts and settlements, fearing attack. The land is farmed, and there are centres of learning, but the overwhelming fact of life is invasion by outside forces. It should be becoming clear by now that Beowulf reflects and expresses the anxieties that would have dominated such a society, but it also offers a sense of something positive. We know from historical evidence that Anglo-Saxon kings such as Alfred (871–99), Athelstan (924–39) and Edgar (959–75) contributed to the forging of one people and one state. This is echoed in the way that Beowulf, as a warrior, stands as a beacon, unselfishly going to the aid of the Danish king and then later, as king, facing the dragon in order to win its treasure for his people. And although he dies without an heir, there is also something impressive in the way that the baton of command is passed on to his successor, Wiglaf. The period before the Norman Conquest used to be referred to as the Dark Ages; the term clearly does less than justice to the achievements of this society, but, if we do accept the description for a moment, we can see how a poem such as Beowulf, with its ideas about leadership and loyalty, stands as a source of illumination in the darkness.

What we also need to recognise in our critical thinking about the text, however, is that a poem like Beowulf, engaging as it does with contemporary concerns, does not spring from nowhere. Beowulf belongs to a tradition of heroic or epic poetry; this tradition can, indirectly, be traced back to Ancient Greece and Rome, and there is something of a parallel tradition in Scandinavian culture. An epic is a long narrative poem (there are 3,182 lines in Beowulf) that operates on a grand scale and deals with the deeds of warriors and heroes. As is the case in *Beowulf*, while focusing on the deeds of one man, epic poems also interlace the main narrative with myths, legends, folk tales and past events; there is a composite effect, the entire culture of a country cohering in the overall experience of the poem. *Beowulf* belongs to the category of oral, as opposed to literary, epic, in that it was composed to be recited; it was only written down much later as the poem that exists today, possibly as late as the year 1000.

In epic poetry there are always threats and dangers that have to be confronted, but even more important is the sense of a hero who embodies the qualities that are necessary in a leader in a hierarchical, masculine, warrior society; the text is concerned with the qualities that constitute his greatness, the poem as a whole amounting to what we might regard as a debate about the nature of the society and its values. Central to those values is the idea of loyalty to one's lord: the lord provides food and protection in return for service. He is the 'giver of rings' and rewards, and the worst of crimes is betrayal. This impression of a larger purpose in *Beowulf* is underlined by the inclusion of decorous speeches and passages of moral reflection, and by the inclusion of quasi-historical stories of feuds and wars that echo and support the main narrative. The fact that *Beowulf* exists within a literary tradition is also apparent in its use of the alliterative metre, which is the most notable feature of Germanic prosody; in *Beowulf*, as in Old English verse generally, there are two or three alliterating stressed syllables in each line, reflecting the pattern of speech and so appropriate for oral performance. The effect is to link the two halves of the lines into rich interweaving patterns of vocabulary and idea. The convention may seem strange to the modern reader, but in its distinctive way it serves, like rhyme, to reinforce the poem's theme of the search for order in a chaotic world.

In the end, however, it is not a simple opposition of the desire for order and the threat of disorder that makes *Beowulf* such an impressive poem. Indeed, if we talk about order versus disorder, the formulation might suggest that literature can convey a static and unchanging ideal of order. But this is never the case. A society is always in a state of transformation. One thing that we know about the period in which *Beowulf* was produced, and which is apparent in the poem, is that pagan values were in conflict with, and gradually yielding to, Christian values. Values and ideas are constantly changing, but the most interesting works of literature are those produced at times when there is a dramatic shift between one way of thinking about the world and a new way of thinking about the world. The most obvious example of this is found in the works of Shakespeare, who was writing at a time when the medieval world was becoming the modern world; part of Shakespeare's greatness, many would argue, is explicable in terms of how his poems and plays reflect this enormous historical shift. In the case of *Beowulf*, we can sense a conflict between a way of looking at the world that focuses on the heroic warrior and, on the other hand, a Christian perspective that is not entirely at ease with some of the implications of the warrior code.

Even from a non-Christian perspective, there are reservations that might be voiced about the heroic life; for example, joy, youth and life will inevitably give way to sorrow, age and death, leaving past glories behind. And there can seem something slightly absurd about the quest for glory; even the greatest warriors might strike us as vainglorious, and as fighting for no real purpose. But the added level of complication that can be sensed in *Beowulf* is the possibility that there is a Christian critique of heroism implicit in the poem. We may well feel that values in the poem that are remote from modern experience – things such as blood-feuds and the celebration of violence in what professes to be an elite society – combine rather awkwardly with a story that might be regarded as a Christian allegory of salvation. In the same way, we may be struck by a gap between the Christian elements in the poem and the stress on a pagan fate that determines human affairs. It is, however, just such instability and indeterminacy in the poem that makes it an important work of literature, for this is how texts function in the period of their production, expressing conflicting and contradictory impulses in a culture. The kind of complication that characterises the best-known literary texts is a matter of how they not only reflect but are also the embodiment of a society caught up in a process of transformation and alteration, of collapse and formation, and of old and new ideas.

'The Seafarer' and 'The Wanderer'

The validity of this last point should become clearer if we look more closely at the Anglo-Saxon period. At such a historical remove, our natural impulse is to think of a static, perhaps rather primitive society. *Beowulf* might actually add to our misconceptions as, superficially, it conveys an impression of a society that is characterised exclusively by violent fighting. We need to understand, however, that the three monster fights in the poem conform to conventional story-types, rather than being in any way a realistic expression of lived experience. We also need to understand that England at this time was certainly not a primitive society. As we noted above, the Anglo-Saxon period runs from the invasion of Celtic England by Angles, Saxons and Jutes in the first half of the fifth century up till the conquest by William of Normandy in 1066. Around the seventh century, there was a period of conversion to Christianity. Even today, we still recollect saints from this period, such as Aidan, and monastic foundations such as Lindisfarne, Whitby and Ripon. The existence of religious orders, the architecture associated with the monasteries, and the scholarship of these learned communities all provide an idea of the sophistication of the society at this time.

In the reign of King Alfred, who lived from 849 to 899, we encounter a leader who established the English navy, reformed the army, promoted education and saved England from the Vikings. During Alfred's reign and in the years that followed, England also developed a system of national and local government, law courts and mechanisms for tax-collecting, all of which were amongst the most advanced in Europe. It is often pointed out that the *Domesday Book* (1086), a great survey of England commissioned by William I, would have been impossible to produce without the Anglo-Saxons' flair for administration. The *Domesday Book* is one of our sources of information about this period. Another is the *Anglo-Saxon Chronicle*, a history of England from the Roman invasion to 1154. It is, in fact, a series of chronicles written in Old English, and begun in the ninth century during the reign of Alfred. As with everything else that informs us about the period, the *Anglo-Saxon Chronicle* conveys an impression of a complex society, a society that was constantly changing, adjusting and evolving.

It is not surprising, therefore, that a vigorous vernacular literary culture existed, although we will never know the precise extent of this because so much has been lost or destroyed over the course of time. In addition to *Beowulf* – and there were probably other epic poems – there was a considerable body of lyric poetry. Most of this is anonymous, although we do know the names of two poets, Caedmon and Cynewulf (the former from the seventh, the latter from the early ninth century), both of whom focused on biblical and religious themes. Probably the most accomplished of the lyric poems is 'The Seafarer'. The poem falls into two halves, and features a speaker who relates the hardship and isolation of a life at sea, at the same time lamenting the life on shore he has known and of which he is no longer a part; there is, paradoxically, both nostalgia for the past and a deep love of the sea despite its loneliness:

> Þær ic ne gehyrde   butan hlimman sæ,
> iscaldne wæg.   Hwilum ylfete song
> dyde ic me to gomene,   ganetes hleoþor,
> ond huilpan sweg   fore hleahtor wera;
> mæw singende   fore medodrince.
>
> [There I heard nothing but the roar of the sea,
> the ice-cold wave. Sometimes, the song of the swan
> I had for entertainment, the cry of the gannet
> and the sound of the curlew in place of the laughter of men;
> the seagull singing instead of mead-drinking.]
>
> ('The Seafarer', ll. 18–22)

In the second half of the poem, however, the speaker moves in a fresh direction, imposing a homiletic gloss upon his recollections. He presents the call to a life at sea as a call to the Christian path of self-denial; life on earth is transient and insignificant in comparison with the idea of heaven.

Just as the tradition of epic poetry informs *Beowulf*, so 'The Seafarer' also draws upon a poetic tradition. Like the other notable Old English poem 'The Wanderer', 'The Seafarer' is an elegy: a complaint in the first-person on the hardships of separation and isolation. In 'The Wanderer' the speaker is an exile seeking a new lord and the protection of a new mead-hall. The poem conveys his sense of despair and fatigue; like 'The Seafarer', the poem employs sea imagery to convey an idea of exile and loneliness, of a hostile universe where human beings are battered and tossed about aimlessly. In the second part of 'The Wanderer', the poet moves from his personal experience to the general experience of humanity, how people suffer in a world characterised by war and the ravages of time. As in 'The Seafarer', comfort can only be derived from the hope of heaven.

Both poems are elegies dwelling on death, war and loss. By the mid-seventeenth century the term elegy starts to acquire a more precise meaning, as a poem of mourning for an individual or a lament over a specific tragic event. In 'The Seafarer', as in 'The Wanderer', however, there is a more general perception of life as a struggle, though one rooted in the poem's culture: the speaker is bereft of friends, but also lordless and so forced to live alone in exile from the comforts and protection of the mead-hall. As in 'The Wanderer', fate and the elements seem to conspire against the solitary human figure. Like *Beowulf*, 'The Seafarer' conveys a characteristic Anglo-Saxon view of life. There is a sense of melancholy that suffuses the poem, a sense of life as difficult and subject to suffering; and that, however much one displays strength, courage and fortitude, time passes and one grows old. There is, too, a stoical resignation in the poem; the kind of response, in fact, that one might expect to encounter in a hard, masculine culture. But the surprise is the delicacy and skill with which the poem reflects upon these matters. Such a poem can still communicate with us today because of the manner in which it articulates both the pain of existence and the search for comfort.

What 'The Seafarer' offers by the end is the idea of religious consolation. It would, however, be a minor, and forgettable, poem if it just offered a Christian answer. The subtlety of the poem lies in the manner in which it is caught between its awareness, on the one hand, of the pain of life and, on the other, its awareness of the comfort provided by religion. But not just that: there is almost a sense in the poem that religion is in some respects a self-consciously adopted literary and ethical frame that is imposed upon an intransigent reality. As with *Beowulf*, we see again how a substantial work of literature is always the product of a society in the throes of change. Indeed, the way in which 'The Seafarer' falls so clearly into two sections suggests two ways of looking at the world that do not quite combine together. It is this ambivalence of the poem, how it looks to both the past and the future as the poet moves between an old, pagan, view of life as a perpetual battle and new values associated with Christianity, that gives it its resonance.

Battle Poems and 'The Dream of the Rood'

Wherever we turn in Old English poetry we encounter two impulses: on the one hand there is a sense of a harsh and unforgiving world, and on the other a sense of Christian explanation and consolation. But there is always the impression that the message of religion is being articulated by poets who are conscious of this as a new discourse, even a kind of novelty. There is also the point that our perception of the literature of the Anglo-Saxon period has been affected by the fact that the poems that have survived were transcribed by monks, and therefore endorse the argument for Christianity. This is less true of some poems than of others. There are, for example, battle pieces, commemorative historical poems, such as 'The Battle of Brunanburh', a poem relating how Athelstan defeated the invading forces of the Scots and Vikings. A poem such as this conceives of life as an armed struggle, and, although composed towards the end of the Anglo-Saxon period, clings on to the traditional values of strength and courage. Much the same is true of 'The Battle of Maldon', which deals with a heroic, yet disastrous, attempt to oppose Viking raiders.

By contrast, other Old English poems are overtly Christian. 'The Dream of the Rood' is a dream-vision poem in which the poet encounters a speaking Rood or Cross. The Cross tells us about the Crucifixion, how it was buried, and then resurrected as a Christian symbol. It thus acts as both a witness to the Crucifixion and as a parallel to Christ, who throughout the poem is compared to a heroic warrior.

Rod wæs ic aræred.   Ahof ic ricne Cyning,
heofona Hlaford;   hyldan me ne dorste.
Þurhdrifan hi me mid deorcan næglum;   on me syndon þa dolg gesiene,
opene inwidhlemmas;   ne dorste ic hira nænigum sceððan.
Bysmeredon hie unc butu ætgædere.   Eall ic wæs mid blode bestemed
begoten of þæs guman sidan   siððan he hæfde his gast onsended.

[I was reared as a cross. I raised up the powerful King,
the Lord of heaven; I did not dare to bend.
They pierced me with dark nails; on me are the wounds to be seen,
the open wounds of malice. I did not dare injure any of them.
They mocked us both together. I was drenched with blood
poured out from that man's side after he had sent forth his spirit.]

('The Dream of the Rood', ll. 44–9)

The poem ends with a religious homily in which the poet speaks of his contrition and hope for heaven. One impulse, after registering the ingenuity of the basic conceit of the text, might be to think that this is an almost formulaic poem of Christian comfort. But what is so powerful is the way in which the speaking Cross conveys a sense of its humiliation and terror as it was chopped down and made into a device for the punishment of Christ as criminal. This is, however, more than compensated for by the pride the Cross now feels in the part it has played in the Christian story. This move from a negative to a positive feeling is echoed in the poet's response at the end of the poem; a life of torment and sin is transformed into a message of hope for the future. But what matters in the poem just as much as this vision of heavenly reward and triumph is the powerful immediacy of the sense of pain and the agony of death.

The sophistication of the conceit in 'The Dream of the Rood', together with the assurance of the poet's craftsmanship, return us again to a fundamental contradiction of the Anglo-Saxon period: that this was a harsh, military society, a society where survival to old age was rare, but also a society in which art and learning were valued, and which had created complex systems of social organisation. In such a culture, however, we are always going to be aware of the fragility of the hold of order over the potential for disaster in life. The sense of a changing and unstable world is evident in the very language out of which Old English literature was created. A language is a culture's most precious possession, for it is the existence of a language that enables a nation to express its own distinctive identity. If a country's language is destroyed or suppressed, something of that nation has been lost forever. Old English is a language that was dominant in England for several hundred years, but it was also a language that was imported, evolved and then, at least in its original form, died.

Old English Language

Old English was spoken and written in various forms for eight centuries, from the fifth to the twelfth century. It derived from several
West German dialects that were brought to Britain by invaders. For
literary and administrative purposes it always existed alongside
Latin. None the less, by the eighth century it was spoken throughout
England, albeit existing in four distinguishable main forms. And it
never stood still; by the ninth century, for example, there was a considerable Danish impact upon the language. But even if it was an
imported and constantly changing language, it was also an extremely powerful and successful language. No other country in Europe at
this time could claim such a strong vernacular literary culture. From
our modern perspective, however, we cannot help but be aware of
the existence of the older Celtic languages that Old English drove out.
Old English was, in this sense, the language of the usurper, the invader and the interloper.

And as we look at Old English in a longer time scale, we become
more and more aware of a curious combination of strength and vulnerability in it as a language. It displaced the Celtic languages, but
with the Norman Conquest the strongest vernacular written culture
in Europe would be overwhelmed and absorbed by another language, or, to be more precise, by two languages. After the Conquest,
English became subordinated to Latin as the language of learning and
religion, while Norman French became the language of the court and
government. Old English continued to be used in some monastic
centres through to the twelfth century, but, existing in isolation, a
standard literary form of the language could not be sustained (Old
English, however, it should be noted, still underlies much of the
everyday vocabulary of modern English, for example in words such
as 'brēad' for bread). After 1066, therefore, we enter a rather strange
period of hiatus in the history of English literature; for almost two
hundred years there is very little in the way of a vernacular literature.
When English texts begin to appear again, there is, for one thing, a
shift from alliterative measure to rhymed metrical verse. From the
point of view of the modern reader, however, the more significant
development is that the new post-Conquest English texts are written

in a form of English that, unlike the Germanic-influenced texts of the Old English period, clearly has some continuity with the English we use today. In a word, Old English is itself replaced by Middle English.

When we look at Old English literature in this broader time scale, we can see a degree of vulnerability in the language. Its strength and success during the period of its ascendancy cannot be denied, but there is always something that pulls in the opposite direction. In literary texts that deal repeatedly with wars, violence and incursions there is perhaps an awareness that it is only wars, violence and incursions that have brought Old English as a language into existence in the first place. In addition, the various dialects of Old English emphasise how the country remained divided. After the Norman Conquest, by contrast, there is a growing recognition of the English language, albeit a language that has evolved and changed considerably (with Old English, French and Latin words integrated into it), as the native tongue that can be asserted against the Norman French of the new invader. The sense, however faint, of Old English as the language that has displaced the older Celtic languages contributes to the dominant elegiac mood in Anglo-Saxon literature: that life is transient, that time passes, and that all earthly things, including perhaps language itself, are insubstantial and subject to change.

2 Middle English Literature

From the Norman Conquest to Chaucer

Everyone has heard of the Norman Conquest of 1066, but why should this be so? Why do we know about this invasion, whereas we might have only a vague awareness that England had experienced earlier waves of invasion and settlement? Some historians argue that the event is not all that significant, that we remember it simply as the last of a series of conquests of lowland Britain, and that it did not have all that much impact on the country. It is true that England, both strategically and culturally, became much more closely involved with France, but possibly the essential pattern of life did not change all that much because of the Battle of Hastings. Other historians, however, would take a different line (in the process, dismissing the alternative view as a rather suspect form of English nationalism). They would argue that it is not the Norman invasion itself that is significant, but how it affected the country, a new political and civil culture emerging, not immediately, but over the course of two to three hundred years. In terms of literature, we see the long-term consequences of the Conquest in the years between 1350 and 1400, one of the great periods of English literature, when Geoffrey Chaucer, William Langland, the *Gawain* poet and others were all writing.

Initially, it is clear, the Conquest can be regarded as a military and political imposition upon England; indeed, until the accession of King John in 1199, England effectively became an extension of northern France. The idea of Saxon subjection is embodied in a change that affected the status of the general mass of the English population; the Germanic concept of the 'churl', the ordinary free man, farming his land but owing personal military service to his lord or king, was replaced by the convention of the feudal villein, bound to the land

and excluded from military service. But there was always resistance to the new system and its new laws. In 1215 the barons forced King John to sign the Magna Carta, the charter ensuring rights against arbitrary imprisonment. And in 1381 there was the Peasants' Revolt, a popular uprising. Interestingly, the revolt took place in the middle of the period when English literature was flourishing again. Both the rebellion and the revival of literary activity can be regarded as signs of a new independence, of a throwing-off of shackles. The developments in the second half of the fourteenth century should not, however, be interpreted simply as a reaction against the Norman French; it is more a matter of old and new impulses (including new impulses in the economic life of the country that developed in the years after the plague, referred to as the Black Death, that swept across Europe in the second half of the 1340s) intermingling, and in the process producing something different. As is the case again and again in English literature, it is the clash of old and new, and how they spark together to start a creative fire, that demands our attention.

This is evident not just in the literature of the Middle Ages but also in the language out of which the literature was created. As a result of the Conquest, Norman French in official and literary contexts, although, obviously, not in the day-to-day life of the majority of the population, drives out Old English. There is very little English literature produced at the highest levels in the period between 1066 and 1200. What exists reflects a small and insular literary culture in retreat, helpless in the face of a continental flowering of the arts that reveals a wide variety of forms and styles. The span from 1066 to as late as 1350 is, indeed, sometimes designated as the Anglo-Norman period, because the non-Latin literature of that period was written mainly in Anglo-Norman, the French dialect of the new ruling class in England. A confident vernacular literature only really re-emerges after 1350, when English increasingly became the language spoken by those who had formerly used French. This fact was given official recognition in 1362, when English became a permitted language in law courts, and in 1385, when English became widely used in schools. But it was a form of English markedly different from Old English, with many lexical loans from French and the deletion of many Germanic words. This reordering of the language once more suggests how the thought processes of two cultures are likely to be found combining in the works of Chaucer and his contemporaries.

A sense of activity and intermingling is very clear in the variety of Middle English literature. In broad terms, we can sum up Old English literature as belonging to a heroic age or heroic culture. 'Heroic' means concerned with epic battles and legendary or mythic figures; when applied to literature, it suggests a formal and dignified poetry dealing with grand concepts such as fate, honour, vengeance and social duty. Its key theme is loyalty to one's lord, or to God. It is a good deal more difficult, however, to find one word that sums up Middle English literature, because the voices we hear are extremely diverse. There are some courtly romances, that call upon continental influences, but there is also a flourishing strain of popular and domestic literature. There are, in addition, religious dramas, prose narratives, lyric poems, and, perhaps most intriguingly, a number of important works by women writers. Amidst such variety, however, it is consistently clear that the English language itself is changing, and that a recognisably different kind of social order is coming into being:

> Ther was also a Nonne, a PRIORESSE,
> That of hir smylyng was ful symple and coy;
> Hire gretteste ooth was but by Seinte Loy;
> And she was cleped madame Eglentyne.   [named]
> Ful weel she soong the service dyvyne,   [sang]
> Entuned in hir nose ful semely,   [chanted]
> And Frenssh she spak ful faire and fetishly,   [elegantly]
> After the scole of Stratford atte Bowe.   [school]
>   (General Prologue, ll. 118–25)

These lines from Chaucer's *General Prologue* (c.1395) describe the Prioress, one of the pilgrims journeying towards Canterbury to visit the shrine of Saint Thomas à Becket, who had been murdered by Henry II. We still need to translate the lines, but many of the words are close to their modern form. Interestingly, the extract focuses on the Prioress's voice, on how she sang and where she learned to speak French. It is as if Chaucer is aware that, in a society in a state of flux, it is the language that people use that provides possibly the clearest indication of the nature of that society and how it is changing.

Julian of Norwich, Margery Kempe, *Sir Gawain and the Green Knight*

The evolution of something new is most apparent in some of the developments in religious writing in Middle English literature. One immediate consequence of the Norman Conquest was a greater degree of control over the English Church. Under Lanfranc, appointed Archbishop of Canterbury in 1070, the church was reorganised, with greater unity and discipline; essentially, the English Church was integrated into the Norman mainstream. Those serving in the church naturally accepted this new dispensation, but in the second half of the fourteenth century we start to hear some different voices. Julian of Norwich's prose work *Sixteen Revelations of Divine Love* describes her visionary experiences. The text exists in two versions, the latter produced after twenty years of meditation. The intervening years, from 1373 to 1393 (the exact dates are disputed), in which Julian was a recluse, were a period of strictly enforced religious orthodoxy across the country. Possibly there was a feeling that the increasing use of English, in the law, education and literature, constituted a threat to the established religious order which still used Latin for all its services. In this context, we can point to the followers of John Wycliffe, who, defying authority, embarked upon a translation of the Bible from Latin into English in the 1380s. In a not dissimilar fashion, one of the most distinctive features of Julian's account of her visionary experiences is the way in which she conveys theological and, indeed, personal concerns in a direct manner to a lay readership through her use of imagery:

> In this sodenly I saw the rede blode trekelyn downe fro under the garlande, hote and freisly and ryth plenteously, as it were in the time of his passion that the garlande of thornys was pressid on his blissid hede, ryte so both God and man, the same that sufferd thus for me. I conceived treuly and mightily that it was himselfe shewed it me without ony mene.
> (*Sixteen Revelations of Divine Love*, ch. 4)

There is, for the most part, nothing all that radical about what Julian has to say, although her idea of Jesus as Mother is tantalising. What really matters in *Revelations of Divine Love*, however, is the manner in which things are said, a manner that speaks to the public beyond the

walls of the religious retreat and without the insistent mediation of a
priest.

Margery Kempe, another prose mystic writer, is a far more controversial figure. She was a married woman, with fourteen children,
who, as she relates in the *Book of Margery Kempe* (*c.*1432–8), had visions
of meeting Christ, in effect claiming a kind of sacred link to God that
was not controlled or sanctioned by the church. The fact of her illit-
eracy (the book, in which she speaks about herself in the third person, was dictated to an amanuensis) is significant; it suggests how her
autobiography is a work that speaks for those who have not previously had a voice, and who are outside the recognised social and
political boundaries:

> On þe next day sche was browt in-to þe Erchebishopys Chapel, & þer
> comyn many of þe Erchebischopys meny, despisyng hir, callyng hir
> 'looler' & 'heretyke', & sworyn many an horrybyl othe þat sche xulde be
> brent.

> [On the next day she was brought into the Archbishop's Chapel, and
> there came many of the Archbishop's meinie, despising her, calling her
> 'loller' and 'heretic', and swore many a horrible oath that she should be
> burnt.]

(*Book of Margery Kempe*, ch. 52)

The fact that she is a woman and mother is also relevant; she speaks
on behalf of those who have contributed a great deal, but who have
received no recognition from the church. The book focuses on the
way she feels she has been on spiritual trial, separated from the
church which has persecuted her. What we see in the *Book of Margery
Kempe* is something repeatedly encountered in English literature: suddenly the voice of the disenfranchised is heard, speaking in a new
way and from a new position. The appearance of such a voice represents and conveys an idea of a broader change in the society of the
day. In the case of Margery Kempe, this woman's intervention is not
an isolated gesture, but symptomatic of how a whole range of new
voices are beginning to be heard in English society starting in the second half of the fourteenth century, in particular as the oral culture
intersects with the developing written culture. As such, the *Book of
Margery Kempe*, while interesting as an account of one woman's life,

also demonstrates how literary texts are closely bound up with the changing history of the country.

One way in which this is particularly apparent in the Middle Ages is in the increasing diversity of literary texts, reflecting an increasingly diverse world. Margery Kempe, we may well feel, writes from the sidelines. At the heart of educated culture, by contrast, is *Sir Gawain and the Green Knight* (c.1375). Even here, though, diversity is apparent. The *Gawain* poet (we do not know his identity, but it is generally assumed that he wrote three other poems, *Cleanness, Patience* and *Pearl*) was writing at the same time as Chaucer, that is the late fourteenth century, but writes in the dialect of the Northwest Midlands, which is unlike, and far less accessible to the modern reader than, Chaucer's English:

> Þ is kyng lay at Camylot vpon Krystmasse,
> With mony luflych lorde, ledez of þe best,
> Rekenly of þe Rounde Table alle þo rich breþer,
> With rych reuel oryzt and rechles merþes.

> [The king was at Camelot at Christmas
> With many a handsome lord, the best of knights,
> fittingly all the noble brotherhood of the Round Table
> with appropriately splendid revels and carefree pleasures.]
> (*Sir Gawain and the Green Knight*, Fitt 1, ll. 37–40)

The existence of a confident vernacular poem in a distinctive regional variation of English attests to the varied energy of English culture at this time. But what is also clear about *Sir Gawain and the Green Knight* is that it owes a very large debt to French literary culture. The poem is a romance, a form that resembles epic in that it features a hero's adventures, but at the heart of romance is the idea of the single hero on a quest. Perhaps the crucial difference between epic and romance, however, is that epic is concerned with tribal warfare (as in the Anglo-Saxon period), whereas romance stresses the importance of a chivalric code. It is a kind of mirror, albeit a distorting mirror, in which a member of the court sees an exaggerated version of the trials he might have to face in life, and is also presented with a model of how he should conduct himself.

Medieval romance developed as a narrative verse form in twelfth-century France, and then spread to other parts of Europe. What we are confronted with in *Sir Gawain and the Green Knight*, therefore, is a poem that owes everything to the impact of French literary models on England. At the same time, though, there is a contradictory impulse in the poem, provided in no small measure by its use of an English setting and the English language. It also calls upon the myth and tradition of Arthur. Gawain is the most favoured knight at Arthur's court (this story, if not the poem, is from the period before later writers introduced the character of Launcelot). Stories about Arthur can be traced back as far as the ninth century. It is, however, Geoffrey of Monmouth in his *History of the Kings of Britain*, written in Latin in the twelfth century, who turns Arthur into a romantic king aided by the magic of Merlin. The Round Table makes its first appearance about 1154, in Wace's *Roman de Brut*. The Arthurian story then continued to be developed in France; so much so that, when Thomas Malory wrote *Morte D'Arthur* in the fifteenth century, he worked mainly from French sources and French ideas. The appeal of the Arthur story in England was that it provided a focus for discussing the state of the nation and expressing an emergent nationalism. At the time of *Sir Gawain and the Green Knight* this was still an embryonic nationalism, as the dominant impulse, politically, culturally and in terms of religion, was still to see England as part of something larger that transcended the nation state – as part, that is, of a knightly or chivalric code sworn to defend the Christian faith and to restore Jerusalem (which had been recaptured by the Saracens in 1187) to Christian rule. In the violent background to much English literature of the Middle Ages are the Crusades, for which the mythic legend of Arthur provided an exemplary model of military conduct.

Sir Gawain and the Green Knight begins at Camelot. On New Year's Day, a figure enters the king's hall; he is gigantic in stature and green in colour. The Green Knight issues a challenge: a member of the Round Table will be permitted to strike a blow with the massive axe the Green Knight carries, but in a year's time this challenger must seek out the Green Knight and receive a blow in return. Arthur accepts the challenge, but Gawain begs for the contest to be his. He strikes his opponent's head off, but the Green Knight picks up his severed head, reiterates his challenge and departs. A year later, seeking the Knight, Gawain stops at a lord's castle, and, during a further test, embarks upon an amorous relationship with his hostess. He then finds the Green Knight, who, after mocking Gawain, delivers nothing more than a light blow on Gawain's neck. The Green Knight then reveals himself as the lord of the castle; he contrived the challenge and the amorous temptation to test Gawain's integrity as a knight. Gawain passed the test in every respect except one; he had kept silent about a gift of a magical green lace belt that he received from the lady.

There are various layers of meaning in *Sir Gawain*, but the major issue is the testing of a knight; it is a double test, of Gawain's courage and honour. In *Beowulf* the hero is tested in conflict, but in *Sir Gawain and the Green Knight* the hero is tested in respect of the entire manner in which he conducts himself. There is a courtly and chivalric ideal that he must live up to. The tension in the story is provided by sex; it is possible that Gawain will be tempted by and yield to his hostess. And to a certain extent he is tempted. What the reader might reflect upon, however, is the gap between the courtly, and literary, ideal and the reality of physical desire. It is as if mundane reality challenges the whole received structure of medieval culture. In the process, the poem explores the nature and limitations of personal integrity, culminating in the hero's acquisition of self-knowledge. In more general terms, though, the experience of the poem might be described as a contest between the romance literary form, with its emphasis on elaborate courtly behaviour imported along with the French language, and a vernacular voice that is consistently ill at ease with this imposed narrative structure. In this respect, the *Gawain* poet echoes what we have seen in the writings of Julian of Norwich and Margery Kempe.

All three authors work within the fold of a received set of values – the framework of the church or the framework of the court – but all three chafe against such authority. It is no doubt the case that French writers at this time also expressed their unease about the rigour and unreality of religious and courtly ideals, but in English writers the articulation of a different position naturally takes the form of asserting their own voice. Indeed, one of the simplest ways of thinking about Middle English literature is to see it as an encounter between received, continental forms and the language, and lives, of the English people. Nowhere is this more clearly the case than in the works of Chaucer.

Geoffrey Chaucer, William Dunbar, Robert Henryson

We should not forget that, for the most part, literature in the Middle Ages remains the preserve of those in power. The intrusion of new voices, however, starts to explain the way in which the literature of the period responds to, but also helps create, currents of change. These currents of change are reflected in the rise of English as a literary language, the vernacular tongue expressing a distinctive sense of national identity, as opposed to Norman French or Latin and their associations with the continent. This is an extreme version of a process that repeats itself throughout English literature; new voices emerge that enable the country to redefine how it conceives and sees itself. There is often, but not always, a sense of these voices as coarse and colloquial: a language closer to the language of everyday life is suddenly heard in contexts that previously excluded the ordinary, the familiar. Of all English writers, none is more intriguingly a participant in such a process than Chaucer.

Everything that we know about Chaucer's life suggests someone at the heart of the established order. When young, he served in the household of Prince Lionel, the son of the king, Edward III. Subsequently, he might have studied law, and he might have visited Spain on a diplomatic mission, but we do know for certain that from 1367 he was an esquire to the royal household. He was with the king's army in France in 1359, and later, 1372–3, he was in Italy, where he might have met the writer-scholars Petrarch and Boccaccio. He sat in parliament, and held various appointments under Richard II. The impression, clearly, is of a man at one with the status quo. Not surprisingly, when Chaucer started to write, in what is regarded as his first phase as a writer, he leaned heavily on French sources and French forms. This is evident in *The Book of the Duchess* (c.1369), a poem on the death of the wife of John of Gaunt, and again in a translation of a French verse romance, *The Romaunt of the Rose* (possibly c.1360), some of which is attributed to Chaucer.

Both poems belong to an established convention: the dream-vision. In a dream-vision, an extremely popular form during the Middle Ages, the poet falls asleep, usually on a May morning. In his dream he encounters either real people or personified abstractions; the characters he engages with represent a broad, if simplified, scenario of life, in which human beings either act as they should or fail to do so. Dream-vision poetry can, as such, be seen as literature that reflects a courtly or chivalric ideal, the dream revealing an ideal which should, but all too obviously does not, pertain to the real world. Chaucer calls upon the dream-vision convention in the two poems mentioned so far, and also later in *The Parlement of Foules* (1372–86), *The House of Fame* (1379–80) and the prologue to *The Legend of Good Women* (1372–86). His liking for the form might suggest that Chaucer was happy to work within the constraints of received literary moulds and ideas, but most readers of these poems sense a degree of complication that goes beyond what we might expect to encounter. There is always a tension in dream poetry, because the form depends upon conveying the disparity between high ideals and human frailty. As we might expect, desire, both sexual desire and the desire for money, is the most common human weakness. But it is possible to argue that Chaucer's dream-vision poems have a more complex psychological dimension, conveying a subtle sense of needs that focus in the unconscious. It might seem misguided to impose a modern concept such as psychology on Chaucer's poems, but they certainly convey an understanding of human diversity that subverts any impression of a simple moral intention in the poems, something borne out by their self-consciousness about their own artifice and language.

As we start to look at Chaucer's works, therefore, what we see are two impulses. On the one hand, there is the debt to a received tradition: he works within an established form that, to some extent, comes complete with an established way of looking at the world. On the other hand, there is a sense of new feelings, new impulses, and new ways of thinking about life that Chaucer adds to the existing form. This is to a large extent a matter of language. It is perhaps easiest to grasp this idea in relation to *The Romaunt of the Rose*. It seems likely that Chaucer translated the first 1,700 lines of this poem, but in a way it does not matter who translated it. The essential point to grasp is that a translation is never a straightforward conversion from what is being said in one language to the same things being said in another language; the act of translation transforms the text, introducing, as in *The Romaunt of the Rose*, a whole way of thinking that is engrained in the English language, and which has no exact parallel in the French language. Consequently, Chaucer, writing in English, inevitably adapts, even as he adopts, foreign literary modes, changing them in a way that reflects broader English cultural and historical concerns as well as more specific circumstances.

We see this again in Chaucer's second phase as a writer, when he began to look towards Italian literary influences. In the years between about 1372 and 1386 Chaucer wrote *The Parlement of Foules*, *The House of Fame*, *Troilus and Criseyde* and *The Legende of Good Women*. The received stories and received forms that he calls upon enable him to explore fundamental questions about life. But, at the same time, working in his own language, Chaucer is adding something new. In *Troilus and Criseyde* (written in the 1380s), for example, we have a tale of courtly love, with the familiar complication that human sexual desire is at odds with a noble ideal. But the freshness of Chaucer's poem is to a large extent a consequence of the way in which he moves towards a sense of Troilus and Criseyde as fully developed individuals, the poem as a whole articulating an idea about the psychological realities of love. *Troilus and Criseyde*, as such, by its rewriting of a familiar story, contributes to a broader movement of cultural change; along with other texts and a mass of historical evidence, it suggests a shift towards a new way of thinking about individual lives, a new way of thinking that will acquire increasing importance in Western society over the course of several hundred years.

It is in Chaucer's third, English phase that he can most clearly be seen to break the mould of what he inherits from earlier writers and to forge something new that resonates beyond its time. The premise of *The Canterbury Tales* is that pilgrims on their way to Thomas à Becket's tomb at Canterbury divert themselves with the telling of tales; the twenty-four stories told constitute less than a fifth of the projected work. Each tale told is, however, a vivid exploration of the personality of the speaker, and the 'General Prologue' also provides an often amusing reflection of the pilgrims' characters. The result is an extremely lively picture of the diverse range of people who lived in England during the late Middle Ages. Less obvious to the casual reader are the conventional formal elements in Chaucer's conception of the work as a whole, and in the design of each tale. Transcending all else is the framework of the pilgrimage; this is a colourful cross-section of the main English social classes (there were three 'estates' or groups – lords, priests and labourers, and Chaucer adds urban and professional people), but, however varied the figures may be, they are united by their sense of a religious purpose in life. In terms of the separate tales, each belongs to an established mode; for example, romance, exemplum, fabliau and sermon. But the stories are often told in such a vigorous manner, and so often focus on human weakness, that we are left with an overwhelming impression of the gap between polite literary forms and the rude untidiness of everyday life. This echoes the pattern in the conception of the work as a whole: the gap between the religious ideal of the pilgrimage and the all-too-human reality of the pilgrims.

It might be argued that this is a disparity that could be identified at any point in history, but what interests us in *The Canterbury Tales* is the fact that we are seeing the social and religious aspirations of fourteenth-century people, and seeing secular and religious failings that are distinctively characteristic of this society at this time. The text, as is the case with any text, cannot be detached from the period of its production; it is, rather, trying to understand the late fourteenth century by seeking to articulate the particular desires and weaknesses of this time in a certain set of circumstances. The colloquial vigour of the poem is highly significant in this respect; there is a kind of polyphonic babble, a range of different and competing voices from the characters that pulls against the sense of a purpose they share on the pilgrimage. As pilgrims they should all speak with one voice, but as people they fail to do so. The experience of each individual story supports this impression; a complex, at times baffling, tale develops within the essentially simple received format so that even the crudest fabliau generates complex questions.

Chaucer is, indeed, so proficient at illustrating human and social diversity that it is tempting to sum him up simply as a writer who is open to the diversity of life. There is seemingly a comic and tolerant tone in *The Canterbury Tales*, as if Chaucer is only ever amused, and never outraged, by human conduct. This stance seems compatible with Chaucer's religious beliefs: perfection is the exclusive preserve of heaven, human weakness is inevitable, and the appropriate response is laughter. If this is Chaucer's position, then this also seems the right moment at which to remind ourselves that the second half of the fourteenth century was characterised by increased religious policing on the part of the church authorities. While the church clamped down on waywardness, Chaucer was content to laugh. But possibly a more complex stance is in evidence in *The Canterbury Tales*, a poem which, despite its popular appeal, originates from a writer who was a loyal servant of the royal court. Chaucer's laughter is warm and generous, but actually a fairly harsh laughter is directed at anybody (for example, the Summoner) who might be judged to be a threat to the established order. What permeates the poem is an assumption that, although people have failings, all reasonable people, including the reader, share the same fundamental values as the poet.

This is perhaps most evident in his attitude towards the Wife of Bath, a strong, independent woman who is not afraid to speak for herself, setting her own experience, gained in marriage, against biblical authority:

> Experience, though noon auctoritee   [*authority*]
> Were in this world, is right ynogh for me
> To speke of wo that is in mariage;
> For, lordynges, sith I twelve yeer was of age,   [*since*]
> Thonked be God that is eterne on lyve,
> Housbondes at chirche dore I have had fyve.
> (*The Wife of Bath's Prologue*, lines 1–6)

But the narrator's amused tone is not really tolerant laughter so much as laughter at the expense of a woman who dares to be different and who does not know her place. The narrator adopts a self-deprecating manner, in which he affects to be the most incompetent story-teller on the pilgrimage; his first tale is cut short by the Host on the grounds of its exceptionally poor quality. Such self-deprecation is, however, entirely consistent with the kind of ironic stance which, while appearing just to laugh at human absurdity, is in reality intolerant of difference. It is part of a kind of ideological sleight-of-hand in *The Canterbury Tales*, in which Chaucer treats the values held by himself and the court as the values that everyone should share. In the same area, a profound sense of the importance of hierarchy permeates the whole; the Knight, who tells the first story, is at the top of the social pyramid, and is treated with due deference. What, therefore, emerges in the poem overall is perhaps a rather reassuring and essentially positive picture of the late Middle Ages. This is aided by the fact that Chaucer excludes uncomfortable evidence that might unsettle things. This was a bloody and violent period, in which no king could ever feel safe or established on the throne, but the poem offers no real sense of unrest in England (the Peasants' Revolt is barely mentioned; Richard II was deposed in 1399, leading to the long period of civil war that we refer to as the Wars of the Roses). On the contrary, *The Canterbury Tales* does not just endorse but actually helps establish an idea of a certain kind of ordered England, a world that we might nostalgically, but incorrectly, assume once existed.

All of this might, of course, seem to constitute a series of reservations about Chaucer, but this is not the case. Indeed, much of Chaucer's power as a writer exists in the way that he seeks to achieve a synthesis. This chapter has dealt with how new voices can pose a threat to the established order. What is so extraordinary in Chaucer is that new voices are given far more exposure and prominence than in any other writer of the period, yet they are all brought within the orbit of Chaucer's masterly control. In particular, Chaucer allows women far more space than the rigid boundaries of patriarchy permitted, opening up areas of experience where they can articulate their desires. But Chaucer also finds room for the aspirations of an upwardly mobile figure such as the Franklin, as well as for the social pretensions of the Prioress and the humility of the Parson, together with stringent criticism of church corruption. In all of this, *The Canterbury Tales* is a work that looks to the future, and also looks to the past, and then, in negotiating between the two, creates a new voice, that of poised conservatism, that will remain central in English literary culture for hundreds of years.

With such ideas in mind, it is interesting to consider the works of a number of writers who, collectively, are often referred to as the 'Scottish Chaucerians'. Gavin Douglas, William Dunbar and Robert Henryson are the main figures involved, all writing in the fifteenth century. The term 'Scottish Chaucerians', however, can mislead. Certainly there is an acknowledged debt to Chaucer in their work, as in James I's poem *The King's Quair* (the King's Book) which draws on *The Knight's Tale*, but it is more accurate to see these writers as part of an independent tradition of Scottish poetic literature. What we see with Douglas, Dunbar and Henryson is the same kind of experiment with form that is found in Chaucer, but one made more vigorous by its use of the Scottish vernacular.

In Henryson's case, this is also a matter of mixing satire with a comic appreciation of human folly, as in his translation of Aesop's fables. Dunbar, however, is a far more courtly writer, producing religious lyrics but also official poems to celebrate James IV's marriage, as well as complaints about his lack of reward. It is perhaps, though, Douglas's translation of Virgil's *Aeneid* into 'Scottis' that tells us most about cultural change during this period. It is not simply that authors find room for other voices in their texts, but they also find ways of incorporating diverse traditions into an increasingly powerful vernacular language, one that can reach both back into the past and across Europe to absorb new influences. In this way the 'Scottish Chaucerians' do not merely follow or imitate Chaucer, but like him suggest the scale of change to come with the rediscovery of the classics in the sixteenth century by writers such as Wyatt and Surrey.

William Langland, Medieval Drama, Thomas Malory

Chaucer is so poised that we can remain all but unaware that there are substantial political tensions behind his works. Other writers get a lot more agitated about the changes that are taking place in medieval society. William Langland, in particular, the author of *Piers Plowman*, is likely to strike us as a writer who, working in a traditional form, looks at the world around him and sees things that give him serious cause for concern. *Piers Plowman*, a religious allegory in alliterative verse, exists in three versions, the revisions being undertaken by Langland over a period of twenty-five years (from the 1360s to 1386). The poet, in a poem that we recognise as a dream-vision, falls asleep on a May morning and dreams of a crowd of people in a field, a field that is bounded by a tower, the dwelling of Truth, and by a dungeon, the house of Wrong:

> I seigh a toure on a toft trielich ymaked;
> A depe dale binethe a dongeon þere-Inne,
> With depe dyches & derke and dredful of sight.
> A faire felde ful of folke fonde I there bytwene,
> Of alle maner of men þe mene and þe riche,
> Worchyng and wandryng as þe worlde asketh.
>
> [I saw a tower on a hill-top, trimly built,
> A deep dale beneath, a dungeon tower in it,
> With ditches deep and dark and dreadful to look at.
> A fair field full of folk I found between them,
> Of human beings of all sorts, the high and the low,
> Working and wondering as the world requires.]
>
> (*The Prologue*, ll. 14–19)

Every kind of person is in the field: honest, dishonest, generous, mean-spirited, and so on. A beautiful woman, who represents the Holy Church, explains certain things to the dreamer; for example, he asks her what is Christ's will, and the woman tells him to love the Lord, to do good works, and to be on guard against duplicity and guile. The poem then moves on with illustrations of corruption. The dreamer subsequently has another vision, of the Seven Deadly Sins, but then, in his role as Everyman seeking salvation, he continues with his pilgrimage to Truth. At the end of the poem he is preparing for the supreme encounter, but it is at this moment that he awakens from his sleep, and realises, to his grief, that the world is as it ever has been.

Piers Plowman can be read simply as a religious allegory, but what we really encounter in the poem is Langland's problems with an increasingly complex and corrupt society. It is essentially a deeply conservative poem; shocked by what he encounters, Langland wants to reassert the value of traditional attitudes and the importance of a straightforward moral frame. But it is not the force of its religious message that impresses the reader of *Piers Plowman* so much as the sense of a tension that is conveyed: the quest for coherence in a world that no longer feels coherent. After 1350, as the Anglo-Norman hold over England slackens, there is an increasing sense of a gap between an idea of order, including religious order, and the actual state of the country; it is as if, in the three elements that constitute the nation – the church, the court and the people – the last of these, the people, are becoming more and more visible and assertive. *Piers Plowman* offers us a dismayed vision of the diversity of English life at this time, of a loss of moral and social direction, but also, paradoxically, by virtue of its mixture of dream-vision and social protest, biblical narrative and poetic symbol, as well as its own vigorous use of English, it actually adds to this sense of diversity.

The *Gawain* poet, Chaucer and Langland are all at work in the second half of the fourteenth century. We might expect a national literature to build immediately on this solid foundation. Curiously, however, there is a distinct lack of major authors and significant texts in the fifteenth century. It is not really until after 1509, the year that Henry VIII becomes king, that English literature flourishes again. Henry VIII was the instigator of the English Reformation, when the English state and then Church broke free from Rome. We can anticipate, from this fact alone, that the era of Henry VIII and his successors will be one of the really important periods in English culture, as it is a period of fundamental change; one cultural formation is overwhelmed by another, and a new way of thinking about the world takes shape. By contrast, the fifteenth century in England, dominated by civil wars, is possibly too chaotic to be conducive to the production of major texts. None the less, there was a great deal of literary activity in this century, partly because of the economic prosperity of a number of towns. In particular, there was a proliferation of popular literature: songs, both secular and religious, ballads, and, perhaps most interestingly of all, mystery plays, sometimes also called 'miracle plays', 'Corpus Christi plays', or, more simply, 'Cycle Plays'.

These were dramatised versions of biblical stories, with a particular emphasis on Christ's trial, death and resurrection. By the middle of the fourteenth century they were being performed in the major towns of England (as well as across Europe). They were acted by the (male) members of trade guilds, each guild working on individual episodes. The plays entertained the public, provided religious instruction, and boosted civic pride and trade. The tradition was in the end suppressed by the Protestant hierarchy around the 1570s, but had been in decline since the Reformation (announced by Henry VIII's declaration in 1534 of independence from papal authority). Some of the best-known surviving texts come from York, Chester and Wakefield. If we remember that church services at this time were in Latin, and that the Bible would not be translated into English until 1526 (there was an earlier translation, the Lollard Bible, associated with John Wycliffe, in the late fourteenth century), it is clear that medieval drama represents the people's sense of their possession, as against the church's official possession, of the word of God. Initially the church encouraged these dramas, but by the fifteenth and sixteenth centuries the church's attitude was more hostile. *The Second Shepherds' Play*, in the Wakefield cycle, with its parody of the infant Christ in the form of a lamb, illustrates the way in which the plays were also becoming increasingly secularised. As is so often the case in the Middle Ages, the voice of the people is in evidence, and, albeit in a way that the modern reader might find it hard to identify as controversial, conflicts with the voice of authority.

That note of conflict is perhaps less easy to identify in the morality plays of the fifteenth century. These were plays in which vices and virtues fought for the soul of humankind. This is the pattern of *The Castle of Perseverance*, the longest of the plays, and of *Mankind* (c.1464). The figures employed are a mixture of personified human qualities, such as Covetousness, and devils – for example, Belial – or Vice clowns such as Nowadays and Nought in *Mankind*. As their name suggests, the morality plays taught or offered a moral lesson, or, as with John Skelton's *Magnyfycence* (c.1500 – Skelton was 'poet laureate' and tutor to Henry VIII), political satire. In the case of the most famous play, *Everyman*, the lesson is one of repentance before death. Everyman, the hero, is summoned by Death to the grave. As his last hours go by he discovers that only his Good Deeds will accompany him to God's judgement. What, though, we remember most is the grim figure of Death summoning Everyman away from his worldly goods. If the conflict in the miracle plays is between an increasingly secular society and church authority, in the morality plays it is between an increasingly affluent society and the moral doctrines of the church.

What we see in the Middle Ages is literary forms and structures of belief coming into contact, and sometimes into conflict, with the English language, with both language and literature changing in consequence. A final, particularly interesting, example of this cross-fertilisation is Thomas Malory's *Le Morte D'Arthur* (1469–70). This is another treatment of the myth of Arthur, but, by a fascinating process of cultural exchange, it is a new version of the British story as taken up by a number of French writers. Malory borrows much of his narrative from three French texts, but also calls upon a couple of English works. The initial impression, however, might be that he is continuing, even as late as 1470, to write in the shadow of an alien culture. At the heart of the story are the values of the court, the notion of chivalry, and the ideal of courtly love; it is as if Malory is striving to maintain the values of an aristocratic elite even while this elite was self-evidently in decline and England suffering military disasters abroad.

But if the work looks to the past in these respects, what we also have to note is that it is written in prose, and prose that is fairly close to modern English:

> So hyt myssefortuned sir Gawayne and all hys brethirne were in kynge Arthurs chambir, and than sir Aggravayne seyde thus opynly, and nat in no counceyle, that many knyghtis myght here:
> 'I mervayle that we all be nat ashamed bothe to se and to know how sir Launcelot lyeth dayly and nyghtly by the quene. And all we know well that ht ys so, and hyt ys shamefully suffird of us all that we shulde suffir so noble a kynge as kynge Arthur ys to be shamed.'

> [So it misfortuned that Sir Gawain and all his brethren were in King Arthur's chamber, and Sir Agravain said thus openly, and not in no counsel, that many knights might hear: 'I marvel that we all be not ashamed both to see and to know Sir Lancelot lieth daily and nightly by the Queen. And we all know well that it is so, and it is shamefully suffered of us all that we should suffer so noble a king as King Arthur is to be shamed.']

(*Morte D'Arthur*, Book 20, ch. 1)

There is, therefore, a fascinating relationship in Morte D'Arthur between the discourse of chivalry and the discourse of everyday life. In this connection, we might also note that Morte D'Arthur was one of the very first English-language books William Caxton, the first English printer, printed in 1485; it was very much part of the vernacular culture. But possibly the most telling aspect of Morte D'Arthur is that, particularly in comparison with Sir Gawain and the Green Knight, it is a valedictory work. The adultery of Launcelot and Guinevere has destroyed Camelot. Even the Round Table is destroyed, and Arthur's apparently dead body is carried to the Isle of Avalon. Morte D'Arthur can be regarded as invoking a romantic ideal in a chaotic century (the 'Wars of the Roses', a sustained period of civil war, continued from 1455 to 1485), but the death of Arthur is equatable with the death of chivalry. The values that the court in the Middle Ages aspired to, even if there was always a huge gap between theory and practice, are, by the time of Morte D'Arthur, a thing of the past (although chivalry remained an important concept in the Tudor court). But if one impulse is dying, with the English language now having developed into something like its modern form, there is, as we move on to the sixteenth century, a sense of being on the edge of further exciting developments.

3 Sixteenth-Century Poetry and Prose

Sir Thomas Wyatt

The literary form most commonly associated with the sixteenth century is the sonnet. This example, 'Whoso list to hunt', is by Sir Thomas Wyatt, who held a number of posts in Henry VIII's court, and was closely involved with Anne Boleyn, who became Henry's second wife:

> Whoso list to hunt, I know where is an hind,
> But as for me, alas, I may no more.
> The vain travail hath wearied me so sore
> I am of them that farthest cometh behind.
> Yet may I, by no means, my wearied mind
> Draw from the deer, but as she fleeth afore
> Fainting I follow. I leave off, therefore,
> Since in a net I seek to hold the wind.
> Who list her hunt, I put him out of doubt,
> As well as I, may spend his time in vaine.
> And graven with diamonds in letters plain
> There is written, her fair neck round about,
> '*Noli me tangere*, for Caesar's I am,   [*Touch me not*]
> And wild for to hold, though I seem tame.'

The poem, written about 1526, is an adaptation of a sonnet by the fourteenth-century Italian writer Petrarch, but, when it refers to hunting a deer that belongs to Caesar, seems to play teasingly, or perhaps anxiously, with Wyatt's own, and now hopeless, pursuit of Anne Boleyn.

There are two points of immediate interest in Wyatt's poem. One is the reliance upon an imported literary form. The sonnet is a poem of fourteen lines, which in its Petrarchan form divides into an eight-line unit and a six-line unit; the octave develops one thought, and there is then a change of direction in the sestet. The form was widely used by Italian poets in the later Middle Ages, usually for love poems. Wyatt and the Earl of Surrey introduced the convention into England in the early sixteenth century; the form flourished, its popularity reaching a peak in the 1590s, with sequences – a series of poems, usually dwelling on various aspects of one love affair – by Sir Philip Sidney, Samuel Daniel, Thomas Lodge, Michael Drayton and Edmund Spenser. The most celebrated sequence, published in 1609 but circulating in manuscript in the 1590s, is by Shakespeare. As in the Middle Ages, English Renaissance writers, it seems, have to turn to the continent to find literary forms they can work with. But, and this is the second main point of interest, whereas writers in the Middle Ages seem to be asserting the value of the English language almost in defiance of the imported literary forms they were using, in Wyatt's sonnet reproduced here – and the same is true generally in the sixteenth century – there is an independent voice that expresses itself confidently without any sense of the form providing a constraint. It is as if the language has come of age. This linguistic confidence is synonymous with a developing national confidence, that the poets feel they can hold their own with continental writers, rather than writing in their shadow. In turn, the nation itself comes to be shaped through the language and to take on its distinctive identity.

This is implicit in Wyatt's sonnet. At face value, 'Whoso list to hunt' might seem a trifling poem. All it says is that the poet is too weary to hunt any more, although he remains intrigued by the elusive deer; others may pursue her, but the fact is that she is another man's property, if, indeed, a man can possess such a wild creature. One thing that adds interest to the poem is the sense of the life of an aristocrat that is conveyed. Hunting deer is the recreation of a courtier; it calls upon the skills required in warfare, but these have been adapted into the rituals of a leisurely pursuit. The reference to the diamond-studded collar underlines the point that this is a society concerned with good style rather than mere utility. Writing the sonnet adds to the overall impression; the complete Renaissance gentleman will be proficient in all the arts, the art of writing just as much as

the art of horsemanship. There is, however, another level of complication evident in the poem. It lies in Wyatt's ability to write indirectly, not just about his pursuit of Anne Boleyn but more generally
about political intrigue; how, as a courtier, he must yield to the
power of the king, and that sexual desire might motivate men as
much as political ambition. There is perhaps always a sense of quarry
– a woman, a secure post – that will remain permanently elusive. And
even the poem's tone is elusive. Is Wyatt just playing with an idea, or
does the poem, written by a man who was not only involved
in intrigues but also arrested on a number of occasions, offer an
unsettling sense of the precariousness of court life, and the complex
link between private and public affairs?

What we can be sure of is the subtlety of Wyatt's performance.
Petrarch's sonnet provides him with a structure in which he produces something that strikes us as entirely original. He takes, that
is, the conventions of the Petrarchan love sonnet, with its hapless
male lover and remote, idealised lady, and invests them with an
ambiguous resonance resulting in a kind of doubleness so that the
poem is at once playful and darkly sinister in tone. What we might
also note is that this poem, and the same is true of a great deal of
poetry in the sixteenth century, is court-based. In the Middle Ages
we often seem to hear the voice of the people, but in the Tudor
period there is an assertion of royal authority. Things are not
allowed to get out of hand; the court asserts its dominance, and this
includes seizing the initiative in literary discourse. This perhaps
begins to explain why the sonnet became established as the
favoured form in the sixteenth century. It is not enough to say there
was a fashion for sonnets; there are always social factors that determine fashions. Wyatt's poem leads us towards an answer. There is
a delight in control reflected in the idea of the poem's set form; life
is complex, and the pressures in life are diverse, but the poet has
asserted an authority over such complications. This matches the
political situation of the sixteenth century. England had experienced thirty years of civil war, the Wars of the Roses, between 1455
and 1485, but the Tudor period, starting with Henry VII in 1485, sees
a move from the chaos of civil war to effective, if authoritarian,
government. The poem also reflects a new respect for learning and

education that became evident in England under the Tudors; the sonnet acknowledges a debt to Italian culture and to the classics, but is also an independent illustration in English of how the intellect can impose a pattern of rational interpretation upon life.

Yet there is always another dimension to sonnets: the two halves of the poem do not exactly match, do not balance each other. Consequently, built into the very structure of a sonnet, there is an idea of life slipping beyond the poet's ability to control it. In terms of imagery, the poet speaks of trying to hold the wind in a net, of trying, that is, to capture something elusive and invisible; and at a simple, but significant, level in this poem, as in many sixteenth-century love poems, the woman evades capture. Wyatt's writing, therefore, can be said to demonstrate his mastery of the intrigues of court and his mastery of the sonnet as a disciplined intellectual composition, but the poem, both in terms of its content and in terms of its intrinsic structure, simultaneously challenges the ability to control and comprehend experience. This could be said to be the central theme of sixteenth-century literature: there is a constant assertion of control, of order, but that control is always being undermined, challenged or doubted. This will become most evident in the 1590s, a decade which can be represented as the period of the great sonnet sequences, but which can also be viewed as almost anarchic in the diversity and excess of its literary and political activity.

Sixteenth-Century Prose and the Reformation

A new confidence in the English language is evident in the strength of vernacular prose writing during the sixteenth century. At the same time, the fact that one of the most important prose works of the century, Sir Thomas More's *Utopia* (1516), was written in Latin reminds us that a variety of impulses were at work at the time. Thomas More was Henry VIII's Lord Chancellor, but resigned in 1532 because he could not agree with the king's ecclesiastical policy and marriage to Anne Boleyn; he was executed in 1535. Henry VIII was the second Tudor monarch. His father, Henry VII, had become the king in 1485, when he overthrew Richard III. Henry VIII came to the throne in 1509. In 1517, Martin Luther's protest against the principle of papal indulgences began the Reformation; this was essentially a protest of the individual conscience against the authority of the Catholic Church.

When, in 1534, Henry VIII was declared 'Supreme Head on Earth' of the English Church it was, on the surface, because he wished to obtain a divorce, but at a deeper level it was a matter of England declaring its independence and separate identity. Henry died in 1547. He was succeeded by Edward VI (aged nine), by Lady Jane Grey (for nine days), by Mary (a devout Catholic), and, in 1558, by Elizabeth I. Her first task was the Religious Settlement of 1559, which imposed the Protestant religion by law, though in such a way that most people could be accommodated within its terms. The Settlement established England as a prime mover in the Reformation cause. The growing strength of England was made apparent in the defeat of the Spanish Armada in 1588. When Elizabeth died in 1603 it brought to an end over a hundred years of Tudor rule, a period which can be characterised as displaying an increasing sense of national confidence and independence.

In the first 45 or so years of Tudor government, however, England was still a Catholic country, and, as such, very much aware of its European identity. This is the context in which we have to consider Thomas More. More is a new kind of figure that appears in this period. In the fifteenth century educated Englishmen began to catch a sense of the cultural and intellectual activity that was flourishing in the Italian city states. The energy of trade and the consequent affluence produced a new interest in recovering and studying texts from classical antiquity, and a new enthusiasm for learning, perhaps best summed up in the term 'humanism'. The poetry of Wyatt and the Earl of Surrey is one manifestation of such humanist activity and of how the Italian Renaissance affected England, but in More's *Utopia* we gain an impression of something rather more weighty. The book looks at European society, offering solutions for some of its ills; it does this primarily by citing, and proceeding to describe, Utopia, a perfect island state. It is a work that reflects a new kind of concern with questions of government and political and social organisation. If we were to make a very crude comparison with earlier texts, we might argue that, while Old English writings focus on loyalty as the key value in a corrupt and harsh world, with religion as the only consolation, in a work such as More's *Utopia* there is a far more positive sense of the human intellect and of human capability.

Yet at the same time, even with More's humanist scholarship, and a new interest in philosophy, literature, history and art, sixteenth-century England was geographically and culturally on the fringe of continental Europe. For men such as More, the question of whether to write in Latin or English was always a difficult one. More's choice of Latin signals an awareness of being part of an intellectual community that extends beyond England as well as a kind of political conservatism (he refused to recognise Henry's divorce and was executed by him). But the choice of Latin also, possibly, conveys a sense of English as still relatively unstable and unproven as a language. Roger Ascham, the tutor to Elizabeth before she became queen, and one of the many interesting intellectual courtier figures in this period, felt he should write in English, even though he found it easier to write in Latin or Greek; indeed, his book *Toxophilus* (1545), which is about archery, includes a significant section on the importance of using English. Ascham's commitment to English was deeply intertwined with his sense of his English Protestant identity. In this connection, it would be hard to exaggerate the importance of the English Reformation in promoting English as the inevitable choice for the writer of prose; at a fundamental level, it is only possible to express one's separate and independent identity in one's own language.

The changes that came about in the sixteenth century are illustrated if we consider the issue of the translation of the Bible. Before the Reformation, the Bible had been translated, but William Tyndale, whose New Testament translation appeared in 1526, was burned as a heretic in Belgium and his translation was suppressed in England. In 1536, however, Henry VIII gave royal licence for an English Bible, which was essentially the Tyndale translation. In 1560, the so-called Geneva Bible was presented to Elizabeth, and became the Bible in standard use for nearly a century; it is, interestingly, less lofty and less Latinate than the King James Bible of 1611. The fact that the Bible was now available in English should be seen in conjunction with the fact that books were now printed, rather than existing in manuscript, and that by as early as 1530, it has been suggested by some historians, over 50 per cent of the population could read.

Many would argue that it is economic activity as much as political or religious factors that prompts social and cultural change. In this respect, it is important to pay attention to the activities of Elizabethan adventurers and the expansion of maritime activity. Richard Hakluyt's *The Principal Navigations, Voyages, Traffiques and Discoveries of the English Nation* was published in 1589, reappearing about ten years later in a greatly enlarged edition. Hakluyt's work is a compilation of ships' logs, salesmen's reports and economic intelligence; it tells the story of English exploration and voyages, including accounts of Cabot's discovery of Hudson Bay and Drake's raid on Cadiz. The particular interpretative power Hakluyt holds is that he takes material as unshaped as a ship's log, but moulds it into a narrative of self-identity; in no small measure, this involves telling a seafaring nation that it is, indeed, a seafaring nation destined to rule the world. Again and again Hakluyt's mariners venture forth into a world that is beset by storms and danger, but they always seem to receive their reward. It is a form of divine providence, and perhaps particularly directed at the English who are suitable recipients of such bounty.

A sense of new horizons coupled with establishing control is evident in the career of Sir Walter Ralegh. Soldier, sailor, courtier, politician, poet and historian, Ralegh seems to embody the idea of Renaissance man as described in contemporary literature such as Castiglione's *The Courtier* (1528), combining intellectual and heroic attributes. Ralegh's unfinished *The History of the World* (1614) reveals something central about the age. The book starts with the Creation and gets as far as the second century BC. This is an ambitious, probably impossibly ambitious, attempt to comprehend the past from the perspective of an Englishman, and through the medium of English. It is, as such, entirely consistent with the expansionist, colonial mission of England in which figures such as Ralegh sought to wrest control of Spanish colonies on behalf of Elizabeth. But the years between 1603 and 1616, when Ralegh was imprisoned in the Tower of London for treason, together with his execution in 1618, suggest the frailty of the concept of control in England during the Elizabethan and Jacobean periods. Dissent, insurrection and rebellion were common during the Tudor period, and were suppressed ruthlessly. As with the sonnet, the initial impression might be of an orderliness under firm authority, but the order that is established is fragile, and forces beyond the tight control of the royal court always threaten to disturb such harmony as has been established.

This is evident in many different ways in the sixteenth century. The dominant voice is that of the courtly aristocrat, as in the case of Sir Philip Sidney's prose romance, *The Arcadia*. Begun in 1577 and then revised in 1580, *The Arcadia* is set in an ancient pastoral world where King Basilius has taken refuge to avoid the prophecy of an oracle, and tells of the adventures of two princes, Musidorus and Pyrocles, who fall in love with the king's daughters. The plot is full of intrigues, while the text itself is punctuated by verse eclogues and songs. As in Shakespeare's late plays, *The Tempest* and *The Winter's Tale*, the effect is to heighten by contrast the themes of love and nature, but, as in all such works, the pastoral ideal is threatened from both within and without, its harmony disturbed by murder and attempted rape.

The Arcadia was first published in 1590, but then revised and added to by Sidney's sister, Mary Herbert, Countess of Pembroke, in 1593. She also continued his verse translation of the Psalms, while her home acted as a literary circle for other writers and thinkers. What may strike modern readers most about *The Arcadia* is its sheer elaborateness intended to convey courtly sophistication, but also a certain eliteness. In this it is at an opposite remove from a work such as Thomas Nashe's *The Unfortunate Traveller* (1594), which can be seen as an early example of the novel in England and which focuses on the adventures of an English page on the continent. Nashe creates a grim picture of a world that is almost anarchically untidy, a world in which the failings and excesses of the ruling class are too apparent. But Nashe was also a vigorous opponent of the growing power of the Puritans and their wish to control both the theatre and writing. In this he represents a dissident stream of literature, including such popular forms as rogue literature and 'coney-catching' pamphlets describing con-tricks played on innocent citizens. Here is a genuine alternative voice to that of the court, a voice rooted in everyday life with all its hazards, but also a voice that is akin to popular journalism and popular fiction. In many ways it is the voice of the future.

It is, though, in the area of religion that the vulnerability of the order established by the Tudor monarchs is most apparent. A new

Protestant dispensation naturally found itself in contention with Catholic orthodoxy, but it also proved insufficiently radical for many in the country. Martin Marprelate was the name assumed by the author of a series of pamphlets issued in 1558–9; these were extreme Puritan attacks on bishops, who were regarded as symbols of the Catholicism still infecting the new Protestant Church. It should be noted again that it is as we enter the 1590s that more and more different voices begin to be heard, asserting their presence in an ever-growing variety of literary forms. Significantly, the government ordered counter-attacks on the Puritan pamphlets, and also introduced censorship; such actions acknowledged the strength of the forces that threatened it politically, but also indicate the way in which works of literature open up and draw attention to the faultlines of change. The Tudor period is characterised by strong central leadership, and this is echoed in a court-based literature that, as in the cleverness of so many sonnets, revels in poise, authority and control. But the very fact of strong government is also a recognition of the existence of disruptive forces in a changing country.

The Sonnet: Sir Philip Sidney and William Shakespeare

There are many examples of popular culture – songs, ballads, some prose fiction – that survive from the sixteenth century, and also texts by writers from a diverse range of social backgrounds, but more than in any other century it is necessary to pay attention to poetry as the preserve of the court, of people who wrote as a civilised recreation. The major sonnet sequences of the century were not written for publication, merely circulated in manuscript amongst a select circle. These sonnet sequences were, for the most part, written by men whose lives were conducted on the public stage, as soldiers and politicians. A key figure here is Sir Philip Sidney, but Edmund Spenser, for example, was at the heart of the colonial administration in Ireland. It was very much a male culture.

But poems by a number of women, including Mary Sidney, Aemelia Lanyer and Elizabeth herself, who translated and wrote a great deal, do survive. One of the best-known poems by Elizabeth is 'The doubt of future foes exiles my present joy':

The doubt of future foes exiles my present joy,
And wit me warns to shun such snares as threaten mine annoy;
For falsehood now doth flow, and subjects' faith doth ebb,
Which should not be if reason ruled or wisdom weaved the web.
But clouds of joy untried do cloak aspiring minds,
Which turn to rain of late repent by changed course of winds.
The top of hope supposed the root upreared shall be,
And fruitless all their grafted guile, as shortly ye shall see.
The dazzled eyes with pride, which great ambition blinds,
Shall be unsealed but worthy wights whose foresight falsehood finds.
The daughter of debate that discord aye doth sow
Shall reap no gain where former rule still peace hath taught to know.
No foreign banished wight shall anchor in this port;
Our realm brooks not seditious sects, let them elsewhere resort.
My rusty sword through rest shall first his edge employ
To poll their tops that seek such change or gape for future joy.

The poem was apparently written in reply to a sonnet sent by Elizabeth's cousin, Mary Stuart, Queen of Scotland, asking to see her. It is a rejection of Mary's request and her attempts to deceive through guile. What, however, is interesting about the poem is not simply its author but its explicit concern with politics. We might, of course, expect this in Elizabeth's case, but it does suggest the extent to which poetry was not merely a courtly pastime but a form charged with political resonance. This is true both of poems such as Mary Sidney's translations of the Psalms and Isabella Whitney's poems about the changing structure of Tudor society. Unlike Mary Sidney, Isabella Whitney came from the lower-middle class, and her writing in the 1570s points to the emergence of a more open literary culture. It is not, however, until the 1640s and 1650s, in a period of political upheaval, that women's voices are heard to any great extent, along with the voices of others who have previously been excluded and kept silent. By and large, the earlier years belong to male writers.

Sidney's sonnet sequence, *Astrophil and Stella*, published in 1591, five years after Sidney died, was instrumental in inspiring the numerous other sonnet sequences of the 1590s, including Shakespeare's. It consists of 108 sonnets and 11 songs, and was written around 1582. The poems are addressed by Astrophil (Greek for 'star-lover') to Stella, his 'star' (derived from Latin). Another context for the poem is provided by Sidney's *The Defence of Poesie* (1579–80), which, with its claim of the superiority of poetry to history and philosophy in questions of moral virtue, reveals the extent to which Sidney was familiar with the classics and European discussions about the nature and function of art. Though entitled a 'defence', the work exudes confidence in the way that it reconciles a careful rhetorical structure with an engaging style. There is an impression of Sidney absorbing continental influences, transferring them to an English context, and writing with an air of independent authority. In a similar way, *Astrophil and Stella* as a sequence takes everything it needs in terms of convention and form from Petrarch, but stands on its own as a major move forward in English poetry. It would be possible to consider the sequence as a whole, which would demand attention to the dramatic coherence of the narrative that develops, and the manner in which the poems, cumulatively, create a sense of obsession, of being caught in a psychological impasse. It is probably more helpful here, however, to consider the issues raised by one sonnet seen in isolation.

In this sonnet the speaker addresses a friend who has rebuked him for neglecting his studies in favour of Stella:

> Your words, my friend, right healthful caustics, blame
> My young mind marred, whom Love doth windlass so,
> That mine own writings like bad servants show
> My wits, quick in vain thoughts, in virtue lame;
> That Plato I read for nought, but if he tame
> Such coltish gyres, that to my birth I owe
> Nobler desires, least else that friendly foe,
> Great expectation, wear a train of shame.
> For since mad March great promise made of me,
> If now the May of my years much decline,
> What can be hoped my harvest time will be?
> Sure you say well; your wisdom's golden mine
> Dig deep with learning's spade; now tell me this,
> Hath this world ought so fair as Stella is?
>
> (*Astrophil and Stella*, sonnet 21)

The friend's words of advice are compared to a corrosive cure for the poet's mind, which has been pulled off its true course by love. What he writes is characterised by vain thoughts rather than weighty matters;

his education in the classics should steady him, rather than make him giddy. By birth, the poet is a man set for great things, but where will such foolishness lead? The poet then, however, in the closing words of the poem, answers his friend: nothing in the world is as fair as Stella. As is so often the case with a sonnet, this might appear to amount to very little. But it is possible to unwrap layer upon layer of complication in the poem's language. At a simple level, the poem tells us a great deal about the education of a Renaissance gentleman. This includes reading the classics, acquiring proficiency as a writer, and generally experiencing a moral education that will prepare a young man for public life. What we are also likely to notice immediately is the cleverness with which the poem conveys its ideas. The most obvious technique is Sidney's play with metaphor, such as when he compares his writing to bad servants; servants, and words, should play their assigned role, rather than stepping out of line. But the poem itself is a witty demonstration of words not being kept in check; indeed, it is characterised by just the kind of irresponsibility that his friend condemns.

At the end of the poem, in a clever reversal, he manages to turn the tables on his friend. He is condemned for writing 'vain thoughts', but when his friend, in a rather hackneyed metaphor, advises him, 'your wisdom's golden mine / Dig deep with learning's spade', the poet wins the argument by the plainness of his closing statement. Again, however, this returns us to the question of whether this is anything more than clever. The answer would seem to be that here, as in many sonnets, questions are raised about the status of writing and its relationship to meaning and truth. The wit that is such a feature of sonnets – the kind of play with language that is apparent in the poem – becomes so self-conscious as to become suspect. The poet is aware that he is constructing a kind of self-enclosed verbal world which seems to relate to the real world, but which is possibly just a form of ingenious pattern-making. This all has particular relevance in sixteenth-century England. Just as the court maintains power but is aware of the fragility of the regulation that it maintains over the country, so Sidney's sonnet seems to acknowledge the precarious nature of the control that the poet maintains. This is particularly an issue in a Protestant country. In a state that has rejected the authority of the Catholic Church, with what authority does the king or queen speak? Is there any sub-stance to titles such as 'Supreme Head on Earth' of the English Church, or is this a little like the spurious control evident in a sonnet, merely a form of ingenious word play?

Can a love poem, however, really be described as having such far-reaching implications as these? Not directly, of course. There is no hidden political agenda in Sidney's poem: it is not about the Protestant and Catholic churches or the position of Elizabeth I in relation to the Pope. But the gender issue in the poem does echo the larger issues raised in the paragraph above. In a love poem, it is usually the case that a male poet addresses a female subject; essentially, he strives to bring her under his control. But the woman remains free and elusive (hence the need to return to her in sonnet after sonnet). The issue of control and the fragility, perhaps impossibility, of control is thus always well to the fore in a love poem. It is this troubling problem that connects to larger social and political questions outside the text.

The issues mentioned here are also central to Shakespeare's son-nets, but Shakespeare takes everything a stage further. This is partly a matter of ability, that Shakespeare can out-perform the verbal gym-nastics of any of his contemporaries. But it is also a matter of Shakespeare writing in the 1590s, as the control maintained by Elizabeth became more and more strained, and also because Shakespeare is outside the established order of the court and more open to an idea of flux and instability. As an illustration of this, the majority of Shakespeare's sonnets are addressed to a man; it is a char-acteristically clever move, for it immediately unsettles the usual con-vention of a love poem, that the male controls the elusive woman. A conventional love poem may question the assumptions inherent in such thinking, but many of Shakespeare's sonnets start by unsettling even our initial expectations and ways of thinking. At a straightfor-ward level, Shakespeare's sonnets obviously have a great many insightful things to say about the experience of being in love, and it would be foolish to deny the way in which they communicate with many readers, but a history of English literature, rather than just drawing attention to the timeless qualities in Shakespeare's writing, should also be concerned with the way these sonnets function in their own time.

Some of these points are evident in the following sonnet:

> When I have seen by Time's fell hand defaced
> The rich proud cost of outworn buried age;
> When sometime lofty towers I see down-razed,
> And brass eternal slave to mortal rage;
> When I have seen the hungry ocean gain
> Advantage on the kingdom of the shore,
> And the firm soil win of the watery main,
> Increasing store with loss, and loss with store;
> When I have seen such interchange of state,
> Or state itself confounded to decay,
> Ruin hath taught me thus to ruminate:
> That Time will come and take my love away.
> This thought is as a death, which cannot choose
> But weep to have that which it fears to lose.
>
> (Sonnet 64)

The poet places himself outside the normal span of life, imagining the process of decay, of buildings razed to the ground, the ocean eating into the shore, and state – in the sense of material existence, but also, as in 'state occasion', meaning worldly grandeur – decaying. He then turns from these lofty themes to the subject of his love, and, in a manner that echoes Sidney's sonnet, switches from verbal ingenuity to a plain statement about his loss. We could point again, therefore, to the textuality of Shakespeare's sonnet, the way in which there is a kind of gap between the verbal game and the reality of loss. And just as in Sidney's sonnet, this raises questions about how we control and comprehend life.

But a rather different picture of daily experience is offered in Shakespeare's sonnet, a picture that does not resemble the courtly impression in a Sidney sonnet. There is a sense of a commercial society: Shakespeare uses the words 'rich', and 'cost' as in finance; there is, with the sea references, an awareness of maritime activity; and 'store' and 'loss' seem to be as much business concepts as images of the changing landscape. There is something deeply significant about this. Over the course of the following centuries, Britain will increasingly see itself as a business-based trading nation; just a few years in the future, the Civil War can be interpreted as a confrontation between the court and the economic interests of a new class of men. Shakespeare's sonnet can be said, therefore, to be moving towards articulating a sense of the new way in which people are beginning to structure, think about and make sense of their lives. But the lack of balance in a sonnet again works effectively; the complicated time shifts, the way in which, as soon as an image is offered, that image is destroyed, and the intrusion of personal concerns into the broader concerns voiced in the poem, all serve to create a sense of disorder that makes the poem unsettling. It is this doubleness, this method of moving beyond the confines of the moment to larger issues of cultural change, and capturing that notion of change in the very form of the text, which enables us to see why the speaker fears the workings of time. Again and again Shakespeare surpasses his predecessors in the sonnet, both in the way that he conveys a new stage in sixteenth-century life, and in the amount of slippage and disturbance that he acknowledges in a poem.

Edmund Spenser

The sonnet might be the form that is most typical of the sixteenth century, but it is, of course, not the only form poets employed. If we take the example of Edmund Spenser: born in 1552, in 1580 he became secretary to Lord Grey de Wilton, Lord Deputy of Ireland, and was given lands there. In 1588 he acted as one of the 'undertakers' for the settlement of Munster, and was clearly part of the establishment of colonial rule in Ireland. It is this that provides the dark background to his work, especially *The Faerie Queene*, his unfinished epic. Committed to an idea of the public role of poetry as a vehicle for developing a Protestant culture in England, his literary career started in 1569 with the translation of a number of texts, including sonnets by Petrarch and an anti-Catholic tract by a Dutch Calvinist. *The Shepheardes Calender*, a pastoral poem, looking back to a lost golden age, followed in 1579; significantly, it includes a panegyric to Eliza (Elizabeth I), the queen of shepherds. In the same year, on the death of Lady Howard, he wrote an imitation of Chaucer's *Book of the Duchess*, and in 1595 he published *Amoretti*, a sonnet sequence, and *Epithalamion*, a marriage poem. *Colin Clout's Come Home*

Again, another pastoral poem, followed, then *Four Hymns* and *Prothalamion,* another marriage poem, in 1596. He then wrote a prose dialogue, *A View of the Present State of Ireland.* His crowning achievement, however, was *The Faerie Queene,* the first three books appearing in 1590, and the second three in 1596. The six completed books together with the 'Mutability Cantos' appeared in 1609, ten years after Spenser's death.

When a poet produces a work on the scale of *The Faerie Queene* there is a temptation to see the writer's earlier works as merely preparation for the great work. With Spenser, as is the case with John Milton and *Paradise Lost,* there is some substance in such a view. Spenser is a serious and moral poet; even the poems in his sonnet sequence are never frivolous in the way that might be said of some other sixteenth-century sonnet-writers. Consider, for example, his ode *Epithalamion,* which appears at the end of his sonnet sequence. The poem celebrates Spenser's marriage to Elizabeth Boyle at Cork, in Ireland, in 1594. Its 24 stanzas represent the hours of Midsummer's Day. In this short extract, Spenser describes his bride:

> Loe, where she comes along with portly pace
> Lyke Phoebe from her chamber of the East,
> Arising forth to run her mighty race,
> Clad all in white, that seemes a virgin best.
>
> (ll. 148–51)

It is the delicate beauty of Spenser's writing that is most apparent. He seems to create a perfect world, a world where happiness is the dominant emotion. There is little evidence of the darker aspects of experience that we encounter in so many works of literature. Yet there is a slight sense of not facing up to the real world in *Epithalamion;* the poem moves so slowly, and the preparations for the wedding are so detailed, that it is as if Spenser wishes to delay the moment of commitment. After Midsummer's day, after the wedding, everything will be a little bit darker. In a related way, we might note how the female figure in *Epithalamion* is contained within the dominant masculine code of writing; the woman is beautiful, but never troublesome, and never given a voice, never allowed to speak.

It is a little surprising to realise that this poem was written in the

1590s, for what we also come across in this decade is a surge of competing voices and different forms. Implicit in *Epithalamion* is an idea of
holding the established order together, but Spenser is holding it
together in a decade where we find evidence of instability, confusion
and change: almost 15,000 people died of the plague in London in
1593, and there were twelve riots in the city in the one month of June
1595. *Epithalamion* seems to belong to a timeless world, but in the
1590s, with Elizabeth growing old, and the absence of a direct heir, it
is apparent that time is running out for the Tudors. The literary diversity of the 1590s is apparent in Shakespeare's first highly productive
decade (Shakespeare in context is the subject of the next chapter),
and the first plays by Ben Jonson. In poetry, there are gloomy
Calvinistic religious poems by Fulke Greville, John Marston's satiric
diatribes, and early works of John Donne, which are mainly verse
satires. *Epithalamion* seeks to offer an impression of a timeless world,
but much of the other activity, particularly satirical writing, that survives from this decade conveys a sense of the furious upheaval of the
1590s.

It is clear that Spenser is fully aware of the complexity of the world
around him. Indeed, as a representative of the English crown in
Ireland, and with the destruction of his house in Ireland in Tyrone's
Rebellion of 1598, he could not have avoided the unrest of the 1590s.
But while a poem such as *Epithalamion* seeks to create a peaceful time-
lessness, *The Faerie Queene* attempts to hold together a unified vision
of the world. As with any poem, it is open to question how to begin
a critical discussion of it, but with *The Faerie Queene* it seems natural to
start with the fact that it is dedicated to Elizabeth I, who, in real life,
in the way she projected an image of herself, and in the manner of her
public statements, provided the coherence that held the country
together. This was supported by numerous agents and servants of the
crown, all dedicated to supporting her authority, but overwhelming-
ly, and almost in the manner of the leaders of some of the former
Communist countries of Eastern Europe, she sought to unite the
country through the force of her personality and even more through
the projection of an image of herself as semi-divine. Spenser's poem
is not only permeated with this sense of Elizabeth but is also very
actively contributing to and helping to create the myth.

One of the ways in which *The Faerie Queene* achieves this mythic glorification of the queen is by retreating to a world of medieval romance where the principles and values of chivalry can be kept alive. Indeed, as he relates stories about knights, Spenser is continuing the tradition of providing a model of conduct for a gentleman, in this instance a Protestant English gentleman. The poem follows the adventures of six knights who encounter threats to their honour and integrity, but, as we might expect, outwit, repel or fight off all such threats. It is, although unfinished, a poem on a massive scale but employs a standard stanza pattern throughout, the so-called Spenserian stanza:

> A Gentle Knight was pricking on the plaine,
>   Y cladd in mightie armes and siluer shielde,
>   Wherein old dints of deepe wounds did remaine,
>   The cruell markes of many a bloudy fielde;
>   Yet armes till that time did he neuer wield:
>   His angry steede did chide his foming bitt,
>   As much disdayning to the curbe to yield:
>   Full iolly knight he seemd, and faire did sitt,
> As one for knightly giusts and fierce encounters fitt.
>
> (*The Faerie Queene*, I, 1.1)

The consistent use of this stanza pattern creates an interesting effect; the poem can flirt with danger, but repeatedly everything is made safe, in effect embraced in and subdued by the untroubled repetition of this soothing stanza pattern. Essentially, the Faerie Queene, aided by her loyal knights, can cope with and subdue every challenge, every hint of insurrection and every sign of danger. There is even a kind of magic about the way in which the court can maintain such good order.

But can such a poem still be interesting to read? There was a time when critics used to focus almost exclusively on the peacefulness, coherence and confidence of *The Faerie Queene*. Critics today, however, concentrate more on the signs of strain in the poem, including, for example, the seductiveness of the idea of a knight abandoning his principles and commitment to moral virtue. Possibly the poem pays more attention to the threats, and takes them more seriously, than some critics would have registered in the past. There is evidence of a lack of poise and control in the poem as threats are considered that, in some way, echo or seem to relate to the Irish experiences of Spenser, especially in Books V and VI where the text is constantly disrupted by violent images and an idea of violent forces. There are people who are so far beyond the pale that the writer finds them repellent; at such points, an anxious quality to Spenser's distaste cannot be concealed.

The most telling point about *The Faerie Queene*, however, is simply the fact that it is unfinished. It was Spenser's death that prevented the poem from progressing further, but it is perhaps just as valid to suggest that the kind of diversity and unrest that we witness by the 1590s cannot really be embraced within the unified vision of one poem, even a poem on the scale of *The Faerie Queene*. In that sense the poem, even as it looks back to Chaucer and the medieval romance tradition, oddly anticipates the modern world where it becomes increasingly impossible to connect everything together.

4 Shakespeare

Shakespeare in Context

Elizabeth I died unmarried and without a direct heir in 1603. It seems more than a coincidence that William Shakespeare's most celebrated works, his major tragedies, were written around this time. *Hamlet* was probably first performed in 1600 or 1601; then, after the death of Elizabeth, *Othello* (1604), *King Lear* (1605) and *Macbeth* (1605–6) were staged in rapid succession. The reign of Elizabeth can be characterised as a successful period in English history, with commercial and military successes (most notably, the defeat of the Spanish Armada in 1588) contributing to a growing sense of national confidence. In addition, Elizabeth's Religious Settlement of 1559, enforcing the Protestant religion by law, cemented a sense of the national identity. But the very idea of imposing a uniform religious identity on people does begin to draw attention to fundamental problems in the Elizabethan period, problems that were to become more acute in the latter years of the queen's reign.

Many people, both Catholics and Puritans, were less than happy with Elizabeth's religious settlement. For Puritans, the official version of Protestantism, with its bishops and retention of some aspects of Catholic ritual, was incompatible with their vision of a much more austere reformation of the church and its services. Such differences of opinion were echoed in politics. Elizabeth, understandably, wished to maintain a tight grip on power, and was notoriously reluctant to summon Parliament. But Parliament during Elizabeth's reign began to display its independence in an unprecedented manner. What we see in both religion and politics is the presence, and growing assertiveness, of a variety of voices all demanding their say in how the country conducted itself. It can, of course, be argued that we would encounter a variety of voices in any society at any time, but it is particularly in the nature of an expansionist trading nation, the kind of nation England was developing into in the late sixteenth century, that it will be characterised by independent voices. The dynamic energy displayed by the merchant class is no less present in religious, political and social life generally, with a similar energy and potential for disruption. The overlapping of business and politics is evident, for example, in 1601 in the way Elizabeth was forced to retreat on the question of the crown's monopoly over granting manufacturing and trading licences.

As long as Elizabeth remained alive, however, she seemed able to hold together conflicting interests in the nation, managing to control or eliminate its dissident members. We can point, for example, to the failure of an attempted rebellion by the Earl of Essex in 1601, an abortive coup that led to his execution (his son, it is relevant to note, was a leader of the Parliamentary army during the Civil War). The means by which the queen held the country together is an intriguing and complex subject, but one important aspect was the way in which Elizabeth projected an image of herself as the embodiment of the nation. As we saw in the previous chapter, literature, especially a work such as Spenser's *The Faerie Queene*, contributed to this image. But the problem with an image is that it is nearly always at odds with, or a covering over of, reality. In the 1590s, in particular, more and more discontented voices were heard in the country, fuelled by various factors: bad harvests, the growing enclosure of commons, poverty and oppression. Even within the court there was impatience with an elderly monarch, who procrastinated rather than accepting change. But the most serious threat was the sense that the unity of the nation might fall apart with the death of the queen, particularly as there was no direct heir. It had been agreed that James VI of Scotland would succeed to the English throne, but when he did succeed, as James I, many of his new subjects were intensely suspicious of his intentions. After all, his mother, Mary Queen of Scots, had been a Catholic – might he not seek to reimpose Catholicism upon the country?

It is in this context – the closing years of the reign of Elizabeth and the opening years of the reign of James I, who increasingly alienated the Puritans with his High Church views, and who also found himself at odds with Parliament – that Shakespeare writes. His plays, in both a light-hearted and a serious way, repeatedly feature rebellious characters who challenge established authority. But they are also concerned with leadership. A substantial number of the plays feature monarchs who, in unsettled times, have established a degree of stability, but just as many feature monarchs and other authority or father figures who fail miserably in asserting control. Drama at any time is the ideal medium for a debate about leadership, as a play's plot is built upon the premise of conflict and confrontation, but this was especially the case in Elizabethan England. The new playhouses, based in London, were close to the very heart of the political life of the country, but also in touch with the new and dynamic forces in society and its expanding business and intellectual environment. Such rapid shifts in a society – London's population soared during Shakespeare's lifetime and its growth outstripped every other city in Europe – destabilise and question accepted structures, raising doubts about order and government. At the same time, it is important to recognise that a play is a performance, an illusion created on a stage, and that a play can self-consciously draw attention to the way in which it is an illusion; in particular, it can draw attention to the manner in which the illusion of order, and especially the authority of monarchical rule, is created. The various elements touched on here, including worries about what might happen following the death of the queen, all come together in Shakespeare's great tragedies at the start of the seventeenth century. The point at which we have to start, however, is when Shakespeare embarks upon his career as a dramatist, in the ferment of new ideas, political activity and social unrest of the 1590s.

Shakespeare's Comedies and Histories

Shakespeare's career in the theatre begins with three plays about Henry VI, written between 1590 and 1592 (the dates for all of Shakespeare's plays are conjectural). It is more illuminating, however, if we look at his first decade as a whole, dividing the plays into three groups. There is a variety of early plays, plays which might be regarded as apprentice works in which Shakespeare is learning his craft: *The Two Gentlemen of Verona, Titus Andronicus, The Comedy of Errors, Love's Labours Lost,* and *Romeo and Juliet.* Then, as the decade progresses, two other groups of plays become distinct. There is a group of English History plays written between 1592 and 1599: *Richard III, Richard II, King John,* 1 *Henry IV,* 2 *Henry IV* and *Henry V. Julius Caesar,* first staged in 1599, is one of Shakespeare's Roman plays, but is considered in this section as it is in many ways the logical culmination of the English History plays, taking up their central concerns, though it considers them in a different context. During this decade, specifically between 1594 and 1600 (or possibly as late as 1602), Shakespeare also wrote his great comedies which, because of shared themes, also demand to be seen as a group: *A Midsummer Night's Dream, The Merchant of Venice, The Merry Wives of Windsor, Much Ado About Nothing, As You Like It* and *Twelfth Night.*

Before turning to the plays themselves, however, we need to consider how such works, which seem to have very little in common with the native English medieval mystery or miracle plays (discussed in chapter 2) came into existence. The Renaissance revival of classical learning and of classical texts prompted an interest in Roman drama which, in turn, provided a model that a number of English writers began to imitate: a five-act structure, dramatic rules to be observed, and established types of plot and character. The influence of these classical models can be seen in Shakespeare's first comedy, *The Comedy of Errors,* which both formally and in terms of content is indebted to the works of the Roman comic poet and dramatist Plautus (c.254–184 BC). It was, however, the Roman playwright Seneca (c.4 BC–AD 65) that English writers turned to for a model for tragedy. By 1574, commercial acting companies were established in London, and Senecan tragedy as it had developed in Renaissance Italy provided a form in which the stage could be littered with dead and dismembered bodies. We can instance Thomas Kyd's *The Spanish Tragedy* (c.1587), in which the revenge hero, whose son has been murdered, bites out his tongue on stage after killing the murderers, and Shakespeare's first tragedy, *Titus Andronicus* (1593–4), which features rape, mutilation and cannibalism. By the 1590s the London stage was thriving, and Shakespeare's company was enjoying considerable popularity, becoming a favourite of the queen – *The Merry Wives of Windsor* was written at royal insistence. But, as a commercial playwright, Shakespeare also occupied a position outside the culture of the court. This leads directly to one of the central questions about Shakespeare's plays: did he write in defence of the established order, or as a sceptical critic of its political values?

It is a question that we can start to consider as we look at *Much Ado About Nothing*. The play begins with the return from war of Don Pedro and his retinue, who are to be entertained at Leonato's house. Claudio falls in love with Hero, Leonato's daughter, and asks Don Pedro to woo her for him. Don John, the villain of the play, manages to trick Claudio into believing that Hero is unfaithful. In the meantime, the other characters contrive to make Beatrice and Benedick, who seem to despise each other, fall in love. Claudio, deceived by Don John, rejects Hero at their wedding ceremony. By the end, of course, the problems are solved, and Claudio and Hero marry, as do Beatrice and Benedick. The play might seem to be just a piece of frivolous entertainment: love creates discord in society, but by the end, as always happens in a comedy, social order is restored. If we look a little deeper, however, we can see a gap between public performance and how characters feel and think. At the wedding, for example, Claudio plays the role required of him until the point where he reveals his disdain for Hero. There is an issue here about the difference between the parts people play in public and a seething discord underneath. Indeed, just behind the good humour of the court, but curiously part of it, is the malevolent villainy of Don John.

The pattern seen here is always in evidence in Shakespeare's comedies: there is always a gap between the attractive idea of social order, represented in the public face that characters present to the world, and the more complex feelings and desires that motivate people. This is perhaps easier to recognise in a dark comedy such as *The Merchant of Venice*, in which Antonio borrows from Shylock, a Jewish moneylender, who accepts as a bond, if the loan is not repaid in three months, the promise of a pound of Antonio's flesh. It is successfully argued in court that the bond mentions only flesh, not blood, and Shylock is defeated; he is forced to give half his wealth to Antonio, and to become a Christian. Life in Venice is, on the surface, polished and urbane, but below the surface are complicated questions about the relationship between money, the law, race, justice and mercy. The play ends with order restored, but has exposed difficult areas of conflict. In *Much Ado About Nothing*, the society represented is one characterised by male rule. This is the conventional order of life. But there is something distasteful about Claudio's attitude towards women, illustrated in the way that he relies upon Don Pedro to woo Hero for him. The woman seems little more than a chattel. Indeed, when he is told that Hero is dead, Claudio is quite prepared to marry her cousin, even though he has never seen her (she turns out to be Hero in disguise). *Much Ado About Nothing* is, then, a play that celebrates the restoration of the conventional order at its conclusion, but which along the way has made some telling points about the assumptions inherent in the established order. This kind of questioning is evident in all of Shakespeare's plays: over and over again he examines the foundations upon which social and political life are constructed, identifying the forces that motivate and shape society. Indeed, central to his plays is the idea that much of social life resembles a performance on a stage, in which people play parts (including the roles associated with their different genders), but that this public performance is an illusion that is easily shattered.

A deconstruction of role-playing is implicit in Shakespeare's comedies, but explicit in his histories. Shakespeare's principal history plays deal with a line of English monarchs from Richard II through to the defeat of Richard III by Henry VII, the first Tudor monarch. The period covered is the century up to 1485, the last thirty years of which were dominated by the Wars of the Roses. The traditional approach to these plays is to suggest that they provided arguments that supported the legitimacy of the Tudor dynasty. Just as Spenser's *The Faerie Queene* endorsed Elizabeth, Shakespeare's history plays can be looked at in the same way: as texts that identify the dangerous motives of rebels, and which, by implication, endorse the manner in which the present monarch deals with troublemakers. This line of argument can be applied with ease to a play such as *Richard II*. The play deals with Richard banishing Bolingbroke and then confiscating his lands to help finance a war in Ireland. Bolingbroke subsequently

invades England and deposes Richard, ascending the throne as
Henry IV. At the simplest level, an inadequate king has been
replaced by a man with more political right to be considered king of
England. But there is more involved than this, for *Richard II* is also a
play that looks at the past as a way of thinking about the present. At
the close of the sixteenth century, as it became clear that the queen
would die without a direct heir, there was a troubled interest in
questions of succession.

Richard is quite unlike Elizabeth, who commanded respect and
loyalty. But what we can see is that, when *Richard II* focuses on the
rhetoric and staging of authority, parallels start to emerge between
Richard's performance as king and the kind of performance we
associate with Elizabeth, though not in any direct or crude way.
The parallels can be seen in the problems associated with the fact
that there might well be a gap between the impression and the real
substance of power. Elizabeth seems more solid and secure than
Richard II, but she is growing old, and the country might be only a
heartbeat away from civil disorder. Similarly, Richard certainly
seems powerful. A single word from him causes the banishment of
Bolingbroke. As if to demonstrate his power, Richard then reduces
the sentence from ten to six years, seemingly in response to the
grief of Bolingbroke's father, John of Gaunt (he is also Richard's
uncle):

> Uncle, even in the glasses of thine eyes
> I see thy grieved heart. Thy sad aspect
> Hath from the number of his banish'd years
> Pluck'd four away. [*To Bolingbroke*] Six frozen winters spent,
> Return with welcome home from banishment.
>
> (*Richard II*, I.iii.208–12)

Generally, there is an impressive quality to Richard's language, something that seems almost god-like. But the truth is that Richard's
words do not carry all that much authority.

Indeed, in a later scene, when Gaunt makes a speech where he
plays with his name, punning on the idea of being physically gaunt,
the status of words, and of language, is not only questioned but also,
in effect, undermined:

O, how that name befits my composition!
Old Gaunt, indeed; and gaunt in being old.
Within me grief hath kept a tedious fast;
And who abstains from meat that is not gaunt?
For sleeping England long time have I watch'd;
Watching breeds leanness, leanness is all gaunt.
                    (*Richard II*, II.i. 73–8)

We become aware of the frailty of any order that is established
through language. At this point, traditional criticism would start to
discuss Richard's flaws as a human being, that he cannot rise to the
challenge of the position he occupies, preferring words to action, but
more recent critical discussions of Shakespeare would identify a
broader issue in the play. Rather than simply being interested in
Richard as a character, the play asks fundamental questions about
the construction and exercise of power in the running of a country.
In particular, *Richard II* looks at how the language of the king, together with the ritualised and stylised way in which he, like any monarch,
or indeed any political leader, presents himself, is crucial in his control of the state. But as Shakespeare looks at these things, there is a
sense of the constructed, and therefore fragile, nature of this hold on
power.

This should become clearer if we think about the characters we
repeatedly encounter in Shakespeare's plays. His focus is nearly
always on rulers, specifically kings, or on father figures in positions
of authority; this is true in the comedies just as much as in the
tragedies and histories. By contrast, Shakespeare's contemporary
Ben Jonson often focuses on ordinary people in London, the kind of
people that, at a later stage in literary history, we might encounter in
novels. In Jonson, a great many of the characters are commonplace
rogues, selfishly pursuing their own private interests; in
Shakespeare the characters are, time and time again, people openly
or covertly challenging, subverting or simply mocking the authority of the leader. The kind of way in which Shakespeare is interested
in political questions is perhaps seen at its clearest in *Julius Caesar*.
The play dramatises the assassination of Caesar when he is at the
height of his power both as a soldier and as ruler of Rome. As is the
case in the English history plays, order and stability seem elusive;

there are rebels (in this case, the conspirators against Caesar), and the hero himself is also fallible. Caesar returns to Rome after his military triumphs, but various figures are beginning to turn against him. A conspiracy develops, in which even Brutus, an old friend of Caesar's, becomes involved. The conspirators murder Caesar. Mark Antony, who has not been involved, swears vengeance for Caesar's death, and is victorious in the subsequent battle at Philippi. Brutus kills himself.

Julius Caesar, as a Roman play, is, of course, at a remove from English life, but deals in a very direct way with contending forces in society, and questions of power and resistance. As such, and the same can be said about all Shakespeare's plays, it deals with issues that were of concern to the Elizabethans, but also engages with problems that are still of concern to a modern audience. Questions about leadership and challenges to leadership were of particular relevance as Elizabeth grew older; it could perhaps be anticipated that, with the accession of James I, there would be a far more unsettled state of affairs, and that the working relationship between crown and country that Elizabeth had established would fall apart. But as well as engaging with current anxieties, *Julius Caesar*, like the history plays, and in a way that is not true of English plays before Shakespeare's, seems to touch upon a political reality that is still relevant today. For example, the play starts with the crowd, who have come out to celebrate Caesar's victory; increasingly, the presence of the people as a whole – as volatile, dangerous and unpredictable as they may be – is a factor that has to be considered in any political equation. Nevertheless, the central issue in *Julius Caesar* is the gap between Caesar's claim to be above ordinary men, a being who is semi-divine like the stars, and challenges to that assumption of authority. What we have to recognise, however, is that the play does not offer a detached commentary on these political tensions; Shakespeare is not in possession of some kind of superior wisdom. On the contrary, the play is a product of the anxieties and uncertainties of the closing years of the Elizabethan period. In an almost instinctive way, as in *Richard II*, *Julius Caesar* senses, teases out, and brings into definition, the undercurrents of thought and feeling that, in retrospect, we see as characterising the period.

Shakespeare's Tragedies

Plays are traditionally divided into comedies and tragedies. Tragedy has its origins in Greek drama, specifically in the plays of the Athenian dramatists such as Aeschylus, Sophocles and Euripides. The central concept is that a major character is afflicted by some kind of suffering, but preserves his or her dignity in the face of this affliction. It is often pointed out that the tragic vision is incompatible with Christianity, in that Christianity offers the good their reward in heaven. In tragedy the hero faces the worst the world has to offer, but there is no sense of compensation beyond the present. It is, furthermore, often argued that the most impressive quality of a tragedy, particularly of a Shakespearean tragedy, is the way in which the main character articulates his sense of the situation he finds himself in. Shakespeare's four principal tragedies, *Hamlet* (1600), *Othello* (1604), *King Lear* (1605) and *Macbeth* (1605–6), appear almost as a sequence in the period before and after the death of Elizabeth. It would seem logical to argue, therefore, that they are plays that are in a very direct way prompted by the political anxieties of this time. But if this is the case, we might wonder why the plays can still so actively hold our interest today. One argument is that these great plays are timeless, offering a particularly insightful vision of the human condition. It is, however, perhaps more convincing to argue that, in the process of engaging with contemporary political concerns, they also convey a sense of fundamental tensions and movements in Western thinking, the legacy of which still affects us today.

This is most obvious in relation to *Hamlet*, and possibly explains why this is commonly regarded as Shakespeare's greatest play. Hamlet's uncle, Claudius, has married Hamlet's mother, Gertrude, just a month after the death of her husband. In addition, Claudius has claimed the throne, ignoring the rights of his nephew. Hamlet discovers that his father was murdered by Claudius. After a great deal of procrastination Hamlet kills Claudius; he is himself killed by Polonius's son, Laertes, who, unlike Hamlet, is an uncomplicated young man who immediately seeks revenge against Hamlet for causing the death of his father and, indirectly, the death of his sister, Ophelia. We can see how the play deals with the issues that concerned the Elizabethans so much, specifically questions of succession and political intrigue at court, but very clearly there is a good deal more going on in the play. In order to make sense of the experience of the work, critics used to latch on to the character of Hamlet, considering how he deals with the moral dilemma he faces. Such an approach to the play had a great deal of theatrical appeal, in that star actors were given an unrivalled opportunity to play the part of an introspective, deep, troubled and thoughtful man. The problem with such an approach, however, is that it seems to reduce the significance of the play in that it makes it little more than a character study.

In these circumstances it makes more sense to search for the larger themes that are implicit in the play, regarding Hamlet himself as simply a device that helps bring these larger themes to life. These larger themes are, as suggested above, in part a matter of the immediate political concerns of the Elizabethans, but what we can also see is the manner in which a corrupt political situation is created at the court, and, rather than acting in accordance with family or tribal loyalties, or (as, for example, was the case with Thomas More in the reign of Henry VIII) in line with the dictates of religion, Hamlet as an individual has to make decisions and choices about his participation in the political process. There is a way in which the burden is placed on the individual in an unprecedented fashion. But there is even more involved than this: the very notion of the individual, a concept which from this point on will feature more and more in Western thinking, is perhaps realised and given substance for the first time in *Hamlet*. There is a shift from a world view where everyone knows their place in a scheme of things to a world view where people are not defined in advance in this kind of way.

And with this shift there comes a new emphasis on the interiority of human beings, on their unknowable qualities as opposed to their known social position. Hamlet himself pretends to be mad, but the force of his acting is to throw into doubt any fixed conceptions about the differences between reason and madness. Suddenly, and in particular in Hamlet's soliloquies, a new interior world is opened up, a world which questions the old certainties of understanding:

> To be, or not to be – that is the question;
> Whether 'tis nobler in the mind to suffer
> The slings and arrows of outrageous fortune,
> Or to take arms against a sea of troubles,
> And by opposing end them? To die, to sleep –
> No more; and by a sleep to say we end
> The heart-ache and the thousand natural shocks
> That flesh is heir to.
>
> (*Hamlet*, III.i.56–63)

And suddenly, too, the language of tragedy has changed, with image following hard upon image, creating an effect of speech confronting the edge of chaos, and of a speaker confounded by contradictions, puzzles and uncertainties as well as pain, anger and grief.

Hamlet deals with a disrupted succession to the throne; an order that is desirable, of one generation following the previous generation in an untroubled way (a fact that would be underlined by Hamlet inheriting the throne from his father who is also called Hamlet), is at odds with the actual state of affairs. *King Lear* also deals with a disrupted succession; the king decides to abdicate in favour of his daughters, but this immediately produces an internecine conflict between Goneril and Regan, Lear having banished their youngest sister, Cordelia, for her refusal to flatter him. She returns with an army to rescue her mad father, who has been driven out of doors by the sisters; Lear and Cordelia are taken prisoner. Cordelia is hanged and Lear dies over her body. Running parallel to this plot is a second plot which sees the illegitimate Edmund deceive his father Gloucester into banishing his legitimate son Edgar; Edmund then betrays Gloucester, who is punished by blinding for helping the mad Lear. Like Lear, Gloucester dies of a broken heart, though reunited with Edgar. Traditionally the play has been thought of as a kind of apocalyptic vision in which the two plots serve to reinforce each other, with the characters acting as symbols of goodness and evil. There is evidence for this view in the play, which has elements in common with both myth and parable: the mad Lear and the blind Gloucester come to self-knowledge through suffering; the vicious cruelty of Goneril and Regan leads to their destruction, but this does nothing to change the world or solve the problems of injustice and poverty the play raises.

On the surface, therefore, *King Lear* might appear to stand free of its historical moment; the play is set in a pagan world, a remote past of elemental storms, unnamed gods and dark landscape. But, as with *Julius Caesar*, this removal of the play from seventeenth-century English society is only true from one angle. From another angle, its concern with the division of the kingdom and the disastrous consequences of Lear's decision to abdicate his responsibilities seems to echo the fears and anxieties that surrounded the death of Elizabeth and the succession of James I; his actions and their consequences reflect the sense of uncertainty and trepidation about what would happen. By the date of *King Lear* James had already succeeded to the throne, but the political worries about the government of the kingdom and its unity remained. It is not a coincidence that the best-known historical event from the period – the Gunpowder Plot of 1605, in which Guy Fawkes conspired with others to blow up the House of Commons – comes at a moment of transition in the constitutional history of the country, England having joined with Scotland in 1603. Similarly, also locking the play into a specific time frame is a concern with the gap between the idea of the king as a semi-divine figure able to command and the reality of his mortality and weakness. It is as if the play is at once concerned that the kingdom will fall apart, but also intensely questioning of any pretensions of kings to be above ordinary mortals. Here we might point to the way James I distanced himself from his English subjects by asserting his divine right to rule, commanding both their obedience and love. The play, we might argue, catches the contradictions of these various contemporary aspects of monarchy and political government, and their complex interaction.

But, as with *Hamlet*, in engaging with immediate political anxieties, the play also starts to grasp a sense of far more fundamental changes in the nature of political and social life, changes that continue to have reverberations even today. Lear and his retinue seem to belong to an older kind of order, conforming to an established set of convictions. But those who set themselves up in opposition to Lear and Gloucester are people of a new kind, with new ideas of political expediency, disdaining traditional loyalties in favour of personal advantage. There is, it can be argued, a kind of premonition of the English Civil War of 1642–60 in *King Lear* in the way that the play recognises an inevitable conflict between those representing the established order in society and characters who are the representatives and embodiment of new impulses within society. The world changes, and the traditional ruling structures and conventions can never cope adequately with the new state of affairs or with the new voices that insist on being heard. Time and time again, Shakespeare returns in the tragedies to a recognition of a moment of deep cultural change, its profound effects registered in the language as meanings accumulate, overloading each word. Some examples of this are stunningly clear: nothing is more powerful in *King Lear* than the way in which the word 'nothing', repeated at key moments, comes to sum up both the negative state to which Lear is reduced and the positive value of Cordelia's love.

Othello is not a representative of the old or established order in society. On the contrary, he is a social outsider, a man who has won his reputation, and achieved his position, by his resourcefulness as a soldier. The way in which this is made most obvious is in the fact that he is an African, a Moorish outsider – some might suggest an interloper – in Venice. Othello secretly marries Desdemona, but her father has him arrested and put on trial for stealing his daughter. The couple are freed and Othello sent to Cyprus as general-in-chief to protect the island against threats from the Turks. Iago deceives Othello into believing Desdemona is having an affair with his lieutenant Cassio; mad with jealousy, Othello strangles her before discovering the truth. Othello then kills himself. Iago's immediate motive is that Cassio has been promoted over his head; he is angered by this breach of the conventions of hierarchy, favour and preference. But this new, and unsteady, situation, where an old set of rules has all but disappeared, creates a state of affairs that is frightening, in that the most extreme anti-social feelings – in particular, Iago's racism – are given a chance to rule. Raw appetite and twisted feelings of desire are both let loose, but also, in Iago's brutal devaluing of women and love, there is a modern cynicism and irony. Here he is speaking to Desdemona about women:

Come on, come on; you are pictures out a-doors
Bells in your parlours, wildcats in your kitchens,
Saints in your injuries, devils being offended,
Players in your huswifery, and huswives in your be
(*Othello*, II.i.109–12)

With the old checks gone, a kind of anarchic situation materialises, symbolised in the play's great storm and the threat of the Turkish invasion. There is a sense of a world that is changing, that is expanding, and, with the disappearance of the old safeguards and safe horizons, new, unstable and destructive forces are released and given the opportunity to wreak havoc.

An anarchic, violent state of affairs is the very essence of *Macbeth*. Stirred on by his wife and tempted by the prophecies of the Witches that he shall be king, Macbeth murders the king of Scotland, Duncan. Then, in order to make himself safe, he has the noble Banquo and his son killed, and also Macduff's family. Duncan's son, Malcolm, however, escapes the slaughter, and, with the help of Macduff, overthrows Macbeth's tyrannical rule and kills him. The plot is short, brutal and violent, with Macbeth's manliness and ambition put to the test by his wife. As in *Othello*, the established order is broken; as in *Hamlet* and *King Lear*, the line of succession is also broken, as if to signal a breaking-up of the old traditional structures as new, ambitious, self-regarding people come to the fore. It is the individual who will determine affairs from now on. There is a gender issue here as well; the world would be manageable if everyone kept to their assigned role, but here is a woman who steps out of line, who refuses to conform to her assigned role. Corrupt, violent forces are unleashed, and again, as in *Othello*, it is a catastrophe that ensues.

In all four of the major tragedies there is a sense of an established order that has collapsed or is in the process of disintegrating. As suggested, this seems to reflect a sense of unrest as James I became king, with the tragedies serving to signal a fear of the breakdown of order as the country comes under new, and indeed foreign, rule. But there is something else involved here as well, something that connects with, and in a sense announces for the first time, the principal thrust of Western experience from this point forward. Over the last four hundred years there has always been a sense of society changing, of things defying comprehension and control as the world seemingly gets bigger and more complex. One of the things that can be said about Shakespeare's plays, particularly his tragedies, is that they not only identify this new sense of the world running out of control, but also manage to give expression to the perception, making it a central feature of the way in which the tragic heroes find the world bewildering. It is because of this that the tragedies still speak to us. It is not that we are like Hamlet or Lear or Othello or Macbeth, but that what they have to say about the way in which the world no longer holds together or makes sense echoes our own impression of a complicated society, and indeed a complicated world, that defies simple analysis and explanation. Wonderfully, the tragedies articulate this bewildering sense of complexity, of things running out of control, of everything teetering on the edge of chaos. The tragedies stand at this edge, looking into the abyss that lies just beyond language.

Shakespeare's Late Plays

Macbeth was followed by *Antony and Cleopatra* (1606–7), *Timon of Athens* (1607), *Pericles* (1608), *Coriolanus* (1608), *Cymbeline* (1610), *The Winter's Tale* (1610–11) and *The Tempest* (1611), and, rather less significantly, *Henry VIII* and *The Two Noble Kinsmen* (both 1612–13). There is perhaps something a little surprising about the direction Shakespeare takes with these late plays; on the one hand, a group of plays about Ancient Rome, and, on the other, a group of plays that are most commonly referred to as romances. It is as if Shakespeare is deliberately taking a step back both from his own time and from the abyss of the tragedies to present plays that adopt a different perspective on the problem of change. With the Roman plays, it is a case of returning to one of the issues at the heart of *Julius Caesar*: Shakespeare examines the reasons why the world's greatest civilisation and empire should have collapsed and disappeared (Rome held a particular fascination for Renaissance England, standing as a kind of model for its own imperial ambitions and self-estimation). With the romances, there is a shift to the world of fairy tale and magic, to the distant, the remote and the improbable, where children are lost and recovered, and time is overcome.

If we turn to *Antony and Cleopatra* first, we can identify something of a difference from Shakespeare's earlier plays in the way that the action shifts rapidly between Rome and Egypt, bringing the two into collision. Mark Antony, the same Antony that avenged Caesar's assassination, is co-ruler of Rome, but has fallen in love with Cleopatra, queen of Egypt and Caesar's former mistress. He abandons his wife and Rome, and crowns himself and Cleopatra joint rulers of the eastern part of the Roman empire. Octavius, Caesar's nephew, defeats them in a sea battle. Antony blames Cleopatra; thinking she is dead, he commits suicide, but lives long enough to discover she is alive. He dies in her arms. Cleopatra then kills herself; she dies as she succumbs to the poisonous bite of a snake. Thematically, what is at the heart of the play is a division between passion and duty. Shakespeare is continuing his exploration of the question of leadership and power, and how Antony is led away from his responsibilities by a passion that destroys him. There is a danger here, as with the tragedies generally, of turning the play into a character study and ignoring its larger ideas, the way in which, for example, the history of the Roman empire has to be seen as pertinent to the current history of Renaissance England, the country that can, even at this early stage of imperial expansion, sense its potential for world domination. We must acknowledge, however, that there are others (including a broad cross-section of general readers, drama critics and theatre audiences), who would challenge the kind of academic, historical and contextual approach to Shakespeare we are commending, arguing that this kind of focus on themes and issues can only operate at the expense of proper attention to the dramatic effectiveness of the plays, and, perhaps more particularly, proper attention to Shakespeare's language.

But this is not necessarily the case; indeed, it can be argued that we are only going to appreciate Shakespeare as a poetic dramatist if we recognise the resonances of his language. Consider the following lines from *Antony and Cleopatra*:

> Let Rome in Tiber melt, and the wide arch
> Of the rang'd empire fall! Here is my space.
> Kingdoms are clay; our dungy earth alike
> Feeds beasts as man. The nobleness of life
> Is to do thus, when such a mutual pair

> And such a twain can do't, in which I bind,
> On pain of punishment, the world to weet   [*know*]
> We stand up peerless.
>   (*Antony and Cleopatra*, I.i.33–40)

Antony says that love is much more noble than Rome, which, as far as he is concerned, can be destroyed. He speaks of Rome melting into the river Tiber, as if it is something that could dissolve, and of the arch of its empire collapsing like a building. He then refers to Cleopatra as his 'space', suggesting something grander, more free and unbounded than Rome. Image follows upon image. The point that needs to be made, however, is that we cannot look at the language of a Shakespeare play in isolation. The aesthetic impression is stunning, but there is far more involved than just beauty, delicacy and ingenuity. The language is so effective because it gives expression to the complex themes at the heart of the play. In this particular instance, for example, it is the aptness and the richness of Shakespeare's use of metaphor that enables him to present a sense not just of the immediate dilemma facing the characters – Antony's defiance of Rome is hedged by suggestions of violence as if to underline the dangerous path he is taking – but of a whole society in ferment. It is not just the lovers who will be affected but the empire, the 'world', the earth and its kingdoms.

What we also need to bear in mind – and this is something that becomes increasingly important during the course of Shakespeare's career as a playwright – is that he is always aware of the play as a play, as a spectacle on a stage. In *Antony and Cleopatra* there is a great deal of attention paid to staging, to the way in which Cleopatra in particular displays herself to the world; an image is projected, and it is the image that the world at large accepts. It is this kind of presentation of a public face that makes life coherent and manageable, but what Shakespeare always manages to suggest simultaneously is the element of feigning involved, that we are constantly aware of the gap between the ordered and organised performance we see on stage and life's more fundamental lack of order. In terms of a critical approach to Shakespeare, an awareness of the theatrical qualities and effectiveness of his plays here coincides entirely with an awareness of how the issues the plays confront are embodied in their dramatic form.

This kind of self-consciousness about the play itself explains why, at the end of his career, Shakespeare returns to comedy, reviving comic form in the late romances. In *The Tempest*, Prospero, the Duke of Milan, has been deposed by his brother and now lives on an island with his daughter, Miranda. He is served by a spirit, Ariel, and a monster, Caliban. Fate draws Prospero's brother, Antonio, near to the island and Prospero conjures up a storm which lands Antonio and his party on the island. There Ferdinand, the son of the king of Naples, falls in love with Miranda. Their betrothal masque, a supernatural dance of spirits dressed as deities, is disrupted by Caliban's plot to kill Prospero. Ariel persuades Prospero to forgive both Caliban and Antonio; he does so, gives up his magic and returns as duke to Milan. To many Prospero has seemed a figure like Shakespeare himself, who gave up his art at the end of his career. Others have seen *The Tempest* as essentially a piece of escapism. These responses, however, miss the way in which the play presents its emphasis on spectacle: how we arrange life into patterns, giving it shape and form, but how, by doing so, we become, paradoxically, even more aware of the randomness of life, its lack of pattern. Shakespeare, it can be argued, returns to comedy precisely because, more than tragedy, it allows us to glimpse the chaos of life that we screen ourselves from. But this should not lead us into thinking that Shakespeare has lost interest in the changing nature of the society of his day. Indeed, *The Tempest* not only deals with issues concerning the construction, deployment and excesses of power, but also deals with a society that is beginning to define itself much more explicitly in terms of its identity as a trading nation and a colonial power.

Shakespeare so effectively offers a sense of the deeper movements of change as the sixteenth century yields to the seventeenth that we might feel there is nothing left for others to say. Essentially, it might be argued that, in dealing with the immediate political anxieties of the Elizabethans, his plays offer a sense of the moment at which the medieval world, which in retrospect can seem manageable and comprehensible, yields to the baffling complexity of the modern world, with its new impulses and new priorities. But Shakespeare, in fact, offers just one perspective on this process of change. If we look more broadly at Elizabethan, Jacobean and, subsequently, Restoration drama, we see that other playwrights all offer their own distinct sense of a changing world; as is so often the case in English literature, it is the variety of voices that can be heard at any one time that demands attention.

5 *Renaissance and Restoration Drama*

Renaissance Drama and Christopher Marlowe

Renaissance drama is a term that embraces Elizabethan drama, Jacobean drama (works written during the reign of James I), and the plays written during the reign of Charles I. It involves three main kinds of theatre: public, private and court. The first public playhouse, the Red Lion, was built at Whitechapel in 1567, in the courtyard of a farmhouse. Regular playgoing in London, however, began in the 1570s.

The Red Lion provided a model for the building of other Renaissance public theatres. It had a raised stage with a trapdoor; above it or near it was a high turret, while around the stage, which thrust into the audience, were scaffolds or galleries for other playgoers. This design was followed for theatres both in Shoreditch, where the Theatre, which replaced the Red Lion, opened in 1576, and in Southwark, where the Globe, built out of the timbers from the Theatre, opened in 1599. The Globe, a public playhouse able to hold up to 3,000 spectators, is the theatre most commonly associated with Shakespeare. Like the Red Lion, it was essentially an amphitheatre, with tiered galleries: those who paid a penny stood before the stage ('the groundlings'), while the seats higher up cost more, the audience, as such, being separated by wealth rather than by social status. The growth of public theatres provides very clear evidence of an expanding economy and the rapid growth of London as a modern capital city to rival those in Europe.

There are, however, other considerations we need to take into account in any discussion of the context of Renaissance drama. Although commercial drama was essentially London-based, the theatres were closed by the authorities during times of plague, leaving the actors without income; as a response, smaller touring companies formed out of the main companies played in the provinces. At the other end of the scale, plays were put on at court for the reigning monarch (the court also produced its own specific kind of drama, the masque). And there was another development: in 1596 a new roofed theatre was built in the Blackfriars (originally a Dominican convent), near St Paul's Cathedral. With benches for spectators and candles for lighting, it was intended to cater for a smaller audience than the Globe, but the residents of Blackfriars objected to its opening. In 1600 an acting company consisting of boys began using it, but in 1609 Shakespeare's company started playing there on a regular basis. By this time Elizabeth I had died, James I was on the throne, and there was a move towards hall-type playhouses which provided an opportunity for new kinds of stage spectacle, including effects made possible by candle lighting. But by 1642, the start of the English Civil War, drama was in decline. The theatres at that point were closed by the authorities until 1660, when, with the restoration of the monarchy under Charles II, they opened in very different circumstances.

Facts like these, about the physical and social context in which plays were staged, start to indicate how it would be misleading to think of the Renaissance dramatic experience in monolithic terms as a single, stable entity. By its very nature, drama is something constantly changing and being changed to suit the conditions of its performance and practice. Most Elizabethan plays were performed in the afternoon, in daylight; scenery was minimal, though the costumes may have been splendid. Realism was not something aimed for; instead, the emphasis was on ideas, on debate, on problems. But other conditions, too, influenced the drama. Plays were subject to licensing, and the authorities were quick to close the theatres not only in times of plague but also following riots or other disorder. It was also the case that Puritan opposition to the theatre meant that the companies had to shelter more and more behind the protection of the court. If we are really going to grasp why Renaissance drama found itself at the centre of a struggle between different interest groups, however, we also need to take into account something else. This is that, as the most prominent and most public form of literature, the drama at all times is at the very heart of social and intellectual change. We can appreciate this point if we think about what drama is and does. Drama stages an action in which a number of people voice different views about the events taking place. It represents the imitation of an action but also, and disturbingly for those in positions of authority, offers an analysis of that action. Whereas in poetry the invisible and unheard voice that speaks the text is single, in drama the voices that we hear are always plural and in dispute. In this way drama comes to reflect tensions and problems in the social order, but also intervenes in them, projecting them into the wider world of its audience. We can see this very clearly in the plays of Christopher Marlowe, the first great dramatist of the Renaissance period.

Marlowe was born in 1564, the same year as Shakespeare. The son of a shoemaker, he was educated at King's School in Canterbury and then Corpus Christi College, Cambridge, gaining his BA degree in 1584, and then his MA in 1587. This was the traditional route for a career in teaching, the church or the law, but Marlowe turned to writing plays, producing no fewer than seven tragedies, as well as the narrative poem *Hero and Leander* (published 1598). He died violently in 1593, in a brawl in a tavern, receiving a dagger wound above the eye. At the time he had been due to appear before the courts on allegations of atheism and treason, and after his death he was accused of blasphemy and atheism by another playwright, Thomas Kyd. Marlowe's death may have been an accident, a quarrel over a bill, or in some way connected with his homosexuality, but it is also possible that he may have been murdered by government agents. Marlowe had, a few years earlier, perhaps been involved in espionage on the continent, and with other criminal activities; in 1589 he was in a street fight in which a man was killed, and in 1592 he was deported from the Netherlands for attempting to pass forged coins. It has often been noted that Marlowe's life is as extraordinary as his plays, both displaying a similar pattern of turning away from traditional values. This is not to argue that his plays reflect his life, but to draw attention to the subversive character of both, and the ways in which they seem to echo each other in their themes of classical learning, violence and rejection of established limits and morals.

Nothing could have prepared the Elizabethans for the arrival of Marlowe's first major play, *Tamburlaine the Great* (c.1587; as with all

Renaissance plays, we are unsure of the date of the first performance and have only a date of publication. It is also worth noting that many plays exist in more than one version). There had been dramatists before Marlowe, but this work was unlike anything that had been seen previously. Thomas Sackville and Thomas Norton had written the first blank-verse tragedy, *Gorboduc* (1561), but the speeches in it are stately, heavy and moralistic. It tells the story of the division of Britain by the king, Gorboduc, between his two sons, an action that leads to civil war and death. The play combines sensational events with a serious moral purpose, and has some claim to be thought of as seminal in the formation of English Renaissance drama, both in its use of blank verse and in its use of Senecan revenge drama as a model. But in the end there is little that is radical about either the content or the form of *Gorboduc*; it offers some traditional advice about the rule of the kingdom and the dangers of division.

Tamburlaine offers something altogether different. It tells the story of a Scythian shepherd chieftain who overthrows the king of the Persians and then overcomes the Turkish emperor before going on to capture Damascus from the Sultan of Egypt. Essentially the action of the play consists of a series of conquests of the most powerful armies on earth; Tamburlaine's ambition and cruelty carry all before him. The only feeling Tamburlaine seems to show is for Zenocrate, the captive daughter of the Sultan, whom he marries. In Part II – the play is in two parts, the second part written to capitalise on the success of the first – Tamburlaine continues his conquests as far as Babylon and is only finally defeated by death. In terms of plot, the play offers little more than a sequence of brutal victories by Tamburlaine over weak rulers who do not deserve to keep power. Where the interest lies, and why the play made such an impact, is in Marlowe's mighty blank-verse lines. Here, for example, Tamburlaine justifies his rebellion against Cosro, the king of Persia (Tamburlaine has previously assisted in overthrowing his brother):

> The thirst of reign and sweetness of a crown,
> That caus'd the eldest son of heavenly Ops
> To thrust his doting father from his chair,
> And place himself in the imperial heaven,

> Mov'd me to manage arms against thy state.
> What better precedent than mighty Jove?
> Nature, that fram'd us of four elements
> Warring within our breasts for regiment,
> Doth teach us all to have aspiring minds.
> Our souls, whose faculties can comprehend
> The wondrous architecture of the world,
> And measure every wandering planet's course,
> Still climbing after knowledge infinite,
> And always moving as the restless spheres,
> Wills us to wear ourselves and never rest,
> Until we reach the ripest fruit of all,
> That perfect bliss and sole felicity,
> The sweet fruition of an earthly crown.
> (*Tamburlaine the Great*, II.vii.12–29)

Tamburlaine argues that the attractions of kingship are so powerful that they caused even Jove, the eldest son of the heavens, to rebel against his father Saturn, just as Tamburlaine is impelled by his aspiring nature. The speech is about the restlessness of ambition, but if we are to grasp its full dramatic impact we need to take into account two things. One is the simple fact that Marlowe gives this speech, with its classical references, the key indicator of civilised values, to a Scythian shepherd, a figure more commonly associated with barbarism; it is a deliberate reversal of traditional assumptions, as if learning itself will inspire men to greatness. The second aspect has to do with the actual language and rhythm of the speech. It is full of large-scale images of the heavens and earth, so that it has a grandeur and resonance, building to a crescendo in the last two lines. The language is on a scale that matches as well as expresses Tamburlaine's heroism.

As is the case with all Marlowe's heroes, Tamburlaine can be seen as a figure of Renaissance man overthrowing the old order of religion and the law in order to achieve his full human potential. Closely connected with this is the idea of the overreacher: Marlowe's heroes aspire to a kind of godhead, craving divine power, but overreach themselves and, like Icarus in classical myth, who drove his father's chariots too near the sun and crashed into the sea, fall from the zenith of their achievements. Such a pattern gives the plays a tragic

structure of rise and fall, and also fits in with the epic nature of
Marlowe's plotting, which adds incident to incident rather than
exploring one situation in detail. This, however, is less true of *Doctor
Faustus* (*c.*1592), Marlowe's most famous play. It tells the story of a
man who sold his soul to the Devil for twenty-four years of power,
knowledge and pleasure. At the start of the play Faustus, tired of traditional learning and science, turns to magic, calls up the devil
Mephistophilis and makes a compact with him. In return for his soul,
Faustus will be given whatever he desires. The central section of the
play shows Faustus enjoying his power, but not gaining the kind of
knowledge of heaven and hell that he thirsts for. As time runs out –
the bargain is for no more than twenty-four years – and his eternal
damnation approaches, Faustus hovers between despair and belief.
The play consequently seems to teach a moral lesson in the fashion
of the earlier morality plays, but also questions the limits placed on
human knowledge by an apparently vengeful God. This doubleness
of the play is evident both in its form, which employs Good and Bad
Angels to dramatise the divisions in Faustus's conscience, and in its
language, most famously in Faustus's final soliloquy:

> Ah, Faustus,
> Now hast thou but one bare hour to live,
> And then thou must be damn'd perpetually.
> Stand still, you ever-moving spheres of heaven,
> That time may cease and midnight never come!
> Fair nature's eye, rise, rise again, and make
> Perpetual day. Or let this hour be but
> A year, a month, a week, a natural day,
> That Faustus may repent and save his soul.
> *O lente, lente, currite noctis equi.*   [*O slowly, slowly, you horses of the night*]
> The stars move still, time runs, the clock will strike.
> The devil will come, and Faustus must be damn'd.
> O, I'll leap up to my God; who pulls me down?
> See, see, where Christ's blood streams in the firmament.
> One drop would save my soul, half a drop. Ah, my Christ!
>   (*Doctor Faustus,*V.ii.143–57)

As in *Tamburlaine*, the language is cosmic, visual and spectacular.
Throughout the plays there is a sense of new worlds being explored,

where human knowledge aspires to new heights, but also a sense of limits and boundaries. In that combination of elements Marlowe's plays reflect the changing world of the early modern period. In 1543 Copernicus had expounded the belief that the sun, not the earth, was the centre of the universe, and that the planets moved around it. In 1628 William Harvey was to announce his discovery of the circulation of the blood. Both the heavenly and human bodies were no longer what they had once seemed. Marlowe, writing between these dates, and from a different discourse, articulates a similar sense of change, of a universe in which knowledge and power are shifting away from those who had previously possessed them. With that change comes a shift in how the world is conceived. What Marlowe's plays particularly illustrate is the force of language itself in shaping and altering the world, as he questions the fixed hierarchies of old and opens up new perspectives. At the same time, however, his plays acknowledge the continuing power of the established regime: Faustus is damned, Tamburlaine dies, and Edward II, in the play that bears his name, is tortured to death for permitting his homosexuality to conflict with the role that he is expected to play as king. In the stress they place on death and violence, Marlowe's plays (the other significant work we have not mentioned so far is *The Jew of Malta*, performed about 1592, but not published until 1633) expose the fear that helped maintain the old order in power despite the subversive voices that were raised against it.

Elizabethan and Jacobean Revenge Tragedy

Nearly all Renaissance tragedies incorporate some element of revenge, but the revenge play proper starts with Thomas Kyd, author of *The Spanish Tragedy* (*c.*1587). A friend of Marlowe, with whom he shared lodgings, Kyd was arrested and tortured in 1593, dying the next year. He may have written a lost pre-Shakespearean play about Hamlet, but what is certain is that *The Spanish Tragedy* provided a model of both plotting and content for later revenge drama, influencing both Shakespeare and other dramatists. On stage we see the ghost of Don Andrea, a Spanish nobleman killed in battle. He is with the spirit of Revenge. They watch as the son of Hieronimo, the hero of the play, is murdered. His body is found in his father's garden. Hieronimo, half mad with grief, seeks justice from the court after he discovers the identity of the murderers, but to no avail. Consequently he takes his own revenge by means of a play in which the murderers, Lorenzo and Balthazar, participate and die. Hieronimo then bites out his tongue before killing himself. A central figure in the play is Belimperia, Don Andrea's lover, who helps Hieronimo with his plot. She is, in fact, indirectly responsible for his son's murder by her brother Lorenzo, a Machiavellian villain who delights in intrigue.

The Spanish Tragedy provided a formula that other plays followed: there is a ghost, a play within the play, a Machiavellian villain, and a grieving, distracted hero who gives vent to his feelings in agonised soliloquies. But these are simply matters of form and content. There are other, deeper reasons for Kyd's success which have to do with the play's central theme of the breakdown of justice. Justice is meant to flow from God through the king to his subjects, but in The Spanish Tragedy this vertical system of justice has broken down. The political problem the play dramatises is the question of what Hieronimo should do after he discovers that the court is responsible for his son's death. Should he take revenge or be patient and wait for God to punish vice? Is revenge a duty or a sin? And who is to authorise such bloody action? Essentially, these are questions of action, questions about how human beings should act when faced by intolerable situations. The Protestant Reformation had placed a new kind of responsibility on the individual for making decisions about moral behaviour; Protestantism focused on the conscience of the individual, but conscience alone, Kyd seems to suggest, does not seem sufficient to cure the wrongs of the court which threaten the social body.

What Kyd devised in The Spanish Tragedy was a structure that permitted the exploration of political and moral questions that seem to have no answer. In that sense the play dramatised a central crisis of the Renaissance as the era shifted from the old certainties of the medieval world to the new priorities of the early modern world. But what the play also shows is the kind of violent cost there was in this process of change. There was, of course, violence in the medieval era, but the violence we witness in the revenge tragedies, inaugurated by The Spanish Tragedy, involves not only that directed against other people but also a violent rendering of the human subject. The best-known example of this violent splitting of the human being is Shakespeare's character Hamlet, but Hieronimo, too, suffers a kind of madness in grief. The seismic shift in the Renaissance is towards this discovery that the world inside human beings is just as complicated and just as chaotic as the world outside.

The Spanish Tragedy was enormously popular. As already noted, it influenced Hamlet, and also the other great revenge tragedies: The Revenger's Tragedy (1607) by Thomas Middleton (or possibly Cyril Tourneur), The White Devil (1612) and The Duchess of Malfi (1617) by John Webster, Women Beware Women (1621) and The Changeling (1622), again by Middleton, and John Ford's 'Tis Pity She's A Whore (1633). These are the major revenge plays, but we can add Shakespeare's Titus Andronicus to the list, together with Tourneur's The Atheist's Tragedy and George Chapman's The Revenge of Bussy D'Ambois, both performed around 1611. As the revenge formula was reworked, it changed, with dramatists ready to exploit the new opportunities afforded by indoor staging to create macabre scenes of gothic darkness, as in The Duchess of Malfi where the Duchess's brother Ferdinand hands her a dead man's hand and shows her the bodies of her dead children and husband made out of wax. The plays hover at the edge of the comic grotesque, sometimes deliberately overstepping the mark, as in The Revenger's Tragedy where the revenger Vindice dresses the skull of his dead lover as a courtesan and puts poison on its lips before the Duke kisses it. Not content, Vindice forces the Duke to watch his bastard son committing incest with his wife even as he dies. What begins to become apparent, and is perhaps apparent even as early as The Spanish Tragedy, is that the violence that marks these plays is only one aspect of their excess. Everything about the plays is extravagant, sensational, and only just under control. At times the plots become bewilderingly complicated, as in The Revenger's Tragedy where Vindice is hired to kill himself, and where only he, in the final scene, can explain what has happened.

What we particularly need to note, however, is that the violence of the revenge plays links them very directly to events outside the theatre. There is a sense in which these works seem to be a kind of premonition of the Civil War to come, in which those outside the court

will take arms against it. This is not to say that Hieronimo or Vindice
are symbols of parliamentary opposition to the king. Rather, it is to
suggest, as critics have done recently, that the violence of the revenge
plays points forward, and that the plays, while not necessarily
approving of the revenge figures they show, see no obvious alternatives to their violent actions. If we ask what Hamlet or Hieronimo or
Vindice should do, how should they act, there appears to be no
answer: in the end they are forced to kill the king. It is in this sense
that the revenge plays seem to embody the inevitability of political
change by force.

There is one element missing from this account so far, which is a
recognition of the prominence of women in Renaissance drama. In
Marlowe and Kyd women are type-cast: Zenocrate is beautiful, while
Bel-imperia is fought over by men. Bel-imperia does, it is true, play a
part in Hieronimo's revenge, just as Lavinia does in Shakespeare's
Titus Andronicus, but there seems little room in these plays for women
as distinct individuals. With the Jacobean tragedies of Webster and
Middleton, however, the focus shifts. In *The Duchess of Malfi*, it is the
Duchess who is the play's tragic centre and who articulates its main
themes of desire and ambition. But in this case the ambition is not for
crowns or territory, as in *Tamburlaine*, but for a kind of domestic, private space in which her family can live beyond the control of the
state. In Middleton's *The Changeling* it is sexual desire that is central to
Beatrice-Joanna's plight as she finds herself caught up in the nets of
male society. If *The Spanish Tragedy* raises the question of how to act in
a corrupt society, these later plays focus on the question of how
women are to survive in a world that restrains and restricts them. The
plays look at marriage and love in a society governed by patriarchal
politics and economics. The tragic deaths of women in Jacobean
drama arise not from flaws in their characters, but from the material
circumstances in which they are placed, where their desires are seen
as too threatening to be allowed to continue. And yet it is clear that
the plays approve of these dangerous women and elicit sympathy for
them. As such, the plays reflect a shift taking place in the Renaissance
that involved new thinking about the family and the role of women.
Set for the most part in Italian courts, Jacobean revenge tragedies
prove, paradoxically, to be just as much about domestic issues as

about state politics, but, in addition, they also testify to the way in which domestic issues of love, marriage, children and the family were becoming issues of state politics. As such, they stand at a crucial intersection of cultural change between older social formations and the modern world.

Ben Jonson and the Masque

It is not easy to fit Ben Jonson into the pattern of Renaissance drama, but it would be totally misleading to leave him out. Jonson was born in London, the son of a clergyman, and educated at Westminster School, where he acquired a good knowledge of the classics. At first he worked as a bricklayer, but subsequently, after military service in Flanders, became an actor and playwright. In 1598 he was involved in a duel with a fellow actor whom he killed, but managed to escape hanging. His influence on English literature is in some ways greater than that of Shakespeare. Jonson was the first unofficial poet laureate, being given a pension by James I in 1616. In the same year he published his collected *Works*, raising drama to the status of other literary texts. In addition to plays he wrote poetry, and (after his death) his prose work *Timber: or Discoveries*, which discusses poetic and dramatic principles, was published in 1640. Jonson is also known for his influence over younger writers (the 'sons' or 'tribe' of Ben, including the poets Thomas Carew and Robert Herrick). In everything he wrote Jonson is likely to strike us as deeply conservative and yet also remarkably innovative.

Jonson's first major play was *Everyman in His Humour* (1598). By humour Jonson meant the governing passions of human beings, such as greed, lust and ambition, passions which he exaggerates for the purpose of satire. In Renaissance and medieval physiology, a humour was a bodily fluid; excess of one particular fluid was felt to unbalance the temperament of people, making them, for example, melancholic or sanguine. In Jonson's plays, set in the expanding economy of London and amongst its merchant class, avarice is nearly always the ruling passion that dominates, but folly, too, is found everywhere. At the centre of *Everyman in His Humour* is the deceitful servant Brainworm who exploits the jealousy of the merchant Kitely and the credulity of his wife. Other figures include a cowardly boasting soldier, Bobadill. Kitely suspects that his brother-in-law, Wellbred, and his friends have sexual designs on his wife and on his sister Bridget. Brainworm tricks all the parties into meeting at the house of a water-bearer where confusion and misunderstanding reign until Justice Clement restores order. The play is a characteristic piece by Jonson, combining satire, knock-about farce and a kind of surreal comedy in which, for a while, the world is dominated by ruling passions that threaten to reduce everything to chaos.

On the surface, Jonson's seems to be a comic world that is informed in a very simple way by a recognition of humankind's propensity for foolishness. Underlying the plays, however, is a darker premise: that people are greedy, lustful and liars, and that society is governed by vice rather than by virtue. It is this that makes Jonson a conservative playwright He is an advocate of tradition and traditional behaviour, and against the kind of radical change that was taking place, especially in London, where a rage for new building seemed to sum up a city in ferment. What Jonson favours is the restraint associated with ancient, and especially Roman, civilisation. This is evident in the form of his plays, particularly his tragedies, such as *Sejanus* (1603), which conform to the classical unities of time, place and action, restricting what can be shown so that it corresponds with what is probable. There is a distrust of the fancy and imagination in Jonson that allies him, rather oddly, with Puritan opposition to the theatre, the Puritans being equally distrustful of the power of the stage to deceive. But Jonson also delights in the mad behaviour of those on stage, as he manipulates everything towards impossible situations only to resolve them at the last moment.

This is evident in his great comic dramas, *Volpone* (1605), *The Alchemist* (1610) and *Bartholomew Fair* (1614), which exploit to the full the idea of people driven by humours. In *Volpone*, Volpone (the 'fox') pretends to be near death. His would-be heirs and friends visit him, hoping to gain from his will. Meanwhile, his servant Mosca (the 'fly') extracts costly gifts from them by suggesting that each is to be the sole heir. But Volpone overreaches himself. He leaves everything to Mosca and pretends to die, but Mosca then blackmails him. In the end Volpone goes before the court to confess all and is punished by being cast in irons, while Mosca is sent to the galleys. In addition to the main plot there is a subplot involving the foolish Sir Politic Would-be, an English traveller mocked for his absurd schemes and who is only brought to his senses when his friend pretends to have him arrested for treason. The play satirises the greedy folly of humankind, as does *The Alchemist*. Here the plot turns upon the desires of the characters for instant wealth based on the pseudo-scientific hope that base metal can be turned into gold. But in addition to this, what we also see played out on the stage are the wild fantasies of the characters tricked by Subtle and Face, and also by their own gullibility and self-delusion. The action, like that of *Volpone*, becomes ever more complicated as the pace increases to a kind of frenzy until all is resolved by the return of Lovewit, the owner of the house where the action has taken place.

What may strike us about Jonson's plays, as well as their caustic satire, is their sheer ingenuity, as if Jonson delights in showing off his skill in a masterly exhibition of plotting and timing. On the page this can make the plays hard to follow, but on stage everything works perfectly. This is certainly the case with *Bartholomew Fair*, set at the annual fair in Smithfield, London, where the public are duped or dupe themselves, Puritans are exposed as hypocrites, wives turn into prostitutes, and Justice Overdo, the overseer of law and order, is arrested as a criminal. On the surface the play is about the ridiculousness of vice, but its self-conscious artifice steers it towards a carnivalesque celebration of idiosyncrasy. As such, and paradoxically, Jonson's satire seems to celebrate behaviour that falls outside the scope of the social and the restrained; the result is a certain ambivalence about the social order.

Jonson's delight in artifice and elaboration, so evident in his comedies, presents us with a clue to the other aspect of his dramatic achievement: the masque. Masques were fashionable at court, especially during the reign of James I. They were spectacular entertainments combining verse, music, dancing, disguises and visual effects. They were performed indoors, often by professionals, while the masquers were played by members of the court. The latter remained silent; only the actors spoke, thus preserving court decorum by separating ladies and gentlemen from common players. A masque nearly always ended with dancing, with both spectators and the courtly masquers involved, but not the actors. The plot was usually symbolic, with virtue triumphing over vice. This is the case in Milton's *Comus* (1634) where the Lady resists the sexual temptations of the pagan god Comus and preserves her virginity. *Comus*, however, has little of the spectacle that normally accompanies the masque and so could also be described as a pastoral drama, Comus disguising himself as a shepherd, as do the Lady's brothers in their attempt to rescue her.

It was Jonson who established the masque as a definite form. He liked to add an anti-masque at the beginning, a burlesque or parody of the main masque. This fits in with the pattern of Jonson's comic writing, in that the purpose of the anti-masque was satiric while the main masque was educative and moral. For example, *The Masque of Queens* (1609) opens with a grotesque dance of witches before these are banished by the entrance of the queens of the title, parts taken by Queen Anne, the wife of James I, and her ladies. They represent the moral virtues as opposed to the witches who stand for the world of evil. The transition in the masque is accomplished by the use of stage machinery: the world of hell disappears on stage to be replaced by a building representing the House of Fame. The machinery and building were designed by Inigo Jones, the architect, who was also the most famous of the masque designers who worked (and quarrelled) with Jonson.

It should be obvious that masques were expensive entertainments, elaborate and spectacular, but also oddly insular. They were intended as entertainments for the court, but they were also meant to glorify the court as ideal, orderly, and virtuous. The lack of dialogue between the common actors and the silent courtiers, however, seems to symbolise the rift between the court and the common world outside, a rift that, with the accession of James and then his son Charles, was to develop into political confrontation. There is a way in which the masque as a form seems to have been designed almost in opposition to the public drama, and while the public drama moved towards a kind of realism, the court retreated into myth and illusion. The invention by Inigo Jones of movable scenery and the use of elaborate machinery was, however, to have a lasting effect on drama. Ironically, when the theatres reopened after the Civil War it was the court style which was to dominate, not the public arena theatre. The court may have been deluded in its self-image, but it was Jonson and Jones's designs that were to hold sway rather than Shakespeare's Globe with its open stage and minimal scenery.

Restoration Drama

In 1660 Charles II returned to England from France following the end of Oliver Cromwell's Commonwealth and the re-establishment of the monarchy. Charles I had been executed in 1649, and from that date until 1660 England had been a Commonwealth, with Cromwell as Lord Protector. With the restoration of the king there came a change in cultural direction. The returning court was heavily influenced by French fashion and ideas, especially by a more secular view of the world. In addition, there were also other changes taking place outside the court which gave a new tone to life. For example, the Great Plague in London and then the Fire of London led to major rebuilding of the city, including Sir Christopher Wren's new churches, most notably St Paul's Cathedral, finished in 1710. The Royal Society for Science was founded in 1662; it advocated a plainer style of writing and thinking, taking its inspiration from figures such as Francis Bacon.

When the theatres reopened after their official closure in 1642, they were not the open-air arenas of the Renaissance, but indoor theatres with movable scenery. The audience was no longer the public at large, but mainly drawn from fashionable circles. The theatres were, in fact, shunned by respectable people, partly on religious grounds, partly on the grounds of the bawdiness of some of the plays, partly because actresses were now on stage, but mainly, one suspects, because the theatres were seen as the preserve of the aristocracy and those in positions of authority. There were just two companies allowed, that of Davenant (who claimed to be a son of Shakespeare), and that of Killigrew, and just two theatres. These retained a thrust stage, but employed a proscenium arch, giving the familiar picture frame effect. The most famous theatregoer of the age who has left a record of the plays he saw is Samuel Pepys.

The theatrical menu consisted of three types of play: operas, heroic tragedies and comedies. The first of these were fairly bombastic pieces, but the second category merits attention. These tend to be plays showing a hero choosing between love and honour, and are set in faraway places associated with romance, such as Granada or Venice. They usually generate wonder rather than offering any real intellectual probing of issues. This is not true of John Dryden's tragedies, however, especially *All for Love* (1677), a rewriting of Shakespeare's *Antony and Cleopatra*. Such rewriting of Shakespeare was common; the Restoration thought well of Shakespeare, but felt his language needed refining. In particular, his use of metaphors was frowned upon and replaced by plainer language. In addition, Dryden cuts back the scope of Shakespeare's play, bringing the action within the confines of neo-classical taste. This is symptomatic of an important change that takes place after the Restoration: whereas the Renaissance seems to take the whole world as its canvas, with the restoration of the monarchy there comes about an urge to confine, limit and order life. This includes the ordering of sexual life, the main subject of Restoration comedy.

The central male dramatists of this period are Etherege, Farquar, Wycherley and Congreve, but in addition we need to take note of the contribution of Aphra Behn, the first major woman dramatist in England. Restoration comedies are sometimes referred to as comedies of manners, and this gives us a clue as to their main area of debate: the manners and morals of fashionable society. They are town comedies, laughing at the expense of fops and country squires. The dominant theme is sexual intrigue, but sometimes, as in Wycherley's *The Country Wife* (1675) the tone is bawdy, cynical and voyeuristic. In *The Country Wife*, the hero, Horner, pretends to be impotent in order to gain free access to women's bedrooms. His name alludes not only to giving married men horns, in other words cuckolding them, but is also a homophonic pun on the word 'honour', a euphemism for chastity. The puns implicit in Horner's name sum up the action of the play and its exposure of sexual hypocrisy. The Country Wife in the play is Margery, who is married to the cruel and vicious Pinchwife. Tempted by Horner, she falls in love with him, but is forced to return to her husband. Meanwhile, Pinchwife's sister escapes marriage to the fortune-seeker Sparkish, and marries her true love Harcourt. The sentimentality of this second plot, however, cannot disguise the raw sexuality of the play in places, and this together with other similar plays provoked a famous attack on the stage by Jeremy Collier in his *Short View of the Immorality and Profaneness of the English Stage* (1698).

We can see that the comedies of this period play with sexual innuendo and focus on the physicality of sexual behaviour, but why should they have provoked such anger? One answer might be found in a shift in culture marked by the Restoration. Restoration comedy seems to revert to a libertine tradition that existed before the Civil War; its rakes and dandies seem to be throwbacks to the Caroline court. After 1660 society started to move towards a more ordered structure, with more rules and regulations, both written and unwritten. Polite social manners started to displace honesty about people's sexual drives and appetites. What was taking place on the London stage seemed to be offered almost in open defiance of the values of an emerging middle class, the people who felt they were the real generators of business and wealth in the country. Restoration comedy puts immorality on public display, but the instinct of the middle classes is always towards privacy, secrecy and concealment.

To express that another way, we are, in the years between 1660 and 1700, moving into the age of the novel, where the private reader is asked to consider matters of taste and judgement on his or her own, away from the public world of the theatre. An impression of moving into a new world can be grasped from Congreve's play *The Way of the World*, written in 1700. This is a very different kind of play from Wycherley's *The Country Wife*, although it is again concerned with honour and sexual betrayal. At the centre of the play's satire is Lady Wishfor't, an old woman susceptible to the charms of both young and old men. She controls the fate of her niece, Millament, loved by Mirabell, a rake figure who has previously seduced Mrs Marwood and Mrs Fainall, Lady Wishfor't's daughter. In a complicated series of manoeuvres, Mirabell outwits his enemies to keep control of Mrs Fainall's property and so protect her and Lady Wishfor't from the blackmail of her husband. The context of the play is not just the rakish codes of the court but the property world of the merchant classes, with a focus on marriage where there no longer seems any room for love. It is against this background that Mirabell and Millament draw up a contract about how to behave in marriage, and how to preserve respect for one another. It is the existence of such a contract that indicates the new way of the world that Congreve is dealing with. Before, there was a world of romantic imagination and foolish desire, such as in the comedies of Shakespeare, where marriage is the ending of a love story. In Congreve's play love and marriage have become integrated into the legal and financial structures of society.

A changing social structure is also apparent in other ways in these plays. First, there is the presence of actresses on stage. The parts given to women may not seem very liberated, with stereotypes of fools, flirts, and man-eaters, but the stage gave women a chance to earn a living in a profession, and also made them visible in society. In this context, we need to consider Aphra Behn. Praised by Virginia Woolf as the first professional woman writer, Behn led a varied life, including spying for Charles II during the war against the Dutch. Her first play was *The Forced Marriage* (1670) but it is for *The Rover* (1677–81) that she is best known. The play takes place at carnival time and, in line with both Restoration and romantic comedy, involves the love affairs of a series of parallel couples. The action focuses on four cavaliers, followers of Charles II, and their meetings in Naples with various English women. The Rover is Penniless Willmore, loved by Hellena. He, however, desires the rich courtesan Angelica Bianca, seduces her and then leaves her to marry Hellena. Other couples pair off, apart from the foolish Blunt who is duped by a prostitute. Seeking revenge for his injured manhood, he threatens to rape Hellena's sister, Florinda, who is saved at the last minute by Valeria, Hellena's kinswoman. It is a cold moment in the play, and suggests how Restoration comedy often lets slip the mask of the social world to reveal something more brutal. It is this as much as anything that the Restoration period perhaps signals: that, in the world after the Civil War, any kind of social order can only be a disguise or mask which cannot really hide the harsh realities that underlie the pretence of social and political order. Restoration comedies, with their mixture of social types, offer us an impression of the changing nature of fashionable society, but they also reveal the fragility of the veneer of civilised behaviour.

6 Seventeenth-Century Poetry and Prose

John Donne

John Donne, the poet who does so much to mould our impression of the first half of the seventeenth century, was born into a Catholic family in 1572. His father was a prosperous London ironmonger and his mother the daughter of a dramatist, John Heywood. He entered Lincoln's Inn, to train as a lawyer, in 1592, and in 1596 joined a naval expedition against Spain. On his return he became private secretary to Thomas Egerton, Lord Keeper of the Great Seal, and was briefly the member of parliament for Brackley, but a clandestine marriage to a relative of Egerton's led to the termination of his employment. It was in this decade that Donne probably wrote most of his love poems. Moving away from Catholicism, his attention, both in poetry and prose, began to turn more and more towards religious concerns, and in 1610 he published his most notable prose work, *Pseudo-Martyr*, which argued that English Catholics should agree to the Oath of Supremacy and swear allegiance to James I. It was around this time that Donne wrote his 'holy sonnets', poems which reflect a dark sense of despair. In 1615 he took orders in the Church of England, and almost immediately was made a royal chaplain by James I. In 1621 he was appointed Dean of St Paul's, a position he held until his death in 1631; in this final decade he continued to write, especially sermons.

The details of Donne's life help us grasp the way in which a writer at the start of the seventeenth century was also likely to be a participant in the broader public life of the country. But the same could be said of writers during the reigns of Henry VIII and Elizabeth I. The moment we look at Donne's poetry, however, it becomes apparent that he is breaking away from the ways of writing that are characteristic of the sixteenth century. This is why, even though they were mainly written in the 1590s, Donne's love poems are usually discussed in a seventeenth-century context. His originality is evident in a poem such as 'The Sun Rising':

> Busy old fool, unruly sun,
>   Why dost thou thus,
> Through windows, and through curtains call on us?
> Must to thy motions lovers' seasons run?
>   Saucy pedantic wretch, go chide
>   Late school boys and sour prentices,
>   Go tell court huntsmen that the king will ride,
>   Call country ants to harvest offices;
> Love, all alike, no season knows nor clime,
> Nor hours, days, months, which are the rags of time.
>
>   Thy beams, so reverend and strong
>   Why shouldst thou think?
> I could eclipse and cloud them with a wink,
> But that I would not lose her sight so long;
>   If her eyes have not blinded thine,
>   Look, and tomorrow late, tell me,
>   Whether both th' Indias of spice and mine
>   Be where thou leftst them, or lie here with me.
> Ask for those kings whom thou saw'st yesterday,
> And thou shalt hear, All here in one bed lay.
>
>   She's all states, and all princes, I,
>   Nothing else is.
> Princes do but play us; compared to this,
> All honour's mimic, all wealth alchemy.
>   Thou, sun, art half as happy as we,
>   In that the world's contracted thus.
>   Thine age asks ease, and since thy duties be
>   To warm the world, that's done in warming us.
> Shine here to us, and thou art everywhere;
> This bed thy centre is, these walls, thy sphere.

Essentially, Donne chides the sun for disturbing him and his partner in bed in the morning. Donne's way of handling this theme, however, suggests that the poem is more significant than its trivial subject matter might initially lead us to believe.

'The Sun Rising' starts abruptly, almost aggressively, and as soon as it starts there is a rapid sequence of images which accumulate so quickly that it is difficult to take them all in. Moreover, as Donne introduces images he seems to turn them inside out, playing with them, creating a sense of a mobile and confusing world. The sun might traditionally suggest warmth and security, but when Donne's mind gets to work on the image the result is restless and unnerving. We can relate this impression to other qualities that are always in evidence in Donne's poetry: there are sudden leaps in imagery, a twisting of ideas, paradoxes and unexpected reversals. The result is to suggest a giddy world, a world that we can barely get the measure of. Donne's tone, the fact that we are never quite sure whether he is being serious or not, contributes to the feeling of uncertainty; nothing seems secure, reliable or trustworthy. The words that best describe the content of the poem are, in fact, the words that we might use to talk about its form: formally 'The Sun Rising' is difficult, bewildering and even exhausting in its twists and turns of syntax and metre, but by being so it creates an impression of a difficult, bewildering and exhausting world.

Such playful complexity could be regarded as simply a reflection of Donne's temperament, but something more general seems to be implicit, which is a changing sense of the world at the start of the seventeenth century. This can be appreciated if we compare Donne and the typical poets of the sixteenth century. Sixteenth-century poetry is both complex and varied, but the writers for the most part work within conventional lyric forms, whereas Donne and many other seventeenth-century poets favour unorthodox and personalised lyric forms. Donne did, admittedly, write sonnets, but the sonnet was losing its popularity. Changes in form could be seen as merely a reaction against the poetic norms of a previous age, but, more significantly, a change in form enables Donne to move from the sonneteers' conventional sense of an idealised love to a sense of love as a mysterious and untidy complex of physical desire and spiritual impulse. It is as if the old tradition works with fixed ideas, but for Donne the notion of familiar patterns is a thing of the past. The reasons for such a change are complicated. Something similar was happening across Europe as the medieval world yielded to the modern world; the term Baroque (from the Italian word for 'rough' or 'unpolished' but also meaning 'extravagant'), which is used extensively in relation to seventeenth-century music and architecture, can also be applied to Donne's poetry. More specifically in an English context, however, we can point to a changing and expanding sense of the world prompted to a great extent by the growth of trade; but there is also a new sense of the individual, a development that has to be seen as an aspect of the Protestant faith in a Protestant country. Suddenly, or so it seems, the world is not only bigger but also more puzzling, and the sense of being an individual in this world is also more complex.

The issues involved are reflected in the concept of the 'conceit'. A conceit is a far-fetched metaphor in which a very unlikely connection between two things is established. Donne employs them extensively in his poetry, as when, in 'A Valediction Forbidding Mourning', he describes lovers' souls as being like the two legs of a pair of compasses. A sense of strain seems to be intended. Donne is trying to comprehend the early seventeenth century, a century that seems to contain a bewildering variety of impressions, and, as trade and science develop, there is more and more in the world that seems to demand consideration. Donne's conceits establish links between disparate aspects of experience, but the links are precarious, as if connections can only be made in a desperately fanciful way. One way of thinking about conceits is to see them as the final expression of a medieval view of life, in which every aspect of experience is linked as part of a comprehensive religious pattern in existence. And this leads us to what is perhaps the central paradox of Donne's poetry: he is the most original writer of his generation, but he is also a traditional writer who would like to recover an old form of all-inclusiveness. He might have become a Dean in the Anglican Church, but a Catholic impulse towards the all-embracing vision survives in Donne's poetry.

This is clearest in his religious poems, where he searches for truth and is disturbed both by doubt and by the distractions of daily life. In 'Good Friday, 1613. Riding Westward', for example, the poet is travelling towards the west, but is conscious that, in doing so, he has turned his back on the east and, by implication, Christ:

> There I should see a Sun, by rising, set,
> And by that setting endless day beget;
> But that Christ on this cross did rise and fall,
> Sin had eternally benighted all.
>
> (ll. 11–14)

Part of the attraction of religious faith is that, as here, it can embrace contradictory aspects of experience. Christ reconciles opposites: he rises and falls, he dies and lives. Donne's response, however, is unexpected:

> Yet dare I'almost be glad I do not see
> That spectacle, of too much weight for me.
> Who sees God's face, that is self-life, must die;
> What a death were it then to see God die?
>
> (ll. 15–18)

He is discomfited, asking awkward questions about his own predicament. At such moments, as Donne complicates and confuses his position, language seems to be stretched as far as it will go before collapsing. There are parallels with what we see in Shakespeare's plays, in particular *Hamlet*, at the start of the seventeenth century: a new sense of life's complexity is acknowledged that is so extreme that the language of literature is pushed to its limits. Indeed, what Charles Lamb said about Shakespeare's works from this period can also be applied to Donne: 'Shakespeare mingles everything, he runs line into line, embarrasses sentences and metaphors; before one idea has burst its shell, another is hatched out and clamorous for disclosure.'

In 'Good Friday' there is a particularly provocative sense of the individual's relationship to God. The poem ends:

> O think me worth thine anger; punish me;
> Burn off my rusts and my deformity;
> Restore thine image so much, by thy grace,
> That thou may'st know me, and I'll turn my face.
>
> (ll. 39–42)

This might seem to be Donne, piously dedicating his life to Christ, but, rather than Donne turning to Christ, Christ is more or less instructed to become aware of Donne. Nothing, we can see, is as it should be; nothing is clear-cut or straightforward any more. What we are confronted with in this poem is true generally of Donne's poetry, both in its secular and religious forms. The syntax of the poems together with every image used enacts a sense of life as in a bewildering state of disarray, with every steady point of reference compromised. Such a stance, it should become clear, sets the tone for much of the seventeenth century.

From Ben Jonson to John Bunyan and Andrew Marvell

It is easy to construct a coherent overview of seventeenth-century poetry; whether such an overview has any validity, however, is open to question. Spenser, as the greatest non-dramatic poet of the six-teenth century, continued to be an influence, but we have to wait until John Milton to see a poet as ambitious as Spenser. Milton, how-ever, has to be seen as rather detached from the poetic fashion of his day, whereas Donne both typifies and dictates the fashion. The so-called Metaphysical poets of the 1630s, 1640s and 1650s – George Herbert, Richard Crashaw, Henry Vaughan and Andrew Marvell – all work in a manner initiated by Donne. Ben Jonson, on the other hand, favoured a more restrained form of social poetry. Amongst those who fell under his influence were the 'Cavalier' poets: Richard Lovelace, Sir John Suckling and Thomas Carew, as well as Robert Herrick and Edmund Waller. Jonson would also, in the course of time, prove a major influence on the neo-classical approach of John Dryden, the writer who, specifically in his satirical poems, seems to embody the spirit of the Restoration period.

What complicates the issue immediately is the fact that writers who were influenced by, say, Jonson, were just as likely to have been influenced by Donne. The real problem in presenting an overview of the century's poetry, however, is the fact that a summary creates an impression of coherent change and development, whereas a more accurate impression is of variety and confusion. Indeed, in poem after poem there is an emphasis on the perplexing nature of life, a stance that is substantiated by the use of rhetorical devices such as paradox and antithesis, conceit and hyperbole. These rhetorical devices convey a sense of the complex and contradictory nature of experience. The security, such as it was, of the medieval world has been left behind, the poetry of the seventeenth century reflecting a world that has, in a variety of ways but perhaps most clearly with the execution of King Charles I by Parliament, in 1649, been turned upside down.

When we think about the intellectual, spiritual, political and social ferment of the seventeenth century, it becomes apparent that the traditional picture of the literary landscape of the period can be redrawn. The established canon of great writers represents a certain view of cultural history, but if we wish to acknowledge untidiness rather than a clear pattern in the century we need to consider writers who used to be overlooked. We could, for example, look at a woman writer such as Aemilia Lanyer, whose *Salve Deus Rex Iudaeorum* (1611) combines religious meditation with courtly elegance:

> Thy Mind so perfect by thy Maker fram'd
> No vaine delights can harbour in thy heart,
> With his sweet love, thou are so much inflam'd,
> As of the world thou seem'st to have no part;
> So, love him still, thou need'st not be asham'd,
> Tis He that made thee, what thou wert, and art:
>   Tis He that dries all teares from Orphans eies,
>   And heares from heav'n the wofull widdows cries.
>
>   (ll. 41–8)

The effect of blending courtly language of love such as 'sweet' and 'inflam'd' with biblical allusion and phrasing is to create an affinity between God and woman. In particular, in *Salve Deus Rex Iudaeorum* Lanyer suggests a deeper connection between Christ and women and offers a feminised image of Christ who in turn reflects back a mirror image of woman. As a result, the poem achieves a much more intense questioning of religious and social hierarchies by its claim to a spiritual superiority for women. It is, however, the combination of religious and courtly concerns that gives the poem its vitality.

Women poets in the period tend to lean in only one of these directions – the religious or the courtly – depending to a great extent upon their allegiances in the Civil War. As we might expect, religious poetry is often associated with radical Protestantism. Anne Bradstreet, who emigrated from England to America, is the best-known woman poet in this tradition, but there are others of considerable interest, such as An Collins, who, in her *Divine Songs and Meditations* (1653), conveys a sense of her poems as humble and personal:

> Lascivious joy I prayse not,
> Neither do it allow,
> For where the same decayes not
> No branch of peace can grow;
> For why, it is sinister
> As is excessive Griefe,
> And doth the Heart sequester
> From all good: to be briefe,
> Vain Delight
> Passeth quite
> The bounds of modesty,
> And makes one apt to nothing
> But sensuality.
>   ('Another Song exciting to
>   spirituall Mirth', ll. 66–78)

The poem in form and language is restrained and almost prosaic in its rejection of 'vain delight'. There is little room here for the kind of play with courtliness evident in Lanier's poem above. What is stressed, quite simply, is 'modesty'. A complication is that this same sense of humility may symbolise the weakness of a woman's role, that the woman occupies a humble position which she has no alternative other than to accept.

A rather similar sense of the woman's role in life is evident in the courtly verse associated with the Royalists, for example in the work of writers such as Aphra Behn, Katherine Philips and Anne Killigrew, although it is the case that Behn voices a powerful sense of woman's sexuality and desire, as, for example, in 'The Willing Mistress', a song in her play *The Dutch Lover*:

> His charming eyes no aid required
>   To tell their softening tale;
> On her that was already fired,
>   'Twas easy to prevail.

> He did but kiss and clasp me round,
>   Whilst those his thoughts expressed:
> And laid me gently on the ground;
>   Ah who can guess the rest?
>
>   (ll. 17–24)

Behn was attacked for her immodesty and openness about sex, but there is an undisguised mockery here of the courtly pretence that love was merely a matter of verbal sport or that women were simply the victims of witty seducers wihout desires and sexual knowledge of their own. It might be argued that much of Behn's poetry and that of other women writers is inferior in quality to the works of well-known male poets, but that is precisely the point: the seventeenth century was, even in the revolutionary years, a masculine culture in which a woman had to struggle to be heard. A case in point is Mary Wroth, the first Englishwoman to write a long romance (*The Countess of Montgomery's Urania*, 1621) and also a sonnet sequence (*Pamphilia to Amphilantus*, 1621, appended to *Urania*). She was the most prolific woman writer of the post-Elizabethan period, and, even though she came from a distinguished literary family (her uncle was Sir Philip Sidney), she ran into trouble because of her seeming criticism of the court of James I and its scandals. As a result, the *Urania* had to be withdrawn from sale.

A parallel point could be made about the writings of the members of the many obscure religious sects that flourished in the seventeenth century, such as Mary Mollineux, a Quaker, whose poems *Fruits of Retirement* were first published in 1702 but date some twenty years before that:

> Thus Modesty, and Spotless Innocence,
> Is often to its self a sure Defence.
> This is the Virgin's Ornament, whereby
> Beauty's adorned; for this doth Beautify,
> Where fading Colours flourish not, and may
> Be term'd a *Dow'r*, whose Worth shall ne'er decay.
>   ('Of Modesty', lines 45–50)

An author such as Mary Mollineux might lack something, indeed just about everything, in terms of literary quality, but such voices need to be listened to if we are to grasp the nature of this turbulent society.

The variety of seventeenth-century voices is more apparent in prose than in poetry. As with poetry, there is an established history of prose writing in the seventeenth century; this traces a movement from texts such as Francis Bacon's *Essays* (1597), Robert Burton's *The Anatomy of Melancholy* (1621), Izaak Walton's *The Compleat Angler* (1653) and Thomas Browne's *Hydriotaphia* (or *Urn Burial*, 1658) through to stylistically far plainer texts at the end of the century. John Bunyan's *The Pilgrim's Progress* (1678) is one text that illustrates the new plainness in writing. Its manner is at a far remove from the fullness of rhetorical expression that characterises works earlier in the century. They reveal a habit of mind which can be described as all-inclusive, whereas Bunyan, with his Puritan convictions, concentrates upon a single example, his hero, Christian, on his journey through life. It is a work that seems to foreshadow the development of the novel in the early eighteenth century as Bunyan dwells on the individual and the importance of personal experience. While a work such as Burton's *The Anatomy of Melancholy* might seem to focus upon a state of mind, in the end it is much more an all-embracing reflection upon life. By contrast, Bunyan, within the framework of a general religious allegory, focuses very much on his hero's state of mind.

While this is the broad pattern of movement in prose works during the seventeenth century, the texts which are amongst the most interesting are those with a political dimension. Milton in *The Reason of Church Government* (1642), for example, challenges the established church, and in the same year, after his wife deserted him to return to her Royalist relations, wrote a number of pamphlets defending divorce on the grounds of incompatibility. His *Areopagitica*, published in 1644, is a plea for freedom of the press. As with all Milton's prose works, it challenges established beliefs and practices. In recent years, interest in this kind of radical thinking has led to a lot of attention being paid to the publications of extreme religious and political groups, such as the Ranters and Levellers, and, perhaps most interesting of all, Gerrard Winstanley's Digger tracts, published between 1648 and 1651, and his final work, *The Law of Freedom* (1652), which puts forward a proposal for a chillingly authoritarian communistic commonwealth.

Winstanley never used to feature in the standard syllabus of an English literature course, but if we are to grasp the seventeenth century

– particularly the fact that in under fifty years the country could move from the relative order of the court of Queen Elizabeth to the execution of King Charles I – it is important to look at writing from the period that conveys the turmoil of new thinking. An interesting insight into the temper of the age is provided in the writings of Margaret Cavendish, who at the outbreak of the war, in 1642, found herself, along with her sisters, under siege from the Parliamentarians at Welbeck Abbey; the sisters ran the estate until it was taken by the opposition in 1644. The sisters' co-written play, *The Concealed Fancies*, deals with these events. This might seem to indicate that Cavendish was very much a voice from the old order in society, but her account of her life, *A True Relation of My Birth, Breeding and Life*, offers a provocative sense of the problem women experience as a result of the fact that their identity is defined through men. Her first volume of verse, *Poems and Fancies* (1653), is also extremely interesting in that it displays her active interest in developments in chemistry and natural philosophy, but also a self-consciousness about her writing:

> Reading my Verses, I like't them so well,
> *Selfe-love* did make my *Judgement* to rebell.
> Thinking them so good, I thought more to write;
> Considering not how others would them like.
> ('The *Poetresses* hasty Resolution', ll. 1–4)

Cavendish is by no means a radical writer, but in a distinctive way challenges an elite masculine culture by confronting its norms. A writer such as Winstanley is angrily at odds with the inherited order, but Cavendish provides evidence of just how many strands of new thinking can emerge in a period of political and social upheaval.

As perhaps might be expected, some of the most powerful new voices in prose come from religious groups and sects, such as the Fifth Monarchists, who believed that Christ's Second Coming was at hand and that he would reign for a thousand years. A remarkable figure in this context is Anna Trapnel who, in January 1654, fell into a trance. Her prophecies in the trance were published in verse as *The Cry of a Stone* in the same year. Also in 1654, her *Report and Plea* appeared, which is an account of how she was called to Cornwall to preach and her arrest and interrogation there on a charge of witchcraft:

> After that day wherein I was thus carried forth to speak for Christ's inter-
> est, the clergy, with all their might, rung their jangling bells against me,
> and called to the Rulers to take me up. That I heard was the speech of Mr.
> Welstead: and others said, 'The people would be drawn away, if the rulers
> did not take some course with me.'

The narrative continues with a dramatic account of Anna's cross-
examination by Justice Lobb and her witty defence. Anna is clearly
perceived as a threat, as someone whose apocalyptic language is dan-
gerously radical, but also as a woman acting outside social and gender conventions by taking on a public role. Throughout the period,
women prophets were constructed as transgressive figures, and the
Report and Plea itself is part of a subversive, transgressive literary tradition which both opposes and ridicules authority.

Literature, of course, reflects social and intellectual upheaval, but it
also helps define and bring into existence new states of feeling and
new attitudes of mind. There is evidence of this, perhaps surprisingly, in the works of George Herbert, who, even though he employs the
devices of metaphysical verse, is likely to strike the reader, at least initially, as a reassuring, essentially traditional, poet. One of his 'Jordan'
poems begins:

> Who says that fictions only and false hair
> Become a verse? Is there in truth no beauty?
> Is all good structure in a winding stair?
> May no lines pass, except they do their duty
> Not to a true, but painted chair?
>
> ('Jordan I', ll. 1–5)

These are the typical ingenious and paradoxical gestures of
Metaphysical poetry, but what Herbert is actually doing is playing off
thinking in this mould against a straightforward belief in God. It can
be argued that Herbert employs metaphysical images merely as a sort
of smokescreen; they do not represent a genuine state of perplexity,
but stand as illustrations of the false thinking of the age, and behind
their cover Herbert sneaks in a simple Christian message. This view is
less than fair to Herbert, however, as at times in his poems there is a
much more alarming sense that the old secure convictions are falling
apart. In 'The Collar', for example, he writes:

> I struck the board and cried, 'No more;
>   I will abroad!
>   What? shall I ever sigh and pine?
> My lines and life are free, free as the road,
>   Loose as the wind, as large as store.
>   Shall I be still in suit?'

>   (ll. 1–6)

The poem arrives, in a way that seems predetermined, at a point where he makes his peace with God, but what dominates during the course of the poem is a sense of an inner spiritual state that is restless and frustrated. There is, as in a great deal of seventeenth-century poetry, a dramatisation of individual feelings that are awkward and troubling, and a fear (even if somewhat glibly dismissed at the end of the poem) that the old framework of convictions no longer provides all the answers.

We can see the crumbling of secure convictions in a number of Ben Jonson's poems. 'On My First Son' deals with the death of a child:

> Farewell, thou child of my right hand, and joy;
> My sin was too much hope of thee, loved boy:
> Seven years thou wert lent to me, and I thee pay,
> Exacted by thy fate, on the just day.

>   (ll. 1–4)

What is striking in Jonson's poem is the directness of the statement of his pain and the absence of any consolatory religious message. What, however, Jonson's poems start to put together as a replacement for old convictions is a secular scheme of values, something that is most apparent in 'To Penshurst', a poem that celebrates balance and proportion, moderation and restraint:

> Thou art not, Penshurst, built to envious show,
> Of touch or marble; nor canst boast a row
> Of polished pillars, or a roof of gold;
> Thou hast no lantern, whereof tales are told,
> Or stair, or courts; but stand'st an ancient pile
> And, these grudged at, art reverenced the while.

>   (ll. 1–6)

By the end of the century, and even more so in the eighteenth century, the social code that Jonson promotes and defends here will be central in English culture, but when Jonson shapes this code of moderation it seems rather like a form of retreat from a period that leans towards enthusiasm, radical ideas and extreme beliefs. Possibly Jonson's conversion from Anglicanism to Catholicism, a few years before Donne made the move in the opposite direction, suggests that he needed a more absolute framework of values.

This sense of an uncertain and alarming world is widespread in the works of the 'Cavalier' poets. At first sight many of their poems seem mere trifles; for example, we might consider 'Delight in Disorder', by Herrick (who is more accurately described as a follower of Jonson than as a Cavalier):

> A sweet disorder in the dress
> Kindles in clothes a wantonness.
> A lawn about the shoulders thrown
> Into a fine distraction.
>
> (ll. 1–4)

The poem as a whole adds little to what is conveyed here: that slightly disordered clothing is sexually alluring. Behind the poem, however, is an awareness of the increasingly restrictive character of Puritan England in the 1630s and 1640s; it is a poem that defies the spirit of its time, both in terms of its theme, and by virtue of being a playful poem about sexual desire. A poet who chooses not to write about politics or other weighty matters can, in fact, be making a political statement simply by his refusal to be serious, his refusal to do anything other than tinkering with trifles. Herrick's poem, it is clear, could only have been written at one precise moment in English history.

It would be wrong, however, to regard Puritan England as uniformly grey and joy-denying. A tremendous variety of people were united in their support of the Parliamentary cause. Andrew Marvell, for example, who served as tutor to the daughter of the leader of the parliamentary army, and later as assistant to Milton, when Milton was Latin Secretary to the Commonwealth, is hard to identify as conforming to any Puritan stereotype. He is equally hard to pin down as a poet, as he combines the inventiveness of Donne with the moral seriousness of Jonson. In his most famous poem, 'To His Coy

Mistress', we see the playful, casual and witty qualities that are, in fact, in evidence in all his poems, but beneath the light subject matter – trying to seduce his woman friend – there is a darker tone as the poem confronts human mortality and the remorseless destruction of time:

> But at my back I always hear
> Time's winged chariot hurrying near;
> And yonder all before us lie
> Deserts of vast eternity.
> Thy beauty shall no more be found,
> Nor, in thy marble vault, shall sound
> My echoing song.
>
> (ll. 21–7)

This leads us towards the other quality evident in Marvell's poetry, the desire to find new reference points in a fluid situation. This is perhaps easiest to see in 'An Horatian Ode upon Cromwell's Return from Ireland', which initially appears to be a straightforward eulogy. As we look more closely, however, we are likely to realise that Marvell's attitude is ambivalent, and that there are limits to his revolutionary and nationalistic enthusiasm; possibly Cromwell has been too ruthless in his treatment of those who oppose him.

Marvell's poem enables us to pull together some of the strands in this discussion of seventeenth-century poetry and prose. There is, in the century, a widespread sense of perplexity, reflected in and leading to disarray and upheaval in both religion and politics. But what also becomes apparent is that, if old convictions are faltering, there are those who are only too eager to embrace new forms of discipline. Politically, during the revolution, there is a new authoritarianism; there are also many who are keen to put forward their views about how society should be reorganised in accordance with their beliefs. But what we also see in the century is the development of a new, essentially secular, code of moderation. Just as Marvell is tactfully critical of Cromwell, on the restoration of the monarchy he becomes an eloquent yet cautious critic of Charles II, in particular of his failure to promote religious toleration. But it is too simple to describe Marvell as a moderate; it is a view that imposes the political vocabulary of the modern world on the very different world of the seventeenth century. There are many aspects of Marvell's whole manner of thinking that are simply irretrievable today. For the sake of argument, however, if we do designate Marvell a moderate, it helps us appreciate something of absolute importance about Milton, who by any definition, both in poetry and politics, is an extremist.

John Milton

One way of approaching Milton is to consider him as a writer at an opposite remove from Donne in terms of religious sensibility. Donne questions everything and refuses to untie the knots he creates, yet at the back of Donne's poetry is the remnant of a Catholic desire to embrace all of experience in a comprehensive and traditional world picture. Milton, by contrast, a Puritan, and indeed the most eloquent defender of Cromwell's regime, engages in fundamental religious and political rethinking. Donne in a sense looks, almost longingly, towards the past, whereas Milton is interested in the future and in establishing a new order.

Milton was born in London in 1608. His father was a scrivener (a copier of legal documents), and, it is worth noting in the context of a century where changes of religious allegiance seem widespread, a Catholic who joined the Church of England. In the course of time, Milton himself would come to regard the Church of England as tyrannical as the Catholic Church. His early works include 'L'Allegro' and 'Il Penseroso' (both 1631), two masques (*Arcades*, 1633, and *Comus*, 1634), and an elegy (*Lycidas*, 1637). In 1638–9 he travelled abroad, mainly in Italy; his travels extended his intellectual and poetic interests, but also added to his hostility towards Catholicism. On his return to England Milton began the second phase of his writing career, producing political prose against the monarchy and supporting the republican cause. Overall Milton wrote on a vast range of topics, but there is always one informing idea: that the English people are special and elect, having been chosen by God to create a new state separate from the past and based upon individual freedom and choice.

Paradise Lost has to be seen in this context. The major complicating factor, however, is that it is a poem that was written in response to the

dashing of Milton's hopes for the country. Although it was not published until 1667, the poem began to be written sometime in the 1650s
as Milton started to realise that the religious and political revolution in
England was an experiment that seemed doomed to fail. Old tyrannies
had simply been replaced by new; the liberties of freedom and choice,
so fundamental to the Protestant faith, were, if anything, more rigor-
ously denied than in the past. There were also factional divisions:
Parliament and the army were perpetually in conflict, with Parliament,
almost inevitably representing landed and vested interests, never proving radical enough for the army. Following the death of Cromwell in
1658, his son succeeded him as Lord Protector, but was unable to provide the strong leadership the country needed. With tension continuing between the army and Parliament, the House of Commons began
negotiations for the restoration of Charles II. If we look at Milton in this
context, the first thing that is apparent is that he welcomes change, and
that, in both his poetry and prose, he is concerned with questions
about the governance of society. In the wake of the failure of England's
religious and social experiment, however, *Paradise Lost* endeavours to
make sense of the fact that the hoped-for new and better social order
had not come into existence in Puritan England.

The poetic form in which Milton confronts this problem is the
epic. Divided into twelve books, *Paradise Lost* tells the story of the fall
of Adam and Eve and their expulsion from the Garden of Eden. In
essence, it is a story of rebellion and punishment. Satan, having
rebelled against God, has been cast out of Heaven with his followers
into Hell. He determines to take revenge, and sets off for the new
world of Earth to find the creatures God has recently created there.
Disguised as a serpent, he finds Eve alone and persuades her that she
will not die by eating the fruit of the Tree of Knowledge, an act for-
bidden by God. After she has eaten, Eve takes more of the fruit to
Adam who decides that he will also rebel against God's command
and share in her fall. Immediately their innocence vanishes; they
have sex, and are then ashamed of their nakedness. The archangel
Michael tells Adam that they must leave Paradise, but that the Son of
God will redeem humankind from the Fall, though Sin and Death
have now entered the world.

A number of features stand out in the poem. Everything, as one might expect in an epic, is on a grand scale: the story encompasses the battle between Heaven, Earth and Hell, looking at the history of the world from the Creation through to the final Flood which will destroy everything. Crucially, it is Milton's language that establishes the poem's stature. Part of this involves Milton's use of epic similes and allusions drawn from earlier writers, including Homer and Virgil, which lend the poem resonance and richness. But the poem also calls upon dramatic devices, such as the use of soliloquy, and visual spectacle, so that the reader is constantly surprised by new perspectives and new sights. We can see that Milton draws upon the whole tradition of Renaissance art, in which the visual interacts with the verbal to create a complex impression. Such complexity is seen again in the way the poem combines classical learning with religious faith, so that behind the poem lies the force of Christian humanism, the belief that classical teaching and Christianity were complementary.

All of this might seem at a distance from questions of the governance of society and the failure of Cromwell's experiment. What makes *Paradise Lost* such a powerful poem, however, is precisely the way in which the Biblical past is pulled into the present in an intriguing way. Behind the action lies the great central question that troubled all writers in the Renaissance as they confronted a world constantly in flux: whether there really was a divine order governing events, a plan that made sense of the endless twists and turns of history. The nature of Milton's project should become somewhat clearer if we compare *Paradise Lost* with Spenser's *The Faerie Queene*. Spenser's poem is a romance epic. Its main figures are knights who are seduced from their quests by temptresses, but who are then rescued. The action is allegorical, so that we come to understand how each of the knights represents a virtue which is aided by true faith. The temptresses are figures of the Catholic Church. The poem's point is that the true church is that of Protestant Puritanism, and that this will overcome all evil. Milton's poem does offer the ultimate hope of Christ, that Christ will restore humankind to Paradise, but he is much more troubled than Spenser by all the questions that surround God's will.

Running through *Paradise Lost* are the key political questions of freedom and choice. These begin in Book I when the fallen angels debate what to do next. From the perspective of Satan and his followers, rebellion against God was inevitable. Heaven demanded obedience and servitude. The revolt may have failed, but it has left them their freedom. Freedom here may seem heroic, defiant and attractive, but it is clear that the fallen angels have also lost their former glory. In this way the poem begins to construct an analogy with the rebellion of the Civil War and with Milton's own interrogation of established authority. That interrogation deepens in Book IX, with the fall of Adam and Eve. There seems little doubt that Milton blames Eve for wanting to gain knowledge and equality with Adam, and blames Adam for taking the fruit and joining her in sin. Yet Milton knows that the Fall is also an act that leads to redemption by Christ, and that Adam and Eve act of their own free will, but within a framework of history planned by God that makes their actions inevitable. Both freedom and choice seem fraught with contradictions that make simple answers impossible to arrive at. Human acts cannot be separated from the Divine Will, but they are not caused by it.

The divine and the human, politics and religion: these seem to be the essential issues in Milton's poetry, and yet they do not account for the extraordinary impact the poem makes. For that we have to think about Milton's choice of verse form and his poetic technique. *Paradise Lost* is written in blank verse paragraphs. It begins:

> Of man's first disobedience, and the fruit
> Of that forbidden tree whose mortal taste
> Brought death into the world, and all our woe,
> With loss of Eden, till one greater Man
> Restore us, and regain the blissful seat,
> Sing, Heavenly Muse, that on the secret top
> Of Oreb, or of Sinai, didst inspire
> That shepherd who first taught the chosen seed
> In the beginning how the Heavens and Earth
> Rose out of Chaos: or, if Sion hill
> Delight thee more, and Siloa's brook that flowed
> Fast by the oracle of God, I thence
> Invoke thy aid to my adventurous song,
> That with no middle flight intends to soar
> Above th' Aonian mount, while it pursues
> Things unattempted yet in prose or rhyme.
>
> (Book I, ll. 1–16)

Milton asks heaven to inspire his attempt to tell the story of the Fall. The first lines sum up the narrative, but they place the emphasis not on God but on Man. It is as if Milton wishes to reorder the Biblical narrative, beginning not with the divine but with the human. But that can only be done by invoking the heavenly muse. Already we start to gain a sense of why the poem is problematic, and how its form works to give expression to problematic ideas and concepts. The open form of the blank verse allows Milton to bring elements together without the pressure of needing to find rhymes and so close meanings off. Similarly, the long sentences work to include alternatives that open up possibilities. In this way, *Paradise Lost* can concern itself not just with political questions of governance but with the whole question of human action and human identity. In eating from the Tree of Knowledge, Adam and Eve claim an autonomy for themselves based on choice and liberty, whatever the cost. In the same way, Milton draws upon an enormous range of classical references and allusions, as well as the epic form, to search out a new understanding of human freedom.

Paradise Lost came out in 1667. It was followed in 1671 by *Paradise Regained*, in which Milton explores further the theme of temptation and fall; in this case, it is the tempting of Jesus by Satan to prove his godhead. Jesus refuses and refutes Satan's arguments. Initially the poem looks like a continuation of *Paradise Lost*, but it is a debate rather than a dramatic epic, as Milton teases out the implications of the contradiction of Christ's dual nature as man and God's son. As with *Paradise Lost*, Milton confronts fundamental questions in order to arrive at a more open sense of the relationship between the divine and the human. The same point might be made about *Samson Agonistes*, a blank-verse tragedy published in 1671, but which may belong to the period 1647–53. The hero, Samson, has been captured by the Philistines after being betrayed by his wife, Dalila (Delilah); his hair, which gave him his strength from God, has been cut off, and he has been blinded. In prison he is visited by a series of figures who tempt him in various ways. The tragedy ends when, having recovered his strength and faith in God, he goes to the festival of the pagan god Dagon and pulls down the temple on his enemies. The play seems to echo Milton's life, but a larger framework is provided by the idea of spiritual crisis that marks all of Milton's writings. That crisis emerges from the historical moment of the Civil War, which seemed to promise change but which ended with the monarchy being restored. Looking for the reasons for such reversals, Milton turned to the past to see if God's plan still held good, or whether some new understanding of the relationship between religion and politics was needed. His works possibly mark the end of this Renaissance quest for such understanding.

John Dryden

The monarchy, in the figure of Charles II, was restored in 1660 following the failure of Cromwell's alternative republican regime. Politically the monarchy was now strengthened, with new treason laws, censorship and a purge of urban corporations. In religion, the Clarendon Code re-established the Church of England and also, at least theoretically, compelled the nation to conform; other legislation in the 1660s limited religious freedoms and clamped down on dissent. As we might expect, these new political and religious restrictions provoked anger, and such feelings became more extreme with the succession of James II in 1685, who advocated wars against the Dutch as a way of strengthening royal power, and who, choosing to ignore the wishes of the majority of his subjects, appointed Catholics to public office. There was a widespread assumption that, following his eventual death, his Protestant daughter, Mary, married to William of Orange, would reverse her father's actions, but James's persistence with unpopular policies led to Whig and Tory leaders inviting William to intervene. James fled to France in 1688, William becoming joint sovereign with Mary.

It is clear, then, that religious and political disputes continued to dominate English life even after the restoration of the monarchy; indeed, it is political and religious infighting that becomes the most prominent subject in Restoration poetry. The leading poet of this period is John Dryden, who was appointed Poet Laureate by Charles II in 1668. He converted to Catholicism in 1686, and lost his court offices upon the accession of William and Mary. The first thing that needs to be established about Dryden is that he is a very impersonal

poet; there is nothing in his works about his private feelings or state
of mind. On the contrary, he is consistently and, as far as poetry is
concerned, almost exclusively a commentator on matters of public
concern. This is apparent in *Absalom and Achitophel*, a verse satire dealing with the political crisis of the last years of the reign of Charles II.
Charles had no son, and his heir, his brother James, a Catholic, was
feared by many. The Whigs, led by Shaftesbury, attempted to exclude
James from the throne, substituting Charles's illegitimate son, the
Duke of Monmouth. Dryden, using a biblical story with certain parallels, attempted to influence the public against the Whigs, presenting them as anarchic enemies of God's anointed king:

> Of these the false Achitophel was first,
> A name to all succeeding ages cursed,
> For close designs, and crooked counsels fit,
> Sagacious, bold, and turbulent of wit;
> Restless, unfixed in principles and place,
> In power unpleased, impatient of disgrace.
>
> (ll. 150–5)

In terms of literary fashion, Dryden's poetry in this mould, together
with his criticism, had an enormous influence on shaping neo-classical literature in the eighteenth century. Alexander Pope, in particular,
as a verse satirist writing almost exclusively in heroic couplets, is the
direct heir of Dryden. And Dryden, who was also a prolific dramatist,
is, in addition, an important figure in the history of prose writing,
helping to establish what might be regarded as the modern style of
prose, with its closeness to speech and an emphasis on plainness and
clarity.

But the main question that needs to be answered is why, after so
much innovation and variety in the first sixty years of the century,
poetry should have turned so decisively after the Restoration to the
forms of verse satire typified by the works of Dryden. There is no
simple answer. It would seem to have a lot to do with the fact that,
after the excesses of the earlier part of the century, there was an
acceptance by all parties that political and religious disputes needed
to be addressed within the established system and through the established institutions. Parliament might have conceded defeat with the

restoration of the king, and the final two Stuart kings, Charles II and James II, might have asserted their independence of parliament, but the reality was, as the non-violent overthrow of James II illustrates, a decisive shift of power towards parliamentary government. The centre of gravity in the country had, accordingly, shifted from the court to the broader machinations of political life, and the poetry of the late seventeenth century registers and reflects where the heart of the national debate is taking place. In the eighteenth century, as the novel begins to establish itself, it can be argued that this becomes the genre where the central national debate is taking place, although it is a debate to a large extent about the nature of middle-class existence, and, as such, significantly different from the overt political focus of Restoration and Augustan poetry. It must also be pointed out that, in the late seventeenth century, where trade and commercial considerations were of increasing importance, there had been a significant move towards the modern social and economic order, and that one aspect of this was the privileging of social and political concerns at the expense of religious issues. At the beginning of the seventeenth century, Donne's primary concern was his relationship with God. By the end of the seventeenth century, religion was still a fact of overwhelming importance in people's lives, but, as the literature of the period illustrates, there was now an entirely different kind of preoccupation with the construction and conduct of social and political life. The shift to verse satire reflects this new orientation, this new central focus in people's lives.

7 The Eighteenth Century

Alexander Pope

In his poem 'An Epistle from Mr Pope, to Dr Arbuthnot', published in 1735, Alexander Pope attacks John, Lord Hervey, referring to him as Sporus, the castrated boy whom the Roman Emperor Nero 'married':

> Yet let me flap this Bug with gilded wings,
> This painted Child of Dirt that stinks and stings;
> Whose Buzz the Witty and the Fair annoys.
> Yet Wit ne'er tastes, and Beauty ne'er enjoys,
> So well-bred Spaniels civilly delight
> In mumbling of the Game they dare not bite
> Eternal Smiles his Emptiness betray,
> As shallow streams run dimpling all the way.
> Whether in florid Impotence he speaks,
> And, as the Prompter breathes, the Puppet squeaks;
> Or at the ear of Eve, familiar Toad,
> Half Froth, half Venom, spits himself abroad,
> In Puns, or Politics, or Tales, or Lies,
> Or Spite, or Smut, or Rhymes, or Blasphemies.
>
> (ll. 309–22)

Hervey at this time was a close confidant of the prime minister, Sir Robert Walpole, and of Queen Caroline, wife of George II. Pope scathingly represents him as a creature in make-up (Hervey used cosmetics to conceal his pallor) who is always ready to speak for his 'Prompter', the cynical and corrupt Walpole, and who, in a manner resembling Satan in the garden of Eden, is constantly 'at the ear' of the queen. He is seen as an emblem of Walpole's court, and as a threat both to the nation and to Pope himself.

There is nothing new about launching such a satirical attack in a poem. While comedy laughs at human weakness, satire is characterised by a lack of tolerance for human imperfection; it involves an ideal, and condemns those who fail to live up to this ideal. The informing principle can be described as reform through ridicule. The history of satire can be traced back as far as Greek poets in the seventh and sixth centuries BC, but it was Roman satirical poets, in particular Horace – an amused spectator of life's follies – and Juvenal – bitter, misanthropic and indignant – who had the most influence on English literature. This influence begins to become apparent in the late sixteenth and early seventeenth centuries, in, for example, the satires of John Donne and the satirical comedies of Ben Jonson. By about the middle of the seventeenth century, poets writing satirical pieces – such as John Denham, Edmund Waller and Andrew Marvell – began to favour the closed or heroic couplet, where, as in Pope's poem, there is a pattern of every two-line unit rhyming, with every line having ten syllables. It is easy to see why this verse form appealed to satirists: it is an ordered and strict rhyme scheme, and, as such, contrasts with the pageant of human folly that the writers are presenting.

John Dryden, in the Restoration period, perfected the use of the heroic couplet, but then, if it is possible to improve upon perfection, Pope proved even more resourceful in exploiting the possibilities of the form. This is apparent in his 'Epistle to Arbuthnot'. The poem is a verse letter to Arbuthnot, a distinguished physician and celebrated wit. Pope had been attacked in verse by Lady Mary Wortley Montagu, with the assistance of her friend Hervey, and in an 'Epistle' written by Hervey alone. Accordingly, Pope embarks upon a savaging of his detractors, together with a defence of his own character and career. During the course of the poem he creates a sense of frenetic movement and woeful disorder in the world at large. Hervey, in particular, is represented as someone not only untrustworthy in character but also less than a man: he is a creature, a bug, and with his painted face and epicene beauty, sexually ambiguous. He has no controlling principles: when he speaks, he leaps alarmingly from subject to subject. In the final two lines of the extract, we see Pope's technique at its best: everything is pulled together in the order of the couplet, but there is such a torrent of words that anarchy seems close to destroying the very idea of order. This is how Pope's couplets work: a sense of chaos is unleashed, and it is only his skill in restoring the rhyme scheme that retrieves any sense of control. Sometimes, however, as in this extract where 'Lies' and 'Blasphemies' do not quite rhyme, the structure buckles. Significantly, it is when people are presented as ignoring the precepts of religion, when their words become blasphemous, that all hope of order disintegrates. By such subtle touches, Pope conveys a sense of society losing all sense of true values.

Pope's skill in creating a sense of a society that has gone astray cannot be doubted, but the modern reader might have reservations. Can the squabbles between Pope and a small group of his contemporaries really be the basis of great poetry? There are those who might feel that such verse is merely topical, and that Pope fails to engage with issues of real substance. In order to challenge such a view we need to consider another question, which is why satire became the major preferred mode of poetic expression in the late seventeenth and first half of the eighteenth centuries. Dryden set the fashion in the Restoration period (with works such as *Absalom and Achitophel*, 1681, and *MacFlecknoe*, 1682), while Pope is at the heart of a literary culture where satirical verse is dominant. Lyric poems, personal poems and love poems continued to be written by any number of writers, but in this period they have no spark of originality. What also goes out of fashion is the kind of narrative poem that deals with heroic events and heroes. What we have instead is 'mock-heroic', in which an elevated approach is employed for a trivial subject. Pope's *The Rape of the Lock*, for example, deals with the estrangement between two families that resulted from Lord Petrie snipping off a lock of Miss Arabella Fermor's hair. The essence of such a poem is the disparity between high, or heroic, ideals and the sordid and trivial nature of modern life.

It was poems such as this that Pope produced throughout his career. Born in 1688, the son of a Catholic linen-draper in London, his first major poem *Essay on Criticism* was published in 1711, and in the following year the first version of *The Rape of the Lock* appeared (it was expanded in 1714). Initially associated with the Whigs, by 1713 Pope was a member of Jonathan Swift's Tory literary coterie. *Windsor Forest* (1713), a pastoral poem celebrating the political order established under Queen Anne, confirmed his allegiance to the Tories. An important fact to note about Pope is that he was one of a new generation of professional writers. Indeed, it was his translation of Homer's *Iliad* into heroic couplets, appearing in 1720, that helped secure his financial independence. A translation of the *Odyssey* followed in 1726, together with an edition of *Shakespeare's Works* in 1725. Yet, although Pope was part of a new commercial economy, he was deeply at odds with the trade-based and, to Pope, unprincipled direction in which Walpole (British prime minister from 1721 to 1742) was leading the country. *The Dunciad* (1728), another mock-epic poem, laments the prevalence of dullness in contemporary literary culture while subjecting it to scathing satire. It was revised and enlarged, appearing in a final revision in 1743, by which time Colley Cibber, the Poet Laureate, was the central figure, reigning over an empire of chaos. Other significant works are an *Essay on Man* (1733–4), and four *Moral Essays*, in 1731–5. What we see in all these poems is a concern, echoed in Pope's commitment to classical literature, with values in public life, a concern that finds an appropriate focus in verse satire.

But why is satire so much the preferred form of poetic expression at this time? One explanation frequently given is that the orientation of people's minds had changed by the early eighteenth century. Evidence to support this view is found in a poem by Matthew Prior, a poet and diplomat associated with William III, who had become king in 1688 along with his wife Mary. They were succeeded by Mary's sister, Anne, in 1702. On the death of Anne in 1714, Prior returned to England from France, where he had been engaged in Franco-British peace negotiations, and, under George I, was arrested and imprisoned. *Carmen Seculare* (1700) is a eulogy to King William:

> Let Him unite his Subjects Hearts,
> Planting Societies for peaceful Arts;
> Some that in Nature shall true Knowledge found,
> And by Experiment make Precept sound;
> Some that to Morals shall recal the Age,
> And purge from vitious Dross the sinking stage;
> Some that with Care true Eloquence shall teach,
> And to just Idioms fix our doubtful speech . . .
> Through various climes, and to each distant Pole

> In happy times let active Commerce rowl . . .
> Nations yet wild by Precept to reclaim,
> And teach 'em Arms, and Arts, in WILLIAM's Name.
>   (*Carmen Seculare, For the Year 1700. To the King,*
>   ll. 440–7, 470–1, 486–7)

Prior's vision is of a rational society, committed to scientific enquiry, morally respectable literature, supervision of the language, and under the guidance of a constitutional monarch in a world where trade acts as a civilising force. It is as if the extremism, religious fanaticism and political absolutism of the seventeenth century is now a thing of the past. In Britain, this new mood is often regarded as a reaction against the kind of excesses witnessed in the Civil War period, but the fact is that other European nations were also committed to a new kind of rational thinking at the start of the eighteenth century.

The new spirit of the age is reflected in the terms that are commonly associated with it. The label 'The Augustan Age' is applied to the period from approximately 1700 to 1745. The original Augustan Age was the period of Virgil, Horace and Ovid under the Roman emperor Augustus (27 BC–AD 14). Writers such as Pope, Addison and Swift not only admired the Roman Augustans but also drew parallels between the two periods, imitating their literary forms, their emphasis on social concerns, and their ideals of moderation, decorum and urbanity. The term Augustan Age overlaps with talk of the 'neo-classical period', which could be said to extend from 1660 to 1800. Characteristically, neo-classical writers were traditionalists, respecting the Roman writers who were felt to have established the enduring models. A lot is revealed in the manner in which Pope constantly revised his own works. As against a conception of art that would see a poem as a moment of inspiration, Pope laboured over his poems. He is always resistant to extremism and hostile to wilful individualism; his emphasis is always on the need to submit to a restricted and defined position in the order of life. He admires forms such as epic and tragedy, but is too modest to embark upon them; he can contribute most by mocking excess.

The problem with this description of Augustan principles, however, is that it does not really begin to explain the power of the satirical works produced during the first half of the eighteenth century. Nor does it acknowledge in any way an unbalanced, almost desperate, quality that is often present in Pope's allegedly rational verse. There was a time when historians used to refer to the 'Peace of the Augustans', as if in a quiet and orderly way a new kind of more reasonable society was developing in the early eighteenth century. But this is not how it would have seemed at the time. Indeed, for Pope the world was changing in a way that induced both fear and panic. What begins to explain the informing dynamic of Pope's verse is if we see him as desperately trying to commentate upon and to resist, but in the end being confounded by, a changing social, political, economic and cultural order.

Society is, of course, always engaged in a process of change. Sometimes, as in the English Civil War or the French Revolution, the process of change is dramatic and apparent. At other times, the process is less dramatic, but perhaps just as significant. This is the case in the eighteenth century. English society is becoming more competitive, with more emphasis on trade, and the emergence of new interest groups. As discussed in the next chapter, the emergence of the novel in the early eighteenth century is both a product and reflection of these changes. And this changing economic and social order was complemented by a changing political order. The rise of Walpole as the first prime minister reflects a significant shift in power from the monarch to parliament. The whole pattern of English life was being transformed. Pope himself, a writer living by his pen, is, however, not just a commentator on but also an embodiment of the new economic and cultural order which sees the growth of subcultures in London, such as that of 'Grub Street' hack writing and journalism scorned by Pope in *The Dunciad*.

It is as a consequence of these kinds of changes that a satirical writer like Pope emerges, endeavouring to establish mythical points of reference, mythical ideals of stability, which are connected with ideas of tranquillity, of rural withdrawal from the new political and economic regime. It is this dimension of Pope's works that makes him far more than a chronicler of petty squabbles. His poems are trying to comprehend, while at the same time being a reflection of and embroiled in, the deep currents of change in the period of their production. It is this

that helps explain some of the more extreme features of Pope's writing. There is, for example, an almost rabid contempt for women in a
number of his poems (though this can combine with sympathy for
their position in a pretentious but also brutal society), which might
be seen as a fear of otherness, a fear of everything and everybody that
does not resemble himself. The form this misogyny often takes is an
association of women with dirtiness and filth, Pope displaying an
almost obsessive desire for sanitised order that he can understand
and control. At the same time, another feature of Pope's poetry, and
which is characteristic of some conservative thinkers and writers, is
that, as much as he wants a world that will stand still, there is a desire
for confrontation and violence, for some form of final struggle with
the forces of anarchy and change. This might seem a dismissive view
of Pope, but it is rather a recognition of how a writer is the product
and reflection of all the contradictory forces of the period in which
he or she is writing. Pope is a conservative writer, deeply offended by
the world he describes, but at the same time he is the writer who
offers the sharpest sense of just how British society was altering in
the early eighteenth century.

In this respect it is particularly important to grasp that Pope is not
entirely a reactionary figure, that in a very significant way his verse
reveals the new way in which people began to think about and see
themselves at this time. Implicitly, and sometimes explicitly, at the
centre of Pope's poetry is Pope himself. In a traditional scheme of values such as that found in the Middle Ages, the individual would have
an appropriate sense of their own insignificance in relation to God
and in the general scheme of things. But in the early eighteenth century, as we see in the rise of the novel, there is a new emphasis upon
the individual as the focus or centre of his or her own world. In a
rather similar way, and in a manner that we do not encounter before
the eighteenth century, Pope places himself at the centre of his own
poetic narratives, controlling their pace, offering his balanced couplets as the epitome of good sense, honesty and civilised values.
Consequently, although Pope might appear to look entirely to the
past, reproducing the pattern of received literary models, what he
actually offers again and again is a new form of narrative reflecting a
new sense of the significance of the self. There is a giddy world full of

people who have lost any sense of proportion, but Pope constructs himself as a still point, a point of reference. These elements, that are central in Pope, appear repeatedly in eighteenth-century literature and help us make sense of social, political, economic and cultural change. There is a sense of trying to comprehend, at times to define, this changing society, and, increasingly so as the century advances, a focus on the self as perhaps the only thing that can be relied upon in a bewildering and increasingly anarchic world.

The Augustan Age

A consideration of eighteenth-century literature must always return to the fact that the revolution of 1688, which resulted in William III being declared King, is as important an event in British history as the execution of Charles I in 1649, for it marked the introduction of con-stitutional monarchy and a new political and social order, Britain establishing political arrangements that reflected its emerging char-acter as a dynamic trading economy. The new political order, char-acterised by parliamentary antagonism between the Whigs and Tories, is most clearly summed up in the figure of the Whig prime minister, Robert Walpole. For Walpole, the essence of politics was the pursuit of harmony within a propertied society; this meant tak-ing measures to encourage trade and, as far as possible, limiting the country's involvement in costly military disputes, while profiting from any wars that did take place. But this grand vision combined in practice with a ruthless and cynical control of patronage in order to maintain his own grip on power.

The new confrontational politics of Whigs and Tories meant there were many who might, by birth, have expected to be at the heart of public life who found themselves excluded. Jonathan Swift, at odds with Walpole's leadership of the country, is such a figure. But more is involved than just a feeling of personal exclusion. For Swift, as for Pope, there is a sense of the nation changing in ways that are disqui-eting. It is the eighteenth-century novel that provides the fullest pic-ture of an expanding, trade-based country, with new voices jostling to be heard. In particular, the novel charts the coming into existence of a new kind of middle-class person; indeed, the novel can be regarded as the genre in which such people write themselves into the public record. But wherever we turn in the eighteenth century, for example in developments of journalism in Grub Street or in the growth of the book trade, there is evidence of a society marked by novelty and innovation that is always connected with the developing economic strength of the nation. Indeed, during the course of the century, the wealth of the country increased dramatically, while a series of successful wars, before the setback of the American War of Independence (1775–83), saw a significant advance in Britain's status on the world stage. But even with military and material success, life became more, rather than less, confusing.

A sense of the shifting social order of the early eighteenth century is apparent in the writings of Swift, who, like Pope, presents a society that is beyond both his taste and comprehension. Swift, born and educated in Dublin, but who always insisted on his Englishness, enjoyed political favour during the reign of Queen Anne, when he was a prolific pamphleteer in the Tory cause. His reward for loyal service was his appointment to the position of Dean of St Patrick's Cathedral in Dublin; initially he held the office as an absentee, but, when the Whigs came back into power, in 1714, Swift left England and took up his Deanery in Ireland. For some years he lapsed into silence as a writer, but in the 1720s he began to write on Irish matters, in particular denouncing the conduct of absentee English landlords. Significant works from this period include a series of satiric pamphlets, the *Drapier's Letters* (1724), and *A Modest Proposal* (1729), another satiric pamphlet, which, ironically, recommends cannibalism (or more accurately, the rearing of children by the poor for consumption by the rich) as the only solution to Ireland's economic problems. It was also in this period that Swift produced his most celebrated satirical work, *Gulliver's Travels* (1726), in which Lemuel Gulliver recounts journeys to imaginary locations. Swift, who wrote such a miscellaneous range of works, many of them outside the established literary genres (*Gulliver's Travels*, for example, cannot be described as a novel, even though it was influenced by Defoe's *Robinson Crusoe*), and who repeatedly adopts an elusive ironic stance, is one of the most difficult authors to pin down. Yet the very elusiveness of Swift makes him an apt commentator on the early eighteenth century.

Swift's core convictions are, in fact, very simple: he is a Christian and an Englishman, and as a Christian aware of England's colonial responsibilities in Ireland. But the world he lives in has lost all touch with simple controlling values. The first two books of *Gulliver's Travels*, where Gulliver visits Lilliput and Brobdingnag, reflect the kind of political infighting that characterises the early eighteenth century. In the third book, contemporary scientists are held up to ridicule. In the fourth book, set in the land of the Houyhnhnms, horses are endowed with reason, unlike the depraved all-too-human Yahoos, but reason is clearly not the only thing that matters in life. Perhaps the most significant difference between Swift and Pope is that, whereas Pope has a clear set of moral convictions, Swift as a satirist offers no solutions and very little to hold on to. It is the same in his writings on Ireland. He adopts such a complex set of masks, deceiving and misleading the reader all the time, that there seems no steady point of reference. This, however, seems an appropriate response to the political and social world he is engaging with.

At the same time, it is important to note that Swift is not a detached ironist; much more is involved than merely undermining convictions and challenging the reasoning process. In all of Swift's writings there is a loathing of, and yet an obsession with, human physicality. There is a disgust at the physical grossness of humanity, yet Swift can never resist describing this physical grossness. In this respect, he is very much like Pope. Indeed, both correspond to a certain pattern of right-wing thinking that incorporates contempt for women and a desire for confrontation and violence; revulsion leads to the wish that a tangibly corrupt society will consume itself. It follows that, although Pope and Swift are the two most celebrated writers of their period, they are also, oddly enough, unrepresentative, in that they are so much at odds with what was actually emerging in terms of a new, more polite society. They position themselves as critics of the excesses of early eighteenth-century life, but display a degree of excess in their own works that is inconsistent with developments in British life, in particular developments in British middle-class life. This becomes apparent the moment we turn our attention from the Tories Pope and Swift to the Whig Joseph Addison.

Addison defended the Whigs in the weekly periodical the *Examiner*

(1710), contributed to Richard Steele's *Tatler* (1709–11), and collaborated with Steele on *The Spectator* (1711–12). Addison and Steele's essays might strike the modern reader as inconsequential, for all they do in *The Spectator*, for example, which appeared on a daily basis for 555 issues, is to present what purport to be the views of a small club of gentlemen from different walks of English life. The contemporary significance of these essays, however, is enormous: they are central in the reformation and development of manners in providing ordinary men and women with a guide to a life of virtue within a commercial society. Pope and Swift looked at the society of their day and saw little to praise, but Addison, although a less substantial figure in literary history, is helping to formulate a new set of reference points for a society that is increasingly determined to see itself as polite and respectable. As the critic Bonamy Dobrée observed of Addison: 'He is the perfect representative of what the age was trying to be, the man who more than anybody else helped society to go the way it wanted to go.'

One aspect of social change in the early eighteenth century is the increasing visibility of women in literary life. If at one time the stuff of literature had been heroic deeds and epic encounters, as we enter the eighteenth century there is, particularly in the novel, a growing emphasis on ordinary life. Attention shifts to those involved in day-to-day commercial and political activities, with a complementary emphasis on domestic experience. It is in just such areas that women at this time can compete on equal terms with men. The writings of Lady Mary Wortley Montagu provide a vivid example. Her husband was the English ambassador to Constantinople, where the couple lived from 1716 to 1718. In a series of letters home she describes life in the Ottoman court, the letters constituting a fascinating example of how public and private life interconnect. Montagu also wrote verse pictures of contemporary society, in *Town Eclogues* (1716) and *Court Poems by a Lady of Quality* (1716), but she is best known for her letters, in particular to her daughter, Lady Bute. It might, of course, seem odd to include Montagu's letters in a history of English literature, yet the very fact that she is best known for her letters tells us a great deal about the position of women in her day. Montagu was on the fringes of literary life, but never quite at the centre, never able to get her voice heard in the kind of way that would have been possible for a man. Her letters, none the less, offer a sense of the increasingly complex and varied life of an upper-class woman in the new century as well as of the growing diversity of literary production.

The impression of diversity would be borne out if we had space to consider the works of a number of eighteenth-century women writers, women such as Ann Finch (Countess of Winchilsea), Elizabeth Thomas, Elizabeth Tollett, Sarah Dixon and Mary Leapor. Even more than Montagu, these were writers on the fringes of the dominant male culture, but in many ways this is what makes their works interesting as each so clearly represents another voice and another stance within the Augustan period. The following lines, influenced by Pope but providing an altogether opposite perspective, are from Mary Leapor's 'An Essay on Woman':

> Woman, a pleasing but a short-lived flower,
> Too soft for business and too weak for power:
> A wife in bondage, or neglected maid;
> Despised if ugly; if she's fair, betrayed.
>
> (ll. 1–4)

Leapor was encouraged and supported by Bridget Freemantle, but died in poor health in 1746. Her poems were published after her death. Like so many others, Leapor's was only a quiet voice commenting from the margins.

Montagu's letters were not published until 1763, the year after her death. Consequently, they represent a retrospective comment on the Augustan age, rather than making a direct contribution to that period. As such, they can be contrasted with James Thomson's *The Seasons* (1726–30), four blank-verse poems which combine description of the natural scene with passages of philosophy and morality, and celebrations of British history, industry and commerce. They seem to be poems designed to appeal to the growing middle-class audience, combining an appreciation of nature with a positive sense of the country's destiny. It is easy to be dismissive about poems such as *The Seasons*, which clearly constitute an expression of popular taste and feelings, but if we are to come to terms with the eighteenth century we have to understand how writers such as Pope and Swift are a product of the same dynamic, but also contradictory, social forces that produced Thomson. The difference is that, while Pope and Swift see nothing but decay, Thomson sees the development of something new and vital.

One aspect of a new eighteenth-century mood was patriotism. It was Thomson who wrote 'Rule Britannia', the poem appearing in his masque *Alfred* in 1740. A developing sense of the importance of national identity emerged during the course of the eighteenth century, largely because of the country's growing economic and strategic power. But what we also have to appreciate in a new age with new priorities is that new narratives – new ways of framing and shaping experience – appear. In the Tudor era, a sense of national pride found its focus in the figure of the monarch, but by the eighteenth century it is the nation itself that increasingly provides people with a sense of who they are and their place in the general scheme of things. There is an interesting contradiction, however, in this new sense of national identity, for what we really encounter in the eighteenth century is an increasingly diverse range of voices and conflicting interests. Under such circumstances, nationalism assumes importance as a uniting concept, but it is one that will come under increasing strain in the political conflicts of the late eighteenth century.

Edward Gibbon, Samuel Johnson

A shift in power, from the monarch to parliament, is evident in the way that the names of a number of eighteenth-century politicians still have a certain resonance even today. Walpole has already been referred to. He was succeeded by Henry Pelham from 1743 to 1754. William Pitt the Elder, a Tory, was at the heart of British politics for much of the 1750s and 1760s, and Lord North, a Tory, was prime minister from 1770 to 1782. The century ends with William Pitt the Younger, Tory prime minister from 1783 to 1801. Tracing a succession of well-known politicians, however, creates a misleading sense of continuity in what was actually a disputatious century. The Jacobites, supporters of the House of Stuart, posed a potential threat, especially in 1715, and again in 1745 when an invasion of England from Scotland, intended to enthrone 'Bonnie Prince Charlie', penetrated as far as Derby. The country was also drawn into a series of wars (the War of the Spanish Succession, 1701–14, the Seven Years' War, 1756–63, war against the Americans between 1775 and 1783, and protracted wars against revolutionary France which only finally came to an end in 1815). Military success did, however, lead to a growth in trade and a rapid expansion of the British empire.

At home, rather than a new political order steadily emerging, there was a recurrent sense of crisis. This was particularly the case in the second half of the century. Up until about 1757, there was a kind of pact between George I and then George II and the Whigs. After 1757, however, things began to fall apart. In particular, as we approach the end of the eighteenth century, there is a far greater sense of confrontation between conservative and radical figures in politics. Essentially, the country was changing at a rate that outpaced the ability of political institutions to respond to and govern that sense of change. What was happening in Britain was echoed on the international stage, with the American colonies asserting their own identity to the point where they finally rebelled against British authority.

We have to wait until the Romantic period to see this spirit of challenge and rejection being openly expressed in literature. What we see before the Romantic period are seeds being sown, and the emergence and development of new voices. But what we also see in the eighteenth century is a large number of writers trying to get hold of and to comprehend the process of change. It is the novel as a genre that illustrates this most clearly, as writers construct new narratives for a new century, but we can also point to works such as John Gay's *The Beggar's Opera* (1728), Oliver Goldsmith's *The Deserted Village* (1770), and the plays of Richard Sheridan, such as *The School for Scandal* (1777). These works seem to confront the teeming variety of eighteenth-century life, but there are other works that seem more intent on summation and definition; essentially, works that strive to bring things under control.

For example, it might be assumed that Edward Gibbon's *The Decline and Fall of the Roman Empire* (1776–88) is a work that could have been produced at any time, but it is distinctively a product of the eighteenth century, more specifically of the Enlightenment. This is a term used for the movement throughout Europe in the eighteenth century towards secular and rational views of humanity and society. There is, for example, the appearance of the *Encyclopaedia Britannica* (1768–71), a product of the Scottish Enlightenment. In more general terms, however, the publication of such an ambitious work can be seen as part of an impulse to define anew, to take command of all experience and interpret it in ways that are in keeping with the modern world. Gibbon's *Decline and Fall* shares the same impulse. It might appear to be a work that is exclusively concerned with the past, but what we actually encounter here is historiography being reinvented. A new narrative is being imposed, a new narrative that has to be called into existence because the world has changed. One aspect of Gibbon's work is his antagonism towards Christianity, which led him to view history in a secular and philosophical manner. This includes his account of the rise of Christianity within the Roman empire, which he presents as explicable in political and social terms, rather than seeing it as a matter of divine providence.

The impulse to provide new explanations for a new age is evident again in Samuel Johnson's *Dictionary*. Dryden, Defoe and Swift, amongst others, called for the introduction of an Academy that could regulate the language, which was changing as rapidly as the world was changing. If the language could not be made to stand still, then it at least needed some stability and coherence; shared standards of correctness could then emerge. It is against this background that we have to consider the appearance of Johnson's *Dictionary*, published in 1755 after eight years' labour. Johnson's massive work of definition is an attempt to take control of, even if it cannot arrest, a changing world. Other works by Johnson, although slight in comparison with the *Dictionary*, have a rather similar aim. His *Lives of the English Poets* (1779–81), for example, takes stock of the English literary tradition. It does so, moreover, in a way that differs from older habits of critical commentary; there is a manner of thinking in Johnson's literary criticism that has threads of continuity with the kind of critical thinking that is still in evidence today.

Indeed, the more closely one looks at Johnson the more it becomes apparent that he has moved on from the world of the Augustans, reflecting patterns of thought that are closer to those of our own world. This is evident in works such as *The Vanity of Human Wishes*

(1749) and *Rasselas* (1759). Initially, Johnson might appear to be an Augustan or neo-classical author, intent on promulgating general truths about mankind; poetry, in this scheme of thinking, should examine the species rather than the individual. But what complicates the picture in Johnson – partly as a consequence of the publication of James Boswell's *Life of Johnson* (1791) – is a strong sense of the complex individual that keeps on intruding into the picture. There is a darkness, a sense of melancholy, that is always apparent just behind the social façade and the emphasis on common sense. This impression that can be detected in Johnson overlaps with the rise of sensibility in the second half of the eighteenth century.

Sensibility

If we compare Britain in, say, 1720 with Britain in 1780, it is apparent that the country had modernised and advanced in all kinds of ways. By 1780 Britain was a relatively liberal decentralised state; there was no tendency towards democracy, but there was a parliament responsive to the requirements of the propertied public. Essentially, by the 1780s Britain had a middle-class political culture. There was also a new national confidence and assertiveness, based upon a sense of secure and balanced government and a sound economy. In short, between 1720 and 1780 there had been a transformation of Britain in social, cultural, religious and economic terms.

This change can be observed if we consider developments in women's poetry and writing. At the beginning of the eighteenth century there is just a small number of women poets getting their collections of verse into print; by the end of the century the figure has risen to thirty. Initially there seems to have been a reaction against women writing, partly because of the reputation of Aphra Behn, whose plays and poems from the 1680s, as well as her lifestyle, offended middle-class notions of respectability. By the 1730s, however, different conditions, to a certain extent, started to prevail, with women such as Anna Seward and Mary Jones finding it easier to get published in the growing magazine trade and by subscription. As the century moved on, there seems, too, to have been a change of heart by men in their attitude towards women writers, with authors such as Samuel Richardson and Dr Johnson offering practical help and support, especially to Charlotte Lennox. Certainly, by the 1780s we can speak of women playing an active part in literary circles, with figures such as Hannah More, Elizabeth Montagu and Fanny (Frances) Burney all prominent. Again, by the 1780s women were not only producers of fiction and poetry but also a major part of the reading public. Not all women, of course. There was still hostility to women writers who did not come from the middle and upper classes, and who might represent a threat to the class structure of the new Britain that was emerging out of the Augustan period.

One aspect of this new Britain was the cult of sensibility. Sensibility originally meant nothing more than physical sensitivity, but by the middle of the century it suggested an emotional, one could even say moral, faculty. As the idea caught favour, it came to suggest a capacity for feeling that included fellow-feeling. It is an attitude that we first encounter in novels, especially those of Samuel Richardson, and this helps pin the sentiment down, for sensibility is specifically the growth of a certain kind of middle-class delicacy, a feeling associated with women but extending to a domestic sensitivity that men, too, could understand and embrace. Sensibility also has to be seen as a consequence of affluence, of the growth of a polite middle-class culture. Indeed, in the 1760s, 1770s and 1780s, contrasts were often drawn between the sensibility and respectability of the middle classes and the degeneracy of upper-class life.

What is also apparent in the cult of sensibility is that, after the austerity of Augustan culture, there was a desire and a search for the sublime in literature, and perhaps in life generally. Something had been set in motion that was preparing the ground for Romantic literature, although, in the Romantic period, a writer such as Mary Wollstonecraft was dismissive of sensibility as a damaging female stereotype. But this is anticipating the next step; what we need to consider here is how sensibility was widely diffused in the culture of the second half of the eighteenth century as writers began to explore an alternate world to the public and rational world of the Augustans. It is appropriate to start with Thomas Gray's *Elegy Written in a Country Churchyard* (1751). Gray muses upon life, upon human potential, and upon the unavoidable fact of human mortality. What we witness in

the poem is the coming into existence of a certain way of conceptu-
alising private feeling; there is a privileging of personal thoughts,
which obviously endorses a strong sense of the individual. In a traditional elegy the poet works out his or her own position in relation to
an overwhelming sense of the existence of God, but in Gray's poem
the religious dimension is rather less important than the sense of the
authenticity of personal experience.

A full discussion of sensibility would demand consideration of
Edward Young's *Night Thoughts* (1742–5), the poetry of Christopher
Smart, and William Cowper's poems, and, although they belong in a
rather different context, the sentimental lyrics and comic satires of
Robert Burns. We want to conclude this chapter, however, with
William Collins (1721–59), whose small output of poetry combines
classical control with intense lyricism:

> Now air is hushed, save where the weak-eyed bat,
> With short shrill shriek flits by on leathern wing,
>   Or where the beetle winds
>   His small but sullen horn.
>
> ('Ode to Evening', ll. 9–12)

Poems such as 'Ode to Evening', and 'The Passion' are haunting in
tone. It is very clear that Collins is struggling against Augustan literary conventions to find a new form of expression. Collins died at the
age of 38, the last nine years of his life blighted by mental illness. In
all, he produced under 1,500 lines of verse.

Despite the originality of some of his work, there is clearly something rather scrappy and incomplete about Collins's poetry. Nobody,
for example, would ever describe Collins as a major poet. But in a history of English literature it is important to note the presence of this
kind of marginal figure, for it is so often the marginal figures who are
chipping away at the established edifice, and who are preparing the
ground for something new. Collins is a writer on the outside, a disturbed and alienated figure, but by touching upon dark and hidden
areas of experience he anticipates at least one aspect of where English
literature will turn next. He also highlights a central paradox of sensibility: on the one hand, sensibility was a respectable middle-class
feeling, to be cultivated and almost flaunted, but sensibility also

begins to delve into the dark side of the mind. As we will see in the next chapter, something similar is evident in the novel by the end of the eighteenth century as the novel of sensibility was succeeded by Gothic fiction; no sooner had the individual mind been put at the centre of literature than writers were discovering the more alarming and repressed aspects of that mind. But some of this is already implicit in the poetry of Pope, who tries to establish his own character as a still point in a turning world, but who in the process exposes the more obsessive and disturbed aspects of his own mind.

8 The Novel:
The First Hundred Years

Daniel Defoe

The novel as most people think of it today first appeared in England in the early eighteenth century with the publication of Daniel Defoe's *Robinson Crusoe* (1719). By the time Samuel Richardson's *Clarissa* (1747–8), Henry Fielding's *Tom Jones* (1749) and Laurence Sterne's *Tristram Shandy* (1759–67) had been published, the genre was not only well established but its distinctive features were also apparent. The opening sentences of *Robinson Crusoe* illustrate a number of these characteristics:

> I was born in the year 1632, in the city of York, of a good family, tho' not of that country, my father being a foreigner of Bremen, who settled first at Hull. He got a good estate by merchandise, and leaving off his trade lived afterward at York, from whence he had married my mother, whose relations were named Robinson, a very good family in that country, and from whom I was called Robinson Kreutznaer; but by the usual corruption of words in England, we are now called, nay, call our selves, and write our name, Crusoe, and so my companions always called me.

The qualities in evidence here might not be typical of all novels, but can certainly be found in a great many.

For a start, there is Defoe's plain style. Other novelists might adopt a different manner – Fielding, for example, exudes patrician authority – but the style of a novel always determines its content, and Defoe's businesslike style serves his purpose in conveying a world of commerce and middle-class life. This is important: the novel in England by and large reports upon the experiences of middle-class people who have to work for a living. Indeed, it can be argued that the novel emerged in the early eighteenth century precisely because a new kind of commercial society was taking shape at this time. The novel serves as a mirror for this new middle-class audience, a mirror in which they can see, albeit with some exaggeration, the dilemmas of their own lives reflected. Such novels tended to be realistic and secular. Up to and including the seventeenth century, people organised their lives principally in relation to God. Defoe, like other eighteenth-century novelists, remains a devout Christian, but if we consider the name Kreutznaer – it means 'the fool of the cross' – we can see that the religious echo in the name disappears as he becomes Crusoe. The change in name suggests a move towards secular experience, towards assessing the world, as Defoe does here, in terms of class, social mobility, family and possessions. In just a few sentences, therefore, the opening paragraph of *Robinson Crusoe* tells us an immense amount about the various cross-currents at work in society in the early eighteenth century.

In a good many novels, as in *Robinson Crusoe*, the story is of someone making their way in the world. We can anticipate from the opening of *Robinson Crusoe* that Defoe's hero will reject the secure life of his father. Characteristically, the hero or heroine in a typical novel is not at ease with the established order, and sets out to create his or her own life. In this respect it might be noted that the life of Crusoe's father, in which he has established the parameters of his own existence rather than passively accepting the position in life he was born into, could constitute the plot of a novel. It has all the qualities associated with material advance on the basis of individual resourcefulness that we find in Crusoe's story. If this is, however, a story told in novels over and over again, every separate telling of the story will feature a number of concerns that are distinctively the product of a particular historical moment. In the case of *Robinson Crusoe*, the novel appears at a moment when the balance of the relationship between human beings and God seems to be changing. Defoe is, quite possibly, concerned about this. If we return to the opening paragraph, the passage might seem to suggest a turning away from religion, as if this is inevitable over the course of time, but it is also quite possible that Defoe is dealing with a worrying drift away from religion. Taking this a step further, it could even be suggested that Defoe, on the basis of how he handles the issue of names, displays scepticism about the whole notion of identity, drawing attention to the way in which Crusoe becomes, in effect, a self-named person. There seems a kind of presumption about the way in which Crusoe selects his name, jettisoning the religious association. Rather than simply offering a mirror to middle-class life in the early eighteenth century, therefore, it could be argued that Defoe, as he foregrounds Crusoe's change of name, reveals a broader anxiety about the loss of a religious dimension in life, and questions the new concept of the self coming into existence at that time, a concept of the self that will be at the centre of the future development of the genre.

A further aspect of the same issue is apparent in how Defoe handles the question of patriarchy. Crusoe shapes his life in the shadow of, and in relation to, his father. It is a power relationship in which the child will need to assert himself. But what it also involves is a direct parallel to the way in which the individualistic, entrepreneurial middle-class character in the eighteenth century asserts his independence from God the father. As *Robinson Crusoe* continues, it is clear at every point that far more is at stake than just a realistic account of Crusoe's experiences. The story involves Defoe's character being shipwrecked on a desert island, fending for himself, gaining a companion in Man Friday, and, eventually, as other people arrive on the island, establishing a community and asserting his role as leader. A recurrent image in the earlier stages of *Robinson Crusoe* is a fear of being swallowed up by the sea, an image that can be interpreted, broadly, as a fear of being overwhelmed by chaos, or, more specifically, as reflecting guilt, sexual anxiety and fear of punishment. But as much as Crusoe might fear the sea, he is also drawn by it. He is restless, always wishing to move on, this personality trait reflecting a new kind of restless energy that came along with the growth of trade, expansion of horizons, and new possibilities at the start of the eighteenth century. Arriving on the island, Crusoe starts to assume control of his environment; this is the novel's most direct expression of the new economic resourcefulness of the early eighteenth century. Through his strategic awareness and possession of the necessary technology, Crusoe is able to establish a vibrant economy. This involves the management of resources, and also the management of men. The newcomers on Crusoe's island include a sea captain and the men who have mutinied against him; Crusoe, having established that the captain is prepared to accept his authority, moves swiftly to shoot the mutineers. It is a matter of social discipline, of asserting his command through punishment.

For the modern reader, however, perhaps the most intriguing element in *Robinson Crusoe* is the relationship with Man Friday. This could be regarded as simply the arrival of a companion, but the complicating factor – implicit in the fact that Crusoe names the newcomer, and then imposes his language and his religious beliefs upon him – is that this is a relationship of racial and colonial superiority. At this point, some readers will ask whether this is an aspect of the novel that Defoe is aware of; that is to say, is he deliberately drawing attention to a questionable master and slave relationship, or is this a meaning that is only apparent to a modern audience? The question of Defoe's intention, however, is beside the point. We look at a text in order to see how it expresses the complex cross-currents of the period of its production, rather than trying to pin down the stance of the author. Consequently, if we look at the details in the Crusoe–Man Friday relationship, the effect should be to make us appreciate even more just how many-layered *Robinson Crusoe* is in reflecting the varied elements at work in English society as it took an economic leap forward at the start of the eighteenth century.

Defoe has, in fact, been called the poet laureate of the market system, as he writes so enthusiastically about, and with such a commitment to, the emergence of this new economy. But the really compelling level of interest in his works always lies in the way in which his novels also reveal the complications, contradictions and limitations of this market economy. This is evident in *Robinson Crusoe*, and equally evident in Defoe's second novel, *Moll Flanders* (1722), which deals with a young woman making her way in life. Beginning as a servant made pregnant by her employer's son, Moll then has to fend for herself even if this involves stealing and selling her body. By the end of the novel she has adopted a pious religious tone as she looks back on the wicked life she has led, but there is a telling sense in *Moll Flanders* of a huge gap between moral and religious platitudes and the conduct that is necessary for survival in a commercial society. In this respect, *Moll Flanders* is a good deal more radical than a great many novels that follow it. Time and time again, later English novels focus on how a young woman finds a husband. *Moll Flanders*, however, follows a rather different course. Moll does marry, but she is, in her own unorthodox way, a businesswoman negotiating a role for herself in a male-dominated society.

Defoe is one of the most prolific writers in the eighteenth century; indeed, one of the most prolific writers in the entire history of English literature. In addition to *Robinson Crusoe* and *Moll Flanders*, his novels include *Captain Singleton* (1720), *A Journal of the Plague Year* (1722), *Colonel Jack* (1722) and *Roxana* (1724). He also wrote poetry, political pamphlets, economic commentaries, a family conduct book, works of history, and a guidebook to the whole of Britain. There is something extraordinary about this torrent of works. His publications provide the best evidence there is of a new class of people, with new energy and new values, coming into existence at the start of the eighteenth century. But what his productivity also indicates is that this new class of people needed to be written into existence. In a sense, they did not know who they were until they could turn to Defoe for written confirmation of their social being. And in some ways this holds good for all the novelists who follow Defoe, that what the novel does is affirm the presence of a social group in the larger canvas of society.

Aphra Behn, Samuel Richardson, Henry Fielding, Laurence Sterne, Tobias Smollett

Defoe's novels appeared at the moment when a particular formation of a mercantile and commercial culture was taking shape. So far-reaching were the consequences of this change in the economic life of the country that the novel after Defoe concerns itself almost exclusively with how those in possession of new wealth and a new confidence organise their private lives. It is the fact that Defoe's novels coincide with such a distinct development in the economic and social life of the country that helps explain why he is usually acknowledged as the first English novelist, and why so little is said about the writers of prose fiction that preceded him.

The plain fact is that there were novels before *Robinson Crusoe*. This chapter focuses on the hundred years from the appearance of Defoe's novels to the publication of Jane Austen's works, but literary historians have traced the novel genre back as far as the Ancient Egyptians in the twelfth century BC. In England, we can point to Sir Philip Sidney's pastoral romance *Arcadia* (first published 1590) as an important landmark in the evolution of the extended prose narrative, and there were a number of other significant works in the same decade, such as Nashe's *The Unfortunate Traveller* (1594). But the kind of steady progress from the pastoral romance to the novel that we might expect to encounter in the seventeenth century did not take place. John Bunyan's *Pilgrim's Progress* (1678) is an allegory that, in a number of respects, begins to anticipate the concerns of novels, but there was very little else before 1713, when William Congreve (the Restoration dramatist) published *Incognita*; he not only referred to it as a novel but also offered his definition of a novel in the preface to the work. He argued that, unlike romances, novels 'are of a more familiar nature; come near us, and represent to us Intrigues in Practice, delight us with Accidents and odd Events, but not such as are wholly unusual or unprecedented'.

The exception to this generalisation about the lack of novels in the seventeenth century is Aphra Behn's *Oroonoko* (c.1688), a work which, quite justifiably, has in recent years commanded more and more attention. It is the story of Oroonoko, the grandson of an African King, who is in love with Imoinda, the daughter of the King's general. The King commands that Imoinda be taken to his harem; when he finds out that she is in love with his grandson, he arranges for her to be sold into slavery; at the same time Oroonoko is captured by an English slaver. He encourages his fellow slaves to escape, but they surrender on the promise of a pardon. Oroonoko himself, however, is flogged. Accepting that their situation is hopeless, Oroonoko kills Imoinda, but before he can kill himself he is taken prisoner again, and executed in the most savage manner. Given the extraordinary quality of Aphra Behn's narrative, and given that she also wrote other novels – *The Fair Jilt* and *The Lucky Mistake* appeared in the same volume as *Oroonoko* – it might be thought odd that Defoe, rather than Behn, is regarded as the first English novelist.

The reason would seem to be that it is Defoe, rather than Behn, who establishes a range of concerns that will become central in the subsequent history of the novel. Defoe tells a story to which all of his readers can relate; Behn, by contrast, narrates an exotic story, and an exotic story that seems to fail to establish a tradition. In fact, however, this is not the case. *Oroonoko* belongs in the tradition of imperial romance, a genre that looks at the relationship between the English and other races. *Robinson Crusoe*, in the relationship between Crusoe and Man Friday, actually covers rather similar ground. Imperial romances always focus on the body, on the extent to which it is a commodity that can be bought and sold, and the attitude the members of a so-called civilised society adopt, or should adopt, towards abuse of the human body. *Robinson Crusoe* in this respect not only touches upon slavery but also includes cannibalism, the most extreme transgression of any civilised social code, as a theme. Imperial romances reappear at various points in the history of the novel, most notably at the end of the nineteenth century, with works such as those of Rider Haggard. The dominant tradition in the English novel, however, is not foreign-based but domestic. And domestic in two ways: the events take place in Britain, and the story, more often than not, centres on events within a family home.

This is certainly the case in the works of the next significant novelist after Defoe. Samuel Richardson, a master printer, wrote *Pamela* (1740) when he was 51. It was followed by *Clarissa* (1747–8) and *Sir Charles Grandison* (1753–4). *Pamela* concerns a servant girl who resists the advances of her employer; eventually she becomes his wife. *Clarissa* is a far more complex novel. *Pamela* could be described as a comedy: danger threatens, but the story ends happily. *Clarissa*, on the other hand, is a tragedy; the threat of sexual violence in *Pamela* is realised in Richardson's second novel. Clarissa, a beautiful young woman, is encouraged by her family to marry a rich neighbour, Solmes, but is also being pursued by a notorious, if charming, rake called Lovelace. Clarissa eventually decides to run off with Lovelace. She is imprisoned in a brothel, where Lovelace drugs and rapes her. She escapes, and seems to be regaining a sense of her integrity and moral worth, but subsequently dies as she cannot come to terms with what she has experienced. At the end of the novel, Lovelace dies in a duel with Clarissa's cousin, Colonel Morden. The differences between

Richardson's two novels indicate how the potential of the novel began to be fully appreciated in the course of the eighteenth century.

Pamela is a fairly simple work. Like Defoe's novels, it is about someone making her way in the world. Pamela, very much like Defoe's heroes and heroines, has to fend for herself. She is on her own, and to a large extent, even with a predatory male as her employer, her fate is in her own hands. The eventual result, as it so often is in the English novel, is financial prosperity and domestic security; the heroine is rewarded, the reward being accommodation within the circle of safe and civilised society through marriage. The novel is, as such, a relatively simple moral fable for its audience, about how the ordinary person can thrive in the modern world. The sexual threat to Pamela gives the novel a slightly salacious edge, but it must also be acknowledged that there is a great deal of astuteness and delicacy in the way that Richardson recognises that a woman, without a career as a possibility, has to trade upon her physical attributes while resisting the notion of herself as a commodity. *Pamela*, to this extent, hints at complex issues, but it does not prepare us in any way at all for the psychological depth and emotional intensity of *Clarissa*.

When the novel in England focuses upon the individual in a domestic setting, it usually considers either a young man making his way in life or a young woman seeking a husband. *Clarissa* starts by acknowledging the complexity of a woman's position in the marriage market, but where it really excels is in its grasp of the nature of the feelings of all those involved. Even Lovelace, for example, is a psychologically complex character, caught between the desire for seduction and revulsion at his own moral corruption. What we see in *Clarissa* can be described as an internalisation of problems. The church had always represented an external source of authority in people's lives. The church remained an important influence upon people's lives in the eighteenth century, but increasingly choices in life were becoming a matter for the individual conscience. *Clarissa* does justice to this growing sense of human experience as essentially private and inward. Yet it does more than this; *Clarissa* is not simply reporting on a new attitude that emerged in the eighteenth century, but also helping to write this new attitude into existence.

A sense of psychological complexity is something that the modern reader takes for granted; in a sense, we still live in the tradition of novels such as *Clarissa*, accepting their stance as normative. But Richardson's view of human behaviour is only an interpretative frame imposed upon people and events. In this respect, it is interesting to see that some other writers in the eighteenth century resisted this way of looking at life; it was still possible at this time to believe that there was no such thing as individual inward complexity. This is evident in the novels of Henry Fielding, a writer prompted to start writing novels by his distaste for what he saw in Richardson's *Pamela*. His first work, *Shamela* (1741), was a parody of *Pamela*, featuring a heroine who artfully manipulates her honour in order to secure a husband. This suggests the essential difference between Richardson and Fielding: in Richardson's novels, the conflicting elements within the mind demand careful consideration; in Fielding's novels, people can be judged instantly on the basis of generally agreed social or moral truths about human nature. The difference reflects the social background of the two writers. Whereas Richardson was a businessman, and, as such, very much part of the new order, Fielding was a gentleman and magistrate, and a defender of traditional views and values. The gap between the two writers is apparent over and over again. For example, Richardson deals with sexual themes but is a puritanical writer, whereas Fielding takes a straightforward delight in bawdiness.

Tom Jones (1749) starts with Tom being found as a baby by Squire Allworthy. As he grows up, he falls in love with Allworthy's niece, Sophia Weston, but his relationship with Molly Seagrim, a gamekeeper's daughter, leads to his expulsion from the squire's house. He sets out for London, where he drifts into an affair with Lady Bellaston. After many complications, it is revealed that Tom is the son of Allworthy's sister, Bridget, and, therefore, heir to the estate. He is now in a position to marry Sophia. It is the revelation that Tom is the rightful heir that tells us most about Fielding's stance. In a Defoe novel, people are launched into the world and have to create their own identity and social role. Fielding challenges this model of middle-class individualism; *Tom Jones* ends with the main character assuming the place that is his by right in the traditional order of things. In a rather similar way, the novel features a series of sexual escapades, but these seem to have no psychological or even moral implications for the characters involved. This is a traditional comic stance: people are bound to stray off course, but everything will sort itself out in the end. In a curious way, however, Fielding, just as much as Defoe or Richardson, accepts that things are changing in the eighteenth century. *Tom Jones* acquires its energy from being a defence of a view of life that Fielding knows is imperilled.

The fact that new ways of thinking about human nature were developing in the eighteenth century, together with an awareness of how the novel as a genre has validated this new view of human nature, is at the heart of the most extraordinary novel from the century, Laurence Sterne's *Tristram Shandy* (1759–67). By the middle of the century novels were telling one story over and over again: the narrative of a person's advance in life. The distinctive quality of *Tristram Shandy* is that it dissects the narrative conventions that are used in, and which have given validity to, this story. Sterne, though, unlike Fielding, is not a conservative writer; he is actually interested in the new emphasis on human psychology. But he is also acutely aware of the role of the novel as a genre in constructing a new way of thinking and feeling, something foregrounded through the novel's actual style.

Tristram Shandy professes to be the autobiography of Tristram, but from the outset there is disruption of the linear and progressive pattern that we might expect. The story starts before Tristram's birth, as he describes his own conception, and from that point on he finds it all but impossible to write a chapter without digressing. It actually takes the best part of three volumes before Tristram is born. Chapters are deliberately out of sequence, and Sterne also employs tactics such as the use of a black page when a death occurs. The effect is a quite brilliant deconstruction of all the ways in which novels presume to arrange and interpret people's lives. But *Tristram Shandy* can also be associated with the eighteenth-century cult of sensibility, in that it focuses on delicate and sensitive emotions and their importance in contributing towards a civilised society.

Alongside Richardson, Fielding and Sterne, the other notable midcentury novelist was Tobias Smollett, a Scotsman. His principal works are *Roderick Random* (1748), *Peregrine Pickle* (1751) and *The Expedition of*

Humphrey Clinker (1771), novels that add an important extra dimension to our understanding of the eighteenth century. Roderick Random qualifies as a surgeon's mate but lacks money for the bribe that could secure him a commission in the navy. He is seized by a press-gang and forced into service as a common sailor, but becomes the surgeon's mate on the ship. Returning to England, he is shipwrecked and then robbed. Eventually, after a series of bizarre adventures, he meets up with a wealthy trader, Don Roderigo, who turns out to be his father. *Roderick Random*, like *Robinson Crusoe*, is obviously about a young man setting out on a journey and making his way in life, but the ending, where he discovers his true father, makes the journey circular, as in *Tom Jones*, as if the voyage was not entirely necessary. Smollett's traditional stance is also apparent in his use of the picaresque, a loose form of narrative in which the hero wanders along falling into a miscellaneous mixture of traps and diversions. All this suggests that Smollett has no real interest in his hero's state of mind. But what we do get in Smollett is an impression of the harsher aspects of the mercantile economy of the eighteenth century.

Roderick Random offers an unblinking view of the brutality, inhumanity and rapaciousness of eighteenth-century life. When Roderick is on the ship, life on board is harsh and extreme: authority is corrupt, the living conditions are appalling, and the medical treatment is brutal. *Roderick Random* was written in the same decade as 'Rule, Britannia!', but Smollett focuses on less positive aspects of the nation's life; in particular, he focuses on tensions in the social construct rather than offering a sense of national unity. This becomes most apparent in the volatility and violence of the language in the novel. There is an explosive rage that cannot be contained, the extreme language breaking through all the polite forms. This is accompanied by physical violence; in Smollett's novels the language is always at the edge of spilling over into direct aggression and assault.

From Eliza Haywood to Mary Shelley

The eighteenth century is a contradictory century. Behaviour was gross and physical in a way that is unimaginable today. Novels, such as those of Fielding, Sterne and Smollett, are full of a coarse humour and brutality that even some of their contemporaries found unacceptable. And a rapidly expanding commercial economy was quite complacent about exploiting people. Yet, at the same time, this was a society beginning to establish new standards in polite behaviour. The novels produced in the course of the century reflect the tension between these two different images of Britain, but, as the century wore on, it was the new, refined standard of the emerging middle class that gained the upper hand.

There is an anticipation of future developments, of the move towards a new, more refined idea of human conduct, in, for example, the career of Eliza Haywood, who moved from picaresque, although never coarse, fictions – such as *The Fortunate Foundlings* (1744) and *Life's Progress Through the Passions* (1748) – to domestic narratives of upper-middle-class life – such as *The History of Miss Betsy Thoughtless* (1751) and *The History of Jemmy and Jenny Jessamy* (1753). What is perhaps most surprising in terms of the development of this new framework of middle-class ideas is that Fielding, in *Amelia* (1751), began to reveal the influence of Richardson, shifting from the comic style of *Tom Jones* to a form of domestic realism. Amelia and her husband, Captain Billy Booth, find themselves threatened with financial and sexual ruin at the hands of an aristocratic villain. This is a repeated motif in the new fiction of the eighteenth century: the respectability of the middle class is defined by indicating how they differ from the villainous upper class.

Other novelists that can be associated with the emergence of domestic realism and a new code of manners – a development that begins to become apparent at roughly the mid-point of the century – are Frances Sheridan (*Memoirs of Mrs Sidney Biddulph*, 1761), Charlotte Lennox (*The Female Quixote*, 1752), and Fanny (Frances) Burney. In *Evelina* (1778), Burney's heroine observes the London scene, but is rather timid about becoming a participant. *Cecilia* (1782), her second novel, focuses more on the social and financial pressures that bear down upon the heroine, who is brought to the edge of death by her guardians. Essentially, in both novels the central figure is trying to negotiate a position for herself in the dynamic, hectic, and often cruel society of the late eighteenth century. The heroine obviously wants to fulfil herself, but at the same time she must maintain a ladylike sense of decorum and passivity. Burney, like many eighteenth-century novelists, can be seen as helping to construct a social code, a framework of civilised values for a commercial society dominated by male values. It is at this point that a reader familiar with the works of Jane Austen, which appeared between 1811 and 1818, will appreciate that the stance Austen adopts – of a concern for correct and moral behaviour – is one that had been slowly taking shape over a considerable period in what we might call the novel of social manners.

One aspect of this was the cult of sensibility. In this new domestic order there was no place for traditional masculine aggression, and during the second half of the eighteenth century the male personality became softened and refined. The most extreme expression of this is in Henry Mackenzie's sentimental novel *The Man of Feeling* (1771). Harley, Mackenzie's hero, sets off to find his fortune. His good nature makes him vulnerable, and, consequently, he is duped by scoundrels and cheats. But he is to be admired because of his gentleness and his intense sympathy for others. Samuel Richardson's third novel, *Sir Charles Grandison*, operates in a similar area, with a hero whose actions are always motivated by the intensity of his feelings and his instinct for good conduct. Sterne's *A Sentimental Journey* (1768) simultaneously mocks and celebrates just such a sentimental standard of behaviour.

The emphasis of these novels is on the cultivation of finer feelings. But *The Man of Feeling* is not a novel that many people today would bother to read, while *Sir Charles Grandison* is a far less substantial novel than *Clarissa*. The fact is that these novels retreat into the simplifications of a moral stance. In this respect they differ from the cluster of major novels in the middle of the eighteenth century, which offer a complex engagement between an emerging idea of the self and the social reality of the period. The sentimental novel, by contrast, takes its eye off the world as it really is. Much the same thing could be said about Gothic fiction, a type of novel very popular from the 1760s onwards until the 1820s. Typical plots hinge on mystery and suspense; delving into the realm of the fantastic and the supernatural, many of the writers seem to revel in cruelty and terror. Works such as Horace Walpole's *The Castle of Otranto* (1764), Charlotte Smith's *Emmeline* (1788), Ann Radcliffe's *The Mysteries of Udolpho* (1794) and

Matthew G. Lewis's *The Monk* (1796) seem to explore the unconscious mind.

But if these novels do not engage directly with the real world, it is clear that some of them, albeit in an indirect way, engage with very substantial, and very real, issues. The pattern of 'flight and pursuit', for example, that is such a mainstay of Gothic fiction, can be taken as a reflection of the period of the French Revolution: a tyrannical regime, oppressed victims, and punishment for transgression. There are elements of this in Fanny Burney's last novel, *The Wanderer* (1814), and C.R. Maturin's *Melmoth the Wanderer* (1820). Perhaps the most interesting of these novels, however, is Mary Shelley's *Frankenstein* (1818), which, like the works by Burney and Maturin, belongs very firmly in the Romantic period at the start of the nineteenth century. It tells the story of Victor Frankenstein, who constructs a monster and endows it with life. The monster is benevolent, but is regarded with loathing and fear; not surprisingly, its benevolence turns to hatred, and it destroys its creator and his bride. It is possible to argue that there are two realms in the novel: one, the public realm, is dominated by language and law; the other, private, realm, is secret, even incommunicable. The latter is the realm of Frankenstein and his monster. It is a world that exists outside society and language, containing only the monster and his creator.

As in *Frankenstein*, many Gothic novels, in particular the more politicised Gothic novels of the early nineteenth century, focus on characters who are excluded from or in a problematic relationship with the dominant discourse of society. There is often a feminist dimension to such thinking: *Frankenstein*, for example, seems to reflect Mary Shelley's anxieties about her own role as someone creating and living by language, yet conscious that language, along with literary creation, is usually regarded as a masculine preserve. At the same time, the sheer power of the novel and its concern with suffering mark it off as doing something different from run-of-the-mill tales as it examines society from a position outside the usual boundaries. As ever, what distinguishes a novel is the way in which it stretches the set conventions. In the case of *Frankenstein*, it is a novel that pushes the Gothic conventions to their limits, in the process creating a challenging sense of the individual in conflict with society.

Walter Scott and Jane Austen

The Romantic period, from about 1780 to 1820, is characterised by a great many dissenting voices, such as Mary Shelley's. She is one of many authors who see themselves as outside or in opposition to the established realm of authority. A number of these writers are considered at the end of the next chapter. It would be possible to construct a history of English literature, especially from this point forward, that concentrated entirely on these subversive writers. For a more mainstream thread of the English novel in the opening decades of the nineteenth century, however, we have to turn to Sir Walter Scott and Jane Austen.

Scott was the most popular novelist of his day. Already established as a poet, in 1814 he started a second career as a novelist with the publication of *Waverley*. It was followed by other novels, for example *The Heart of Midlothian* (1818), set in seventeenth- and eighteenth-century Scotland. With *Ivanhoe* (1819), he moved to England in the Middle Ages. Scott's novels (which initiated a taste for historical fiction) usually deal with a time of change, when one social formation is giving way to another. We can see how this corresponds with much of what has been said in this book in general and in this chapter in particular about literature focusing upon periods of transition. As with other novelists considered here, Scott considers the transition from an aggressive masculine culture to a more restrained, rather feminised culture. In *Waverley* and a number of the other Scottish-based novels he deals with how the presence of the English has forced changes in the traditional, clan-based fighting life of the Scots.

Jane Austen's novels appear at a time when the rougher manners of the eighteenth century are starting to be a distant memory, and when a new social formation has been clearly established. She focuses on the everyday play of relationships within a small group of people in the property-owning middle class. There are six novels: *Sense and Sensibility* (1811), *Pride and Prejudice* (1813), *Mansfield Park* (1814), *Emma* (1816), and *Northanger Abbey* and *Persuasion* (1818), which were published together the year after Austen died. Every new writer of note has, to a greater or lesser extent, his or her own new voice, but some are more recognisable than others. Certainly, most readers would be able to identify immediately the understated, ironic and totally distinctive voice of Austen. It is the polite voice of polite society, but with nuances of wit and a teasing ironic inflection that consistently make it far more than just the voice of polite society.

In all Austen's novels there is a sense that she is a writer with a case to present, and who presents her case professionally and with perfect control. *Emma*, a novel focusing on the development and moral growth of its heroine, offers plenty of evidence of this clarity of purpose. Emma lives with her father. Her governess leaves the household to marry a neighbour, Mr Weston, and Emma, who relishes acting as a match-maker, makes a protégée of Harriet Smith, an illegitimate girl of no social standing. George Knightley, a friend of the family, disapproves of Emma's attempts to manipulate Harriet. Emma half-believes that she is in love with Mr Weston's son by his first marriage, Frank Churchill, but eventually realises that, without actively considering it, she has always assumed Knightley will marry her. This, together with the revelation that Frank is already engaged, forces Emma to examine her conduct and resolve to behave better. Knightley proposes to Emma, and is accepted. Emma, as is apparent in this summary, matures: she changes from being vain, self-satisfied and insensitive to the needs of others. Essentially, she has fallen in line with, and come to accept the wisdom and value of, the code of conduct for personal behaviour that should operate in polite society.

The discussion could end there, with a sense of the moral development of Emma, and a comment on how Jane Austen's style, in particular the understated but devastating way in which she can demolish the pretensions of those who think too well of themselves, reinforces her social message. The problem with such a response, however, is that it makes Austen appear to be a kind of static novelist, rather than a novelist responding to a changing world. It is as if the eighteenth century starts with a new kind of character, but by the time we get to Austen, exactly a century after Defoe, these characters have their own homes, and are totally in control. Superficially it might appear that, whereas Defoe deals with a fluid society, in Austen everything has become very fixed and secure. But this is not necessarily the case, and Austen, in fact, starts to become a lot more interesting the moment we realise that she, too, is dealing with a society that is in the throes of change. It can be pointed out, for example, that she is writing on the eve of the Industrial Revolution, when the country-house-based order of life she describes is about to fall apart. London is no more than a presence in the background of Austen's novels; thirty years later, when we arrive at Dickens and Thackeray, London is at the very centre of the novel in England. The period which Austen deals with can, therefore, be seen as a period of imminent social change, where the social formation that had evolved, and which she concentrates on, was about to change shape again. These imminent changes in the economic and class arrangements of England will put an enormous strain on the kind of families she features in her novels.

In *Emma*, everyone has their place in the social hierarchy; nobody moves up or down in society, and Emma and Knightley, who are snobs at the beginning of the novel, are snobs in exactly the same way at the end. In short, Austen defends the position of people who not too long ago were social newcomers themselves against a fresh wave of social newcomers. But there is also a way in which she knows that the little social enclave she is dealing with is caught in a rather unreal time warp. If we adopt this approach, taking the view that a substantial work of literature is always about how one way of life is yielding to another, Austen's image alters. Rather than being totally assured and self-confident, her works start to seem fraught, anxious and possibly a lot more substantial; rather than talking about the moral values of Austen, our attention turns to a more ambitious project in which she illustrates how one social formation is under threat and yielding to another. Her novels might simply involve a handful of characters in a rural setting, but behind the particular example is a sense of a far broader process of social, political, economic and cultural transition.

This can perhaps best be seen in *Mansfield Park*. Mansfield Park is the family seat of the Bertram family. Fanny Price, Lady Bertram's niece, is brought to live with the family. She is befriended by Edmund Bertram, but his sisters Maria and Julia seek only to humiliate her. While Sir Thomas Bertram is off visiting his estates in the West Indies, Mansfield Park is visited by Henry and Mary Crawford from London. They tempt the sisters to throw off restraint, resulting in Maria entering into marriage with a Mr Rushworth, and then an adulterous elopement with

Henry Crawford. Julia also elopes, while Edmund is tempted by Mary Crawford to give up the idea of becoming a clergyman. Edmund resists and finally marries Fanny. For all its tidiness, it is an uncomfortable ending to the novel in its perfunctoriness. There can be little doubt that the old way of life symbolised by Mansfield Park is under threat both from outside and inside, and the Bertram family clearly lacks any real moral energy to sustain this way of life and to defend it against the clever London socialites Henry and Mary Crawford. It is no accident that Austen alerts us to the real-world economics of Sir Thomas's plantation or to the equally real collapse of sexual restraint in his own home. The forces of change are too powerful to be controlled, even by Austen's irony.

9 The Romantic Period

The Age of Revolution

The Romantic period is also referred to as the 'Age of Revolution'. This designates an era from the American Declaration of Independence in 1776 through to Britain's Great Reform Act (which gave many more people the vote) in 1832. At the heart of the period, however, and at the heart of Romanticism, is the French Revolution, with a great deal of the subsequent vocabulary of liberal politics, right through to the present day, deriving from the French experience between 1789 and 1799. During the course of the eighteenth century the French monarchy had made gestures towards reform, but by the end of Louis XV's reign the country was weak, the monarch distrusted, the nobility detested, and the church widely unpopular. Initially, between 1789 and 1792, the Revolution established constitutional monarchy, liberal freedoms, and major legislative reforms. The overthrow of Louis XVI in 1792, however, and his execution in 1793, inaugurated a more radical phase, with authoritarian government and repressive measures aimed at commanding obedience. This is a period referred to as the 'Terror'. This phase of the French Revolution, associated with the extremist leader Robespierre, came to an end in 1794, when there was an attempt to revive more liberal values. But the rule of law proved difficult to maintain in a turbulent period, and in 1799 Napoleon Bonaparte engineered a military coup. This effectively represented the end of the Revolution, although Napoleon did stabilise the revolutionary changes.

The relevance of the French Revolution to English literature might not be immediately apparent. Throughout this book, however, we have stressed that society is constantly involved in a process of transformation, and that literature is both a product and reflection of the change from one way of thinking to a new way of thinking, and an intervention in that thinking. The most admired works of literature are those produced at a time when there are the most dramatic shifts from one way of looking at the world to another way of looking at the world. The French Revolution is just such a period. Indeed, the British historian Edmund Burke realised this immediately, as can be seen in his *Reflections on the Revolution in France*, published in 1790. A conservative, troubled by the enthusiastic and, to his mind, irresponsible English response to the Revolution, Burke argued that it constituted a radical and dangerous break with the past and the overthrow of the old order. His counter-revolutionary thesis produced numerous rejoinders, including Thomas Paine's *Rights of Man* (1791) and Mary Wollstonecraft's *A Vindication of the Rights of Men* (1790; her *A Vindication of the Rights of Woman* appeared in 1792). But what sort of change had taken place in France? The classic Marxist interpretation of the French Revolution is that it constituted a change from an old feudal order to a new capitalist order. In essence, it amounted to the triumph of the middle classes over the aristocracy.

Such a process of change had begun a lot earlier in Britain; in particular, following the establishment of constitutional monarchy in 1688, a new political culture had evolved during the course of the eighteenth century. But, although the political and social conventions of Britain and France altered at a somewhat different pace, what we have to grasp is that, at a more fundamental level, towards the end of the eighteenth century economic developments were taking place that changed the social relations between people, and changed how people saw, and thought about, life. In both countries there was a change from a society in which people accepted their place in a fixed social hierarchy to a more dynamic economic order, in which people began to see their own role, and contribution, much more positively. Indeed, one aspect of the French Revolution was a greater sense of human agency: people no longer accepted their passive role, but seized the initiative. There was a new sense of the importance of the immediate moment as against the authority of tradition.

Britain was at the heart of these currents of political, social and cultural transformation at the end of the eighteenth century, but Britain was also drawn into the French Revolution in a direct way.

Hostility between France and Britain led to a protracted period of war between the two countries, beginning in 1793 and only concluding with Napoleon's defeat at Waterloo in 1815. This was a major military commitment over a period of more than twenty years that provoked political unrest in Britain. But the wars between the two countries also, in the long run, fostered British trade and the British economy. The wars in addition, in a rather more elusive way, prompted the British to adjust, or perhaps to reinforce, their sense of their national identity. In rejecting the French experience, there was a convergence at home, a desire to pursue a middle course, that, after the political repression of the war years and its immediate aftermath, affected the development of democracy in nineteenth-century Britain.

There was, then, it is clear, a ferment of new ideas and social transformation at the end of the century. If Pope, at the start of the eighteenth century, sought stability after the turbulence of the previous century, there was, from 1770 onwards, a growing sense of having broken with the past and accepting a world in flux. This is apparent in the literature of the period. In every era of literary history we encounter new voices expressing themselves in new forms; people are, in effect, telling new stories about a new state of affairs. In the Romantic period, however, we encounter a quite unprecedented profusion of new voices, and new voices that display a breathtaking ability to reject old literary conventions and find new forms of expression.

The variety of literature at this time does, though, pose some problems in deciding how to organise a chapter about Romanticism. There are six major English Romantic poets: Blake, Wordsworth, Coleridge, Shelley, Byron and Keats. But too great an emphasis on these writers creates a sense of solid coherence that is rather at odds with what was actually happening in literature at this time. The real character of the Romantic age is conveyed in the fact that it provided an opportunity for an extraordinarily diverse range of voices. In particular, while at every point in the history of English literature there is increasing evidence of the existence of women writers, it is in the Romantic period that women become central in an unprecedented way. They are no longer writing from the fringes but are at the very heart of political and social turmoil. It is tempting to produce an account of Romantic literature that focuses exclusively on such writers, but that would lead to the kind of radically revised narrative of the past that would be inappropriate in a history of literature. The way we have constructed this chapter, therefore, is with a look at the major established poets in the two central sections, and then, in what should be regarded as the climax of the chapter, rather than as an afterthought, we turn to a variety of Romantic authors.

William Blake, William Wordsworth, Samuel Taylor Coleridge

William Blake (1757–1827) was an engraver who also pursued the careers of poet and painter. For a while, he was part of a radical group of thinkers and writers that included Tom Paine, William Godwin and Mary Wollstonecraft. His best-known works are the *Songs of Innocence*, published in 1789, and then, in 1794, the *Songs of Experience* were added. Collections of apparently simple poems, they deal with two contrary states: the state of innocence, in which the world is unthreatening, there are no moral restrictions, and God is trusted implicitly, and the state of experience, which reflects a fallen world of repression and religious hypocrisy. Both books try to imagine life as it might exist outside conventional habits of thinking, and, indeed, see conventional attitudes as the prejudices that destroy and deny life.

This is a typical stance in Romantic literature: that the writer detaches his or her self from received ideas and values. This can lead to fierce social indignation, a feeling that comes across forcefully in 'London', from the *Songs of Experience*:

> I wander thro' each charter'd street,
> Near where the charter'd Thames does flow,
> And mark in every face I meet
> Marks of weakness, marks of woe.

> In every cry of every Man,
> In every Infant's cry of fear,
> In every voice, in every ban,
> The mind-forg'd manacles I hear.

How the Chimney-sweeper's cry
Every black'ning Church appalls;
And the hapless Soldier's sigh
Runs in blood down Palace walls.

But most thro' midnight streets I hear
How the youthful Harlot's curse
Blasts the newborn Infant's tear,
And blights with plagues the Marriage hearse.

The pattern of 'London' is characteristic of Blake's shorter poems: a simple ideal is set against the knotted corruption of modern life. In the final verse here, the child's life is tainted even as it is born. It is the city that is at the heart of the problem, for the city both restricts and exploits people. This is a concept that is encountered again and again in Romantic literature: an idea of the freedom associated with nature is set against the mire of the city.

As might be expected, Blake welcomed the French Revolution as an apocalyptic event that would sweep away old exploitative patterns of social relations and old ways of thinking. Part of what Blake opposed was the rationalism and moderation of eighteenth-century Enlightenment thinking, which he saw as demeaning life: society had become too narrowly committed to the idea of reason and a soul-destroying pursuit of material progress. What Blake lamented was the absence of any sense of the spiritual dimension of experience. If we compare Blake's thinking with the kind of ideas encountered at the start of the eighteenth century, we can see that, as against a notion of shared values and a shared way of thinking, Blake develops a private creed in which his imagination plays a vital role in rediscovering a sense of unity in experience. He consistently stresses the importance of freedom, as opposed to the tyranny that he feels to be characteristic of the government of his day, and attacks negative moralising, which he associates with the church, as opposed to a true sense of religion. One aspect of all this, as seen in 'London', is the corruption of sexuality, which has become debased and commodified. Implicitly and explicitly in the *Songs of Innocence* and the *Songs of Experience*, Blake plays with the alternative possibility of unrestricted sexuality and guilt-free desire.

Blake developed his views in *The Book of Thel* (1789), *The Marriage of Heaven and Hell* (1790–3), *Visions of the Daughters of Albion* (1793), *The Book of Urizen* (1794), *The Four Zoas* (1794–1804), *Jerusalem* (1804–20), and *Milton* (1804–08). The title of this final poem prompts the observation that there are distinct parallels between Blake's thinking and ways of thinking encountered in the English Civil War period. In particular, there is a close ideological resemblance between Blake and Milton, in that both are radical thinkers, both advocate freedom, and both are at odds with established authority and established institutions. It is equally important, however, to note the differences between seventeenth-century radicalism and Romantic radicalism. A central issue is the significance the Romantic generation attached to the imagination. Indeed, the transformation of life through the subjective imagination can be regarded as the central concept in Romanticism. The mind of the writer has become the focus and the centre. If, at one point in history, God was at the centre of everything, by the time we arrive at the Romantics God has been displaced sufficiently to establish the individual mind as the organising centre of life.

That might seem to create the possibility of excessively idiosyncratic texts, but thinking does not take place in a vacuum. A great many of Blake's ideas are consistent with the ways in which other people were beginning to think at the end of the eighteenth century. If there is a difference, it is that Blake is far more of a visionary than most of his contemporaries: in castigating radicalism and authority, he calls prophetically for a new humanity based upon imagination, instinct and creativity. Essentially, he writes visionary poetry which envisages a different world. The mood of his early poems in particular is clearly inspired by the spirit of the French Revolution and by a feeling that the moment of apocalyptic judgement is at hand. Just a few years later, people had a far more jaundiced view of the Revolution. None the less, other Romantic writers do share Blake's commitment to vision and the imagination, but they generally avoid the kind of extreme quality that we encounter in his works. It is frequently said that the problem with Blake is that he is too subjective, that, particularly in his long poems, he works too exclusively in terms of a private symbolism that fails to communicate with the reader. This need not, however, be regarded as a limiting judgement.

What is of interest is the manner in which, in the first flush of revolutionary enthusiasm, an English writer breaks away so decisively from received patterns of thinking and writing, in particular those of the eighteenth century with its stress on reason and decorum.

Turning from Blake to Wordsworth, we encounter a less radical writer. Or, possibly not. It can be argued that Wordsworth is actually the most radical of the Romantic poets, simply because he is the most accomplished and subtle poet. Initially enthusiastic about the French Revolution, the reign of 'Terror' in 1793 changed Wordsworth's view. The *Lyrical Ballads* of 1798, a joint collection of poems by Wordsworth and Coleridge, marks a withdrawal from public and political life, the poems, in a language that professes to be close to the language of everyday life, tending to focus on solitary or isolated figures. Whereas Pope and early eighteenth-century writers emphasised the general truths that should be at the heart of poetry, Wordsworth focused on unique experiences and private insights; the characters in the poems in *Lyrical Ballads* are, however, it is implied, also close to a pattern of life evident in nature itself. The importance of these poems might not be immediately apparent, particularly as there is none of the overt political and social thinking that we encounter in Blake. But where the significance lies is in the notion of personal insight. Although Wordsworth is a Christian, life is not perceived in terms of an inherited Christian code. Nor is life discussed in terms of a shared social philosophy. On the contrary, it is the subjective insight of the poet, aided by nature, that sees a pattern in life, in which meaning comes to reside in experience reflected upon in moments of tranquillity.

The issues in Wordsworth's poetry can be seen at their clearest in the poem 'Lines Composed a Few Miles above Tintern Abbey', which belongs to his most productive period, between 1795 and 1807. The poem opens with a description of a rural landscape; as is so often the case in Romantic poetry, the author turns to nature. But what is more important is that Wordsworth then writes about the effect of the scene:

> . . . the heavy and the weary weight
> Of all this unintelligible world,
> Is lightened . . .

> . . . we are laid asleep
> In body, and become a living soul;
> While with an eye made quiet by the power
> Of harmony, and the deep power of joy,
> We see into the life of things.
>
> (ll. 39–41, 45–9)

Truth and meaning are found in the natural world. In 'Tintern Abbey',
this is partly there in the natural world itself, but in equal measure it is
a consequence of what Wordsworth's own mind brings to the view.
Wordsworth's poetry is often admired on the basis of this sense of
harmony in nature that he half-perceives and half-creates; indeed,
even today many people would profess to experience a similar feeling.

But what distinguishes 'Tintern Abbey', and makes it a really complex poem, is the fact that Wordsworth is sufficiently realistic to
acknowledge that the sense of harmony he detects might not exist,
and that it might be simply an invention of his imagination. Indeed,
the more closely one looks at the poem the more it becomes apparent that Wordsworth is not just concerned to express his personal
vision but to discuss, analyse, and even question, his vision. Thus,
rather than simply being a poem in which Wordsworth is concerned
to present his insight into the 'life of things', 'Tintern Abbey' can be
seen as a more ambiguous work that examines the subjective imagination. Many of Wordsworth's finest poems follow this pattern. He
encounters something natural (a landscape or a character) on which
he imposes an interpretation, but then questions the activity he has
engaged in. While impressing the reader as the most uplifting of the
Romantic poets, Wordsworth consequently also comes across as a
hesitant, self-questioning Romantic. Why this is important is that, in
the midst of embracing the new ways of thinking that characterise
the late eighteenth century, Wordsworth examines the status and
validity of these new ways of thinking; his poems, consequently, not
only provide evidence of how ways of thinking changed in the
Romantic period, but also show him examining these new ways of
thinking. If Blake conveys the revolutionary fervour of Romanticism,
what makes Wordsworth a more complex poet is that, as well as
expressing the spirit of Romanticism, his works, in a philosophical
manner, analyse the nature of Romanticism.

This is clear in *The Prelude*, Wordsworth's longest poem, which was published after his death in 1850. The poem, at epic length, draws upon Wordsworth's life, recollecting his childhood in the Lake District. But the poem then becomes a discussion, exploration and analysis of his response to his own childhood experiences. A helpful way of considering *The Prelude* is to look at it in the tradition of epic and to think about how it differs from its predecessors. Whereas an epic poem such as Milton's *Paradise Lost* amounts to a kind of encyclopaedic synthesis of all experiences, *The Prelude* can only piece together a picture in terms of the author's personal experiences, and his personal interpretation of his experiences. Milton tries to make sense of the world in relation to his awareness of the existence of God; Wordsworth, by contrast, is at the very centre of the world he presents. In a sense, it is only the poet himself, and his own imagination, that matters. But, as is the case in Wordsworth's shorter poems, the strength of *The Prelude* resides in the fact that, as well as conveying the mood of his childhood, Wordsworth moves on to examine the manner in which ways of thinking and seeing changed in the light of the dawn of the French Revolution, specifically the new privileging of the individual. In *The Prelude*, it is the 'I' that is the narrator who is the principal subject of the narrative.

The *Lyrical Ballads* collection was a joint venture with Samuel Taylor Coleridge. These two writers, Wordsworth and Coleridge, have a great deal in common, but there is also much that separates them. Coleridge, as is the case with Wordsworth, can present a totalising vision, in which he unites all the disparate elements of experience into one coherent picture. This is apparent in the most extraordinary manner in 'Kubla Khan':

> In Xanadu did Kubla Khan
>   A stately pleasure-dome decree:
> Where Alph, the sacred river, ran
> Through caverns measureless to man
>   Down to a sunless sea.
>
> (ll. 1–5)

Coleridge's imagination has created a make-believe, alternate world. While Wordsworth limits himself to his own experiences and the materials of everyday life, Coleridge leaps into a fantasy world. And powerfully so: there is something magical about Coleridge's vision, and the intense and exotic manner in which Xanadu is created. But this is more than a poem of escape. Indeed, one reason why the poem works so well is that there is always a tension between the dream and reality, with dark notes of sexual anxiety and military confrontation intruding into the perfect vision. 'Kubla Khan' reaches after totality, but we are also aware of the unreality, and even frightening quality, of Coleridge's vision.

Not all of Coleridge's poems are so exotic. As is the case with Wordsworth, Coleridge often turns to nature, and writes of how imagination can perceive a sense of harmony in the natural scene. In his 'conversation poems', however, such as 'Frost at Midnight' (1802), Coleridge's most common theme is the inability of his imagination to sustain itself. There are lines in the poem where a vision of something that transcends the untidiness of daily life is offered to the reader, but the most emphatic stress is on how Coleridge cannot make the move he craves from fragmented, and troubling, reality to a coherent vision. If Wordsworth's most consistent theme as a poet is a questioning of his own imagination, Coleridge's is the failure of his imagination.

This is, in part, the theme of *The Rime of the Ancient Mariner*, first published in the *Lyrical Ballads*. A mariner shoots down an albatross, and his ship and its crew are punished by spirits. The crew die from thirst, while the mariner lives on, the albatross hung around his neck. When he recognises the beauty of the world and prays for his sins, the albatross falls from his neck. In essence, it is a story of sin and penance as the mariner wanders the earth, unable to find rest in conventional religion. The wedding guest to whom he tells his story is wrapt in both wonder and fear, afraid of the uncanny figure and his strange narrative in which disturbing symbols mix with alarming characters such as Life-in-Death. While, however, the poem dramatises Coleridge's sense of a world no longer redeemable by Christian faith, its power testifies to the way in which poetry itself comes to take on a new role in Romanticism, the way in which it can enable us to look differently at the world and its meanings.

In addition to poetry, Coleridge also has a considerable reputation as a prose writer, in particular as a philosopher and literary theorist. In his later years he worked on, but never completed, an ambitious project (the *Biographia Literaria*, 1817) in which he attempted to reconcile German philosophical radicalism, Christian theology and a Romantic vision. His inability to complete this work is significant. A more superficial writer might have stitched together a glib synthesis, but Coleridge, as much as he might wish to construct a new view, is always aware of the difficulty of doing so. The problem lies in abandoning traditional forms of knowledge and knowing, and substituting arguments that rely upon the subjective views of the individual. In essence, what we see in Coleridge, and in a great deal of Romantic writing, is a partial rejection of old habits of thinking, but also tremendous uncertainty about the ideas that are taking their place. The consequence is that much of Coleridge's work is fragmentary and incomplete; the old order has fallen apart, but it proves impossible to put together a coherent new order. In Coleridge's writings we are always aware of his anxiety, his despair, and a sense of mental sterility. In verse, his inability to find a way forward makes him a kind of tragic figure within his own poems. In the end, however, it is not Coleridge as an individual that interests us so much as the more universal figure of the bereft individual in a complicated world, where old sources of comfort and reassurance no longer seem accessible.

Lord Byron, Percy Bysshe Shelley, John Keats

A new way of looking at both the individual and the world at large is also at the heart of the poetry of Byron, Shelley, and Keats, three writers conventionally grouped together as the second generation of English Romantic poets. George Gordon, Lord Byron, was, in fact, the most famous and popular poet in the Romantic era. He spent much of his life in exile from England, dying in 1824, at the age of 36, in Greece, where he was organising forces fighting against the Turks for Greek independence. These biographical details are consistent with the character-type that always appears in Byron's poems: the Byronic hero is a solitary, somewhat misanthropic figure, defying nature, and cursed with guilty secrets, usually of a sexual nature, from his past. But if this figure outside social convention seems to have something in common with the solitary figures in Wordsworth and Coleridge's poetry, what must also be acknowledged is that Byron was scornful of the philosophical affectations of his contemporaries, stressing wit and common sense as against imagination.

In addition, as against the emphasis on withdrawal from society that we find in Wordsworth's poetry, Byron is politically engaged, with a particular hatred of hypocrisy and tyranny. There is a consistent stress in his poems on the importance of independence, an ideal that connects with ideas of sincerity and natural spontaneity. In his poetic dramas *Manfred* (1817) and *Cain* (1821), for example, Byron reflects on the tension between the potentialities of the individual and the restraints of the world in which the individual lives. There is a desire to strike out a new path, surpassing conventional behaviour and conventional morality, but at the same time the texts betray a sense of guilt, as well as nostalgia for the old order, in this lonely, isolated stance. *Don Juan* (1819–24) again features the typical Byronic hero, but what is particularly apparent here is Byron's good-humoured ironic stance: he takes his hero seriously, but also treats him dismissively. Don Juan is gallant, charming and reckless, and led by desire. Politically, this is fairly straightforward, in that *Don Juan*, as with Byron's other works, articulates the language of liberty, but there are clearly complications when the hero is a sexual libertine.

The political dimension of Romantic literature is even more apparent in the works of Percy Bysshe Shelley. Influenced by the political radicalism of William Godwin, Shelley was expelled from Oxford for publishing a pamphlet 'The Necessity of Atheism' (1811). Opposed to the tyranny of king, church and family, he decided at this time to devote his life to a vision of liberty. His first long poem, *Queen Mab* (1813), amounted to a forthright statement of his views. His radicalism is again evident in *The Mask of Anarchy* (1819), a poem that deals with the Peterloo Massacre of that year, an open-air meeting at St Peter's Field in Manchester in support of parliamentary reform where the yeomanry and hussars charged the crowd, killing eleven and wounding five hundred. Of Shelley's shorter works, perhaps the most typical is 'Ode to the West Wind', a poem that bears a slight resemblance to the poems of Wordsworth and Coleridge in that it laments the loss of an original spontaneous vision. At the heart of

Shelley's thinking, however, is the idea that there is an eternal, rational order, a pattern for all our finest values: beauty, harmony, justice and love. Characteristically, his poems are cloudy and blurred, with images of indistinct, shadowy things, as he invokes an ideal that can be sensed but not described. As against these elusive ideals, there exist the rigid forms of organised religion, the political system, and moral codes. Shelley, probably the most politically radical of the Romantic poets, and, as such, the most optimistic, consistently nurtures a belief that faithful adherence to ideal values will result in the transformation of human society. But his poems also reveal an awareness that the forces of change can prove destructive.

Shelley's poem responding to the Peterloo Massacre serves as a reminder that the world had moved on from the French Revolution. In 1819, thirty years after the Revolution, British society was extremely unsettled. The long series of wars against France had come to an end in 1815, and, with the release of 300,000 men from the army and navy, there were people looking for work, political unrest, and almost unprecedented government repression. The demonstration by 100,000 people at Peterloo, together with its aftermath, represents a moment of tension and confrontation that is symptomatic of a deep sense of malaise in Britain at this time. In addition, the Industrial Revolution was now under way, accentuating class and social divisions. It might seem surprising at this point, therefore, to turn to John Keats, who might appear the least political of poets. But there is a deeply subversive quality to Keats's verse.

The most obvious thing about Keats is that he is an extremely distinctive new voice, something that was apparent when an early reviewer referred to him as a member of the 'Cockney School'. What the modern reader is most likely to notice is the rich sensuality of Keats's writing, but the fact that this has broader social implications might not be immediately obvious. The beautiful quality of Keats's verse is apparent in 'La Belle Dame Sans Merci':

> I met a lady in the Meads,
>   Full beautiful – a faery's child,
> Her hair was long, her foot was light,
>   And her eyes were wild.
>
> (ll. 13–16)

It is a work that explores sexual attraction and sexual frustration, becoming a poem about the intensity of desire and the intensity of its defeat. The knight's sexual needs are conveyed, but also his fear of the woman. What is so new about Keats's writing is the kind of attention he pays to, and the manner in which he evokes, a private psychological state. If Romanticism put the individual imagination at the centre of literature, Keats, in a way that is in part echoed in Gothic fiction, begins to explore the darker side of the mind, in particular the sexual imagination.

Such a way of writing might seem to be something other than political, but Keats can be regarded as searching for sources of value, support and consolation that are different from those inscribed in the dominant religious and political systems of his day. In 'Ode to a Nightingale', one of a series of reflective odes which are Keats's most celebrated and well-loved poems, the poet revels in the bird's song, indulging himself in feelings of excess. It is as if he escapes from the real world, until the end of the poem where he re-establishes his awareness of the everyday world. Traditionally the poem has been praised for the poise with which it maintains a balance between the ideal of escape and the necessity of the return to reality, but a sense of poise in the poem seems less important than the extraordinary way in which a sense of excess is evoked. There is again a political dimension to Keats's writing. It is not the pragmatic, overt politics of Byron or Shelley, but a more oblique refocusing of the relationship between the individual and society, in which, through a concentration on human emotional and physical needs and desires, a new kind of resource is found in the self and private feeling. Not that such a clear position is ever formulated in Keats's poetry; his works do not offer anything even remotely resembling a philosophy, and even in his very short poetic career, Keats dying at the age of 26, his ideas changed rapidly.

If Blake, Wordsworth and Coleridge place the subjective imagination at the heart of literature, by the time we get to Keats there is a sense of the self, a sense of desire and an awareness of sexuality that has a different qualitative value. This is apparent in the language of Keats's poems. Wordsworth's plain style, which aims to be close to the language of everyday life, represents a very self-conscious rejection of poetic artifice, and, by implication, of inherited ways of both writing and thinking. But Keats, in the desire-driven excess of his verse, reconceives how people see and think about themselves in an equally radical manner. As we progress through the nineteenth century, it will be apparent that questions concerning the self, sex and desire are at the heart of a great deal of literature, and in a way that is very different from the kind of emphasis on sexual matters that we encounter in, say, the poetry of John Donne, where God, social values and the public world of morality are always there as points of reference. The difference lies in the fact that in Keats, and in a great deal of subsequent literature, it is something deeply internal, often concealed, and just as often dark and alarming, that is being explored. The significance of Keats in the overall history of English literature is that he plays a central role in constructing this new kind of internalisation of experience.

Radical Voices

When we consider the Romantic period, it is important to acknowledge the range of new voices that become audible at this time. By its very nature, a literary movement that challenges the past should provoke a babble of new voices; they will have a family resemblance, in that they are all the product of the same historical era, but we need to be alert to the variety of these voices. And what we also need to be alert to, and prepared to admire, is writers whose works might seem half-formulated or only half-completed, and writers who jolt from one position to another, or from one literary form to another, as they proceed from text to text. Romantic literature is, inevitably, work in progress. The attention that is routinely paid to the six best-known Romantic poets can rather obscure this fact. They are such well-known writers that, as we noted ealier in this chapter, a sense of overall coherence is conveyed that is misleading. The vitality, variety, and half-developed quality of Romantic writing become apparent, however, the moment we turn to less well-known writers. They enable us to get closer to the spirit of a period characterised by fragmentation and diversity.

Mary Wollstonecraft, the figure who can be regarded as initiating modern feminism, is probably the most significant of these other writers in the Romantic period. *A Vindication of the Rights of Woman* (1792) argues that women must be educated for citizenship. This is one of the works that Wollstonecraft wrote in immediate response to the French Revolution, and it is interesting to see that the basis of her argument is that, if women are ignored and trivialised, this will undermine the Revolution. Wollstonecraft afterwards lived in France during 1792 and 1794, the period when the optimism of the early rev-olutionary period yielded to extremism and violence; her *An Historical and Moral View of the Origin and Progress of the French Revolution* (1795) is at heart a critique based upon Enlightenment cultural and economic thinking. This was followed by *Letters Written during a Short Residence in Sweden, Norway and Denmark* (1796) in which, behind the label of 'female philosopher', she presents herself as woman, intellec-tual, lover, social critic, mother and revolutionised consciousness. After this she started to write a feminist novel *Maria; Or, the Wrongs of Woman*. Her private life was complicated, with a number of suicide attempts, but in 1797 she married William Godwin; she died some six months later, following the birth of their child, Mary Wollstonecraft Shelley, the author of *Frankenstein*.

What we see in Wollstonecraft is an ability to combine political and social analysis with a revolutionary ideology of individual rights. This is also true of her husband William Godwin, who, like Mary Wollstonecraft, turns to a variety of literary forms to work through and develop his ideas. His *Enquiry Concerning Political Justice* (1793) is probably the most extreme manifesto for restructuring the social and political order published in the Romantic period. A year later, in 1794, his novel *Caleb Williams* involves a re-working of, and, as such, a fresh twist to his social ideas. A one-time member of the Godwin–Wollstonecraft circle was Amelia Opie. Her novel *Adeline Mowbray* (1804) is based upon Wollstonecraft's life, but, when we look at Opie's own life as a whole, what is most striking is the way in which a writer at this time could respond to the new opportunities offered by moving in a very different direction. Essentially a moral writer, Opie's *The Father and Daughter* (1801) was extremely successful. She also published poetry (*Poems*, 1802, and *The Woman's Return*, 1808), but in 1825, after becoming a Quaker, she abandoned novel-writing for the Bible Society and charitable works. Her efforts on behalf of the anti-slavery movement resulted in a work – *The Black Man's Lament* (1826) – that illustrates vividly the extraordinary variety of literature in the Romantic period.

Elizabeth Inchbald, another friend of Godwin's, combined writing novels (*A Simple Story*, 1791) with a career as an actress and dramatist. There is, indeed, a thread that connects these authors, which is the fact that the novel was now proving more and more popular as a genre, both for straightforward domestic narratives and as a means of developing social and political ideas. Charlotte Smith enjoyed considerable success as a novelist, with works such as *Emmeline, or the Orphan of the Castle* (1788), but she also wrote children's stories, sonnets and a number of long poems. Mary Robinson, an actress, and for a while the mistress of the Prince of Wales, wrote a number of novels which are essentially sentimental melodramas, but they are informed by a note of social protest. This gained a more explicit form in a treatise, *Thoughts on the Condition of Women, and on the Injustice of Mental Insubordination* (1798). Another writer who demands attention is Felicia Hemans, who published fourteen volumes of verse, and whose poems characteristically explore the contradictions of her and other women's lives. If this is a writer playing the kind of role that might be expected of a woman author, the same cannot be said of Catherine Macaulay, a Whig historian, political theorist and educationalist. Her eight-volume political history of the seventeenth century was published over a period of twenty years, between 1763 and 1783, but she was active as a writer until the end of her life, challenging Edmund Burke on two occasions, and in *Letters on Education with Observations on Religious and Metaphysical Subjects* (1790) she dealt with matters such as prison reform, capital punishment, slavery, and the treatment of animals, as well as educational questions.

It would be possible to keep on adding to this list of Romantic writers – the poet John Clare and Thomas De Quincey, best known for his autobiography, *Confessions of an English Opium Eater* (1821), are two other really notable figures, and this is also the time at which Jane Austen was writing – but the essential point is that at no earlier period in literary history do we encounter so many writers from so many backgrounds writing in such a variety of forms. What is also evident is not just a new energy in political and social analysis, but also a new sense of the self, including a sense of the interior self. Paradoxically, throughout this time of political turmoil, George III remained on the throne, from 1760 to 1820, creating an illusion of continuity and certainty, although, in a way that seems in keeping with this period, the king was afflicted with mental illness. He was succeeded by George IV and then, in 1830, William IV became king. Keats, Shelley and Byron were all dead by this time. Coleridge died in 1834. Only Wordsworth lived on into the Victorian era.

10 *Victorian Literature,*
1837–1857

Charles Dickens

Queen Victoria succeeded her uncle, William IV, as sovereign of
the United Kingdom of Great Britain and Ireland in 1837. In the
same year, Charles Dickens published the first monthly instal-
ments of *Oliver Twist*, a novel that tells us a great deal about the
early Victorian period. The story concerns Oliver, an orphan child
of the workhouse, who is apprenticed to an undertaker, but then
runs away and encounters the Artful Dodger, who introduces him
to Fagin in the London slums. Fagin is the organiser of a set of
young thieves, and an associate of Bill Sikes, a violent criminal,
and Nancy, a prostitute. After a series of complications, Nancy
reveals that Fagin is being bribed, by the boy's half-brother Marks,
to corrupt Oliver. Nancy's betrayal is discovered, and Sikes murders her. In the pursuit that follows, he accidentally hangs himself.
Fagin is arrested, and Oliver is adopted by a benevolent Mr
Brownlow.

An obvious target of the novel was the New Poor Law of 1834,
which confined paupers to workhouses. A deeper issue, however, lies
behind the immediate issue of the Poor Law; this is the way in which
Britain in the first half of the nineteenth century was having to intro-
duce new legislation and new mechanisms of social regulation in
order to control an increasingly complex society. The period around
1837 was one of unprecedented change as an agricultural country was
transformed into an industrial one. The very appearance of the landscape was changed by the railways, a physical alteration that also
affected how people saw and related to each other. By 1851, well
before anywhere else in Europe, more people lived in towns than in
the countryside. These technological and demographic changes

altered the fundamental rhythms of life. Old communal patterns of existence vanished; in a large town, such as London, and also in the new large industrial towns in the north, such as Manchester, each person encountered was not only a stranger but also potentially a threat. As early as the 1830s, a new sense existed of being an individual, and having to fend for oneself in the urban world. In the past, people knew precisely who they were, as they probably continued in the same occupations, and in the same homes, as their parents, but in a town it became necessary to think about one's identity and how one related to other people. It also became necessary for the government to think about how to regulate this changing society; in particular, the government had to think about how to deal with the surplus elements in society, the incidental casualties of economic progress.

Dickens, in his characteristically populist way, challenges the inhumanity of aspects of the new social legislation. But Dickens also shares the anxieties of his time about potential disorder. The most alarming elements in *Oliver Twist* are Fagin and his gang, the violent Bill Sikes, and, although she has a heart of gold, the prostitute Nancy. Dickens throughout his career was fascinated, and yet repelled, by anarchic forces within society. It is a fear of criminality that is most apparent, but Dickens also deals again and again with the transgressive power of sexuality. What is also apparent, however, is a fear of the mob, of a threatening herd of working-class people such as the crowd that pursues the murderer Sikes. *Oliver Twist*, then, like Dickens's other novels, looks at the question of how to control an increasingly complex society, but in doing so – and this is one reason why his novels are so effective – offers a vivid sense of the dangerous forces that threaten this society.

There was, it is true, a precedent for the kind of plot Dickens employs in *Oliver Twist*. In the years before 1837, the novel as a genre was characterised by novelists reworking old forms and developing new ones. There were novels of manners and sentiment, featuring life among the upper class and middle-class aspirants; one variety of the novel of manners was the 'silver-fork' novel, preoccupied with fashionable society. There were Gothic novels, and parodies of Gothic novels (such as Jane Austen's *Northanger Abbey*), and, by contrast, novels of ordinary life. Extremely popular were historical novels, as influenced by Walter Scott. But Dickens owes most to the Newgate novel, a form of fiction that dealt with the lives of criminals. A typical Newgate novel, however, such as Edward Bulwer-Lytton's *Paul Clifford* (1830) or Harrison Ainsworth's *Rookwood* (1834), is a loose and episodic picaresque tale; *Oliver Twist* has altogether more focus. An aspect of this is the way in which Dickens endorses emerging middle-class values. Oliver's salvation takes the form of being absorbed into a middle-class family. This is an important idea in the Victorian period: domestic order acts as a refuge and sustaining structure in a changing world.

What we can add to this is the way in which Dickens time and time again deals with the progress of a male hero who, as with David in *David Copperfield* (1849–50) and Pip in *Great Expectations* (1860–1), comes to terms with the world as he embraces middle-class values. At the same time, however, Dickens's heroes often have uncomfortable doubles: David Copperfield is shadowed by Uriah Heep and Steerforth, both of whom reveal the kind of dark sexual urge that David attempts to conceal or deny in his own life. It is as if, in embracing a new middle-class code, Dickens is equally aware of the precariousness or vulnerability of the new respectable social conception of the self, of the buried life that is hidden beneath the veneer of polite manners.

There are, too, other important aspects of Dickens's art. In all his novels, Dickens presents the teeming variety and abundance of the nineteenth century, but it is actually a carefully controlled vision. The working-class characters are frequently eccentric, but, because they are so, they do not represent a threat. The lower classes, in effect, become a kind of carnival backdrop to the moral advance of the middle-class heroes and heroines. The story that is usually told in a Dickens novel is a story of social reconciliation and reconstitution. The characteristic hero or heroine is an orphan, who moves from a position of deprivation and oppression towards being inside a middle-class circle of kindness and care. Success is associated with the bourgeois virtues of industriousness, honesty and charity, while time and time again the novels are concerned with the development and strengthening of individual identity. The heroes often struggle with sexual desire, but by and large they manage to control both their sexual needs and their moral nature. We can see this in a character such as Arthur Clennam, in *Little Dorrit* (1855–7), who, in the face of adversity, including uncertainty about his parentage and identity, tackles life manfully, and is duly rewarded. But this is only towards the end of the story. There is often play with characters' names in Dickens's novels, and it is often only at the end of a novel that a character, as is the case with Esther in *Bleak House*, gets to know who he or she really is, and how he or she relates to other people.

A lot of this might seem to suggest that Dickens uses the novel form to provide reassurance for his readers: it is as if the novels hold out answers, in terms of specific ideas about identity and social class, that offer hope in an increasingly complicated and mechanised urban world. The constructive element of what Dickens offers is certainly important: a text such as *David Copperfield*, in particular, provides a role model for an idea of the self. This is a central aspect of the Victorian novel: it helped people in the nineteenth century make sense of their lives, including guidance on how they could construct themselves in a changing world. But this only works so well in Dickens's novels because, simultaneously, he provides a full impression of the complexity of this new age that prompted these new narratives of the self.

We can see this in *Bleak House* (1852–3). Dickens's novels become darker and darker during the course of his career, a development that is initiated with *Dombey and Son* (1848), a disturbing tale of a father who has no love for his daughter. *Bleak House* concerns Esther, the illegitimate daughter of Lady Dedlock, and her peripheral involvement in a court case about an inheritance, Jarndyce and Jarndyce, that has dragged on for years. The novel might end happily, with Esther marrying Dr Allan Woodcourt, but the reader is aware of a gap between the bewildering narrative structure and the orderliness of the story's outcome. This is an impression that starts to be created on the opening page of *Bleak House*:

> Fog everywhere. Fog up the river, where it flows among green airs and meadows; fog down the river, where it rolls defiled among the tiers of shipping, and the waterside pollutions of a great (and dirty) city. Fog on the Essex marshes, fog on the Kentish heights.

The novel starts in fog, and we seem to be lost in a confusing fog. As is increasingly the case with Dickens's novels, the story features death, murder, madness, despair, suicide and hauntings. The characters are disturbed, alienated and lost. This is the disorder of society, and the disorder felt in individual lives. It is, above all else, the dangerous force of sexual desire that haunts and undermines society, something that is reflected in the presence of Esther as the illegitimate child of Lady Dedlock and Captain Hawdon, who is now employed as a law-writer and who goes by the name of Nemo, or Nobody. This is perhaps the most disturbing aspect of *Bleak House*. Even though the novel endorses Victorian values, steering Esther into a rewarding relationship, it is a huge labyrinthine structure built around a missing centre, a dead father. Possibly why Dickens is the most celebrated Victorian novelist is that, to an extent that is not true of any other writer, he is able to render the alarming complexity of nineteenth-century Britain in its many dimensions even while suggesting its essential middle-class nature.

Charlotte and Emily Brontë

A period of around eighteen months in 1847–8 is generally regarded as perhaps the most significant in the entire history of the English novel. There were major novels by Dickens (*Dombey and Son*), William Makepeace Thackeray (*Vanity Fair*) Elizabeth Gaskell (*Mary Barton*), Charlote Brontë (*Jane Eyre*), and Emily Brontë (*Wuthering Heights*). This huge wave of major novels is more than a coincidence. In the first half of the nineteenth century, Britain experienced unprecedented economic and social change, all the various forces seeming to build to a climax around 1847–8. The novels that appeared at this time are a response to these social developments. But more is involved than just a response. An old discourse, an old way of thinking about the world, is losing relevance, and the novel as a genre is actively involved in creating a new discourse, including new ways of talking about people, society and the individual. It is very clear at this time that social change was affecting at a fundamental level the way in which people saw themselves and how they felt about how they related to the world at large.

Charlotte Brontë's *Jane Eyre* might, initially, strike us as having very little to do with the economic and social changes of the 1840s. Indeed, the novel might appear to be a simple love story that could have happened at any time in history, or no time at all. Jane Eyre is an orphan who lives with her aunt, and then attends Lowood School. After some years as a pupil and then as a teacher, she becomes a governess at Thornfield Hall, looking after Adèle, the ward of Edward Rochester. Jane agrees to marry Rochester, but at the wedding service it is revealed that he already has a wife, Bertha, a lunatic who is confined upstairs in his home. Jane flees, is taken in by a clergyman, St John Rivers, and his family, and takes up a post as the local schoolmistress. St John proposes to Jane, but she rejects him and returns to Thornfield Hall, Rochester's house, which is a blackened ruin. Bertha is dead, and Rochester maimed and blinded by the fire from which he sought to rescue Bertha. Jane and Rochester marry, and the novel ends with an account of marital bliss.

Jane Eyre could be regarded as a Cinderella story, in which the poor girl marries a prince. But, even though the story is set at a remove from urban and industrial Britain, there is a great deal of contemporary relevance in the way that it examines the position of women in Victorian Britain and in the remarkable way that it presents the heroine. In addition, although *Jane Eyre* might appear to lack the broad social awareness of a Dickens novel, this is not really the case at all. Towards the end it is revealed that Jane is heir to a fortune that her uncle has made in Madeira; Bertha, Rochester's wife, is of mixed race, a woman he married in the West Indies; and St John asks Jane to join him in missionary work in India. In short, the novel shows a consistent awareness of the economic life of early Victorian Britain, in particular its colonial dimension. Once we become aware of the colonial issue in the novel, we begin to gain a sense of how *Jane Eyre* is situated in the society of the day: it is aware of, and to a certain extent examining, the complex economic and social life of early Victorian Britain.

In acknowledging this, however, we need to recognise how ways of looking at Victorian fiction have changed in recent years. There was a time when critics used to emphasise the moral development of Jane: that she is a hot-headed young woman who matures, learning to act with more caution. The book could thus be seen as a kind of guide to the Victorians as to how they should behave. The problem with such an approach is that it is too quick to dismiss troublesome elements in the story. The people from the colonies, the working-class characters, and women, in particular women such as Jane, are all awkward figures, challenging the complacency of male middle-class society, and all the more so as it was the people in the colonies, the working class and women who contributed so much to the prosperity of Victorian Britain. Quite simply, early Victorian Britain might have been reconstructing and reconceiving itself as an ordered and morally respectable society, but there were those who remained outside this new middle-class discourse.

Accordingly, recent criticism of *Jane Eyre*, rather than focusing on the containment of Jane's voice as she makes an accommodation with society, has looked at the extraordinary nature, and demands, of that voice. Lowood School, imposing conformity and discipline, may be taken as an illustration of a kind of regimentation that was increasingly a feature of Victorian life. Jane, however, consistently challenges the authority of the school and its director, Reverend Brocklehurst. Almost wilfully, Jane places herself in the position of social outsider. She has an opportunity to become an insider when Rochester proposes to her, but what is most interesting in the novel is the way in which, verbally, she duels with Rochester, asserting her independence and refusing to yield. If a woman does not conform in Victorian society, however, she is punished, and the usual form this takes is incarceration. Bertha, who is mad, but can also be seen as a woman who refused to conform to the expectations of respectable society, is locked away. If Jane will not conform, she, too, might be locked away. The threat is all the more real because it is difficult for Jane to establish a conventional relationship with other people.

Indeed, the impression that comes across is that Jane is strong and independent, but also vulnerable and confused. What is significant here is the kind of conception of the individual that Brontë offers. In Romantic literature, there is frequently a sense of the rebel or lonely outsider at odds with society. By the time we get to *Jane Eyre*, there is a sense of how, in a society where people are increasingly separated from their place of birth and their families, individuals are much more exposed, much more on their own. This is one of the central issues that Victorian texts return to. Socially, what we see in Victorian Britain is the emergence of a more regulated, more disciplined society; rapid social change demands a greater degree of social control. But, at the personal level, rather than individuals just slotting into this structure, there is a sense of the lonely and complicated position of the individual. Typically, therefore, we see two things in Victorian novels: a new sense of social order, which is increasingly a middle-class social order, and simultaneously, and paradoxically, a developing sense of psychological complexity, of the problems that an individual experiences in such a society.

Jane Eyre ends with social reconciliation and reconstitution: Jane becomes part of the established order. But throughout the novel there are contradictory elements in her character. She sees herself as an outsider, but is always quick to judge others according to conventional values. In essence, she is at odds with, but also craves, middle-class respectability. This is a common contradiction in Victorian literature. Dickens, for example, is the most thorough-going sceptic about all the institutions of his day, but also a defender of middle-class society. In the case of Charlotte Brontë, her heroines are rebels, but very much middle-class rebels. What we need to appreciate, however, is that, in 1847–8, rather than merely describing an existing conception of middle-class individualism, Brontë is engaged in actively constructing this notion of individualism. It follows that Victorian readers looked to the novel as the genre that could provide an understanding of, even a vocabulary for articulating, what it meant to be an individual in nineteenth-century Britain.

The kind of psychological complexity that we experience in *Jane Eyre* is taken much further in Charlotte Brontë's *Villette* (1853), where a central focus of concern is desire. The Victorians valued marriage in a way that had never been the case previously; for the Victorians, marriage was the central mechanism of social regulation and control, tidying young people away into neat domestic units, and regulating the potentially dangerous force of sexuality. In Dickens's novels there is always a sense of sexuality as the anarchic energy that can disrupt the smooth-running of society. In Brontë, sexuality is equally anarchic, but there is also something highly compelling about the way in which she creates a new discourse that can do justice to her heroines' sexual feelings.

Villette is the story of Lucy Snowe, a teacher in a girls' school in the Belgian town of Villette. She gradually falls in love with Paul Emmanuel, another teacher at the school. He is obliged to depart for the West Indies, but leaves Lucy in charge of her own school, and with a promise to return in three years. At the end, however, it is possible that he has died. In some ways this is the same story as *Jane Eyre*: an isolated young woman who asserts herself, finds herself, and finds a partner. But in *Villette* everything is cast in more extreme terms, and a compromise with society is never really achieved. At the end, Lucy is fantasising about a future that will probably never be realised. The novel is astute in its grasp of how power is wielded in society; there are extraordinary episodes, such as when Emmanuel is directing the school play, acting out all the parts and making the girls imitate his performance. He is, almost literally, putting words into the girls' mouths. The complement of this awareness of male power in society is the sense of Lucy as someone who is deeply isolated.

The manner is which *Villette* suggests Lucy's needs, anxieties and desires is astonishing. Victorian society developed an ideology of what was considered normal and respectable, with people deviating from this shared standard being judged as aberrant or dangerous. The other side of this, however, was the simultaneous development of a complex sense of the self, and this is what *Villette* conveys so well; indeed, the novel is helping to formulate this new sense of self by offering a language for it. This new notion of self did not actually conflict entirely with Victorian social morality; on the contrary, it is a central element in the thinking of the Victorians and an important constitutive feature of the social formation. An advanced liberal capitalist society not only proved flexible enough to accommodate a new idea of the individual but actually sustained itself by nurturing just such a sense of the individual. This is perhaps the principal reason why it is this complicated, intricate relationship between the individual self and society at large that Victorian novelists returned to time and time again.

What this also indicates, however, and perhaps rather surprisingly, is something rather parochial and insular about the subject matter of Victorian literary texts, and about the Victorian period generally. The Victorians managed a vast empire but at no point saw themselves as part of a broader European culture, as had been the case up until at least the seventeenth century. Their favoured form, the novel, focuses almost exclusively on domestic life. And the very term Victorian, unlike, say, Romantic, which suggests a way of thinking that transcends borders, implies an insular concern with British society. For the modern reader, Victorian literary texts are amongst the most compelling, but we should recognise that this is possibly because they address topics that are close to our own lives; we need to retain an awareness that, in some respects at least, the horizons of literature were reduced by the Victorians.

Obviously, though, this does not reduce in any way the impact of many nineteenth-century novels. Consider Emily Brontë's *Wuthering Heights* (1847), for example, which tells the story of the love between Catherine Earnshaw and Heathcliff. It is a novel that seems to be caught between an old way of life and the new world of the Victorians. The house of Wuthering Heights is an open, communal space. It is set against The Grange, a house of private rooms and private spaces. The architectural change suggests how the Victorians, increasingly, not only demanded their own private space, but also how, psychologically, they withdrew into themselves or detached themselves from other people. One of the many things that could be said about the relationship between Catherine and Heathcliff is that, in seeing themselves, as the imagery stresses, as one person, the novel rises above the Victorian ideology of separate individuals and separate lives. *Wuthering Heights* develops the idea of a passion that is so intense that it transcends individualism, but one reason why the novel can do this is because it has grasped how Victorian society is restructuring itself. A second generation emerges at the end of *Wuthering Heights*, the children of Catherine and Heathcliff, a generation more moderate and disciplined in its behaviour. This, essentially, is the direction in which the world is heading. But, in its representation of the relationship between Catherine and Heathcliff themselves, *Wuthering Heights* confronts us with an extreme alternative to the new social discipline that characterises early Victorian Britain.

William Makepeace Thackeray, Elizabeth Gaskell

In 1851, Britain held a Great Exhibition in a Crystal Palace in Hyde Park in London. The social, industrial and political unrest that characterised the 1830s and 1840s was displaced by a spirit of burgeoning confidence in the 1850s. In this context, the Great Exhibition can be seen as a triumphalist statement, an invitation to the whole world to reproduce itself in the image of the middle-class Englishman. Industry – the exhibition was a celebration of industrial productivity – declared the existence of a world of identical and interchangeable parts; excess and instability were eliminated. The world's products were on display in the Crystal Palace; it was as if everything could be collected, catalogued and controlled under the roof that the British had constructed.

Victorian literature to a large extent embraces this sense of the nation's identity, but, as we might expect, literature also draws attention to stresses and strains in the nation's self-image. In William Makepeace Thackeray's novels what we see is a refusal to become enthusiastic about, and at times even to accept, the new values of the Victorian era. Perhaps most markedly, Thackeray appears to reject the new narratives of the Victorians. For example, in Victorian fiction the typical heroine, as in *Jane Eyre*, is frustrated by the lack of openings for her abilities within a gendered society but eventually settles down in that society. In Thackeray's *Vanity Fair* (1847–8), by contrast, the heroine, Becky Sharp, is conniving, cynical and nasty – a woman on the make. It is as if Thackeray knows how women are now presented in literature, but refuses to endorse this new vision.

There was a time when Thackeray was seen as the equal of his contemporary Dickens. Even in his lifetime, however, reservations were voiced. Some readers felt Thackeray was old-fashioned, and certainly his works – with the exception of *Vanity Fair* – have sometimes proved less than compelling to modern readers. Yet it is possibly the old-fashioned qualities of Thackeray that make him interesting, for his is an awkward, reactionary voice, resisting the new assumptions at the heart of a great deal of early Victorian fiction. Thackeray's reputation was established with the publication of *Vanity Fair*, the subtitle of which, 'A Novel without a Hero', begins to suggest his

scepticism about the kind of commitment to the complex, introspective hero or heroine that we see in the works of several of his
contemporaries. The reader is invited to share in the trials of Jane
Eyre or David Copperfield, but we are not required to have much
sympathy for Vanity Fair's Becky Sharp. Thackeray's approach to
characterisation is, essentially, comic and external. Vanity Fair as a
whole amounts to a satiric representation of a society consumed by
a new desire for material goods, most of the characters being motivated by the simple lusts of greed and self-interest.

Setting his novel at the time of Waterloo (1815), Thackeray gives
himself an opportunity to reflect on the tremendous social changes
of the first half of the nineteenth century. At a time when novels were
playing a vital role in creating a new middle-class sense of self-worth,
Thackeray fails to oblige. Rather than finding value in middle-class
experience, as many of his contemporaries did, he castigates it as selfish. Even Dobbin, the most honourable character in Vanity Fair, and
the nearest we get to a middle-class hero, is viewed patronisingly.
Thackeray's lack of commitment to the middle-class subject and the
discourse of individualism, together with his lack of commitment to
the associated values of marriage and family, establishes him as the
awkward outsider in the early Victorian novel. His distance from the
norm is particularly apparent in The History of Pendennis (1849–50),
which appeared in the same year as David Copperfield. The two novels
feature similar stories, but whereas David Copperfield is centrally concerned with the construction of a successful middle-class identity,
Pendennis concentrates on the hero's loss of a role and direction in his
life. The leisurely pace of Pendennis, which can prove off-putting to
modern readers, is possibly an important aspect of its achievement –
that the novel seems deliberately to stick with a rhythm that is at
odds with and disrupts the new rhythm of Victorian life.

It is in The History of Henry Esmond (1852) that Thackeray engages
most directly with new Victorian ideas about individual identity. Set
in the reign of Queen Anne, the novel shows an old military order
yielding to a new social structure in which the individual is at the centre, acting in accordance with the dictates of individual conscience.
The novel might, therefore, be read as an articulation of a more sensitive set of values that is replacing a defunct code. But Henry

Esmond is not necessarily a positive figure. He can be seen as totally self-absorbed, setting himself up as a kind of god at the centre of his own world. In this reading, *Henry Esmond* exposes the shortcomings of the new Victorian emphasis on the self. Thackeray's refusal to participate in the kind of thinking we find in the novels of his contemporaries is often, as in *Vanity Fair* and *The Newcomes* (1855), accompanied by a devastating critique of materialism. By the end of his career, in *Philip* (1862), Thackeray's disillusionment with contemporary culture had become a lot more bitter, but the harshness of *Philip* (one of the most overtly racist Victorian novels) helps us appreciate the subtlety of Thackeray's position in his earlier novels. There, having lost confidence in the old order, Thackeray remains teasingly sceptical about the new values of Victorian Britain as reflected in, and in part created by, the novels of his contemporaries.

Elizabeth Gaskell provides an example of the positive spirit that is encountered in a great deal of fiction in the 1850s. By the 1860s, a sense of failure was becoming widespread; there was an awareness that material prosperity had not actually improved people's lives. In the 1850s, however, particularly in social and industrial novels – such as those of Charles Kingsley (for example, *Yeast*, 1848, and *Alton Locke*, 1851) – there is an optimistic sense that society can heal its wounds and advance decisively. This is evident in Gaskell's *North and South* (1854–5), a novel, fundamentally, about social reconciliation and overcoming hostility and division. It tells the story of Margaret Hale who, when her father resigns his living as a clergyman in the south of England, accompanies him to Milton-Northern (Manchester). There she finds herself in conflict with a mill-owner, John Thornton, trying to persuade him to take a sympathetic view of his workers' problems. Eventually his attitude softens, and they marry at the end of the novel. There are some works of literature that seem to come complete with an interpretation, and *North and South* is one of them. It is admirable that a novelist should engage with the new reality of industrial Britain, and the dynamic of this novel is conciliatory: it wants to heal rifts and divisions within society, notably between employer and worker. But the novel also presents two distinct versions of middle-class ideology, and attempts to reconcile them. One version is a liberal vision of moral responsibility for the general well-being of society and a sense of obligation to the less fortunate; the other middle-class ideology is that of business and profit. In uniting Margaret and Thornton, both sides learn from the other. The emphasis is conciliatory and healing; as such, it is a novel with a moral prospectus for society. And, in this respect, it matches a mood of the 1850s, that, with rising affluence, solutions can be found to the country's problems.

One possible criticism of Gaskell's stance – a criticism that is often levelled against Victorian novelists – is that she seeks a personal answer to a political problem, believing that a modification in the views of individuals can affect the whole nature of society. What is also apparent in Gaskell's novels is her belief that, in the end, everyone should share her vision of middle-class values; the workers are assumed to have the same long-term interests as their employers, if only they could see what is best for them. This is a form of ideological thinking that becomes prevalent in the Victorian period: a tyranny of the respectable norm. *North and South*, in representing such a way of thinking, can be seen as one of a number of novels that attempt to rethink Britain in the decade of the Great Exhibition. In suggesting this, however, we also need to be aware of a level of complication and contradiction in Gaskell's work.

North and South seems totally committed to middle-class domestic values, but the Hale family is unhappy and divided. The mother regrets marrying Mr Hale, and Mr Hale is a weak father, who relies upon his daughter to cope with difficult challenges. Their son, Frederick, has been involved in a naval mutiny, and, consequently, cannot legally return to England. There is, it can be seen, a fundamental contradiction at the heart of the text: the novel endorses middle-class values, but these values are also shown as suspect and flawed. Superficially, love, marriage and family life might seem to provide an answer to life's problems, but the more closely one looks at *North and South* the more it becomes apparent that Gaskell is only too aware of the problems associated with love, marriage and family life.

One aspect of the novel that is particularly striking is a sense of sexual agitation that affects Margaret at various points. It is as if there is an irrational dimension to her character that has no place in a polite discourse; indeed, the social and moral discourse of the novel seems to edge out any possibility of an emotional side to life or language. In this respect, we realise again what the Victorians denied or repressed in constructing their social morality. As with the novels of Charlotte Brontë, however, although this sense of Margaret's sexual identity might appear to be at odds with the social theme of the novel, the truth is that an acknowledgement of the complexity of the self – in particular, the complex depths of a female character, whose way of thinking will always differ from the dominant ways of thinking in a male-led society – is really part and parcel of how the Victorians were rethinking their world. In all of Gaskell's novels – novels that include *Ruth* (1853), *Mary Barton* (1848), *Sylvia's Lovers* (1863) and *Wives and Daughters* (1864–6) – the impulse might be towards social healing, but she is always aware of levels of contradiction. As with other novelists of her era, she might be actively involved in the creation of new middle-class values, but she is also sceptical, at times very sceptical, about these values.

Alfred Lord Tennyson, Robert Browning, Elizabeth Barrett Browning

It is clear that the novel in the Victorian period became the dominant form. In a way that is perhaps unprecedented in literature, what we see is a literary genre that connected directly with very large numbers of people, helping them make sense of their lives. But if the novel became the preferred literary form, what role did poetry serve in these years? Poetry, in fact, continued to enjoy a cultural status that set it above the novel. But what is also the case is that, while the novel occupied the middle ground, Victorian poetry tended to engage with some of the more marginal, extreme and unnerving dimensions of Victorian life.

The leading poet was Alfred Lord Tennyson, a writer whose emotional and mental outlook was, as we might expect, very much at one with the feelings of his audience. In Romantic poetry, the individual stance, as a social outsider, is one that represents a new kind of energy. By the time we get to Tennyson, the sense of being on one's own is more haunted and lonely; we sense characters who, distressed by the world, have withdrawn into themselves. This is apparent in poems

such as 'Mariana' (1830) and 'The Lady of Shallott' (1832). There is a feeling of guilt, of not being able to muster any resolve. This feeling is
underwritten by the sensuous, musical quality of Tennyson's style; it
is a style that lends itself to the representation of enervated states.

This extends to strange and disturbed states, and even a homoerotic quality that is at a remove from conventional desire. Time and
time again in Tennyson – and in Victorian poetry as a whole – there
is a delving into the strange and dark depths of the mind. But, as is the
case with the Victorian novel when it explores the unconscious
mind, an alienated sense of the self can exist alongside a great deal
that is conventional in terms of moral uplift and positive in terms of
social resolve. This is evident in *In Memoriam*, published in 1850, a
work that Queen Victoria is said to have valued second only to the
Bible. *In Memoriam*, a long elegy, is dedicated to Tennyson's friend,
Arthur Henry Hallam, who died in 1833, aged 22. Composed over a
number of years, it consists of a sequence of 130 poems in which
Tennyson reflects on the shifting flux of Victorian life while exploring the nature of loss and bereavement.

What is likely to strike us immediately is the dark sense of despon-
dency created:

> Dark house, by which once more I stand
>   Here in the long unlovely street,
>   Doors, where my heart was used to beat
> So quickly, waiting for a hand.
>
> A hand that can be clasped no more –
>   Behold me, for I cannot sleep,
>   And like a guilty thing I creep
> At earliest morning to the door.
>
> He is not here; but far away
>   The noise of life begins again,
>   And ghastly through the drizzling rain
> On the bald street breaks the blank day.
>   (*In Memoriam*, VII)

Tennyson now haunts the street and house where Hallam used to
live, remembering the feelings he used to have. Everyday life has
ceased to have meaning for him, and the poem powerfully suggests

the way in which death has shaken his being. But the poem's very simplicity implies a larger resonance: the loss of Hallam has echoes of the death of Christ. There is no consolation, however, no hope of any kind of afterlife, and Tennyson himself is tormented by his guilt. The poem does not say Tennyson loved Hallam: there is clearly no room in Victorian culture for such homoerotic openness. But what this individual poem, and *In Memoriam* as a whole, suggests is an almost totally disabling sense of loss and confusion. It might seem odd, therefore, that *In Memoriam* itself was enormously popular with Victorian readers. But what the poem as a whole manages to do is to confront the issues that caused so much anxiety at this time, Tennyson expressing the profound doubt his contemporaries felt about how to reconcile religion and science, God and nature, and possibly doubts about the entire domestic ideology they had constructed. He craves the security of companionship and a familiar setting, but the things that provide reassurance are so easily destroyed: the house is 'dark', the streets 'unlovely', and the day 'blank'.

Robert Browning is another poet who explores strange states of mind, plunging into the dark places of the human psyche. He does this, most characteristically, in dramatic monologues, poems in which an imaginary speaker addresses an audience. In 'My Last Duchess' there is an imagined speaker, the Duke, who addresses the representative of the girl he hopes to marry. He inadvertently reveals himself as a tyrant who could not tolerate his first wife's independence; he is despotic, wishing to limit the freedom of another person. This sets the pattern for Browning's dramatic monologues, although they do become increasingly subtle. There is always a tension between the mind of the speaker and the world he or she occupies; there is often a psychologically disturbed will to power that is at odds with the values of any kind of rational or liberal society:

> That's my last Duchess painted on the wall,
> Looking as if she were alive. I call
> That piece a wonder, now: Frà Pandolf's hands
> Worked busily a day, and there she stands.
> Will't please you sit and look at her? I said
> 'Frà Pandolf' by design, for never read
> Strangers like you that pictured countenance,

The depth and passion of its earnest glance,
But to myself they turned (since none puts by
The curtain I have drawn for you, but I)
And seemed as they would ask me, if they durst,
How such a glance came there . . .

(ll. 1–12)

By the end of the poem it becomes clear that the Duke's obsessive
jealousy has destroyed the Duchess, but that, curiously, the jealousy
still lingers together with his discipline of fear. Hovering somewhere
between confession and stream-of-consciousness, the poem takes us
into the disturbed world of the mind, and away from the domestic
and the comfortable concerns that are often the desired goal in
Victorian literature.

If we put Browning and Tennyson together, we can start to gener-
alise about Victorian poetry. What is most apparent is the exploration of strange and submerged feelings. It is as if poetry has become
the medium for dealing with the more awkward aspects of life that
the mainstream, and especially novelists, would prefer to neglect. Yet
the popularity of both Browning and Tennyson says a great deal
about how their subject matter must have chimed with the fears and
anxieties of the public at large. There is a similar exploration of the
marginal in the poetry of Browning's wife, Elizabeth Barrett
Browning. Her best-known poems appear in *Sonnets from the
Portuguese* (1850), but her most important and revealing work is
Aurora Leigh (1857). A novel in verse, the poem charts the heroine's
development as an artist. Refusing the love of her cousin, who wishes her to renounce her writing and work on behalf of the poor, she
establishes herself as a poet in London. Later, in Europe, she meets up
with her cousin again and both confess their love. Described in these
terms, *Aurora Leigh* seems to lack any real substance, but it actually
played a central role in a debate about women, women's writing and
sexual difference in the Victorian period. Whereas the Brontës question male values and examine the role of women in a middle-class
society built around marriage and the home, Barrett Browning, by
questioning the exclusion of women from 'true' poetry, confronts
some very fundamental questions about gendered identity. *Aurora
Leigh* explores the very language of Victorian verse, undermining the

social codes that sought to restrict women's writing, and by extension women's ambitions, to the emotional, the domestic, and the slight. Indeed, it seeks to reverse the assumptions about gender that contributed so much to underpinning the implicit assumptions of conventional writing and the conduct of conventional society.

The feelings expressed in much of what Elizabeth Barrett Browning writes elsewhere, for example in *Sonnets from the Portuguese*, are odd; there is, repeatedly, an articulation of something alienated, denied, hidden and repressed:

> I lift my heavy heart up solemnly,
> As once Electra her sepulchral urn,
> And, looking in thine eyes, I overturn
> The ashes at thy feet. Behold and see
> What a great heap of grief lay hid in me,
> And how the red wild sparkles dimly burn
> Through the ashen greyness. If thy foot in scorn
> Could tread them out to darkness utterly,
> It might be well perhaps. But if instead
> Thou wait beside me for the wind to blow
> The grey dust up, . . . those laurels on thine head,
> O my Beloved, will not shield thee so,
> That none of all the fires shall scorch and shred
> The hair beneath. Stand farther off then! go.
>   (*Sonnets from the Portuguese*, V)

These are the kind of feelings that the Victorians were becoming increasingly aware of, but which, paradoxically, in their respectable, middle-class culture, they also wished to contain and even deny. But the contradiction is not as strange as it seems. Old values, including, to a certain extent, the security of religious values, might have gone in a new age of science, technology, and industrial progress. A new framework of essentially middle-class social and moral values may have been constructed in their place, but these values lacked the ultimate authority and sanction of religious values. The new values helped the Victorians make sense of an increasingly bewildering world, but there was, in the end, an awareness that the real focus of life, and the only thing that could really be known or even trusted, was oneself and one's own feelings.

11 *Victorian Literature,*
1857–1876

Victorian Thinkers

Matthew Arnold's poem 'Dover Beach' deals with a central source of
worry in Victorian life, the loss of religious faith:

> The Sea of Faith
> Was once, too, at the full, and round earth's shore
> Lay like the folds of a bright girdle furled.
> But now I only hear
> Its melancholy, long, withdrawing roar,
> Retreating, to the breath
> Of the night-wind, down the vast edges drear
> And naked shingles of the world.
>
> (ll. 21–8)

Arnold presents a world where everything is frightening and all
familiar points of reference have disappeared. In the poem as a
whole, he clings on to love, but even love seems an illusion. At the
heart of the poem is his loss of confidence in a religious explanation
of experience, in the 'Sea of Faith' that once surrounded the earth.
And yet we also associate the Victorians with a strong sense of religious conviction.

This apparent contradiction is not difficult to explain. As the
world changed rapidly, people craved the security of sound beliefs,
rules and fixed codes. There is, in fact, often an air of quiet despera-
tion to Victorian religion, of clinging on to what one can amidst the
wreckage of change. The problem people at the time faced was that
the old narratives, in particular that of religion, no longer seemed
capable of making sense of their lives. The result was that they sought
new ways of ordering their world, both intellectually and in concrete
terms. As evidence of this we could point to government enquiries,

works of sociological enquiry (such as Henry Mayhew's *London Labour and the London Poor*, 1862) and social legislation (such as a variety of Factory Acts) that attempted to comprehend and then regulate a society that had been transformed by economic changes. We could also point to how the Victorians built sewage systems for cities, how they built vast hospitals and lunatic asylums and prisons, and how they built schools. There had to be a huge physical infrastructure to service and maintain their society. And we could point to the introduction of a police force, and the emergence of the lawyer and the doctor as central figures in society; the day-to-day functioning of life had to be policed, legislated and nursed to an extent that had never been necessary in the past.

In addition to such practical measures, the Victorians also needed intellectual explanations that could help them make sense of a world that had changed and was changing so fast. Arnold, who by the 1860s had stopped writing poetry, is a typical Victorian intellectual in the way that, in his literary, political and educational writings, he analysed the situation in which his age found itself. His most famous work, *Culture and Anarchy* (1869), recommends culture as 'the great help out of present difficulties'. The title is itself significant: Arnold sees no central authority to control the drift of civilisation towards anarchy, and so proposes culture as a source of value that will provide a direction in human affairs. What we might say about *Culture and Anarchy* is that, in essence, it constructs a new narrative as a substitute for the old narratives that seem to have lost their relevance.

There are a number of Victorian writers who, like Arnold, helped the Victorians make sense of their lives. Collectively, these writers – Thomas Carlyle, John Stuart Mill, Matthew Arnold and John Ruskin are the leading names – are referred to as the Victorian Sages. They are writers who interpreted the age for the age, the historians of their own time. The response of the modern reader to these writers is complicated; to an extent they are difficult to read, because they belong so much to their own time. If we read them at all, it is with a certain detachment, seeing how they function in a context. Ruskin is particularly interesting in this respect. He was an art critic and historian who, from his aesthetic concerns, increasingly drew social and moral views; addressing himself more and more to political and economic problems, he condemned laissez-faire economics, and extolled the dignity of labour and the moral and aesthetic value of craftsmanship. In an age when the demands of work dominated people's lives as never before, Ruskin, and the same is also true of William Morris, a poet, designer, writer and socialist, attempted to reintroduce the human dimension into a factory-based economy.

The Victorian Sages provided new narratives that were of great importance to their contemporaries, but when we look at the Victorian period in retrospect we see the appearance of three new narratives that are of a different order altogether; narratives that are as all-embracing as the religious narrative they succeeded, and which are still relevant to people's lives today. The three major European thinkers of the Victorian period are Charles Darwin, Karl Marx and Sigmund Freud. Darwin developed the theory of evolution, Marx was the founder of international communism, and Freud was the founder of psychoanalysis. The new narratives of these three men offer, in each case and collectively, a new means of making sense of all of life. One reads the world on a scientific basis, one in political terms, and one in terms of the importance of the individual mind. The writings of all three men are the astonishing products of an age of uncertainty, and their ideas are still returned to and disputed. But they are also characteristically Victorian ventures. Sometimes people make the point that these new master narratives of the Victorian period can be compared to Victorian colonialism: they are enterprises that reach out to command, control and explain everything, ignoring any awkward local differences that might challenge the dominant authority. If the Victorian period is marked by the arrival of these new master narratives, the twentieth century, as we will see, is the century when all narratives seem to fall apart.

Darwin's *The Origin of Species* appeared in 1859. Its theory of the 'descent with modification' of the human species ran entirely counter to religious belief and teaching, while his arguments about natural selection and the survival of the fittest seemed to place human beings in an evolutionary chain that had little moral or spiritual purpose. Suddenly the world had changed; its history was no longer governed by religion but by the natural sciences. No less revolutionary was the publication in 1848 of *The Communist Manifesto* by Marx and Friedrich

Engels, and then, in 1867, of Marx's major treatise *Das Kapital* (*Capital*), with its analysis of society in terms of its material base and its theory of a struggle between the different social classes for dominance. The new understanding that Marx brought to the organisation and working of society was to have a far-reaching effect on the whole of twentieth-century political and philosophical thinking. Freud's work on psychoanalysis, including works such as *Studies in Hysteria* (jointly published by Freud and Josef Breuer), and his ideas about the way in which sexual repression is reflected in dreams, jokes and language, did not appear until the 1890s, but is consonant with the theories of Darwin and Marx in providing the Victorians, and the twentieth century, with a new master narrative.

Darwin, Marx and Freud all influenced literature, particularly towards the end of the nineteenth century, but the main thing we see in fiction from the 1850s onwards is the development of other new forms of narrative, in particular the realistic novel. By the 1850s the term realism was associated not so much with what was being observed as with a certain way of looking and, perhaps just as importantly, a certain tone of voice, which is that of the middle-class novelist. There is a kind of policing of the fictional world in line with middle-class values; the assumptions of the middle-class observer are taken to be universal standards of morality, propriety and conduct. Essentially a moral frame, a kind of secularised version of an old religious code, is imposed upon life. This might seem to hold out the promise of nothing more than the most tedious moral tracts, but the best Victorian realistic novels habitually contradict, complicate and frustrate the overall scheme of values that they might seem to be advancing, revealing an awareness of the tensions that lie just below the surface of respectable life.

George Eliot

It is partly because the material wealth of Britain was transformed in a very few years that George Eliot seems to be writing about a different world from that of Charles Dickens. While the 1840s can be regarded as a decade of unrest, the period in which George Eliot was writing – *Adam Bede* was published in 1859 and her final novel, *Daniel*

Deronda, in 1874–6 – was an era of tremendous prosperity. Social conflicts and divisions were no longer so apparent; for example, the kind of class division that is so evident in the Brontës and Dickens received far less consideration. In a number of ways, George Eliot seems to be almost the complete embodiment of the mid-Victorian period.

This is apparent, first, in the way that her works always appear to be making a statement. All Victorian novelists focus on the relationship between the individual and society, but George Eliot is the writer who, perhaps more than any other, spells out the duties and obligations of the individual. Her principal theme is egoism; her standard plot is an educational one, in which the central character comes to understand that he or she has been too self-absorbed, and starts to think about his or her social commitment. What Eliot says in her novels cannot be separated from her manner of saying it: her chosen mode was realism, which involves the close observation of ordinary life, but also involves a discourse that she has in common with her readers. It is a discourse that is characterised by a shared understanding of the world and shared values. Some of the elements involved in her narrative method are apparent in the opening sentence of her most ambitious novel, *Middlemarch* (1871–2):

> Miss Brooke had that kind of beauty which seems to be thrown into relief by poor dress.

Eliot does very little in terms of actually describing Miss Brooke. Instead, she calls upon ideas, in particular a shared apprehension that she can identify in her readers. Essentially, it is a middle-class way of looking, disdaining vulgarity and show, and approving of moderation and economy.

This is the essence of Victorian realism: a shared way of perceiving the world, in which the judgements offered are those of all reasonable people. One aspect of this is the simple fact of naming the object. The novel starts with the words 'Miss Brooke'. By naming, in effect labelling, everybody and everything, the world is made both tangible and comprehensible. Nothing eludes definition or understanding. But the perspective is always the polite perspective of the middle classes. In this instance, there is an implicit understanding, and accepted decorum, that 'Miss Brooke', rather than the over-familiarity of 'Dorothea', the heroine's first name, is the correct form of address. George Eliot would not, however, be a very interesting novelist if she merely provided reassurance for her audience, and recent criticism has focused increasingly on elements of anxiety and uncertainty in Eliot's writing. In particular, critics have looked at the way in which she is not entirely sure of, and even undermines, the controlling discourse that she establishes in her novels. In endorsing the dominant values of the society of her time, Eliot is, in a variety of ways, endorsing values that are male-centred, but what we also have to recognise is Eliot's feminism, the quiet anger that often informs her accounts of the situations in which women find themselves.

This is apparent in *The Mill on the Floss* (1860), a novel dealing with Maggie Tulliver and her brother Tom. Maggie is an intelligent girl in a community that has no time for unconventional young women, and which offers no outlet for her intelligence. She becomes friends with Philip Wakem, who appreciates her qualities and sympathises with her interests, but Tom forces her to give up Philip's friendship. Subsequently, Maggie's reputation is compromised through the irresponsible behaviour of Stephen Guest. Tom then turns her out of the house, and she is ostracised by local society. Maggie and Tom are finally, if briefly, reconciled when she attempts to save him from a flood that threatens the family mill; but it is the briefest of reconciliations, for they both drown. Traditionally, critics used to find fault with the ending of *The Mill on the Floss*. There was admiration for the skill with which Eliot evokes rural and domestic life, and for the confident, sympathetic manner in which she enables us to understand Maggie's frustrations and aspirations, but the ending was commonly criticised as rushed and arbitrary. More recently, critics have had nothing but good things to say about the ending of the novel. One point made is that it is an ending that undermines the dominant narrative method of the novel, that is to say, the realistic perspective. Eliot at the end switches to a more extreme and dramatic mode of presentation. This in turn serves to highlight the limitations of the dominant narrative stance in the novel. Eliot's usual voice constitutes a reassuring means of presenting and processing experience, but the ending to the novel suggests how it is possibly a rather limited view, with little room for strong feelings.

Maggie's relationship with Stephen Guest is relevant here. Maggie is drawn to him as a reckless, irresponsible figure. At this point the novel begins to touch upon a form of passionate waywardness or strength of desire that, essentially, has no place in the cautious and respectable code of the mid-Victorians, and which is also, in a way, at odds with Eliot's own moral, if compassionate, voice. There is, as such, a contradictory impulse at the very heart of *The Mill on the Floss*. Eliot writes from a middle-class perspective which, perhaps more than anything else, puts the needs of the community above the desires of the self. When she writes in this way, Eliot is both reflecting a moral and social discourse that was becomingly increasingly a feature of mid-Victorian thinking and helping to establish this way of thinking; that is, she reflects an existing discourse, yet is also adding to the authority of this discourse. But the real level of complexity in the novel resides in the fact that, even as she constructs this way of looking at life, she is also dissecting and deconstructing it. In the case of *The Mill on the Floss*, she is aware of the limitations, and ungenerous, unyielding spirit, of this view of life.

When we turn to Thomas Hardy in the next chapter, we will see an author who is more overtly hostile to middle-class social and sexual morality. In addition, he is an author who consistently and wilfully undermines the voice and conventions of realistic fiction. The force of Hardy's reaction against realism and its associated moral values does, however, help us grasp how central a role the voice of realism played in mid-Victorian Britain. At the same time, what is also apparent is that, even as they were being put together, realistic novels were always taking themselves apart. This is particularly clear in what is probably the finest English realistic novel, *Middlemarch*. The opening section of *Middlemarch* focuses on Dorothea Brooke, and shows how she comes to marry Edward Casaubon, a clergyman some thirty years her senior. As this story develops, a number of other strands are introduced. There is the story of Tertius Lydgate, a young doctor newly arrived in the area, and his courtship of, and marriage to, Rosamond Vincy. Another couple who eventually marry are Mary Garth and Rosamond's brother, Fred Vincy, but in the early stages of the novel she refuses to marry him unless he mends his ways. For Dorothea, the reality of marriage to Casaubon is not at all what she had expected, although they come closer together when she learns that he is terminally ill. But Casaubon extracts a promise from her that, after his death, she will continue with his futile scholarly work; moreover, he leaves a codicil to his will stating that Dorothea will be disinherited if she ever marries a young relative of Casaubon's, Will Ladislaw. Just as Dorothea's marriage has proved a disappointment, so has Lydgate's, whose wife, Rosamond, is extravagant and foolish. Dorothea finds Rosamond and Will Ladislaw together. This is a decisive moment for both women. Rosamond acts unselfishly for once, as she tells Dorothea that Dorothea herself is the woman Ladislaw loves, and, at the same point, Dorothea realises her love for Ladislaw. This paves the way for their marriage.

What can we deduce from this summary? *Middlemarch* is clearly a novel that concerns itself with the ordinary dilemmas of life: with marriages, mainly unhappy marriages, with people's working lives, and their relationships with their neighbours. When characters are at odds with society, it is not so much a consequence of obvious ills in the world but as a result of their own unrealistic expectations. If we extract a moral from the novel – and there was a time when critics were very interested in drawing attention to the sagacity of Eliot's moral views – it resides in the way that characters become less self-absorbed as the novel progresses; their egotism is curbed by a sense of social obligation. In this respect, if we interpret the novel this way, we can see again how Eliot acts as a kind of moral tutor to her audience, guiding them on the right kind of social morality. There is, much of the time, both confidence and reassurance in Eliot's narrative voice, as she explains the maturation of characters, and generalises on the significance of their actions. She has the kind of authority that we might associate with a teacher, a role that she assumes for herself partly because of her own loss of religious faith, and the need she felt to construct a secular social morality in its wake.

But there is, simultaneously, always a level of doubt in Eliot's work, something perhaps not unconnected with her own position in society; she lived with a married man, George Henry Lewes, behaviour which at this time, if it had been more widely known about by the general public, would have scandalised people. But what we also see, in broader and rather more significant terms, is a difference between

Elizabeth Gaskell's generation and Eliot's. Gaskell, as in *North and South* (1855), is, essentially, an optimistic novelist; she is convinced that employer and employee, north and south, and men and women can overcome their differences and work together. By 1870, despite the material advance of the country, realistic fiction generally is far more sombre and disillusioned; the idea of simple social remedies to problems is no longer an option. One, almost trivial, scene in *Middlemarch* features an auction. Scenes of auctions are fairly common in Victorian novels; what they signify, as the goods of a household are sold, is disintegration. A home, and perhaps a family, fall apart in a society where everything has become a commodity. *Middlemarch* is infused with an idea of the fragility of the lives that people have constructed for themselves; there is an edifice of middle-class respectability, but it is so often based upon trade that the threat of bankruptcy and ruin always stalks middle-class Victorians. There is, however, a more fundamental sense than this in the novel of the fragility of core institutions and values. Dorothea's marriage is unsuccessful, and probably unconsummated. We see her on her honeymoon in Rome, sitting alone and crying. One thing that Dorothea has had to face up to in Rome is a world that exists beyond her own circumscribed English middle-class limits. She begins to sense a sexual and emotional dimension to experience that, up until now, has played no part in her respectable experience, and which will have no presence in her marriage to Casaubon. In Casaubon, she has sought a kind of substitute father and the chance of intellectual fulfilment, but there is, or should be, more to life than this.

What we experience in *Middlemarch*, therefore, is a representation of the moral codes and values of polite middle-class English society, values that Eliot herself shares, and which permeate the entire texture of her narrative voice. Yet, at the same time, she is aware of the narrowness of this position, in particular the ways in which such a stance is incompatible with human needs, human desires and human weaknesses. Eliot is, however, not an overt critic, in the manner of Thomas Hardy. But in the margins of the text we sense the limitations, not only of the moral code that has been established but also of social institutions such as marriage. The effect, overall, is a novel that colludes with, and helps formulate, the dominant middle-class discourse of respectable mid-Victorian society, but which also sees the limitations of, and dissects, that discourse. Eliot is not alone in this. What we find in *Middlemarch* is echoed in other mid-Victorian novels. The realistic novel is the form in which middle-class readers see the world being made sense of in terms of their own convictions and values, but it is also the form that takes the most critical look at these convictions and values. This is particularly apparent in a variant of, almost a parody of, the realistic novel, namely sensation fiction.

Wilkie Collins and the Sensation Novel

Wilkie Collins's best-known works are *The Woman in White* (1860) and *The Moonstone* (1868). The first of these novels established a vogue for the sensation novel, a form of fiction that, like the realistic novel, focuses on ordinary middle-class life, but which includes extravagant and often horrible events. 'Sensation' has two applications: the events are sensational, but they also affect the senses of the reader, instilling a spine-tingling fear. And this effect on the body is relevant to the novels in an additional way, for they are works of fiction that often deal with the abduction or abuse of people's bodies. This made a particular impact in mid-Victorian Britain: in the kind of morally respectable atmosphere where people preferred not to talk too directly about various aspects of life, the body makes its presence felt in a rather alarming way.

The Woman in White is, for the most part, narrated by Walter Hartright, a young drawing-master. One evening in London, he encounters a woman dressed in white who is in deep distress. He later learns that she has escaped from an asylum. Hartright then takes up a position in a house in Cumberland, where he finds that Laura Fairlie bears an extraordinary resemblance to the woman in white, whose name is Anne Catherick. Hartright and Laura fall in love, but Laura has promised that she will marry Sir Percival Glyde. After their marriage, Glyde and Laura return to his family estate in Hampshire, accompanied by Glyde's friend Count Fosco. Glyde, desperate to get his hands on Laura's money, and Fosco then conspire to switch the identities of Laura and Anne Catherick; Anne dies of a heart attack and is buried as Laura, while Laura is drugged and placed in an asylum as Anne. With the help of her devoted half-sister, Marian Halcombe, she escapes, and they live quietly with Hartright, but they are determined to restore Laura's identity. Hartright discovers that Glyde has concealed his illegitimacy, but Glyde is killed in a fire. It is Fosco that Hartright then has to turn to in order to extract a written confession. Hartright and Laura are married, with Laura's identity restored.

As is often the case, a summary of a work of fiction, particularly of something like a work of sensation fiction, can make it appear nothing more than a highly contrived story, but it is clear that *The Woman in White* deals with a whole range of issues that were of central concern in mid-Victorian Britain. We can start with the manner of the narration. Walter Hartright constructs the story like a legal enquiry, with statements from a range of witnesses who have been involved in the events. This reflects an age when people increasingly relied upon the processes of law, and were ready to defer to the authority of facts and the cataloguing of facts. In a sense, the novel is attesting that it is a work of realism, in that the events presented are tangible, true and verifiable. And this concern with things tangible and trustworthy is also evident in the inherent assumptions in the novel. *The Woman in White* deals with families and marriage and work; in other words, the core institutions upon which the Victorians established their lives. Even on the first page, we hear about Walter's father who, through working hard and providing for the future, ensured the well-being of his family after his death. In brief, he played the kind of role a man was expected to play in this society. As such, he can, initially, be contrasted with his son, Walter, who has no energy, little sense of purpose or direction in life, and who, in his profession teaching drawing to young women, is an oddly feminised hero, a kind of male governess.

During the course of the novel, the nature of marriage, or at least of the marriages presented in this work, is dissected. The marriage between Glyde and Laura, like the marriage between Fosco and his wife, is a form of tyranny, in which the man exploits and abuses his wife. What also happens during the course of the novel is that characters are abducted and robbed of their identities. Essentially, and in a spectacular fashion, the novel questions and undermines the institutions and things of value that the mid-Victorians, in an increasingly secular age, relied upon: marriage, family and even a sense of one's own identity are shown to be fragile concepts. The arch-villain of the novel is the Italian Count, Fosco, who, as an outsider, mocks all the values that the English believe in; he is quite candid about his villainy, but there is a sense in which nobody believes him because he is questioning beliefs that people do not want to see questioned. The direction in which the novel thus leads is towards undermining the very foundations of middle-class life: everything is exposed as secrets and lies. People play roles that disguise their true, and more sinister, motives.

There is, overall, an effective tension between the methodical and orderly way in which, with his legal documents, Hartright constructs an orderly and methodical investigation, and the sordid truth that is actually revealed. In this the novel reflects the need felt by the Victorians to construct coherent narratives of explanation of their lives, but in the process of doing so undermines all those things, such as marriage, family and individual identity, that they place their trust in. It is perhaps relevant to note that *The Woman in White* appeared at almost exactly the same time as Darwin's *The Origin of Species*, another narrative that attempts, in a spirit of scientific enquiry, to look at the facts and arrive at an overall explanation, but which, in the process, and like *The Woman in White*, tells a story that is worrying and disconcerting in that it is a story of disruption, of violence and mere chance. There is, however, another level of complication in *The Woman in White*, a level of complication that is typically Victorian. Collins appears to be an author who questions everything. One of the cleverest touches is his conception of Marian Halcombe, a strong and capable woman who is frustrated at having to play a woman's role; at points like this, and the same thing is true in all his novels, Collins is even prepared to question the concept of gender roles as a stabilising factor in society. But, during the course of the novel, Hartright, who is initially a feminised hero, becomes more and more assertive and confident, eventually taking entire control of the situation. This is the kind of contradiction that it is not at all surprising to find in a Victorian novel: Collins is ready to question middle-class values, but, as a member of that society, he also embraces, and cannot avoid expressing his commitment to, such values. It is as if, when he frightens himself too much, Collins returns to the security of conventional beliefs.

The Moonstone is just as disconcerting as The Woman in White, and perhaps more so, as its range is so ambitious, including a questioning of the assumptions at the heart of British imperialism. The Moonstone starts with the storming of Seringapatam in 1799, an event that left the British as the masters of Southern India. It is the looting of the Sultan's palace that provides the foundation of Collins's novel. John Herncastle steals the Moonstone during the course of the siege, murdering at least one of the three Brahmins guarding the diamond. Back in England, the diamond is again stolen. It could be argued that the Indian episode is simply an enabling mechanism for the detective novel that follows, but the novel unavoidably raises larger questions. The British soldier behaves 'like a madman' as he steals the diamond; in a few words, Collins has reduced the imperial mission to frenzied plunder. The subsequent theft of the diamond in England is investigated, but the original crime, a crime fraught with symbolic and religious significance, is left uninvestigated. The novel, as it proceeds, pays a great deal of attention to the question of the ways in which the characters support or challenge the legal and domestic order of life in Britain. There are servants, such as Rosanna Spearman and Ezra Jennings, who, to judge by their appearance, would seem to be outside the social compact, but who demonstrate their loyalty. By contrast, some of the most respectable, and respectable-looking, characters are utter rogues.

As with The Woman in White, therefore, The Moonstone, albeit in the guise of an entertaining, almost trivial novel, questions some core assumptions of the mid-Victorian period. The British presence in India is seen as exploitative and rapacious rather than as beneficial. This is all the more evident because Britain, steeped as it is in criminality, does not in reality possess a set of values that can be set above the values of the east. Indeed, in order to get at the truth about the Moonstone, one of the characters, Franklin Blake, has to use opium; he has, that is, to rely upon the apparent irrationality of the east, together with a morally suspect product from the east, to sort out a mystery in the west. Overall, in The Moonstone, the focus becomes the extent of criminality and transgression in Britain, which is contrasted with the integrity of the Indians, as reflected in the conduct of the Brahmins.

Other sensation novelists are rather less ambitious than Collins, but the informing logic of their novels is always the same: they look at respectable society, viewing it with a set of respectable middle-class convictions that they share with their readers, respectable middle-class convictions that, to a large extent, have only evolved during the Victorian period. But they then expose these convictions as hypocritical, fragile and damaging. Some sensation novelists, however, are rather more conventional than others. Mrs Henry Wood's *East Lynne* (1861) is the story of Lady Isabel Vane who marries Archibald Carlyle but then deserts him to go abroad with Sir Francis Levison. After he abandons her, she is disfigured in a train crash. She returns to England, works, unrecognised, as a governess to her own children, and asks for her husband's forgiveness on her deathbed. This is a novel that plays with adultery, and plays with a questioning of marriage, but its core convictions are, it is clear, sentimentally moral.

By contrast, Mary Elizabeth Braddon's *Lady Audley's Secret* (1862) is a radical text. Robert Audley, investigating the disappearance of George Talboys, discovers that Lady Audley, the wife of his uncle, Sir Michael, is married to Talboys. She faked her death, and married Sir Michael bigamously. She tries to kill Robert, but he survives to hear her confession that she pushed Talboys down a well. Declared insane, she is committed to an asylum. For a long time regarded as nothing more than an entertainment, in recent years *Lady Audley's Secret* has commanded attention as a novel that looks sceptically and critically at the roles that are imposed upon women in Victorian society, and at the complicated truths that might lie behind a façade of marriage and respectability.

Anthony Trollope, Christina Rossetti

A rather similar tension is evident everywhere in mid-Victorian fiction. The novelists favour stories about middle-class life and ordinary domestic experience; the novels are then narrated in a tone of voice that clearly identifies with the ruling social and moral principles of such a society. The novelists, it is important to note, are simultaneously constructing and endorsing these values; the values might exist in society at large, but readers have to turn to fiction for written confirmation of the existence of these values. But in the very process of putting such a picture together, and in fictionalising it, the novelists escape the limitations of the core institutions and the limitations of the moral and social values of their era. To an extent, and perhaps not always consciously, they are able to stand outside those values and see their shortcomings.

Anthony Trollope, who, initially, is likely to strike the reader as the most resoundingly confident and reassuring of middle-class writers, provides a fascinating example of a novelist who is altogether less secure and complacent than he might initially appear. We can see this in *Phineas Finn* (1869), written around the time of the Second Reform Bill of 1867, which extended the right to vote to working-class men in towns. The novel tells the story of Phineas Finn's rise to parliamentary power through a series of romantic attachments. But his life as a rising star of British politics is short-lived. Dispirited after losing his government salary for voting in favour of the rights of Irish tenants, Phineas turns down the chance of power and money and returns to his native Ireland to marry his sweetheart and to work on behalf of the poor. This romantic narrative is the vehicle for an analysis of parliamentary society, an analysis that seems at first simply to celebrate the British political system; there is, Trollope seems to suggest, a kind of genius to this system, a reassuring quality in the fact that Britain possesses political institutions that are not only the envy of the world but provide a framework that is flexible enough to accommodate unexpected developments and changes in fortune.

But there is also a self-evident self-congratulatory smugness about this system, with its parties and procedures, its pettiness and atmosphere of a gentleman's club in which political opponents feel no rivalry outside the debating chamber. The thought that may occur to the reader is that the parliamentary system is perhaps just a futile game, a pretence that is irrelevant to the true material state of the nation and with few real connections to those it claims to represent. Quite plainly, it is a system that excludes and wastes the talent of women, who can only act in a private capacity, supporting, or frustrating, the ambitions of their husbands, who, in this novel, are, for the most part, career politicians. But the system is also limited and parochial in outlook. That parochial quality is underlined by the presence of Irish members, in particular Phineas Finn, who is able to see issues from a position outside the narrow confines of a system which cannot accept difference, a system which cannot really acknowledge that Ireland and the Irish might have interests that differ from the interests of the English. What is so good about the novel is that it examines the political foundations of British life in the nineteenth century and, in equal measure, sees both the strengths and weaknesses of the British way of doing things; its understanding and presentation of the nature of British political life is incisive and commanding in a way that remains relevant even today, but it also takes apart the system it celebrates.

Trollope is at his most gloomy and pessimistic in *The Way We Live Now* (1873–4). Augustus Melmotte is an apparently wealthy financier involved in a scheme to promote the Central American railway. All are eager to help him and he has no trouble being elected to Parliament. The railway deal is a confidence trick, however, and Melmotte is exposed. He commits suicide. Meanwhile his daughter is betrayed and duped by the dissipated aristocrats who pursue her for her wealth. Everything in the novel is a sham, a deception, and built on nothing, with widespread corruption and profligacy. Though the novel has a conventional happy ending, in the form of a marriage, there is a sense of living on borrowed time, and of everything being about to fall apart, as, arguably, it will do in the last twenty years of the century, as the narrative form developed by the mid-Victorians, their discourse of realism, starts to disintegrate. *The Way We Live Now*, with its satiric picture of a decadent society ruined by gambling and greed, seems to predict not simply the end of the Victorian era but the end of the Victorian narrative of middle-class progress and respectability.

In some periods of English literature we are acutely aware of voices from the margins – the excluded, the disaffected, those who are outside the mainstream – intervening and having something new to say in their own distinctive accents. Even an established poet such as John Keats occupies this kind of position; his is the voice of the intruder. What is perhaps most apparent in mid-Victorian literature is that the critical and dissenting voices do not come from outside the consensus. On the contrary, it is the mainstream authors, those who seem to speak most authoritatively in the established voice of literature, who are the critics. We could consider, for example, Margaret Oliphant, the author of many novels and also a prolific reviewer and contributor to periodicals. As her career continued she lapsed into producing increasingly undemanding accounts of domestic life, but at her best, in a novel such as *Miss Marjoribanks* (1866), there is an astute sharpness in her understanding of ordinary lives and social conventions. Her best works add to the impression that middle-class society and middle-class values are so well established at this time that, rather than being challenged from the outside, they challenge themselves. But there are other voices in mid-Victorian literature, voices that, perhaps not surprisingly, tend to make their presence felt more often in poetry than in prose. However, not always so. We could point, for example, to a vein of fantasy in Victorian writing; the way in which a work such as *Alice's Adventures in Wonderland* (1865), by Lewis Carroll, plays with an alternative logic, calling upon the world of dreams. It is, of course, a children's classic, but there is a great deal going on in Carroll's work in terms of how a different voice constructs a different narrative in the golden age of realistic fiction.

Christina Rossetti's narrative poem *Goblin Market* (1862) is another work that purports to be for children but which explores, in a surprising, even odd, way, enclosed forms of female subjectivity. Lizzie and Laura are two sisters. The goblins try to get the sisters to eat their mouth-watering fruit. Laura does so, paying for the fruit with a lock of hair, but then falls into a decline when she cannot get more. Lizzie tries to buy fruit, but the goblins are angry that she will not eat it and pelt her with it. Laura is, however, able to lick the juices off Lizzie and so is saved by her sister's actions. The poem is at once a kind of fairy tale and erotic fable in which female desire is mixed with sisterly self-sacrifice. What is most remarkable about the poem, however, is the nature and power of the longings expressed, and the extent to which Rossetti gives voice to aspects of sexual needs and feelings that were silenced, excluded or denied by the Victorians at large in their public discourses:

Hug me, kiss me, suck my juices
Squeezed from goblin fruits for you,
Goblin pulp and goblin dew.
Eat me, drink me, love me . . .

(ll. 468–71)

Like Lewis Carroll, Rossetti had to find a literary form outside the dominant mode of the realistic novel in order to articulate a different kind of understanding of what it might mean to be a human being, and a representation of the powerful sexual and emotional drives that surface even in the most simple circumstances.

Rossetti opens up the secrecy and silence that surrounded women's sexuality in the nineteenth century, as did Algernon Swinburne, in works such as *Poems and Ballads* (1866) and *Poems and Ballads: Second Series* (1878), and a number of other poets. As the century moves to its close, however, there will be far more marginal and disaffected voices, as Victorian confidence, and self-confidence, disintegrates, partly at least under the weight of its own success. As the empire expands, so Britain becomes exposed to more and more ideas that will question its ideological base. Paradoxically, Karl Marx, the critic of modern capitalism and industrialism, had fled to London in 1848, and was to die there in 1883. Britain in the nineteenth century had a tradition of admitting foreign political exiles and politically subversive figures; there was a kind of supreme confidence that the British way of doing things was so resilient that the presence of political agitators would affect and change nothing. But, viewed from another angle, what becomes apparent is that Marx's voice is, to a certain extent, consistent with those other voices, both mainstream and marginal, that drew attention to strains in the system. Such voices were to become a lot more direct and strident in the last twenty-five years of Victoria's reign.

12 Victorian Literature, 1876–1901

Thomas Hardy

Thomas Hardy was the most significant novelist in the last quarter of the nineteenth century. He achieved fame with *Far from the Madding Crowd* (1874), and went on to produce a series of novels, including *The Return of the Native* (1878), *The Mayor of Casterbridge* (1886), *The Woodlanders* (1887), *Tess of the D'Urbervilles* (1891) and *Jude the Obscure* (1895). Prompted in part by the hostile reaction to the last of these novels, Hardy then turned exclusively to poetry, which had always been his preferred medium.

Hardy's novels are set almost exclusively in a tract of Southwest England that he calls Wessex. The choice of location is significant. George Eliot clearly has a finer and fairer mind than most of her readers, but the overall impression in her novels is that she writes from the centre of a social and cultural consensus. Hardy, by contrast, making use of Wessex, writes from the margins; there is consistently a sense of standing outside and questioning established values. Other late Victorian authors adopt different approaches, but a similar effect is often achieved; there is a sense of disintegration, with a steady centre falling apart. By the end of the century there is, again and again, an impression of social institutions – such as the family and marriage – crumbling, and of authors adopting a sceptical attitude towards conventional morality.

In the case of Hardy, such scepticism is apparent as early as *Far from the Madding Crowd*, which tells the story of Gabriel Oak and the woman he loves, Bathsheba Everdene. Bathsheba, however, marries the dashing Sergeant Troy, who has abandoned Fanny Robin, the only woman he ever really loved; she dies, along with their new-born child, in the workhouse. Troy is not a man to be constrained by marriage; at odds with his wife, he disappears. He is assumed to have drowned. Bathsheba is now pursued by a gentleman farmer, William Boldwood. She promises Boldwood that, if in six years there is no indication of her husband being alive, she will marry him, but Troy reappears with the intention of reclaiming his wife. Boldwood murders his rival. As for Bathsheba, she finally marries Oak. The novel, therefore, ends conventionally, with marriage and social renewal, but Hardy's novels, including *Far from the Madding Crowd*, actually place far more emphasis on the failure of relationships, the breakdown of marriages, and even divorce.

The implication is that the conventions and institutions society has established in order to promote the well-being of that society are simply at odds with the reality of what people are like. It is an awareness that extends to the novel form itself: the novel as a genre relies upon a number of plot conventions, such as a movement towards marriage as a device for resolving and concluding the story, but Hardy, characteristically, is likely to indicate a gap between the neatness of a fictional convention and the untidiness of individual actions. For example, at one point in *Far from the Madding Crowd* Bathsheba, as she starts to face up to the failure of her marriage, flees from Troy and sleeps in the open air. The next morning, as she awakens, she sees a ploughboy on his way to work and a schoolboy on his way to school. There is a similar moment in George Eliot's *Middlemarch* as the heroine, Dorothea, after a sleepless night in which she examines her life, looks out of the window and sees people going about their daily business. It is a decisive moment in Dorothea's life: she realises that she must accept her part in the general scheme of things rather than focusing, selfishly, upon herself. The scene in *Far from the Madding Crowd* could almost be described as a parody of this moment. Bathsheba goes through the motions of the kind of character-changing experience that heroines have in novels, but does not change at all; she remains fickle, immature and self-absorbed. The basis of her attraction to Troy was emotional and sexual, and there is no indication that she is now going to start acting in a different, more rational way.

All of Hardy's major characters are romantic, impractical or simply disorganised in the management of their lives in the same kind of way as Bathsheba. A great many English novels focus on an individual coming into collision with society. In an Eliot novel, even though the narrative is complex and has contradictory strands, the hero or heroine tends to adjust his or her behaviour to achieve a working relationship with society. Even Wilkie Collins, author of *The Woman in White*, who adopts a more sceptical attitude than Eliot and most of his contemporaries, presents characters who by the end of the work have usually established a secure, even conventional, niche in middle-class society. The typical Hardy hero or heroine, by contrast, with actions dominated by the heart rather than the head, cannot establish a working compromise with society. It might be felt that this is merely an individual quirk on the part of Hardy, that he is a novelist drawn to romantic, emotionally driven characters. But more is involved than just the peculiar bias of Hardy's mind. Hardy's rejection of established patterns of social reconciliation in fiction is symptomatic of a wider collapse of a consensus, and even the collapse of a confidence in rational debate, that becomes apparent at the end of the nineteenth century. There is a widespread feeling that society cannot hold together; that larger, disruptive forces are at work that promote a fundamental instability.

Some of the ways in which Hardy establishes a different, late-century perspective involve nothing more than a minor adjustment of a literary convention; the consequences, however, can be substantial. For example, *Middlemarch* starts with the name of the main character, Miss Brooke. Hardy nearly always holds back the names of his characters; before being named, they are identified simply as men or women engaged in some form of activity. The effect is to suggest that there is something elemental about people that is more fundamental than their social identity; a basic quality exists before, and quite separately from, the rather limiting social identity that is imposed upon them. In a rather similar way, Hardy frequently quibbles over the naming of a place; often, as with Lower Longpuddle or Weatherbury, in *Far from the Madding Crowd*, he provides alternative place names. The effect is to distance himself from the conventional social order; society names people and places, but in doing so brings them under its command. In Hardy's novels, there is consistently a sense that something more is in evidence than just the imposed order of society. This stance necessarily has implications for the manner in which Hardy narrates his novels. In distancing himself from the conventional social order, he needs to stand outside the established discourse of that social order; that is to say, certain ways of seeing and judging are implicit in the omniscient manner of narration that we witness in many realistic novels, but Hardy, choosing to remove himself from a standard social outlook, must also detach himself from a conventional narrative voice. There is, consequently, always a sense in a Hardy novel that the narrator's voice is self-conscious, turning on itself, drawing attention to itself and frequently drawing attention to the fallibility or partiality of its judgements.

This combines with a story in which, most commonly, the characters are not rebels by choice, but simply because their natures lead them to be. Society, however, will not tolerate rebellion. As there is no possibility of social reconciliation – no possibility, that is, of these characters finding a quiet and complaisant role in the villages or towns where they live – Hardy's novels almost invariably end with the death of the major characters. Right through to the very end of the novels in which they feature, they are estranged from society and its dominant values. *Far from the Madding Crowd*, ending with a marriage, is the exception. But it is still a novel that breaks with tradition. The most obvious way in which it does this is in its emphasis on sexuality. The force of sexual desire is apparent everywhere in the novel, even, for example, in something as trifling as a description of the first day of June: 'Every green was young, every pore was open, and every stalk was swollen with racing currents of juice.' It would be fair to say that the most distinctive quality of *Far from the Madding Crowd*, and the thing that invests the novel with a joyous and exuberant energy, is the way in which it rediscovers, and takes a delight in presenting, aspects of sexual experience and feeling that the novel has, perhaps throughout the entire Victorian period up to this point, been denying, sublimating or repressing. Sex in earlier Victorian novels is often a dark and guilty secret; sex in *Far from the Madding Crowd* is dangerous but exciting.

The freshness of *Far from the Madding Crowd* is, however, a quality that Hardy cannot maintain. As his career as a novelist continues he focuses in a far more critical way on the discipline and conformity that society imposes upon people; there is always a price that must be paid if characters overstep the mark or choose to defy society's rules. *The Mayor of Casterbridge* is the story of Michael Henchard, a poor man who, having sold his wife at a country fair at the start of the novel, rises in the social hierarchy to become the mayor in his adopted community. There is, though, an extravagant and ferocious dimension to Henchard's personality, something that becomes apparent when he resumes drinking after abstaining for many years. This dangerous side to Henchard puts him in conflict with all those around him, including his daughter. And, as there is no way back for him into the social order of Casterbridge, he dies, at the end of the novel, an alienated and angry man. At one point, Hardy describes a petty incident of vandalism:

> The farmer's boy could sit under his barley-mow and pitch a stone into the office-window of the town-clerk; reapers at work nodded to acquaintances standing on the pavement-corner; the red-robed judge, when he condemned a sheep-stealer, pronounced sentence to the tune of Baa, that floated in at the window from the remainder of the flock, browsing hard by; and at executions the waiting crowd stood in a meadow immediately before the drop, out of which the cows had been temporarily driven to give the spectators room.

The passage conveys a sense of the compactness of the town of Casterbridge, and how the town and the surrounding countryside merge, but what is also conveyed is an altogether more disturbing idea: it is as if the vandal who throws the stone goes on to steal sheep, and is finally executed. Such indiscipline seems natural, but the other side of the coin is that society has instituted a system of law and order to regulate people, and this includes the ultimate sanction of taking the lives of those who step out of line.

In *Tess of the D'Urbervilles* and *Jude the Obscure* Hardy is far more indignant about the way in which social regulations and conventions ruin people's lives. *Tess of the D'Urbervilles* is the story of a country girl who is raped by Alec D'Urberville, and then abandoned by Angel Clare, the man she marries, when he discovers her sexual history. Eventually Tess murders Alec, and the novel ends with her execution. The aggressive nature of a male-dominated society, the harshness of the law, and a lack of tolerance and understanding are all apparent as significant strands in the novel; Tess is the victim, and it is the society that she lives in, together with the people, especially the men, in that society who accept its conventional attitudes and morality that destroy her life. As against the heavy hand of those who pursue, abuse and condemn her, there is a consistent emphasis on Tess as a free and natural spirit. But if Hardy presents Tess's sexuality as, essentially, innocent, he is also aware of a vicious side to human nature, something most apparent in the dark sexual instincts of Alec D'Urberville.

By the time he wrote *Jude the Obscure* Hardy's outlook was very pessimistic. In his other novels there is always an impression of the traditional order of farm life, but in *Jude the Obscure* the hero, Jude Fawley, begins his working life on a farm with a soul-destroying job as a human scarecrow. Jude wants to advance in life, but his ambition of attending university proves an impossible dream. He is trapped into marriage by a farm-girl, Arabella, but then falls in love with his cousin, Sue Bridehead, a married woman. She and Jude set up home together and have two children, but Jude's child by Arabella, Father Time, murders his half-brother and half-sister, and then kills himself. Sue returns to her former husband, and Jude lives alone. The most obvious aspect of *Jude the Obscure* is how the education system, class barriers, religious and moral conventions and the divorce laws all conspire against Jude.

The characters to a certain extent, however, also create their own misfortunes. At the centre of the novel are the nervous and highly strung Jude and Sue, characters who do not belong in any one place, and who, when they move, do not embark on a journey with any kind of clear goal. On the contrary, they move aimlessly from place to place. This is a plot device – also used in *Tess of the D'Urbervilles* – that works very effectively to convey a sense of alienated and dislocated people. It is an idea of character that Hardy uses to good effect in his poetry. Rather than focusing on a hero or heroine who can turn the course of events, Hardy, as in his novels, focuses upon powerless and defeated individuals in an enormous universe. In 'Drummer Hodge', for example, a poem written in response to the Boer War, there is an effect of bafflement, with a small character encountering a world that resists both control and comprehension. In many of Hardy's poems, there are similar feelings of loss, confusion, uncertainty and pain.

But a far more disturbing and extreme quality is in evidence in *Jude the Obscure*. When Father Time kills the other children and himself, a sense of something dark and irrational is exposed; it is as if, in the wake of the kind of compromise that used to exist, something malignantly destructive has appeared. This is more than an idiosyncratic perception on the part of Hardy. Generally in late nineteenth-century literature there is a feeling of having moved beyond an old liberal dispensation, and a fear of brutal, irrational forces that lie just below the surface becomes evident. Repeatedly, texts from this period offer an impression of probing into dark places, including the dark areas of the mind. In brief, the sustaining fictions of an earlier generation fail, and more troubling, disruptive ideas move in to take their place.

George Gissing, George Moore, Samuel Butler, Henry James, Robert Louis Stevenson

In 1877 Queen Victoria was declared Empress of India. It is a moment that might stand as the high point of British imperial self-confidence. But just two years later, in 1879, William Ewart Gladstone, the former prime minister, denounced the imperial policy of the Conservative government. In imperialism there is always a sense of power being abused, of the language of the conqueror silencing all other voices. At the same time, the rise of a politics of empire, race and nation in the late Victorian period can be seen as a sign of weakness: that in a changing world, there was a desire for simple answers and forceful action. By the last twenty years of the nineteenth century, Britain's economic lead over all other nations was beginning to fade. And not only was there increasing economic competition, there was also a growing sense of political, and even military, tension between European countries. In addition, at home there was a mounting awareness of social problems and class hostility. For much of the Victorian period people could focus rather narrowly on their own domestic concerns in a secure environment, but by the end of the century this was becoming more difficult. As old convictions collapsed, many united behind the idea of the nation, but jingoistic rallying cries could not conceal the evidence of a more divided and anxious country.

What we see in the literature of the last twenty years of the nineteenth century is a number of writers trying to engage with these changes, whereas others seem to opt for a variety of forms of escape. The more engaged literature of this period was influenced to a substantial extent by the works of the French novelist Emile Zola. Zola was a 'naturalist', a novelist who reported on life in an exhaustively researched manner, producing works that bear a degree of resemblance to a sociological report. One of his most celebrated novels in this mould is *Germinal*, set in the French coalfields. But any claim to scientific objectivity that we might be tempted to associate with 'naturalism' has no substance. Zola's works are informed by contemporary ideas about the influence of the environment and genetics; whereas most novels focus on the development and progress of an individual, Zola reports on an inevitable decline in people's lives. There is always a downward spiral of disease, alcoholism, poverty or madness. Zola's social thinking has an obsessive dimension, but the ideas in his novels overlap with widely held beliefs in the late nineteenth century, beliefs inspired to a large extent by the writings of Charles Darwin. Supporters of imperialism could claim that Britain's colonial successes confirmed the views of Darwin: that the stronger race would defeat the weaker, and that this was an inexorable law of nature. Such Social Darwinism, however, went hand in hand with fears about degeneration, with anxieties about the triumph of brute force. Consequently, by the late nineteenth century, an interest in evolution, progress and reform went hand in hand with pessimistic fears about regression, atavism and decline.

The novels of George Gissing provide evidence of late Victorian social pessimism (evidence that is also present in medical, sociological, historical and political texts from the period). In novels such as *Workers in the Dawn* (1880), *The Unclassed* (1884), *Demos* (1886), *Thyrza* (1887) and *The Nether World* (1889), Gissing considers London working-class life. Unlike Elizabeth Gaskell, who, when she deals with urban poverty, writes positively, with a conviction that class relations and individual lives can be improved, Gissing despairs, regarding many of the people he presents as little better than savages. In his best-known

novel, *New Grub Street* (1891), his negative social vision connects with a
sense of a culture that has been coarsened by commercialism; his hero
is Edwin Reardon, a delicate novelist who cannot survive in the kind
of vulgar environment where only the most crass or cynical taste success. The impression in Gissing's novels is of a society that has lost
direction because it has lost sight of traditional principles in politics,
religion and morality. His fears focus most clearly, however, on the
idea of the working-class mob. It is an anxiety that he shares with
many of his middle-class contemporaries, an anxiety that the forces of
darkness and irrationality are preparing to take over.

There are some writers of 'slum novels' in this period who offer a
more positive vision. Walter Besant's *All Sorts and Conditions of Men*
(1882), which deals with the setting up of a People's Palace in Stepney,
is the kind of novel in which middle-class characters commit themselves to good works in working-class areas, making a tangible
change in people's lives. In real life Besant actually opened an institution resembling the People's Palace, but the idea fails to carry conviction in a work of fiction. It would seem that the kind of socially
restorative story that Gaskell could construct without too much of a
sense of strain is no longer viable by the 1880s. An impression of an
out-of-date narrative stance is also, and perhaps rather surprisingly,
evident in George Moore's *Esther Waters* (1894). Moore, influenced by
the example of Zola, was intent on producing shockingly direct novels. In *Esther Waters*, the heroine is seduced by a fellow servant,
William Latch. She is dismissed by her employer, and the novel then
charts her life as a new mother. She is about to join a religious sect
when Latch reappears. They marry and set up a public house in Soho,
but his ventures into book-making lead to ruin. He dies, leaving
Esther destitute. *Esther Waters* is a tremendously assured novel that
caused a sensation on its first appearance because of the frankness of
its sexual content. Its originality, however, is rather superficial. The
novel is shocking rather than substantial, with a narrative stance that
is essentially liberal and traditional. Gissing's stance in relation to his
material is more awkward than Moore's, but the consequence is that
Gissing seems to be engaging with real problems, whereas Moore,
with his sentimental emphasis on the moral resistance of Esther,
imposes too coherent a pattern.

In a period when novels, as is the case with Hardy's and Gissing's, increasingly end with the defeat and even death of the main characters, we might wonder what had happened to novels in the *David Copperfield* tradition, about young people making their way in the world and establishing a position in middle-class society. Such novels flourish at the start of the twentieth century (the Edwardian realists Arnold Bennett and H.G. Wells tell a version of this story over and over again), but are uncommon in the 1880s and 1890s. There seems to have been a loss of faith in the goals traditionally pursued by the middle-class hero and heroine, an impression backed up by the evidence of Samuel Butler's *The Way of All Flesh* (published in 1903, but written between 1874 and 1884). This amounts to a denunciation of Victorian values; in particular, it offers a denunciation of Victorian family life. Ernest Pontifex is tyrannised by his father. He is bullied into ordination as clergyman, even though he has lost his faith. In London, he is cheated out of his inheritance, and then imprisoned for six months for sexual assault. He marries one of his family's former servants, but she turns out to be a drunkard. Ernest is relieved to discover that her marriage to him was bigamous, and that he can become a happy recluse, free from all family and marital commitments. What is most obvious in *The Way of All Flesh* is that everything we associate with a certain tradition in Victorian fiction is reversed: the family, marriage, a sound career and religious faith are all shown as having nothing to offer.

In a period when writers started to show unprecedented scepticism about the institution of marriage, it is not at all surprising to find authors focusing on women who have not married, sometimes by choice. The most notorious novel in the latter mould was Grant Allen's *The Woman Who Did* (1895), about Herminia Barton, who refuses to marry on ethical principles, preferring to live with a man. The most substantial novel about single women, however, is Gissing's *The Odd Women* (1893), which deals with the wretched lives of the three Madden sisters. The least fortunate is Monica, the only one of the three to marry; her husband is neurotically jealous, and she dies in childbirth. Her sisters, Alice and Virginia, dedicate their lives to caring for the child. Henry James, an American writer domiciled in Britain, is another novelist who frequently focuses upon the lives of unmarried heroines, sometimes venturing into the unhappiness of his heroines who do marry. In works such as *The Portrait of a Lady* (1881), *The Bostonians* (1886), *What Maisie Knew* (1897) and *The Awkward Age* (1899), together with *The Wings of the Dove* (1902) and *The Golden Bowl* (1904) at the start of the new century, he presents heroines caught up in a web of sexual corruption. They are disturbing novels, examining, in an extremely sensitive way, manipulative, bullying and power-obsessed forms of sexual desire. James's novels are unusual and distinctive, but what he has in common with other late nineteenth-century novelists is a sense of disturbing and irrational forces that lie just below the surface of family life.

As against novelists who engage directly with social and sexual tensions, there are other writers at this time who seem to choose the option of escape. In 1883, with the publication of Robert Louis Stevenson's *Treasure Island*, a vogue for romance develops: stories in which the hero retreats from Britain in order to embark upon a series of vivid, and often violent, adventures. Apart from Stevenson, the most successful of the new writers of romance was Rider Haggard, the author of *King Solomon's Mines* (1885), *She* (1887), and *Allan Quatermain* (1887). The impression that these novels offer of embracing an idea of escape is, however, rather misleading, for the story they tell over and over again involves the hero encountering dark and dangerous powers. In *Treasure Island*, for example, the hero, Jim Hawkins, is up against Long John Silver and his blood-thirsty fellow pirates. The 'enemy' in these novels always represents a threat to the well-being, and even the life, of the hero. This assumes its most astonishing form in *She*, where the hero, Leo Vincey, has to confront an African queen, Ayesha, who threatens both his masculinity and his English identity.

It seems reasonable to suggest that this kind of imperial romance finds an external substitute for the kind of internal threat that is present in the novels of a writer such as Gissing; there are other races encountered by the imperial adventurer that echo Gissing's sense of the working-class mob as an alien race. Indeed, wherever we turn in late nineteenth-century literature there is the idea of something dangerous and irrational that will destabilise society. In Hardy's novels there is, principally, an idea of a natural indiscipline in people, including sexual indiscipline, that is at odds with the requirements of social convention. For the most part, Hardy directs his anger at society and its rules, but in *Jude the Obscure*, specifically in the killings carried out by Father Time, there is a sense of something negative and destructive that has developed, or is developing, in the human temperament. In contrast to Hardy, a number of other novelists offer a more overtly political, and rather distasteful, picture of working-class people, other races in the colonies, and women as a threat to the established order of society. But, in addition, and establishing a psychological emphasis for the coming century, in some novels, the most obvious example of which is Stevenson's *Doctor Jekyll and Mr Hyde* (1886), there is an idea of irrational, concealed or repressed elements within the individual mind that are fundamentally at odds with a sense of humanity's rational identity.

Rudyard Kipling

In the last twenty years of the nineteenth century a great many established values and conventions seem to fall apart. Everywhere we turn there is a sense of disruptive forces that threaten the very idea of a regulated and ordered society. It is in this context that we need to consider the extraordinary literary debut of Rudyard Kipling. The achievement of Kipling in the 1890s, and perhaps the source of his popularity, is that he seems to transcend such uncertainty, presenting a coherent and positive vision. For a brief moment, and even though there were hostile critics, Kipling, in a series of short stories set for the most part in India, seemed to speak for the nation. This, however, was an illusion, for by the 1890s any sense of a coherent national culture was irretrievably splintered. But for a short period at the start of the decade Kipling appeared to offer a new consensus of shared values that could stand as a replacement for the old, now exhausted, liberal consensus.

At the heart of Kipling's early stories – the tales that first appeared in England towards the end of the 1880s – is his reinvention of an aristocratic military code for a democratic age. Essentially, he takes the aristocratic code, puts it in the mouths of working-class soldiers, and sells the illusion to a middle-class audience. There has never been a clearer case of the right author with the right material at the right time. The pattern can be seen in 'His Private Honour', from Kipling's fourth collection, *Many Inventions* (1893). Ortheris, an ordinary soldier, is unjustly struck on parade by a young officer, Ouless. Ortheris broods over his lost honour as a soldier. The problem is resolved when Ouless suggests that, out of the public eye, they settle the matter with a fist fight. The point of the story is that social differences disappear, or are of no consequence, when men agree to abide by the same set of rules. The implicit idea in all these early stories is essentially the same as in 'His Private Honour': there is a set of values that is relevant to all ranks. This code operates in the army but, by implication, can be regarded as a straightforward code that applies to all areas of civilian life.

Kipling's social thinking might strike us as simplistic, but his stories clearly struck a chord with the society of his day. There was a resurgent spirit of conservatism in late Victorian Britain, based largely upon a perceived sense of threat; this was both an external threat, from competing nations and colonial subjects, and an internal threat, from an expanding working class. Part of the achievement of Kipling's soldier stories was to calm such fears, particularly fears about disturbance from below. The shrewdest, and politically most significant, move Kipling makes is that he presents three potentially awkward characters in his stories – the three soldiers at the centre of the tales are an Irishman, a Cockney and a northerner – and then makes them the spokesmen for a shared set of national values. These values, rather than being imposed from above, seem to be a matter of enlightened self-interest. The impact of the stories was extremely powerful – Kipling proved to be a literary sensation in a way that had never been experienced before – and it seems reasonable to suggest that this was because the stories seemed to provide an alternative to a feeling of disillusion that was widespread by the 1890s. There were, from the beginning, dissenting voices – people who deplored Kipling's crassness and coarse tone – but the overwhelming impression at the start of the nineties was that Kipling was saying something that his first audience desperately wanted to hear.

The problem was that, although the early stories offered a seductively neat impression of coherence, this was nothing more than an illusion. The military values that Kipling endorsed in these very specialised stories about soldiers had little, if any, relevance to life as a whole at the end of the nineteenth century. We can appreciate this point if we consider the difficulty Kipling experienced in making the leap from writing short stories to writing a novel. His only genuine attempt at a mainstream novel for adults, *The Light that Failed* (1891), is disappointing. The small canvas of a short story permitted an extraordinary degree of authorial control; opposed positions could be expressed, but ultimately everything was part of a rigidly controlled pattern. In *The Light that Failed* Kipling cannot impose the same tight control. Consequently, the deep divisions within late nineteenth-century life disrupt his work; it is likely to strike the reader as untidy and confused.

What is also the case, however, is that even in his short stories Kipling found it increasingly hard to maintain the degree of control evident in his first publications. In the years leading up to the Boer War it became more and more difficult for him to produce a short story that really convinces. The Boer War helps explain the problem. This was a colonial conflict, lasting from 1899 to 1902, in which, for the first time since the Crimean War, the British were fighting people of European origin (Dutch settlers in South Africa), and, moreover, fighting an enemy that they found extremely difficult to defeat. The problem with Kipling's works as a whole is that, although for a brief moment he offered a vision in which the military virtues are equal to, and can overcome, all threats to good order, in the end a complex world consistently refused to arrange itself in accordance with his simplistic vision.

George Bernard Shaw, Oscar Wilde, Late Victorian Poetry

There are moments in literary history when the theatre renews itself; suddenly, as if from nowhere, a new kind of play appears on the stage. More often than not, these are times when an old set of values is falling apart. The theatre seems to present the best forum for the ensuing debate about the state of the nation. The late Victorian period is characterised by just this kind of revival of drama. The most notable figure is George Bernard Shaw. His early works included *Mrs*

Warren's Profession (1893), a play about a prostitute that was banned for many years, *Arms and the Man* (1894), *Candida* (1897), *The Devil's Disciple* (1897), *The Man of Destiny* (1897), *You Never Can Tell* (1899) and *Captain Brassbound's Conversion* (1900). Shaw's career as a playwright then continued well into the twentieth century. His approach to drama was heavily influenced by the Norwegian writer Henrik Ibsen. It might be more accurate, however, to say that his works were influenced by the image of Ibsen that Shaw chose to extract from the plays; this was Ibsen as social crusader and political analyst.

Shaw's plays, particularly at the start of his theatrical career, were exposés of social hypocrisy. But what must also be acknowledged in Shaw's works from the 1890s is a new kind of social analysis that reflects his commitment to socialism. This is an important aspect of the decade. There was a sense of old discourses losing their relevance; what we see in their place is a variety of new forms of social analysis. Those who were committed to the new assertive imperialism and nationalism of the late century play a part in this proliferation of fresh views, but there was also a resurgent socialism, a new feminist voice associated with the movement for votes for women, and, from those opposed to the Boer War, a fresh expression of liberal values. Consequently, although literature from the late nineteenth century conveys a feeling of a loss of direction and confusion, there was no shortage of voices ready to offer their vision of the path to the future.

Alongside Shaw, the other really notable playwright at the end of the nineteenth century was Oscar Wilde. His plays – such as *Lady Windermere's Fan* (1892), *A Woman of No Importance* (1893) and *The Importance of Being Earnest* (1895) – may appear far more traditional than Shaw's, but in fact they express a radical, and thoroughly disconcerting, vision of society. This is most sharply evident in *The Importance of Being Earnest*, a romantic comedy about polite society. Jack is in love with Gwendolen Fairfax, cousin of his friend Algy, who will only marry a man with the name 'Ernest'. Meanwhile Algy is pursuing Cecily Cardew, Jack's ward. In London Jack calls himself Ernest, the name of his supposed brother, while Algy has invented a sick friend, Bunbury, to visit as a cover for his absences. At the end of the play it turns out that Jack and Algy are in reality brothers and that Jack's real name is, after all, Ernest – he had been lost in a handbag as a baby at Victoria Station by the nurse Miss Prism. Happily, he can now marry Gwendolen since his financial future as well as his identity are both assured.

The plot of Wilde's play will probably strike most readers as both improbable and thin. How can Gwendolen possibly be in love with the name 'Ernest'? How do you misplace a baby in a handbag at a railway station? Isn't there something absurd about Jack calling himself 'Ernest' when that actually is his name? Such improbabilities are deliberate; they are intended to draw attention to themselves as improbable, as lacking in substance. In this they are at one with the dialogue of the play as it dances along on the surface of life, rendering all serious subjects trivial and all trivial subjects serious. Wilde has often been praised for his witty, epigrammatic style, his inversions, parodies and satire, but, unlike eighteenth-century satirists such as Swift and Pope, Wilde has no intention of reforming the world. Rather, what is important about his style is that it is just for the moment and has no purpose beyond itself. Such a style ties in with the play's central metaphor of pretence. Both Jack and Algy invent characters they can use, but everything in this society is fake in a rather similar way; it is only a pretence that names signify any kind of dense reality. What this all amounts to in *The Importance of Being Earnest* is a play that offers a comic view of life which can be described as 'absurd', in which everything is ridiculous and without substance or depth. The whole of life is merely an elaborate charade, in which language serves to cover the lack of anything solid beneath the surface. If the mid-Victorians had solid moral and social convictions, Wilde, as a late Victorian, seems to draw attention to the vacuous emptiness of everything; consequently, although *The Importance of Being Earnest* might appear to be nothing more than a witty and superficial comedy, it in fact offers us a disconcerting new vision of life. It would be possible to trace back a great many traits of twentieth-century literature to *The Importance of Being Earnest*, and to argue that it is the principal work of literature that introduces a certain way of seeing the world.

Wilde cannot be discussed simply as a dramatist; he demands to be considered in a broader context of late nineteenth-century aestheticism. A central principle of aestheticism – which can be traced to

Walter Pater's *Studies in the History of the Renaissance* (1873) – was that art had no reference to life, and therefore had nothing to do with morality. Relating this to the issues discussed in the earlier sections of this chapter, it might be said that aestheticism represents a refusal, or inability, to engage with reality, and a withdrawal into the safety of art. In Wilde's novel *The Picture of Dorian Gray* (1890), a portrait of Dorian Gray ages while the hero himself retains his youthful beauty. Aestheticism, which overlaps at the end of the century with the concept of decadence, became a delicate means of evading materialism, capitalism and the sheer complexity of the era. It prompted a form of poetry in which musical effects are perhaps more important than sense. Notable figures associated with aestheticism were Lionel Johnson, Ernest Dowson and Arthur Symons. Their verse, characteristically, displays an enervated feeling. The favoured time of day in such poetry is twilight; it can be associated with a mood in which the harsh light of day is avoided, yet at the same time there is no sense of probing into real darkness.

These writers remain attractive and interesting to read, but their cultivation of a mood and little else means that there is not really a great deal of substance in what they write. Some would express similar reservations about the works of Gerard Manley Hopkins, a Catholic priest who produced extraordinarily innovative poems about his relationship to God. The most ambitious of these poems is 'The Wreck of the *Deutschland*' (1876). In the years that followed, notable poems included 'God's Grandeur', 'The Windhover' and 'Pied Beauty', but none of his poetry was published until 1918, nearly thirty years after his death. Many regard Hopkins's works as tremendously important poems, anticipating the techniques of modernism, but others see them as a kind of escape from reality into the patterns and techniques of verse. But that, in a sense, is their strength. Hopkins, in particular in his so-called 'terrible sonnets', teeters on the edge of an abyss of despair; it is as if there is nothing left, the last trace of God having been replaced by mere poetics.

It is Wilde, however, a writer who combines many late-century strands of thinking and feeling in his works, who seems to embody in the most complex way a new mood at the end of the nineteenth century. He deliberately positions himself outside conventional manners and morality. The issue of sexuality is always a relevant matter in Wilde's writings (and life), for part of the overall effect is the extent to which he plays with the idea of stepping outside assigned gender roles. It is in the late nineteenth century that the presence of a homosexual subculture first becomes apparent. There is something highly significant about this, in that it reflects again the disintegration of a consensus; even sexual identity becomes something other than fixed, something that is open to question and choice. But what we might also note in Wilde's works, which again and again focus on characters playing a role in society, is the way in which they raise the question of whether there is anything behind the mask. It is an important issue, as questions are being asked about the very concept of identity. Our first impression of Wilde, both as a person and as a writer, may conform to the received image of the outrageous dandy, a man refusing to engage with life, but the contradictions within Wilde's works amount to possibly the most complete expression of a sense of a disintegration of values at the end of the nineteenth century. It is hard to pin Wilde down, but this in itself indicates how he is at a far remove from earlier certainties, just as many of his contemporaries seem at a remove from the more confident convictions of earlier generations of Victorians.

13 The Twentieth Century: The Early Years

Joseph Conrad

Queen Victoria died in 1901. The twenty years following her death saw Joseph Conrad establish his reputation as a novelist, and the climb to fame of popular novelists such as Arnold Bennett and H. G. Wells. D. H. Lawrence published his first novel, *The White Peacock*, in 1911, and went on to write, among other works, *Sons and Lovers* (1913), *The Rainbow* (1915) and *Women in Love* (1921). Henry James was still writing, his novels moving into a new and more complex phase at the start of the century, and E. M. Forster published four novels – *Where Angels Fear to Tread* (1905), *The Longest Journey* (1907), *A Room with a View* (1908) and *Howards End* (1910) – in the space of a few years, followed by a period of literary silence before *A Passage to India* (1924). George Bernard Shaw was at the height of his powers as a dramatist, with plays such as *Major Barbara* (1905), and T. S. Eliot, Ezra Pound and James Joyce all started to publish at this time. Perhaps most intriguingly, the Irish poet W. B. Yeats, who had made his name in the 1890s, developed a new mature voice around the time of the 1916 Easter Rising against British rule in Ireland.

Moving beyond a list of names, the event that defines the first two decades of the twentieth century was the First World War, from 1914 to 1918. Even long-established writers such as Rudyard Kipling and Thomas Hardy were prompted to write startlingly original works that reveal just how profoundly they were affected by the war. More broadly, it is no exaggeration to suggest that the First World War changed fundamentally the way in which people thought and wrote. There is, however, another factor that we have to be alert to in literature. It has often been noted that when a major historical event takes place (for example, the English Civil War in the seventeenth century), literary texts in the decades preceding the event seem to be anticipating it; they are, albeit unknowingly, examining the social and political tensions that are leading to the imminent upheaval. This is certainly true of the relationship between the novels and short stories of Joseph Conrad and the First World War: his works consistently offer a pessimistic vision of the frailty of the civilised order. Indeed, as we read Conrad we are likely to form the impression that this is the first major English-language writer of the twentieth century. In the works of novelists before Conrad there is always a sense that a community used to exist, and that people used to belong to a place and to a family, but in Conrad there is a new, and far more extreme, sense of dislocated individuals in an unrelentingly cruel world.

In *Lord Jim*, Conrad's first major novel, published in 1900, Jim is chief mate on a steamship, the *Patna*, taking a group of pilgrims to Mecca. When the ship appears to be at risk, the members of the crew lower a lifeboat to save their own lives, leaving the pilgrims to drown; Jim watches, and then finally jumps overboard to join the others in the lifeboat. The *Patna* does not sink, and the circumstances of the crew abandoning the ship become public knowledge. A Court of Inquiry is held in Aden. Jim loses his Master's Certificate and afterwards is haunted by his behaviour. Eventually he settles in the trading port of Patusan, where his peaceful life is destroyed by the arrival of thieves led by Gentleman Brown. Jim hopes that Brown can be persuaded to leave without violence, but the son of the local chief is killed. Jim, assuming responsibility for the tragedy, lets himself be shot by the chief. The world presented in this novel, as in many of Conrad's novels and stories, which often have a maritime dimension, is a world of grubby trade, of ships picking up whatever work they can wherever they can, without too many questions being asked. Transporting the group of pilgrims on the *Patna* is a very dubious commercial venture; it is a form of trafficking in bodies, with the packing of too many people on an unsafe ship.

There is a disparity in *Lord Jim* between the Court of Inquiry, where a standard of conduct is codified in a set of regulations, and the reality of the commercial enterprise Jim is involved in, which is not informed by any ethical considerations. When Jim fails to rise to the challenge he has been set on the ship, jumping instead to save his own life, perhaps the real surprise is that a concept of correct conduct still survives at all; it seems an anachronism in the commercial climate of late nineteenth-century colonialism. A number of factors can be identified that help shape Conrad's negative vision. In the background there is the influence of Darwinian thinking, with ideas of a world characterised by ruthless competition and survival of the fittest. But such ideas only have any relevance because they so clearly match the reality of an increasingly competitive, land-grabbing and inhumane late-century colonialism. If this is how Conrad perceives and presents the trading world of his time, the only thing that can be set against such barbarism from the representatives of the West is a concept of civilised behaviour; this might offer some hope, however slight, of redeeming qualities in the agents of colonialism. In this context, the obvious point to make about Jim's dereliction of duty is that, however he might behave subsequently, when he was tested he failed to act properly. He does so, moreover, in a novel that, as it approaches its conclusion, sets Jim against 'Gentleman Brown', a latter-day pirate with nothing but contempt for morals, human life and other such niceties. In the modern world, it seems, a character such as Jim cannot compete with the villain; the villain is bound to win.

Conrad's novel has the effect of drawing attention to a rather sentimental streak that runs through many nineteenth-century novels; whatever their subject matter, time and time again they place their confidence in the figure of the individual who is likely to act in a way that, at least to some extent, mitigates or deflects attention from the worst failings of society. In Conrad's novel, however, we seem to have moved on to a world where the individual can no longer make a difference, where there is no room for such concepts as gentlemanly behaviour. There is a cruel, unrelenting logic to life, and individuals are just pulled down by this general momentum. The heroes in Conrad's novels, as is the case with Jim, might have a place of origin and a family, but there is never any sense of their roots or connections offering them any strength or help. It is relevant to note at this point that Conrad was a Polish sailor who, after his life at sea, settled in England as a writer. There is something significant about a modern writer being an outsider in this kind of way; there is, in early twentieth-century literature, an absence of any sense of being able to gather strength from belonging, from being a part of something. As is the case with Conrad, who wrote in a language other than his native tongue, even words seem untrustworthy.

A general air of scepticism, including scepticism about language, writing and literature, becomes even clearer in Conrad's novella *Heart of Darkness* (1902). Marlow, who is also the narrator of *Lord Jim*, on this occasion relates the story of his journey up the River Congo on a steamboat owned by a Belgian trading company; this firm is known for its ruthlessness in the acquisition of ivory. He begins to hear stories about Kurtz, the company's most successful agent, yet at the same time a man with a reputation as an idealist. After a number of delays, Marlow reaches the Inner Station, where he is confronted by heads on sticks surrounding Kurtz's hut. It becomes clear that Kurtz, rather than standing as an apostle of western civilisation, has taken part in barbaric acts, including human sacrifice and, quite possibly, cannibalism. As Kurtz dies, his final words are 'The horror! The horror!', but on his return to Europe Marlow tells Kurtz's fiancee that he died with her name on his lips. The story ends, therefore, with a sentimental lie; it is as if, in the interest of keeping alive the old reassuring fictions, Marlow chooses to keep quiet about the excesses he has witnessed.

The main way in which a harsh sense of the reality of a world dominated by colonialism is brought to life in *Heart of Darkness* is through references to bodies, in particular the abuse and destruction of people's bodies. There are many grotesque episodes and passages of description in the work, but these find their most extreme expression in the suggestion that Kurtz has engaged in cannibalism, the ultimate transgression. Cannibalism as a topic appears in other novels. It is, for example, of central importance in the first major English novel, Defoe's *Robinson Crusoe*. But traditionally such depravity is associated with non-European people, such as natives, or with dissident characters, such as pirates. Indeed, the mark of Crusoe as a civilised man is that he is appalled and outraged by the existence of cannibalism. *Heart of Darkness* inverts this scale of values. In this work it is the representative of the West who is the murderer and the cannibal. Possibly for the first time in English literature, the representation of white civilisation is associated with the kind of behaviour that the

western imagination generally associates only with uncivilised people and the uncivilised world. Kurtz's conduct suggests that there
might be something rotten at the very heart of civilisation; indeed, it
is possible that the very idea of civilised people and a civilised society
might be nothing more than an anachronistic myth.

The vision conveyed in *Heart of Darkness* anticipates the kind of general collapse that is associated with the First World War. It is as if
everything that the West has spent centuries building up is blown
apart; the war is, of course, associated with physical destruction, but
what also disappears is a traditional structure of values, understanding
and reassurance. Values associated with the individual, including an
idea of the positive contribution an individual can make to society, are
undermined. The things that people cling on to in life – such as their
identity, their sense of belonging to a community, and their sense of
shared human values – are mocked, or shown to be nothing more
than illusions. Life has a cruel and destructive logic of its own, and
individuals are simply sucked into the meaningless, but vicious, cycle
of existence. This undercutting of old values is not only apparent in
the content of *Heart of Darkness* but also in the manner in which the
story is told. *Heart of Darkness* is narrated by Marlow, a created character; this indicates a distancing of the narration from the kind of omniscience we encounter in, say, a George Eliot novel. There is no longer
the possibility of omniscience, because omniscience suggests shared
values and a steady, reliable perspective. All that is now possible is the
partial or fallible interpretation of one observer. And, beyond this,
there is always a rather mannered or stylised quality to everything
Marlow says. We cannot simply look through what he says to see the
world he is reporting on. We are brought to a halt by the prose itself;
we cannot help but notice the role that language plays in structuring
a vision of the world. In a way, Marlow's narration reveals a very
assured literary style, but when we become too aware of a literary style
we also become aware of how language falsifies reality.

This seems to be a deliberate tactic in Conrad's prose. Writing
imposes a grammar, a syntax and, as such, an order on life, but
Conrad's self-conscious prose deconstructs the very idea of coherence that the writing, at one level, is aiming to achieve. The implications of this are substantial. In *Heart of Darkness* there are the events

and the story that is imposed upon the events, but the manner of the narration consistently suggests that there is not really a meaning to be teased out of the tale. This is a view that will become almost a commonplace in the early twentieth century: writers will find ways of writing about a world which, they are prepared to accept, does not make sense. They do it most commonly, as in *Heart of Darkness*, by narrating a story, but at the same time drawing attention to the fact that a story is being imposed. Such texts, and *Heart of Darkness* is one of the first to do this, question our desire for coherence and meaning. It is an approach that seems particularly relevant at the time of the First World War, when events were taking place that were, essentially, too extreme to be accommodated in any narrative. The overall effect in *Heart of Darkness* is that, rather than offering a revelation, the text seems more of a comment on our need for revelation. The narrator embarks upon a journey; as with the traditional heroes of romance, he is on a quest for the truth. But *Heart of Darkness* becomes a form of ironic romance, mocking our yearning for truth.

The Secret Agent (1907) explores similar ideas. Verloc, married to Winnie, works as a double agent, for the Russians and for Inspector Heat at Scotland Yard. He also has connections with a group of anarchists. Verloc obtains explosives, with which he plans to blow up Greenwich Observatory. His wife's brother, a simple-minded lad called Stevie, is killed in the bungled terrorist operation. When Verloc tells Winnie about his role in Stevie's death she stabs him with a kitchen knife. Winnie then plans to leave the country with an anarchist, Ossipon, but he deserts her, and she jumps overboard from a Channel ferry. It is a story of waste, violence and death. Apart from the care that Winnie has lavished on her brother, there is nothing positive in the novel. Human agency is ineffective; people's actions are selfish and destructive; political acts, such as the bombing of Greenwich Observatory, are pointless and mindless. There are, in short, no ideals to pursue.

The consistently negative emphasis of Conrad's novels and tales is, curiously, only reversed in the first work that he completed after the outbreak of the First World War. *The Shadow-Line* (1919) is the story of a sea captain, a challenge, and his success in meeting that challenge. A ship is becalmed on tropical seas. Some of the crew are dying, but the captain, with initial support from his men, copes with the crisis. In a straightforward way, a man's readiness to be tested and a traditional standard of conduct are positioned at the centre of the novel. And very directly at the centre; this is an unusual Conrad novel in that the method of narration is unambiguous, with none of the ironic distancing or undercutting that he generally favours. Essentially, it is a story that has a singleness of purpose dictated by the circumstances of its production. Conrad's works seem to anticipate the general collapse of the First World War, but the actual outbreak of war seemed to demand a straightforward response stressing the interdependence of men, as if to counterbalance the shock of the cataclysmic events.

Arnold Bennett, H. G. Wells, E. M. Forster, Katherine Mansfield

No other novelist writing in the first twenty years of the twentieth century paints such a bleak picture as Conrad. Indeed, we are more likely to be struck by the apparently rather traditional quality of the works of some of the leading novelists of the time. If the realistic novel falls apart at the end of the nineteenth century, at the start of the twentieth it appears to acquire new energy. Two popular realistic novelists in particular demand attention: Arnold Bennett and H. G. Wells. Bennett produced ten substantial novels: *A Man from the North* (1898), *Anna of the Five Towns* (1902), *The Old Wives' Tale* (1908), the Clayhanger trilogy (1910–16), *The Pretty Lady* (1917), *Riceyman Steps* (1923), *Lord Raingo* (1926) and *Imperial Palace* (1930). Wells wrote more than a hundred books and pamphlets in his fifty-year career, including over forty novels. He is best known for his early science-fiction works, *The Time Machine* (1895), *The Invisible Man* (1897) and *The War of the Worlds* (1898), and for novels such as *Kipps* (1905), *Tono-Bungay* (1908), *Ann Veronica* (1909) and *The History of Mr Polly* (1910).

A typical novel by either of these writers is a story about a young man or young woman making his or her way in life. With a novel such as *Anna of the Five Towns*, the title alone tells us a great deal. We can anticipate that it is about a young woman growing up in a particular society; we know in advance that she will find herself at odds with the values and established way of life of this society. And the title also probably suggests that Bennett's style will be straightforward, a kind of clear window on the world. A novel such as *Anna of the Five Towns* is important in that it engages with social, moral and cultural change; in particular, at the start of the twentieth century a novel like this is likely to offer an insight into a changing sexual morality, with an emphasis on a new assertiveness on the part of young women characters. At the time of their publication, therefore, such novels appeared very modern, but in retrospect *Anna of the Five Towns* appears curiously old-fashioned. If we compare Bennett with Conrad, it is Conrad who seems to be probing deeper in analysing the society of his day.

Yet, even if the novels of Bennett and Wells strike us as old-fashioned, there is something intriguing about the renaissance of this kind of novel at the start of the twentieth century. Hardy, as we have seen, dwells on death and despair, but here are novels about people starting out in life. There is every possibility that Bennett and Wells had actually found a new direction for fiction. If we consider *The Old Wives' Tale*, this is the story of two sisters, Constance and Sophia, one of whom follows the traditional path of marriage and motherhood while the other leads an adventurous and unconventional life. It looks like a traditional realistic novel, but it can also be seen as a subversion of realism. As the world changes, the characters lose a sense of who they are and where they belong. At the same time, characters repeat the pattern of the lives of previous generations; as such, there is nothing unique about their lives or identities. This might seem a fairly minor tinkering with realism, but Bennett's innovations work well to convey a sense of living in a world where all familiar reference points have disappeared.

Wells was a slapdash writer compared to Bennett, more concerned with conveying his ideas than anything else. But *Tono-Bungay*, his best novel by a considerable margin, is as effective as Bennett's novels in creating an impression of living in uncertain times. It features George Ponderevo, who becomes a salesman for a quack medicine, and who is later involved in aviation, and then in the search for 'quap', a radioactive material that might revive his family's fortunes. Invention is an issue in the novel, but it is essentially a story about decay: the collapse of the house of Ponderevo foreshadows the forth-coming collapse of Europe. Wells presents a vulgar, commercial soci-ety, bent on its own destruction. In a sense Wells's work complements the novels and tales of Conrad, but whereas Conrad adopts an indirect method, calling upon symbols and metaphors to convey his sense of impending darkness, Wells is direct and trans-parent in his writing.

The novels of E. M. Forster provide a rather similar impression of an old order that is exhausted and has outlived its usefulness. *Howards End* (1910) focuses on the relationship between the Schlegel family, who live on unearned income, and the Wilcoxes, a family in business. The Schlegels are liberal and cultivated, but despise the Wilcoxes, even though they depend upon the Wilcoxes for their income. The Wilcoxes are a snobbish, rather unpleasant middle-class family. An additional complication involves Helen Schlegel who becomes preg-nant by a poor bank clerk, Leonard Bast. Bast then dies after being beaten by one of the Wilcox sons. This undercurrent of violence is possibly the most alarming element in Forster's novel. It is a work that offers a delicate sense of fluctuating class and social relationships in England before the First World War, but there is also a sense throughout of a violent explosion that might entirely destroy this old order.

The explosion came with the First World War. *A Passage to India*, which was published in 1924, is far more ambitious than Forster's pre-war novels, even though it had been planned ten years before and reflects the India of that period. The earlier novels are almost parochial, dealing with the legacy of Victorian middle-class liberalism; they gen-erally involve characters who unthinkingly conform to established social standards and conventions. This is also true of *A Passage to India*, which focuses on British officials and their wives in Chandrapore, and their encounters with the local Indian intelligentsia. As in some of the earlier novels, Forster contrasts British culture and a foreign tradition that has qualities that are missing in the British way of life, but the scale of the contrast is much more extreme here. There is a deeper sense of the emptiness of the British tradition, which is adequate for routine matters and day-to-day business and administration, but which, in the wake of the war, is exposed as lacking any real core of purpose or conviction. As is the case in T. S. Eliot's *The Waste Land* (1922), Forster's thoughts turn to religion, in particular seeing something in Hinduism that is lacking in the West. The quality that is apparent in these and other post-war works is a sense of a void waiting to be filled, a direction that is being sought. Forster's pre-war works seem to be awaiting the apocalypse; after the war there is a sense of political, cultural and spiritual emptiness.

   D. H. Lawrence, as we will see in the next section, is the author who proves most active in trying to fill that void, in trying to find a new direction. Beforehand, however, it is interesting to see how the concerns discussed here overlap with the position of women before and after the war. The first twenty years of the century might have been a time of crisis for the West, but they were also years in which opportunities for women increased dramatically, though not without bitter struggles. A case in point is Katherine Mansfield. Born in New Zealand, she moved to England and, later, France to pursue a literary career. Locked into a disastrous marriage, like George Eliot she broke with social convention by living with a man. She is best known for her collections of short stories which are characterised by their multiple points of view, and by their attention to detail and atmosphere. The titles of collections such as *In a German Pension* (1911) and *Je Ne Parle Pas Français* (1918) suggest the way in which Europe assumes increasing importance in almost every aspect of life in the early decades of the twentieth century; a wider world has displaced the old sense of domestic security and the insular convictions of English life.

   There is, consequently, something profoundly symbolic about a story such as 'The Daughters of the Late Colonel' (1922), where two daughters watch their father die. On the surface, it seems slight enough, the story of a man dying, but the details imply much more:

> He lay there, purple, a dark, angry purple in the face, and never even looked at them when they came in. Then, as they were standing there, wondering what to do, he had suddenly opened one eye. Oh, what a difference it would have made, what a difference to their memory of him, how much easier to tell people about it, if he had only opened both! But no – one eye only. It glared at them a moment, and then . . . went out.

A representative of the old order is dying. The comic tone here cannot disguise the bullying contempt of the father for his daughters, nor the sense in the story as a whole of their wasted lives under his regime. But, at the same time, with his death there is just the slightest possibility of a different kind of future not governed by patriarchy and military bravura. It is as if the death of the colonel signals the death of a whole way of life which, looked back upon, now seems absurd in all its gestures and pomposity.

D. H. Lawrence

D. H. Lawrence was born in 1885 at Eastwood, a small village in Nottinghamshire. His father was a miner. Lawrence was, therefore, doubly removed from the cultural and middle-class dominance of London, and has come to be seen as the voice of working-class fiction standing outside the confines of polite society. His life itself was fraught with battles against the authorities in one form or another, especially the censors who objected to the frankness of his writings about sex, specifically in *Lady Chatterley's Lover* (1928). After ill health forced him to give up teaching, Lawrence eloped to Italy with Frieda Weekley, the wife of a university professor. The couple went on to live in Australia and New Mexico and finally Vence, in the south of France, where he died in 1930. There is something characteristically modern about the lack of rootedness in this life-style, just as there is about every aspect of Lawrence's career. Lawrence hated the First World War, but also the social conditions of England which he regarded as responsible for destroying spontaneous feelings. His reputation rests not just on the achievement of the major novels (*The White Peacock*, 1911; *Sons and Lovers*, 1913; *The Rainbow*, 1915; *Women in Love*, 1921), but also on his short stories, poetry, plays and essays. His output was both distinctive and disconcerting to a society incapable of or unused to confronting the issue of human sexuality. If Conrad offers a sense of the bleakness of the opening years of the twentieth century, Lawrence anticipates, and in part creates, the sexual revolution that was such a feature of the twentieth century as a whole.

It is all but impossible to keep details of Lawrence's life separate from his writings. This is especially the case with *Sons and Lovers*, an autobiographical novel based on Lawrence's early years. It tells the story of Paul Morel's development as a young man and his ambitions to become an artist, ambitions nurtured by his mother but also frustrated by her jealous possessiveness. Her marriage to Walter Morel is deeply unhappy, while her relationship with Paul is intense and passionate to the point that both his father, and Miriam, his girlfriend, are finally excluded from Paul's life. He finds some fulfilment, or perhaps just release, in his intensely physical affair with a married woman, Clara Dawes, but it is only with the death of Mrs Morel that Paul gains release from his mother's grip on his emotional life. He is left at the end, however, with very little to hold on to. Whereas in a traditional novel the hero or heroine usually comes to terms with society by the close of the narrative, *Sons and Lovers* breaks with this pattern: Paul turns his back on his community at the end, striking out on his own.

There are other ways, too, in which Lawrence's novel breaks with the conventional patterns of fiction. Initially the novel might look like a traditional realistic novel, relating a familiar story about a young man making his way in life. But the style of the novel is very different. Much of its power comes from its use of heightened, sensuous language that attempts to convey inner emotional feelings; time and time again, it is as if the feelings a character experiences are reflected in a physical response, the body experiencing sensations that mirror a state of mind. But also present in the novel is a constant undercurrent of violence and destruction: relationships no longer hold together, families are fragmented, and the social world of the novel seems unable to accommodate or sustain individuals. Lawrence explores the possibility of his hero entering into new relationships, in which he is no longer hampered by the burden of the past, but complementing this exploration of private life is a more general sense of social unease; there is an impression of the potential for violence in life that seems to foreshadow and anticipate the destruction that was to come in 1914.

The Rainbow, which came out in 1915, is another Lawrence novel informed by a sense of conflict. It can be argued that it is a work of fiction that exists between two formal conventions. On the one hand, it is an extraordinarily vivid social history, a realistic novel that tells the story of the lives of a small number of people in a specific community. These people are the Brangwen family. They are farmers, and the novel tells their story across three generations, extending from Tom Brangwen who marries an aristocratic Polish exile Lydia Lensky, his nephew Will who marries Lydia's daughter Anna, and their daughter Ursula, a teacher who is involved with another figure with a Polish background, Skrebensky. He wishes to marry Ursula, but, in a way that could be considered characteristic of a new, or at least more widely shared, feeling in the early twentieth century, she is reluctant to sacrifice her freedom and her career for the dubious benefits of marriage. This dynastic genealogy provides the novel with its linear framework, tracing the changes in a family and looking at how individuals come to terms with or rebel against the social and religious codes that govern their lives. In essence, the struggle is between conformity and freedom, which includes a form of sexual freedom; it is a contest between deadening obedience and trusting one's emotional instincts.

But, in addition to being this kind of realistic novel, *The Rainbow*, calling upon the narrative conventions traditionally associated with the romance, is also a novel that starts to move on and forward, looking for something new, something to fill the void of modern life. The choice of the metaphoric title – the promise of something new after the destruction of the flood – indicates this, as does the emphasis on a new kind of woman in the figure of Ursula, a woman seeking independence and a life outside marriage. Other novelists in this period seem to focus on waste, ruin and despair, but Lawrence starts to construct a quest for a different way of living as well as a different way of writing. The challenge is to move beyond realism while not losing the particularity of lived experience, as Lawrence searches for a new way in which human beings can relate to one another.

This becomes more obvious in *Women in Love*. Once again there is a solid realistic picture in the novel, with the main narrative focusing on the relationship of Ursula (the same Ursula as in *The Rainbow*) and Rupert Birkin, a school inspector, and her sister Gudrun's affair with Gerald Crich, a wealthy mine-owner, which ends with his death in the Austrian Alps. As in earlier novels, there is an emphasis on the violence that destroys human relationships – Gerald accidentally kills his brother when he is a boy, and his sister Diana drowns – but in the case of Gerald it is connected with a particular social class and ideology. The ruthless management that Gerald exercises at the mine also informs his personal life; the result is that his relationship with Gudrun is characterised by a growing destructiveness and sense of emptiness. Birkin recognises this, and offers Gerald an intimate male friendship based on love; it is not quite homosexuality, more a set of feelings intended to complement their relationship with the sisters.

What Birkin seems to embody in the novel is an attempt to construct something new in terms of personal relationships, something that has both a political and a spiritual dimension to it. *Women in Love* is, in this sense, manifestly about how to live in the modern world and survive its mechanistic philosophy, about the place of reason, and about the importance of spontaneous feelings and instincts. But it is also about modern people. The characters move in the intellectual circles of their day, and the conversations are as much about art and culture as about relationships. It is as if Lawrence is trying to resolve the schism he sees between nature and culture, desiring to make whole again what has been rent asunder by war and violence. In a number of respects, Lawrence might, therefore, be regarded as a visionary writer, working in a Protestant tradition that runs back through Blake and Milton, writers who also looked for a fundamental restructuring of society and human values. Such writers, it must be said, can irritate, annoy and even infuriate some, perhaps a great many, of their readers.

In the case of Lawrence, a lot of people consider his works offensive; not, as was the response at the time of their publication, because of their sexual explicitness, but because of Lawrence's sexual politics. His novels do tend to focus on male self-realisation; time and time again this is achieved at the expense of women. Particularly in *Women in Love*, it might be felt that the women are only present in order to help Lawrence work out Birkin's intellectual and philosophical position. What we also have to consider, however, is that Lawrence's emphasis on sex, on personal fulfilment and on self-discovery is not simply a case of the author voicing his personal obsessions. Such concerns are, in fact, a large strand in Western thought and politics in the twentieth century: that what matters above all else is the individual and his or her sensibility. In connection with this, it is important to note that we do not turn to Lawrence for a message. As readers of his novels, we do not have to share or even sympathise with his convictions. What we are interested in with Lawrence, as with any writer, is how he expresses the mood and the anxieties of his time. Lawrence anticipates the destruction wrought by the war, and then tries to fill the void.

Georgian Poetry, War Poetry, W. B. Yeats

The term 'Georgian poetry' is used in relation to five anthologies of poetry, edited by Edward Marsh, published between 1912 and 1922, during the reign of George V. The poets represented included A. E. Housman, W. H. Davies, Walter de la Mare, John Masefield, Ralph Hodgson, Edward Thomas, James Stephens, Robert Graves, Edmund Blunden and D. H. Lawrence. The signal sent out by the anthologies was that the new century created the possibility of a new energy in and a new direction for English poetry. The aesthetic verse of the 1890s (the poetry of writers such as Lionel Johnson, Arthur Symons and Ernest Dowson) can, quite reasonably, be regarded as the exhausted last gesture of Romantic poetry. In the Georgian volumes there is a more direct and colloquial approach, with more of an attempt to engage with real issues and real life. But it is sometimes the case that the originality of certain works of literature fails to command attention because other writers come along and do more interesting things. This is the case with Georgian poetry; the works of W. B. Yeats, Ezra Pound and T. S. Eliot are innovatory and substantial to a degree that makes the Georgians look almost inconsequential. This is to be regretted; there is a great deal of interesting verse in these anthologies, but for the most part it remains unread, while still being used as a yardstick against which other new writing at the time is measured.

There is, for example, a clear contrast between Edward Thomas's 'Adlestrop' and the war poetry of Wilfred Owen or Siegfried Sassoon (writers conventionally grouped together, along with a number of others, such as Charles Sorley and Isaac Rosenberg, as the 'war poets'). Adlestrop is a small village in Gloucestershire. The poem recalls how Thomas's train stopped there briefly one afternoon:

> What I saw
> Was Adlestrop – only the name
> And willows, willow-herb, and grass,
> And meadowsweet, and haycocks dry
> (ll. 7–10)

This is, essentially, rural poetry, celebrating a certain vision of rural England as an unspoilt paradise. The moment is all the more significant given the date of the poem; it was written in 1915. In such a poem the war is at a distance; its threat, by implication, is to nature and the landscape of England, but there is also a chilling emptiness in the poem: there is no one on the platform, and no one comes to the train. Behind the poem, then, lies a sense of impending death, but this in the end serves only to intensify the stress on the value of the rural idyll of England.

If Thomas celebrates the beauty and richness of England, Sassoon sets out to shock, satirising the authorities responsible for the war. In a poem such as 'They' the soldiers reply to a bishop's platitudes about death by relaying the grim details of how 'George lost both his legs; and Bill's stone blind'. Earlier in the century Conrad had written of the horrors of cannibalism and human sacrifice, but it is the war poets who offer us the sharpest sense of the barbarism that overtook civilisation and destroyed forever the old order and its supporting myths. Each poem is itself a kind of explosion; the recurrent imagery is of landscape sunk in mud and a world torn apart by shells as the war destroys the young men of Europe. This is the recurrent theme and nightmare of Wilfred Owen's poetry, of the mass, senseless slaughter of young men, as in 'Anthem for Doomed Youth':

> What passing-bells for these who die as cattle?
> – Only the monstrous anger of the guns.
> Only the stuttering rifles' rapid rattle
> Can patter out their hasty orisons.
> (ll. 1–4)

Elsewhere Owen writes of the futility of men's lives as they returned emasculated and disabled from the front. It is a gloomy picture, unrelieved even by the flashes of tenderness shared between the men in the trenches. And yet, for all its honesty in responding to the war and its terrifying consequences, there is, strangely, a looking back in Owen's poetry, a kind of yearning for the past. In the lines above, the frame of reference for the poem is provided by religious ceremony and the associated rituals, as if that might somehow restore a dimension of decency to the deaths on the field of battle. If there is a criticism that can be levelled against the works of the war poets, it is this looking back, as if the only way to make sense of the war was to cling to outmoded forms of thinking even while recognising, as in Sassoon's poem, that these ways of thinking did not match the world of the Somme, the river in northern France where, in 1916, unimaginable numbers of soldiers perished.

A different perspective is afforded by the poetry of Ivor Gurney. Wounded in 1917, Gurney was sent back to the front in the same year and was in the battle at Passchendaele. Like the Somme, this was another major battle with terrifying numbers killed. In 'The Silent One' Gurney writes of the death of a soldier from Buckinghamshire on the barbed wire of the trenches. The poem features a dialogue between Gurney and his commander who asks him in a 'finicking accent'

> 'Do you think you might crawl through there: there's a hole.'
> Darkness, shot at: I smiled, as politely replied –
> 'I'm afraid not, Sir.'
>
> (ll. 10–12)

The poem dramatises what both Sassoon and Owen point to, that the war is not, as Thomas would have it, remote from England but informed by its social hierarchy and class values. The politeness and 'finicking accent' may seem out of place, but what Gurney implies is that at the heart of the war is the deceit of language itself, which betrays men, leading them into death and violence. More particularly, it is the language of the old patrician code which now seems to find a new home on the battlefield of modern warfare. There is a social and political dimension to such language: Gurney shows it to be a factor contributing to the slaughter of war even as it pretends to offer and represent a civilised code of behaviour. This is an important aspect of the works of the war poets: they discover how barbarity has its roots in the very words that we use to shape and order our world.

It might seem natural to associate war poetry with the men who fought, but those who remained at home were also, of course, deeply affected by the First World War. In recent years there has been renewed interest in the war poetry and prose of a number of women writers, in particular Alice Meynell. Born in 1847, and publishing her first volume of poems in 1875, she was, in addition to being the mother of eight children, engaged in a wide variety of social issues and humanitarian projects, including the woman's suffrage campaign. Describing herself as a Christian Socialist and a feminist, what is fascinating about Meynell's First World War poems is the manner in which she combines a personal and lyrical approach, that often focuses upon the theme of religious mystery, with the enormous and public subject of war. This can be seen in 'A Father of Women':

> Like to him now are they,
> The million living fathers of the War –
> Mourning the crippled world, the bitter day –
> Whose striplings are no more.
>
> The crippled world! Come then,
> Fathers of women with your honour in trust,
> Approve, accept, know them daughters of men,
> Now that your sons are dust.

(ll. 21–8)

Meynell's war poems make a powerful impact on their own, but become even more interesting when we consider how she adds to the range of voices and responses we can detect in Britain in the war years. In particular, there is an awareness of gender issues that is seldom addressed directly in the work of male writers.

We will, of course, never know in what direction poets such as Edward Thomas and Wilfred Owen might have developed if they had survived the war. In the case of W. B. Yeats, by contrast, we have a writer with a career that extends from the 1880s to the outbreak of the Second World War. Born in Dublin, Yeats spent his early years between London and Sligo, his mother's home county in north-west Ireland. He studied art for a while, but by the 1890s he was deeply involved both with editing and writing poetry and also with the founding of the Irish National Theatre at the Abbey Theatre in Dublin. Yeats was manager of the theatre, but also wrote plays for it, the most successful being *Cathleen Ni Houlihan* (1902). Throughout his career Yeats continued to write plays which, like his poems, drew upon myths, folklore, the occult and contemporary Irish politics. The most significant period for his poetry begins in 1919 with the publication of *The Wild Swans at Coole*, and then *Michael Robartes and the Dancer* (1921), *The Tower* (1928) and *The Winding Stair* (1933), poetry characterised by its symbolism and by its sparse yet rich style. Yeats is central to the revival of Irish literature, beginning with his early poetry in *The Wanderings of Oisin and Other Poems* (1889), followed by collections such as *The Countess Kathleen and Other Legends and Lyrics* (1892), *The Land of Heart's Desire* (1894) and *The Wind Among the Reeds* (1899), as well as prose works, studies of Irish culture and essays. The result is an enormous body of work, and a body of work that changes as the world changes.

Yeats's earliest verse, as in *The Wanderings of Oisin* (1889), could be said to represent a mixture of Romanticism, nationalist idealism, Irish mythology and mysticism. A good impression of Yeats in the early stage of his career as a poet is provided by 'The Lake Isle of Innisfree', where he writes about how he longs to escape from the city to Innisfree.

> I will arise and go now, and go to Innisfree,
> And a small cabin build there, of clay and wattles made:
> Nine bean-rows will I have there, a hive for the honey-bee,
> And live alone in the bee-loud glade.
>
> (ll. 1–4)

There is an implicit contrast here between the complications of the everyday world and the simplicity of Innisfree, where everything seems idyllic and harmonious. This is apparent in the lazy, reverie-like quality of the poem, as if the abrasiveness of life has been left far behind. It is an effective and attractive poem, but, as most readers will sense, this is really a poem of escape, a poem expressing a desire to avoid engagement.

By the second decade of the twentieth century, however, Yeats's desire for escape might have seemed almost offensive. A parliamentary bill for Home Rule in Ireland had received Royal Assent, but, owing to the outbreak of the First World War, the Act was not implemented. Consequently, at Easter 1916 there was a rising in Dublin. In 1918 the independence of Ireland was affirmed, but fighting between the forces of the British Crown and supporters of Sinn Féin continued until 1921. In that year the Irish Free State came into being. It is clear that Yeats's poems acquired a new strength of expression as they engaged with these political changes. In 'Easter 1916', for example, he writes of the people he has met in the streets of Dublin; they are people he once scorned, but their deaths in the Easter rising have made them into heroes and martyrs.

Yeats describes one of the rebels:

> A drunken, vainglorious lout.
> He had done most bitter wrong
> To some who are near my heart,
> Yet I number him in the song . . .
>
> (ll. 32–5)

Yeats is confused: this man who seemed so awful has become a hero. He writes of what has happened to the man:

> He, too, has been changed in his turn,
> Transformed utterly:
> A terrible beauty is born.
>
> (ll. 38–40)

The rebels, including this lout, disrupt both the calm of Ireland and the civilised calm of Yeats's mind, but there is something inspiring about their actions that makes them fit subjects for celebration in verse; what they embody is heroism and the promise of a new dawn for Ireland, even if this new order overturns the kind of aloof civilised order that Yeats has clung on to.

The movement in Yeats's approach from the dying years of the nineteenth century to the period of the First World War may be said to represent a more general movement discernible in literature at the time: the nature and scale of the political upheaval forces writers to become engaged, and such engagement demands formal innovation, in that it is necessary to find new rhythms in writing to capture and convey a new, more urgent rhythm in life. Yeats's poems in response to Ireland's political changes do not in any way amount to a political manifesto; on the contrary, what they convey is the contradictory and confused feelings of a writer living through such times. But what perhaps finally distinguishes our sense of Yeats as a poet, enabling us to talk about a level of poetic development beyond his poems from the immediate period around 1916, is the manner in which a changing social and political climate demands a reconsideration of how poetry engages with life. This is, again, a development that we find in other writers besides Yeats. Essentially, in the post-war period we can refer to Yeats as a modernist writer. What this means is that basic ideas about life and art have been so disrupted by the events of the period between 1914 and 1918 that the writer has to reconsider in a fundamental way the relationship between the civilised activity of writing and what might now appear to be an uncivilised world.

This kind of complete reconsideration of the relationship between the activity of writing and life itself is apparent in a poem such as 'Sailing to Byzantium'. It is a poem in which Yeats seems to turn his back on Ireland; he wants to escape from a world where people grow old and die, and so imagines himself as the court poet in Byzantium, who will

> sing
> To lords and ladies of Byzantium
> Of what is past, or passing, or to come.
> (ll. 30–2)

The idea might seem elevated, but in reality he is nothing more than the court gossip. We might contrast this with the poem's opening evocation of Ireland:

> The salmon-falls, the mackerel-crowded seas,
> Fish, flesh, or fowl, commend all summer long
> Whatever is begotten, born and dies.
> (ll. 4–6)

What is apparent is a teeming sense of life in this opening stanza, conveyed in its rich and abundant imagery. But there is also a tension in the poem between the complexity and variety of life and the coherence and order of art, a tension that is a recurrent issue in modernist writing. In a very self-conscious way, such writing looks again and again at the possibility of creating or finding order in a disorderly new century.

14 The Twentieth Century: Between the Wars

T. S. Eliot

These are the opening lines of T. S. Eliot's *The Waste Land* :

> April is the cruellest month, breeding
> Lilacs out of the dead land, mixing
> Memory and desire, stirring
> Dull roots with spring rain.
> Winter kept us warm, covering
> Earth in forgetful snow, feeding
> A little life with dried tubers.
> Summer surprised us, coming over the Starnbergersee
> With a shower of rain; we stopped in the colonnade,
> And went on in the sunlight, into the Hofgarten,
> And drank coffee, and talked for an hour.
> Bin gar keine Russin, stamm' aus Litauen, echt deutsch.
> And when we were children, staying at the arch-duke's,
> My cousin's, he took me out on a sled,
> And I was frightened. He said, Marie,
> Marie, hold on tight. And down we went.
> In the mountains, there you feel free.
> I read, much of the night, and go south in the winter.
>
> (ll. 1–18)

Eliot was an American poet, playwright and critic, who lived in England from 1915. His first volume of poems, *Prufrock and Other Observations* (1917), was followed by *Poems* (1919) and *The Waste Land* (1922). *Poems 1909–25* (1925) and *Collected Poems* (1936) reveal a developing religious tendency in his verse, an impression that is consolidated in *Four Quartets* (1943). His plays include *Murder in the Cathedral* (1935) and *The Cocktail Party* (1950). His most notable critical work is probably *The Sacred Wood* (1920), which sets out his views on the poetic tradition. Eliot became a British subject in 1927, and was awarded the Nobel Prize for Literature in 1948.

Of all his works, it is *The Waste Land*, with its innovatory technique, that continues to command the most attention. It was published in 1922, the same year as James Joyce's *Ulysses*, and which can be viewed as the key year in modernist writing. It is easy to deduce that *The Waste Land* expresses a mood of disillusionment that was prevalent after the First World War, but much of the poem remains baffling to readers encountering it for the first time. It is a long poem, divided into six sections, each of which has a somewhat cryptic title, such as 'The Burial of the Dead' and 'A Game of Chess'. Long poems are often narrative poems, where the reader can follow the story, but *The Waste Land* clearly does not operate in this manner, consisting instead of a disjointed sequence of verse paragraphs. The content of any one of these paragraphs, such as the opening lines above, is likely to prove confusing, principally because of the absence of a single thread of meaning; individual lines often appear to head off in unexpected and unanticipated directions.

If we look a little more closely, however, a number of things start to fall into place. For example, we might detect an overall movement of a kind of journey through a dry, or waste, land in search of water, which could be seen as a sign of both physical and spiritual nourishment. *The Waste Land* is a poem that breaks new ground in a dramatic manner, but even in the most innovatory works we are always going to encounter patterns that have existed in literature for thousands of years. *The Waste Land* can, quite reasonably, be described as a quest, and in this respect it bears a striking resemblance to many early twentieth-century texts, starting with Joseph Conrad's *Heart of Darkness*. The idea of being on a journey or quest is never all that apparent in nineteenth-century realistic fiction, even though such a pattern does underlie a great many works, including, for example, George Eliot's *Middlemarch*. Thomas Hardy makes more of the journey, although in *Tess of the d'Urbervilles* and *Jude the Obscure* his characters tend to go round in circles getting nowhere. In the early twentieth century, however, the idea of the quest becomes more and more apparent in literature; as in the works of D. H. Lawrence, there is a sense of searching for a new order that might exist beyond the present state of confusion. In T. S. Eliot's poetry, and increasingly so as the years passed, there is a sense of searching for some kind of spiritual consolation, some enduring set of values beyond the post-war sense of a void.

This, however, is to anticipate a great deal. *The Waste Land* starts with a reference to April as the cruellest month. Conventionally we think of April as the season of spring and renewal, but Eliot refers to it in a very different light. It is a cruel month; there is even something chilling in the signs of growth that are in evidence, with lilacs blooming out of 'the dead land'. Essentially, *The Waste Land* sets up an idea of a life-giving, beneficial renewal in the natural order and pits this against a vision of a world that has become hard and unyielding. A theme has been established for the poem as a whole: Eliot is confronting a dispiriting world, but it is likely that he will be seeking some sign of hope or promise in this waste land. The disconcerting shifts from image to image in the opening sequence of the poem help to convey the appropriate impression of a disordered world. The sense that comes across is of a rootless existence, of a wandering life on the continent. The line in a foreign language ('Bin gar keine Russin, stamm' aus Litauen, echt deutsch') adds to this impression. It is not even necessary to understand the line to feel its effect; it adds to the sense of a world where nothing seems to make sense any more. If we do translate it, however, the line ('I am not Russian at all; I come from Lithuania; I am pure German') provides an insight into an aspect of Eliot that has troubled many readers over the years. The line deals with racial purity; throughout *The Waste Land* there is a sense that degeneration is linked to race, the poem using descriptions of racial characteristics to create a sense of seediness and corruption. Some critics deny there is a problem, but many accept that Eliot is a great poet with unpleasant political views. As always, the issue needs to be set in context. It does not excuse Eliot if we say that others held similar views at this time, but it does add to the challenge of his work that he reflects fears and anxieties of his time, incorporating widely held views not only about how but also about why his society is in decay.

Eliot's politics, as is the case with the politics of most of the major modernist writers, are an awkward and complex matter, which we have only a small amount of space to touch on here. Suffice it to say that, surprisingly often, modernist writers turn towards right-wing ideas in their search for stability and order, largely in response to their fear that various forms of decadence were undermining the whole of civilisation. This becomes evident in the way Eliot's fragmented poem creates an image of a world out of joint. *The Waste Land* is a fragmentary poem in three ways: each verse paragraph seems to bear only a loose relationship to the previous verse paragraph; line by line, there are disconcerting shifts from image to image; and the individual images are disconcerting. Consider the start of the second verse paragraph:

> What are the roots that clutch, what branches grow
> Out of this stony rubbish? Son of man,
> You cannot say, or guess, for you know only
> A heap of broken images, where the sun beats,
> And the dead tree gives no shelter, the cricket no relief.
>
> (ll. 19–23)

Images of disorder are prominent: this is a world of stony rubbish, where nothing grows. We are confronted with a world of 'broken images', a world where everything has collapsed into pieces. But by incorporating images such as 'roots' and 'branches' Eliot also points to what is missing, which is signs of growth. Some of the images, however, seem to imply more. 'Son of man', which alludes to the biblical figure of Ezekiel, might also suggest 'Son of God'. If this is the case, then it starts to become evident how Eliot just hints at the need for, or his desire for, the concept of a religious dimension to experience.

What is far more apparent, however, is the sense of a painful and bewildering world. We witness it, for example, in a sudden, seemingly inexplicable shift to the character of Madame Sosostris:

> Madame Sosostris, famous clairvoyante,
> Had a bad cold, nevertheless
> Is known to be the wisest woman in Europe,
> With a wicked pack of cards. Here, said she,
> Is your card, the drowned Phoenician Sailor.
>
> (ll. 43–7)

The particular images in evidence here also add to an impression that is sustained throughout the poem, which is of the cheap and sordid nature of modern life. It is a society in which people turn to fortune-tellers rather than trusting in any traditional sense of God. At the same time, the introduction of the Tarot cards reasserts what is perhaps the central theme of the poem, which is the search for meaning in the present waste land, in the post-war void.

What we also need to consider, however, is the way in which a great many lines in the poem contain literary allusions; that is to say, Eliot has incorporated phrases and words from other texts into this poem. For example, the opening reference in the poem to April is an inversion of the opening line of Chaucer's *Canterbury Tales*. These fragments from other works underline how the post-war world has collapsed into fragments, but they also suggest that writers in the past had a sense of wholeness. The effect is not uncommon in modernism; the author draws attention to how authors in the past have been able to perceive a pattern in life. Essentially, the modernist writer takes a step back, examining how literary texts relate to the world they reflect. This leads to a certain kind of self-consciousness about language and, indeed, every aspect of writing, which is again a feature of modernist texts. *The Waste Land*, disrupting the continuity and logic that we normally expect to encounter in a literary text, forcibly draws our attention to the manner in which traditional texts conspire to make life coherent and meaningful. In a sense, every modernist writer distrusts the implications of writing.

As a whole, *The Waste Land* is a poem that conveys a dark mood at the end of the First World War, but tantalises us with a variety of images of hope:

> In this decayed hole among the mountains
> In the faint moonlight, the grass is singing
> Over the tumbled graves, about the chapel
> There is the empty chapel, only the wind's home,
> It has no windows, and the door swings,
> Dry bones can harm no one.
> Only a cock stood on the rooftree
> Co co rico co co rico
> In a flash of lightning. Then a damp gust
> Bringing rain
>
> (ll. 385–94)

These lines appear towards the end of the poem. We feel consider-able relief as rain comes. But *The Waste Land* remains a poem where hope is hinted at rather than stated. Here, for example, there is an image of a chapel, which carries obvious implications, but the point is not developed. As readers, we are searching for things to hold on to amidst the ruins, and in this respect we shadow the process of the poem itself, which also appears to look for things that work in a bro-ken world. But the poem does not deliver any kind of answer; instead, in its self-conscious way, it seems, like many modernist texts, to be as much concerned with examining literature's quest for truth as with the truth itself.

James Joyce

The term modernism is used widely in relation to the creative arts in the first half of the twentieth century. For example, cubism in the visu-al arts is one branch of modernism. Cubism, founded by Pablo Picasso, involves dissecting the form of an object and separating the pieces so that it is reduced to flat, slightly angled planes. This parallels the man-ner in which modernist literary texts not only establish a break with established ways of looking but also draw attention to the way in which a work of art views, presents and interprets what it sees. What the comparison with cubism also draws attention to is that modernism was an international movement in the arts, and one particularly asso-ciated with capital cities; time and time again, the classic texts of mod-ernism are about huge, anonymous and dispiriting modern cities.

James Joyce's stories and novels, however, are set in a small capital city, Dublin, where people still know each other. Joyce published a collection of short stories, *Dubliners*, in 1914, and this was followed by *A Portrait of the Artist as a Young Man* (1916), serialised by Ezra Pound in the *Egoist* in 1914 and 1915. It was also in 1914 that Joyce began *Ulysses*, which appeared serially in a New York magazine, *The Little Review*, from 1918 to 1920, when it was banned after a prosecution instigated by the Society for the Suppression of Vice. It was published as a book in Paris and London in 1922, but the book was banned in Britain and America. *Ulysses* is an account of the thoughts and experiences of Leopold Bloom, a Jewish advertisement canvasser, and Stephen

Dedalus, a school teacher, who is also the central character in *A Portrait of the Artist as a Young Man*. It is set during a single day in Dublin. Bloom's day is structured to parallel the wanderings of Odysseus in Homer's epic poem. *Ulysses* was followed by Joyce's final work, *Finnegans Wake*, in 1939.

The first thing that can be said about *A Portrait of the Artist as a Young Man* is that it is in some ways the same novel as D. H. Lawrence's *Sons and Lovers*: an artistic young man who is trapped by his family, and particularly at odds with his father, tries to break free by establishing relationships with women. Both young men, as they grow up, are opinionated and annoy other people. And at the end, both young men escape, Stephen leaving Ireland, and Paul Morel turning his back on his birthplace and walking towards the city. But if the two novels have a great deal in common, they also have a great deal that sets them apart. Most obviously, there is the extraordinary manner in which *A Portrait of the Artist* is written. The truth is that the style of *Sons and Lovers* is just as original and innovatory as that of Joyce's novel, but *A Portrait of the Artist* is wilfully odd.

From the outset, Joyce finds ways of distancing his novel from the structures of perception that characterise nineteenth-century fiction:

> Once upon a time and a very good time it was there was a moocow coming down along the road and this moocow that was coming down along the road met a nicens little boy named baby tuckoo. . . .
>
> His father told him that story: his father looked at him through a glass: he had a hairy face.
>
> [. . .]
>
> > O, the wild rose blossoms
> > On the little green place.
>
> He sang that song. That was his song.
>
> > O, the green wothe botheth.
>
> When you wet the bed first it is warm then it gets cold. His mother put on the oilsheet. That had the queer smell.
>
> His mother had a nicer smell than his father. She played on the piano the sailor's hornpipe for him to dance.

We can see that this is about a child's earliest memories. Initially he encounters a 'moocow', and then his father and mother are introduced.

The novel is conveying the way in which the child begins to understand who he is and how he relates to other people. A growing awareness of how the world is structured is also apparent in Joyce's use, or lack of use, of punctuation. The first paragraph is unpunctuated, but Joyce then introduces punctuation, which steadily becomes more complex. It is as if at the beginning there are just individual words, like 'moocow', and then strings of words, but as we acquire language we learn how language is organised, especially in its written form, to structure experience. As the opening continues, the child encounters additional ordering frames that we call upon in life, including politics and religion. By the end of the first page, even though the opening impression is baffling, it is clear that Joyce is examining the family, political and religious structures that Stephen has been born into; in addition, the self-conscious use of language forces us to consider the ways in which language and the patterns of fiction help shape the world.

The point about the patterns of fiction is evident in the way that the opening sequence sets up a pattern for the novel. Stephen is caught in a situation that he does not like, challenges those in authority, feels elated, but is then punished for his presumption. This pattern is repeated in the five chapters of the novel. There is also a repeated pattern in small incidents. At one stage, Stephen is sitting in a maths lesson at school. The class has been split into two teams: York and Lancaster. Stephen does not enjoy the competitive atmosphere, but what is worse is that the history of another country, England, is being imposed upon these Irish schoolboys. He drifts off into a reverie, a daydream in which he imagines a magical land where a green rose might exist. But his reverie is interrupted, and he finds himself back in the sordid real world. Stephen again and again drifts off in this kind of way; repeatedly, it is as if he leaves the real world for the world of art. But if he is ever to succeed as an artist he will have to engage with the real world, rather than conceiving of art as an escape from reality.

There is a similar pattern in Stephen's encounter with a prostitute at the end of the second chapter:

> She passed her tinkling hand through his hair, calling him a little rascal.
> – Give me a kiss, she said.

> His lips would not bend to kiss her. He wanted to be held firmly in her arms, to be caressed slowly, slowly, slowly. In her arms he felt that he had suddenly become strong and fearless and sure of himself. But his lips would not bend to kiss her.

At one level, Stephen has escaped from the morally oppressive religious climate of Dublin, finding liberation. But the encounter is also humorous; it is as if Stephen can romanticise the encounter, with ecstatic prose, but cannot engage himself physically. Rather than overcoming any sense of sexual anxiety, he has simply sought the security of a romantic discourse, reflected in his romantic thoughts. Time and time again, Stephen, for all his air of being a rebel, seeks the security of the old structures. This is evident again in the way that, just after his meeting with the prostitute, he accepts the security of religious faith, albeit for a short period.

At this stage of the novel, as at every stage, the book laughs at the way in which Stephen takes himself seriously. What this amounts to is the presence of irony, which could be said to be one of the most distinctive features of modernist texts. In this instance, Stephen's story is told, and to a degree taken at its face value, but Joyce also mocks his character, and mocks the way in which novels pay serious attention to such characters. The result is double-edged: we are offered a story about a young man's development that we can become genuinely involved in, but there is also a level of detachment that laughs at the kind of comfort the reader derives from a familiar narrative structure. It is, indeed, the failure of the old sustaining structures – religion, family, nationality – that seems to be the most prominent issue in A Portrait of the Artist, and this links with the self-conscious manner of the narration, that takes a step back from the conventional, and familiar, structures of fiction.

Ulysses, like A Portrait of the Artist, also takes a step back at every stage, examining not just life but also the role of writing and language in how we perceive and structure experience. There is a possibility, however, that we could read, follow and enjoy A Portrait of the Artist without even registering the ways in which it is a modernist text; that might involve ignoring many aspects of the novel, but it would be possible to read it as a reasonably traditional education novel about the development and progress of a young man. It is not, however, possible to read *Ulysses* in the same way as, from the outset, it is apparent that form in this novel is far in excess of what seems to be necessary for any traditional idea of content. Consider the opening of the 'Sirens' chapter, for example:

> Bronze by gold heard the hoofirons, steelyringing Imperthnthn thnthn-thn. Chips, picking chips off rocky thumbnail, chips.

To a far greater extent than is true of *A Portrait of the Artist*, *Ulysses* is not just drawing attention to life but also to the activity and idea of writing.

This is apparent in the sentence-by-sentence texture of the novel, and also in the overall use of the Homeric parallels between Joyce's text and the original epic poem, the *Odyssey*. Much has been made of the parallels, but it is worth asking whether there are any real similarities between the episodes in Homer's work and the lives of Joyce's characters. Or is it simply that any fictional structure can be imposed in an almost arbitrary fashion on everyday, essentially shapeless and meaningless, experiences? This extends to the manner in which Bloom and Stephen meet up, and establish a relationship, during the course of the novel. Is this a significant meeting of father and son, as in the *Odyssey*, with Stephen finding a substitute for his own father, who has failed him? Or is the very idea of a reconciliation of father and son, and, with it, the idea of the restoration of coherence and continuity, just a literary cliché? Rather similar questions are raised by the way in which the 'story' of *Ulysses* ends with the two men together, to be followed by a final chapter, which is a long monologue from Bloom's wife, Molly. It is as if a structure has been completed with the meeting up of the two men, but the woman remains untidily outside the neatness of the story, and, as such, the neatness of a work of art. There is a self-mocking dimension in Joyce's approach here. In a masculine fashion, he has built an elaborate model, in which all the connections with Homer's epic and between the characters are established, but Joyce then has to concede that the woman remains outside the model he has built, the story he has already finished telling. Clearly, when we consider a work that functions in this kind of way, as readers we are not merely engaged with the details of the lives of the characters presented; any kind of meaning we derive from the text is not dependent upon the straightforward picture of life that is presented. Instead, we are forced to confront more abstract questions about how we structure and presume to make sense of life through fiction and narrative.

At one point in *Ulysses*, in the 'Nestor' chapter, Stephen, working as a schoolmaster, sets a riddle:

– This is the riddle, Stephen said.

> The cock crew
> The sky was blue:
> The bells in heaven
> Were striking eleven.
> Tis time for this poor soul
> To go to heaven.

– What is that?
– What, sir?
– Again, sir. We didn't hear.
Their eyes grew bigger as the lines were repeated. After a silence Cochrane said:
– What is it, sir? We give it up.
Stephen, his throat itching, answered:
– The fox burying his grandmother under a hollybush.

The riddle in some ways resembles a traditional literary text: clues are laid, and the reader links the clues together in order to arrive at a solution. In a realistic novel, for example, we assess all the little details that we are offered both about the people and the society in which they live, and on the basis of the evidence we have accumulated we arrive at an interpretation. But it is a false process, and *Ulysses*, as in this riddle, exposes the absurdity of the whole idea of a series of clues pointing to an answer. The reservation some readers might have is whether any kind of real satisfaction can be derived from a text such as *Ulysses* that refuses to tell us things in the way a traditional novel might. But it can be argued that this is how a novel had to be at this time, teasing the reader with the possibility of meaning but frustrating the desire for meaning. As Europe emerged from the First World War, not only had the old structures of explanation and understanding been blown apart, but also the world itself had become complex and chaotic in a way that seemed to deny and defy comprehension. At the same time, it is evident that modernist writers such as Joyce consciously set out to find new ways of writing in order to defamiliarise what had become staid and conventional. Ezra Pound's words, 'Make it new', seem to define this spirit of experimentation, of trying to remake the world through representing it differently.

Virginia Woolf

The typical nineteenth-century novel, as is the case with *David Copperfield*, *Jane Eyre* and *Adam Bede*, uses the name of the main character as its title. This is such an obvious point that we never stop to think about it, but it is, in fact, a very significant gesture, for what it asserts is a certain view of the importance of individual identity. By contrast, some of the most significant modernist novels employ a metaphoric title, such as Lawrence's *The Rainbow* and Virginia Woolf's *To the Lighthouse*. The change is more than mere coincidence. What these metaphoric titles, which often play with images of darkness and light, imply is a different kind of quest for truth. But what is also the case over and over again in modernism is that the emphasis is not so much on any answer that is arrived at but on the process of searching. In the period of disillusionment following the First World War, there is a sense of all of Europe trying to pick itself up after the disaster and trying, without a great deal of success, to find a fresh direction.

If we consider the novels of Virginia Woolf, for example, we can see that there is a constant sense of searching for a new way of representing the world, a new way of thinking about people and their experiences. Woolf herself was born into a literary family and is particularly associated with the Bloomsbury Group, a set of intellectual and artistic friends who met at the house she shared with her sister in London at Gordon Square, Bloomsbury. These included, amongst others, the novelist E. M. Forster and her husband-to-be, Leonard Woolf. Together the couple set up the Hogarth Press whose policy was to publish new and experimental works such as Eliot's early poems and *The Waste Land*, as well as some of Woolf's own work. Her first novel, *The Voyage Out*, appeared in 1915, followed by *Night and*

Day (1919). Both of these are essentially realistic works, but with her next novel, *Jacob's Room*, published in 1922 (the same year as Joyce's *Ulysses*), she broke with the realist tradition and established herself as a leading modernist writer. This is evident in her most famous works, *Mrs Dalloway* (1925), *To the Lighthouse* (1927) and *The Waves* (1931), but also in *Orlando* (1928), an oblique, fantastical biography of the poet Vita Sackville-West, and in her last work, *Between the Acts*, which appeared in 1941. Plagued by mental illness, she committed suicide in the same year.

The Voyage Out tells the story of Rachel Vinrace's journey to South America on her father's ship, her engagement there to Terence Hewet, and, following a fever, her death. In many ways the novel is a rewriting of earlier prose narratives, in particular journey fictions, such as Conrad's *Heart of Darkness*. There is, however, a distinct difference: this time the adventurer is a woman. In addition, while the novel includes marriage and romance, and so can be seen as fitting in with a romantic tradition in fiction (romantic, that is, in the sense of love stories, as opposed to the other meaning of romance, which suggests a quest narrative, although *The Voyage Out* clearly is a quest narrative at the same time), the emphasis of *The Voyage Out* falls upon the distinctively twentieth-century complications in the relationship experienced by Rachel. In this respect, the novel can be said to be about a journey into womanhood and sexuality, a journey that parallels in some ways Lawrence's exploration of sex in a modern patriarchal society. As with so much twentieth-century fiction, the voyage 'out' is also a voyage 'in' to the recesses of the mind, a quest that Woolf was to pursue in all her work.

Indeed, what Woolf was especially interested in was rendering a more subtle sense of identity than could be found in the traditional novel. In a famous essay, 'Mr Bennett and Mrs Brown', she attacked what she saw as the crude characterisation of Arnold Bennett, arguing for a presentation of character that recognised the internal consciousness, the inner experience of people. In order to achieve this, Woolf abandoned the kind of realism she used in *The Voyage Out* in favour of a much more fluid technique, a style closer to poetry than prose. Her approach is often referred to as 'stream of consciousness', a technique also employed by Joyce in *Ulysses*, but inspired by the method of Dorothy Richardson's long novel *Pilgrimage*, begun in 1915. Like Woolf, Richardson explores the subjective experience of her heroine. It is more than coincidence that both use stream of consciousness in works that place women at their centre. Both are concerned with the intricacies of personal relationships and how these can be rendered more truthfully in prose fiction, but, more importantly, both are concerned with the position of women, their rights and their place in political and social life, and their complex identities.

Much of this can be seen in *To the Lighthouse*, a novel about the Ramsay family. The setting is their holiday house. The first section is entitled 'The Window' and concerns Mrs Ramsay's thoughts as she sits at a window with her son James. Out at sea is a lighthouse flashing in the darkness in the same way that Mrs Ramsay illuminates the imaginative life of her family. The middle section, 'Time Passes', covers the war years 1914–18, while the house is empty, and Mrs Ramsay's death. In the final part, 'The Lighthouse', Mr Ramsay visits the lighthouse with his son James, symbolically healing an earlier quarrel. At this moment, too, Lily Briscoe, a painter friend of Mrs Ramsay, completes her picture of the house inspired by Mrs Ramsay. The novel dispenses with plot and instead is organised around the symbols of the lighthouse and the painting, but what strikes us most is just how wonderfully Woolf conveys the mood of each moment, as here, in section five of the book, when Mrs Ramsay is thinking about the house and her children:

> At a certain moment, she supposed, the house would become so shabby that something must be done. If they could be taught to wipe their feet and not bring the beach in with them – that would be something. Crabs, she had to allow, if Andrew really wished to dissect them, or if Jasper believed that one could make soup from seaweed, one could not prevent it; or Rose's objects – shells, reeds, stones; for they were gifted, her children, but all in quite different ways. And the result of it was, she sighed, taking in the whole room from floor to ceiling, as she held the stocking against James's leg, that things got shabbier and got shabbier summer after summer.

These are very ordinary thoughts reinforcing Mrs Ramsay's role as wife and mother, but there is a sufficient piling up of details to make us stand back and wonder about the tone of the novel and about how we are to read such domestic scenes. Simultaneously, complicating our response, there are subtle shifts between the present, the past and the future, as the passage hints at the coming war as 'things' get 'shabbier' and 'shabbier'. Or perhaps it is family life itself that is shabby, Woolf offering a critique of the family, with its gender assumptions and routine ordinariness.

What has been said so far might create the impression that Woolf, as an important modernist writer, is, none the less, simply echoing the formal procedures and political and social concerns of the other modernist writers we have discussed up to this point. But this is only half the story. Woolf's unique importance lies in her recognition that the traditional myths and structures have excluded women, they have been excluded both from society and from writing in their own voice. Her works, consequently, both her novels and her essays, demand to be recognised as constituting a highly significant, indeed ground-breaking, feminist critique of the exclusion of women from economic independence and education. This is the central theme of *A Room of One's Own* (1929), in which she analyses the figure of 'woman' both in male texts and in writings by women, and where she considers the broader issue of the ideological oppression of women. In order to counter the suggestion that 'there has never been a woman writer as great as Shakespeare', Woolf invents a sister for the bard, Judith Shakespeare, and shows how she is destroyed by society. It is a characteristically challenging move on Woolf's part as she confronts patriarchy and its authoritarian power. If *To the Lighthouse* remains Woolf's most remarkable novel, *A Room of One's Own* is her most enduring contribution to changing the ways in which we live and think today.

That, in turn, can alter how we respond and interpret the past. In this chapter we have reproduced the standard view of the modernist movement, with Eliot and Joyce as the two dominant figures, while Woolf is to some extent seen as a supplementary figure. But in a movement such as modernism, which questions the inherited order of things, there are, as in the Romantic period, opportunities for a wide variety of new and different voices to assert their presence. It would be possible to construct an account of modernism in literature that did not focus on the two dominant male figures; not only would such an account pay more attention to various women writers, but it would also want to challenge the parochialism of focusing exclusively on English literature (a term that becomes open to question as soon as we acknowledge that Eliot and Joyce are, respectively, American and Irish). A fuller account of modernism in literature, intent on re-reading the past, would want to look at writers such as H.D. (the American poet Hilda Doolittle), Gertrude Stein (the American autobiographer, essayist and poet; see, in particular, *Tender Buttons*, 1914, a work influenced by cubism), Dorothy Richardson (the English author of a sequence of thirteen novels called *Pilgrimage*, the first of which, *Pointed Roofs*, was published in 1913), Djuna Barnes (the American author of *Nightwood*, 1936, an account of bohemian life in Europe in the inter-war years), and Harriet Monroe (the American poet and critic). It is significant that a number of these authors were American women based in Europe; as with T. S. Eliot, they were external voices breaking into what might be regarded as someone else's conversation. What becomes apparent when we list such authors is not only the fact that it would be possible to read and interpret the modernist movement with different emphases, but also the fact that American critics, and students, are likely to have different points of reference in constructing a view of modernism. Time and time again in interpreting literature, what we see depends to a large extent upon the position from which we decide to look. It might be argued, indeed, that this was the main effect of modernism, to make us aware of the way we look at the world, by changing it.

The 1930s

Britain was not involved in a really major war for a hundred years from the defeat of Napoleon at Waterloo in 1815 to the outbreak of the First World War in 1914. It was a very different story in the first half of the twentieth century; just twenty-one years after the conclusion of the First World War, the Second World War commenced in 1939. A war is often followed by a period of economic recession, with a large surplus labour force seeking work, but generally the countries of Western Europe have shown great strength in bouncing back to good health after a conflict. This, however, was not the case in the 1920s and 1930s. Britain experienced a General Strike in 1926, and 1929 witnessed the Wall Street Crash and the start of the Great Depression. Britain's second Labour government, with Ramsay MacDonald as prime minister, had been elected in 1929, but in 1931 a National Government was formed under MacDonald (this was a coalition government, a form of goverment that is only ever contemplated at a time of major crisis). In 1933 Hitler was appointed Chancellor of Germany, in 1934 Stalin started a purge of his political enemies in the USSR, while 1936 saw the outbreak of the Spanish Civil War. In 1938, the year of the Munich crisis, the British prime minister Neville Chamberlain agreed to Hitler's territorial demands on Czechoslovakia, but in 1939, following the German invasion of Poland, Britain declared war on Germany. The Second World War continued until 1945.

It is against this background of political, social and economic unrest that we need to evaluate the literature of this period, in particular the works of the generation of writers that succeeded figures such as Eliot, Joyce and Woolf. Significant names associated with the 1930s include W. H. Auden (*Poems*, 1930, and *Look, Stranger!*, 1936), Evelyn Waugh (*Vile Bodies*, 1930, and *A Handful of Dust*, 1934), Noël Coward (*Private Lives*, 1930), Henry Green (*Living*, 1929), Aldous Huxley (*Brave New World*, 1932), George Orwell (*Down and Out in Paris and London*, 1933), Christopher Isherwood (*Mr Norris Changes Trains*, 1935, and *Goodbye to Berlin*, 1939). The decade also saw the publication of early poems by Dylan Thomas, the debut of Samuel Beckett, with *Murphy* (1938), and important works by Elizabeth Bowen, with *The Death of the Heart* (1938), and Graham Greene, with *Brighton Rock* (1938). Many of these authors are still known and widely read today, but it is noteworthy that the decade produced no writer, with the possible exception of Auden, of the reputation of Eliot, Joyce or Woolf. A point that some critics would also make is that the new authors of this decade seem to have retreated from the kind of innovations that we associate with modernism. But literature is always a response, as well as a contribution, to the period of its production. It was the fundamental change that the First World War amounted to that produced a fundamental change in literary form. This was one of the watersheds of history, after which people would never write again as they had in the past. The 1930s, by contrast, was a decade of serious political tension, but in some ways an aftershock from the First World War. Writing from the period tends, therefore, to be an attempt to engage with contemporary political tensions, rather than amounting to a fundamental reconsideration of the nature of writing.

This is very clear in the early poems of W. H. Auden who, in the late 1920s and the 1930s, was associated with a group of writers, including Christopher Isherwood and Stephen Spender, who were committed, at that time, to a Marxist social vision. Auden's poems from this decade deal directly with specific social and international crises. It is always a characteristic of a significant work of literature that it will reflect the fears and anxieties of the period of its production, and this is sharply apparent in Auden, who deals with a world that seems worryingly ready to embrace fascism and just as willing to abandon consideration for the individual. We can see this in a poem such as 'Spain 1937', where he can accurately be described as the voice of his generation:

> To-day the makeshift consolations; the shared cigarette;
> The cards in the candle-lit barn and the scraping concert,
>   The masculine jokes; to-day the
> Fumbled and unsatisfactory embrace before hurting.
>
> The stars are dead; the animals will not look:
> We are left alone with our day, and the time is short and
>   History to the defeated
> May say Alas but cannot help or pardon.

(ll. 85–92)

A vivid sense of the political tensions of the 1930s is also apparent in the works of Christopher Isherwood, who worked as a teacher of English in Berlin from 1930 to 1933. *Mr Norris Changes Trains* (1935) and *Goodbye to Berlin* (1939) are very direct accounts of a decadent Berlin in the last days of the Weimar Republic. In the latter work, in particular, there is a sense of living on borrowed time. Stability and a sense of tradition have been lost in the frenzied atmosphere of Berlin, which is a modern city as we experience it in modernist texts. But such frivolity cannot last forever; in the background there is a sense of threat, of the Nazi party about to call a halt to the way of life described. What is also apparent in *Goodbye to Berlin*, however, is a contradiction that is repeatedly present in socialist writing from this period. The narrator of *Goodbye to Berlin* characterises himself in the following manner: 'I am a camera with its shutter open . . .'. There is a detachment apparent throughout, a sense of an English observer who retains his individuality and will not become involved. It could be said that a great deal of socialist writing from this period, including the works of Auden, is essentially little more than middle-class dabbling with working-class politics. In his later work, for example, Auden turns to Christianity, but is also interested in developing a philosophy of individualism. Auden, Isherwood, and a number of their contemporaries, such as Stephen Spender, Cecil Day Lewis and Louis MacNeice, seem to lose a sense of direction and relevance after the 1930s, in that their personal concerns never really again coincide with the general concerns of their contemporaries.

In the thirties, however, there is evidence everywhere of a strong interest in social and political issues. It was in this decade that George Orwell started to write, works such as *Down and Out in Paris and London* (1933) and *The Road to Wigan Pier* (1937) looking at poverty in modern life. Orwell also fought in the Spanish Civil War, reporting on his experiences in *Homage to Catalonia* (1938). He is considered in more detail in the next chapter, as he published his most important works immediately after the Second World War. A novelist who superficially seems to be working in a similar area to the social and political writers of the 1930s is Henry Green, but his works in fact offer a far more oblique form of social commentary. *Living* has an industrial working-class setting, but *Party Going* (1939) takes place over the course of a few hours in a fog-bound London railway station. One of the things that is most distinctive about Green's novels is that he avoids the kind of rendering of consciousness that we see in, for example, the novels of Virginia Woolf. On the contrary, he relies upon the spoken words of his characters to convey a complex sense of social relations.

Green's novels indicate that writers were experimenting in a great variety of ways in the 1930s, and that the complexity of the period is missed if too much emphasis is placed on the more overtly political texts. And even in the area of politics, a great many options were available to writers. There is, for example, the emergence of the dystopian novel. A dystopia is the opposite of utopia; the dystopian novel is not a report on a perfect country but a vision of the worst possible state of affairs. There are nineteenth-century precedents for the dystopian novel, but it comes into its own in the 1930s with Aldous Huxley's *Brave New World* (1932). The essence of Huxley's method is to select tendencies evident in the society of his day and then to work them through to a nightmare conclusion, showing a society where any sense of individual freedom has been lost. It is an approach echoed in Orwell's *Nineteen Eighty-Four* (1949), and also indicates a concern that links many texts from the 1930s, which is that the modern state will increasingly neglect the rights and freedoms of the individual. It is an understandable fear during the decade of fascism, but the fear really goes beyond the immediate issue of fascism, seeing an incompatibility between the interests of any modern state and the interests of the individual.

The overall impact of the 1930s, therefore, is of a decade in which literature became increasingly concerned with contemporary political and social issues. In their own way, the plays of Noël Coward, and other texts from the 1930s, such as Richard Hughes's *A High Wind in Jamaica* (1929) and J. R. R. Tolkien's *The Hobbit* (1937), are also obliquely engaged with political questions. But the impression that the reader possibly takes away from the 1930s is that there is not a clear-cut or discernible literary character to the decade. There are a lot of authors we still read, but it is difficult to link them all together and arrange a sense of an overall pattern. It might be tempting to think that this is because the 1930s is still, in terms of literary history, a relatively recent decade, and that the job of sifting out what really matters has not yet been completed. But it is actually a different consideration that we have to take account of. In the 1920s, the major texts of modernism all have a family resemblance. But in the 1930s we possibly begin to witness the true aftermath of the First World War, which is the disintegration of a coherent culture. By the 1930s in Britain there is an unprecedented impression of literary fragmentation, with a host of authors writing in different ways and adopting different stances. A sense of a main drive and purpose, and even a national identity, has fragmented. This begins to explain why the last fifty years of the twentieth century in Britain are characterised by an unprecedented number of interesting works, but the absence of an overall direction.

15 The Twentieth Century: The Second World War to the End of the Millennium

Wartime and Post-War Britain

The Second World War, from 1939 to 1945, involved Britain and the British Empire and Commonwealth, France, America, Russia and China (the Allied powers) fighting Germany, Italy and Japan (the Axis powers). This might, in Winston Churchill's memorable phrase, legitimately be referred to as the British people's 'finest hour', but victory in the war could not disguise a fundamental problem in Britain. The depression of the inter-war years meant that, in 1939, Britain entered the war with limited resources; by the end of the war, the country was virtually bankrupt. Financial and also political leadership of the world now moved decisively to the United States.

In Britain, in the immediate post-war period, there was, however, a spirit of optimism, a sense that the country was entering a new era of prosperity. The post-war Labour government's creation of the Welfare State, with what was, at that time, the finest free health service in the world, offered the promise of a better life for everyone. But so much of the country's economic power had been eroded that there was never enough money to pay for the health, education and welfare provision people had come to expect. Throughout the fifties, sixties and seventies, with the British economy continuing to decline, the country had to make a series of painful adjustments. Initially, Britain had to accept that it was no longer a dominant player on the world stage. As the years went by, it had to come to terms with the fact that it was also on the margins of Europe; even at the start of the twenty-first century, Britain still finds it impossible to define the nature of its relationship with its European neighbours. Britain also had to adjust to a new economic reality; that much of its industrial infrastructure was old and inefficient, that British working practices left a lot to be desired, and that, perhaps due to complacency, there had never been enough investment in research, new plant and new skills. Such problems found vivid, even alarming, expression in the almost total decline of the British car industry in the 1980s. At a rather more intangible level, Britain and the British people had to adjust to a sense of national decline and loss of national self-confidence; as sometimes happens, a sense of weakness can find expression in belligerence, lack of manners and aggression.

The last twenty years of the century – the years of the Thatcher, Major and Blair governments – saw attempts to tackle some of Britain's fundamental problems. The country's principal weakness was its economy. Margaret Thatcher as prime minister focused her energies on revitalising the economy; keen to promote a competitive, entrepreneurial society, there were times when she seemed utterly unconcerned with social welfare provision. In fact, two main stances can be identified in British politics in the last twenty years of the twentieth century, both of which prioritised business: one group of politicians argued that the economy mattered, and that the benefits of greater prosperity would work their way down through society, while another group maintained that economic prosperity could be the bedrock on which the government could gradually improve public services. The economic changes within Britain as a result of these policies, accompanied by a sustained boom in the world economy, meant that by the end of the twentieth century many people enjoyed a standard of living that they could never have envisaged fifty or even twenty-five years earlier.

Yet at the same time a feeling persisted that there was something fundamentally wrong in Britain. It was clear that the health and education services were far from satisfactory. Despite the fact that the British people were working harder than ever before, poverty in some areas of the country was as bad, if not worse, than ever. And people were worried about levels of crime and social indiscipline. These are, of course, concerns that are felt in all countries, but in Britain there was possibly the added feeling that the country had lost a sense of where it was heading; indeed, whether it was heading anywhere at all.

It is, of course, hard to make sense of recent history. But there is one thing we can be sure of, which is that, in centuries to come, when historians look back at this period they will look at how events were reported in newspapers and on television, but they will also look at novels, poems and plays to capture a sense of the mood of the nation. It is not that poets, playwrights and novelists are more astute social commentators than their journalistic contemporaries; indeed, more often than not they are probably unaware of the deeper resonances of their own works. But a literary text can often convey the deeper currents of change and concern within a society; even unknowingly, a literary text can touch on the issue behind the surface issue, the story behind the story.

We can start to appreciate the truth of this proposition if, initially, we consider the literature of the Second World War and texts that look back to the war. The point has often been made that the Second World War did not lead to the production of the great, if painful, poetry that we associate with the First World War. But this is understandable; there was not the same sense of an apocalypse, of being at the end of everything. What we tend to witness, in the poetry of Keith Douglas, Alun Lewis and Charles Causley, for example, is a sense of individuals caught up in events that they can neither comprehend nor control; more often than not, they are decent people in a world that has become indifferent to decency. There is something of this in the increasingly highly regarded wartime fiction of the Anglo-Irish novelist Elizabeth Bowen. *The Heat of the Day* (1949) concerns a suspected pro-German traitor, Robert Kelway, and his relationship with a divorcee, Stella Rodney, in wartime London. Stella is told about Robert's apparent crimes, but refuses to believe her informant. Stella's son, Roderick, inherits an estate in Ireland, and then discovers the uncomfortable truth about his parents' divorce. Another strand in the novel involves Louie Lewis, a young woman whose adulterous relationship results in the birth of a child.

What the novel conveys is a sense of emotional dislocation. In a time of war, old points of reference, old values and old convictions have gone. Readers today might be interested in the wartime setting of *The Heat of the Day*, but are likely to become more caught up in the lives of emotionally vulnerable and exposed characters. The influence of

Henry James, who frequently deals with innocent characters in a corrupt world, has often been noted, but whereas James deals with the rottenness lurking in European civilisation, in Bowen's novel, as in her stories set in the London Blitz, *Ivy Gripped the Stairs* (1946), there is an awareness that there are no secure places any more. In the First World War, the battle was always elsewhere, but in the Second World War, with aerial bombing of British cities, safe refuges were, literally and symbolically, being destroyed.

It is a recurrent feature of British Second World War novels that they recall an order that used to exist. Evelyn Waugh's trilogy, *Sword of Honour*, features Guy Crouchback, a decent man who has no place in the modern world. The values he has lived by, including his Catholicism, have no relevance in a world that has changed so much. The *Sword of Honour* trilogy is made up of *Men at Arms* (1952), *Officers and Gentlemen* (1955) and *Unconditional Surrender* (1961). Together the three can be described as a *roman fleuve*, a series of novels, each of which may be read separately but which constitute a continuous narrative. As a genre, it is quietly traditional; in a steady and coherent way, the novels in a *roman fleuve* explore the extended moral and social development of an individual over a long period. It is a genre that is most associated with the Second World War and the years immediately before and after. Another example is Olivia Manning's *The Balkan Trilogy* (1960–5), which deals with the lives of British expatriates before and during the German invasion of the Balkans in 1941. The most ambitious British *roman fleuve* is Anthony Powell's *A Dance to the Music of Time* (1951–75), several volumes of which are set during the Second World War. The appeal of all these novels lies in the tension between the moral perspective they seek to maintain and the extreme threat to any moral code posed by war.

If an old structure of values disappears, however, the modern state is likely to move in to fill the void with its own rules and systems of regulation. George Orwell's most famous works, *Animal Farm* (1945) and *Nineteen Eighty-Four* (1949), dystopian fantasies about totalitarian states, both focus on the limitations on individual freedom that could occur in the near future. The story of *Nineteen Eighty-Four* takes place in a Britain that is now part of a European superstate. Winston Smith transgresses state rules by having a love affair with Julia Smith. Under interrogation, he eventually betrays Julia. She, he later discovers, has similarly betrayed him. But it does not matter, for they no longer love each other; they love the party leader, Big Brother. In Orwell's novel, surveillance and control of the individual are more extreme than they have ever been; the very notion of privacy and a private life is all but eliminated. In the post-war period Orwell's works were seen as referring to Russia and the form of Stalinist dictatorship associated with Russia at that time, but it is now apparent that *Nineteen Eighty-Four*, in particular, addresses a broader issue concerning the role of the modern state. The ways in which the state intrudes in people's lives may be more subtle today than in *Nineteen Eighty-Four*, but it is clear that it is a text that with the passing of time becomes more rather than less relevant.

Drama

What connects many of the novels written during the Second World War and novels looking back to the war is an emphasis on an order that has fallen or is falling apart, and on the exposed individuals who then have to make the best of their lives in this unstable society. In addition, there are some novels, as is the case with *Nineteen Eighty-Four*, that look at the structures likely to be established by politicians to fill the void; a state of chaos is acknowledged, but the literary text then speculates on how that chaos is to be managed. These concerns that are evident in fiction obviously reflect a broader debate that was being conducted in all areas of life in a country that had lost its world role and lost a sense of purpose and direction. When values are changing rapidly, however, it is the theatre that can often stage the most effective debate about the state of the nation, capturing and showing a state of flux. This is certainly the case in Britain over a period of about twenty years that begins with John Osborne's *Look Back in Anger* in 1956.

Having said that, however, it seems sensible to start with the major playwright who transcends these, perhaps insular, concerns. Samuel Beckett is, intriguingly, equally an Anglo-Irish and a French writer. Born near Dublin, Beckett made his home in France in the 1930s where he wrote two full-length novels (*Murphy*, 1938; *Watt*, 1953) in

English, together with the trilogy *Molloy* (1951), *Malone Meurt* (1951, *Malone Dies*) and *L'Innommable* (1953, *The Unnamable*) in French. Like Joyce, by whom he was influenced, Beckett uses interior monologue as his major device to convey his sense of a bleak world in which all are isolated. It would, therefore, be reasonable to refer to Beckett as a modernist writer, someone engaged in experimenting with language and literary form in a self-conscious, sometimes parodic way. There are, however, significant differences between Joyce and Beckett. Where we might feel that Joyce is writing in a real context, making references to real history and a particular culture – Ireland in the 1920s – Beckett seems to belong more to the postmodern world. This is the world after the Second World War, a world haunted by its knowledge of nuclear war.

The writers looked at so far are, for the most part, caught up in the void of the Second World War and its aftermath, but there is a way in which Beckett takes us beyond this moment to a much more troubling vision where everything has been utterly changed. The most obvious place he does this is in his plays which, though related to the novels, strike a different note. The plays belong to what, since Beckett, has been called the Theatre of the Absurd, a term used to describe plays where the main feeling of the audience is one of bafflement as they face a world on stage where there is no logic to events or human behaviour: human life seems absurd in its disjointedness and meaninglessness. In *Waiting for Godot* (1952), two tramps, Estragon and Vladimir, wait for Godot, who never comes. We do not find out who he is. The characters fill their time by playing word games. Pozzo and his slave Lucky arrive, but they are not Godot. A boy announces that Godot will not be coming that day. In Act Two, the tree that is bare at the start of Act One has leaves, but almost everything else is the same. What the play adds up to is a bleak vision of life; it is, at once, both comic and terrifying.

With *Waiting for Godot* Beckett changed modern drama forever, and changed, too, our perception of the world. This has to do with the way in which Beckett captures not so much local events at a particular time as a deeper shift in feeling. In brief, what Beckett conveys is the deep sense of anxiety that marks the second half of the twentieth century. That sense of anxiety is connected in the plays with an impression of writing after the Holocaust. In *Endgame* (in French 1957, in English 1958) Nag and Nell, two elderly characters, spend the whole play in dustbins. The play takes place in a single room. At its centre is the blind Hamm, totally dependent on his servant Clov. Outside the room is a wasteland. In *Happy Days* (1961) Winnie is buried up to her middle in a mound of earth, and unable to move. In *Not I* (1973) a disembodied monologue is delivered and all that the audience see is a 'Mouth'. Time and time again the impression created by the plays is of a sense of desolation and sparseness as the characters, like the audience, struggle with the incomprehensibility of their world where there seems no future and no past, only a kind of constant waiting in desperate hope. Equally, language is reduced to circularity and repetition, and isolation becomes the norm.

Beckett shows us the world that we have come to inherit. Like many great writers, he seems to see around the corner of time, anticipating what is to come or to be. He belongs to the second half of the twentieth century, but, moving between French, Irish, and British identities, remains oddly elusive. There is, however, also a great deal of interest in those writers who can be placed rather more neatly in a particular cultural context and a very specific time slot, as in the case with John Osborne and *Look Back in Anger*. First staged in 1956, the year of the Suez Crisis, which marked the end of British imperialism in the Middle East, and which can also be seen as a final empty, and humiliating, attempt by Britain to play a major role on the world stage, the play created a tremendous stir. At the time it was described as a 'kitchen-sink' drama. Audiences at the Royal Court theatre where it was staged were used to polite drawing-room comedies, but Osborne, as was also the case in the plays of Arnold Wesker and Shelagh Delaney, put a new emphasis on domestic realism and everyday life and language. Suddenly the theatre reflected, in a way that had not previously been the case, post-war life in ordinary Britain.

The play tells the story of the marital conflicts of Jimmy Porter and his middle-class wife Alison, intensified by the presence of their lodger Cliff and the visit of Alison's friend Helena. Sentimental and violent, Jimmy drives Alison out, but she returns after a miscarriage. The play ends with a kind of reconciliation. The plot, however, is not the main interest. Our attention focuses on the character of Jimmy, a new sort of hero. University-educated, he now works on a sweet stall, and much of the play consists of his attacks on British society. His speeches, along with his education, position him outside the usual working-class stereotype; consequently, he seems to belong nowhere. For Jimmy, the old structure has disappeared, and the result is that he is an isolated figure without any place. But his bullying attitude towards women is revealing. Cut off from his own class, he seeks reassurance in the old-fashioned pattern of a gender relationship in which he can at least dominate women. The contradiction between Jimmy's analysis of social ills and his shocking treatment of his wife, which, it must be said, was not readily apparent to audiences at the time of the play's first performance, suggests something of the turmoil of the 1950s. Britain emerged from the war years without any clear convictions about new directions or new forms of politics that might guide the country towards new ways of thinking about how to order society. Jimmy is full of a certain kind of energy, but energy that is frittered away in empty speeches; he talks, but he is incapable of action.

The sense of isolated individuals that is conveyed in *Look Back in Anger* is present as well, in a very destructive way, in Harold Pinter's plays, which can be associated with the Theatre of the Absurd, and which clearly owe a debt to Beckett. Pinter's first play, *The Room*, was performed in 1957, followed by *The Birthday Party* the next year, *The Caretaker* in 1960 and *The Homecoming* in 1965. Other plays have followed, but it is these early plays that are generally recognised as Pinter's special contribution to modern drama, in which menace and violence constantly threaten the characters' lives. The plays are oddly realistic in so far as they are concerned with social relationships and in their expression of the difficulties of communication between people. The characteristic Pinteresque exchange is one of silences and pauses, just as the characteristic Pinteresque setting is a room where people retreat from the world that threatens them, although the nature of this threat is never clearly defined. There is, too, something characteristically Pinteresque about the obsessive behaviour of his characters and their disturbed mental states. What Pinter presents is a world where people seem locked in their own non-communicating lines of thought, or in fantasies, so that there is never any chance of a sane or healthy society emerging. Rather, the sense is of individuals trying to gain some assurance about their existence, but never able to articulate their needs. Their words, and language generally, become part of the menace and violence they are seeking to escape, but from which escape is impossible.

If Pinter's plays are comic, they are so in an uncomfortable way. This may be because they deal so often with people who are almost normal, with very ordinary lives, living on the edge of violence. In Act Two of *The Caretaker* Mick's spring-cleaning in a darkened room with a vacuum cleaner proves to be a moment of pure terror for a tramp, Davies, who has been invited into the house by Mick's brother. As Mick explains, however, the cleaner has to be plugged into the light socket, throwing the room into darkness, before the bulb is put back. The noise terrifies Davies so much that he stands flat against the wall, knife in hand:

> I was just doing some spring cleaning. . . . There used to be a wall plug for this electrolux. But it doesn't work. I had to fit it in the light socket. . . . How do you think the place is looking? I gave it a good going over.
>
> *Pause*
>
> We take it in turns, once a fortnight, my brother and me, to give the place a thorough going over. I was working late tonight, I only just got here. But I thought I better get on with it, as it's my turn.

The language is mundane and unremarkable, with Mick, engrossed in his own actions, indifferent to the fear Davies is experiencing. The familiar domestic world remains in place, but its most familiar routines are now associated with unpredictable, if improbable, threats of violence.

In a different kind of play, Tom Stoppard in *Rosencrantz and Guildenstern are Dead* (1966) focuses on little men in a world beyond their comprehension. Rosencrantz and Guildenstern are the two courtiers in Shakespeare's *Hamlet* who serve as spies on the Prince for the King. Stoppard moves these peripheral characters from the margins to centre stage, so that we come to see *Hamlet* from their powerless position, and, if we know Shakespeare's play, with an awareness that they will die, as they are overtaken by events over which they have no control and of which they have very little understanding. A different slant is found in Joe Orton's plays. Starting with *Entertaining Mr Sloane* (1964), *Loot* (1965) and then *What the Butler Saw* (1969), Orton confronted audiences with a picture of bizarre people with bizarre lives, as he mocked the remnants of a moral order. The odd thing with Orton is that, although these plays proved controversial at the time of their first performance, nobody today would seem very concerned about things that people found shocking at that time. It is as if once a framework of values goes, that framework loses all relevance in people's lives.

This helps us understand why there is such a strong sense of decline and drift in post-war drama. There are, none the less, powerful political writers at work in the British theatre who meet the challenge of examining the 'state of the nation' in an era of decline. We can mention David Hare's plays, including *Plenty* (1978) and *Murdering Judges* (1991), and David Edgar's *That Summer* (1987), about the miners' strike in Britain in 1984–5. Such plays might seem essentially topical, reflecting British life at a particular moment, but they also have a wider relevance in identifying the damaged state of the social body in Britain in the years between 1950 and 2000. This is particularly clear in the violent plays of Edward Bond. In *Saved* (1965) it is urban violence that Bond dramatises, shocking audiences with the stoning to death of a baby, but it is his *Lear* (1971), a rewriting of Shakespeare's *King Lear*, but even more provocatively cruel than the original work, that sums up the state of modern society as Bond sees it. If Beckett seeks to convince us of the absurdity of contemporary twentieth-century society, Bond seeks to show us its appalling and meaningless cruelty.

Behind Bond's play, as is the case with the works of Pinter, Hare and Edgar, lies a recognition of the collapse of old structures of order, but also an awareness of the continuing grip of the past on the present. As old structures disappear, including the traditional authority of masculinity, some dramatists, however, do seek to move forward and adopt new positions. This is evident in the works of the feminist dramatist Caryl Churchill. Her best-known plays are *Top Girls* (1982) and her satire on the Thatcher years, *Serious Money* (1987). In *Top Girls*, women from history – for example, Pope Joan and Patient Griselda, the obedient wife from one of Chaucer's *Canterbury Tales* – are brought into the everyday world of contemporary women to set up an extraordinary dialogue about oppression and the struggle waged by women across the years for recognition. In the 'Top Girls' employment agency Louise is looking for a new job after twenty years in the same firm:

> I've spent twenty years in middle management. I've seen young men go on, in my own company or elsewhere, to higher things. Nobody notices me, I don't expect it, I don't attract attention by making mistakes, everybody takes it for granted that my work is perfect.

Louise's words seem to sum up the whole course of history for women: it is assumed that they will always play the role expected of them to perfection, but they are always seen as inferior to men and, consequently, denied opportunities for self-fulfilment. But Louise's desire to move on is a recognition of the way in which people, and especially women, in the late twentieth century can embrace a new position. Churchill, as such, articulates not just a sense of the past but also a sense of how the social order might be reconstructed differently.

Novels

The earlier novels of Doris Lessing, from 1951 to 1969, offer perhaps the most vivid, if indirect, evidence of how and why people's lives changed in the first twenty-five years after the Second World War. Her first novel *The Grass is Singing* (1951), set in Southern Rhodesia (now Zimbabwe), focuses on the marriage of Mary and Richard Turner, and the murder of Mary by Moses, the African servant with whom she has been sleeping. British fiction over the years has consistently returned to, or at the very least included references to, colonial settings. It makes one realise the extent to which the English over a long period depended on the empire for a sense of self-definition; Englishness was defined both on the basis of difference and on the basis of being at a centre where everything else was peripheral. There are those who argue that with the collapse of an imperial role, most obviously with the withdrawal of the British from India in 1947, the English were left without any way of defining their identity.

The Grass is Singing is a novel that considers the essential frailty and emptiness of colonial power, conveying the sterility and hypocrisy of the lives of the settlers. The novel starts with the mere facts of the murder, as reported by the local newspaper; it then goes on to explore the story behind the headline. There is, throughout the novel, a sense of a colonial order that has been imposed upon Africa without any regard for the land or the native people. It might be felt, of course, that as a novel about Southern Africa The Grass is Singing has little to do with post-war Britain, but what we see here is something that will be repeated over and over again, and that still continues today. Just as the English always relied upon the empire to define their national characteristics, the British novel has continued to call upon outside perspectives in order to discuss Britain. Writers from India and Ireland, in particular, have played a central role in British culture since the Second World War; reflecting on their own post-colonial nations, they inevitably acknowledge the country that has, for better or for worse, been part of their own history. In The Grass is Singing, however, the connection is more straightforward; the British settlers live out a pale parody of Englishness, the defining feature of which is their racist contempt for the Africans.

After The Grass is Singing, Lessing, in a five-volume sequence of novels entitled Children of Violence, tracks the life of a character called Martha Quest. The five novels are Martha Quest (1952), A Proper Marriage (1954), A Ripple from the Storm (1958), Landlocked (1965) and The Four-Gated City (1969). The novels deal with Martha's childhood on a farm in Southern Rhodesia, her involvement in left-wing politics, her marriage, her life in post-war Britain, through to an apocalyptic ending in the year 2000. The pattern is that Martha, seeking something, moves through a series of structures, or temporary solutions, all of which prove unsatisfactory. When it comes down to it, there is just her dislocated individual conscience, but Lessing is also trying to grasp how the individual will relates to and engages with larger historical and political realities. Similar themes are explored in The Golden Notebook (1962).

William Golding is another writer who, sometimes directly and sometimes indirectly, considers the post-war world. Lord of the Flies (1954) looks at a group of schoolboys marooned on an island and their reversion to savagery; as such, it is another novel that considers the frailty of the structure of civilisation. And as in a great many modern texts, we are always only a step away from violence. Characteristically in his novels, Golding speculates on whether there is any meaning in existence. *The Spire* (1964) is about a man driven to build an immense spire for a cathedral; it is to the glory of God, but also a hare-brained scheme. There is a nicely poised ambivalence in the work, Golding wavering between commitment to religious belief and scepticism. In *Darkness Visible* (1979) a horribly disfigured child emerges from the wartime bombing of London. The child, Matty, is convinced that he has been put on earth for a purpose. This seems to be the case when, towards the end of the novel, he saves the life of another child. His action stands as an illustration of the power of love as a force in the world. But any impression that we are being offered a fable with a positive message is countered by the overall effect of *Darkness Visible*, which confronts us with a dark, violent and essentially meaningless world.

A criticism that can be levelled against Golding's novels is one that relates to a great deal of modern British fiction. This is that, although Golding can engage with the present, he is always looking back, recollecting old ways of structuring the world. This is a criticism that can be applied to the novels of John Fowles, in particular *The French Lieutenant's Woman* (1969), which at the time of its publication seemed so innovatory. A modern narrator writes a Victorian novel about the relationship between Charles Smithson and Sarah Woodruff, who has previously been involved with a French sailor. The narrator stresses the gap between the framework of secure beliefs the Victorians needed and the uncertainties of modern life. But Fowles's experimental narrative method cannot conceal the fact that his own convictions are essentially traditional; that he is a middle-class, liberal author, and that he desires and wishes to possess his heroine every bit as much as his hero Charles does. Fowles, it is clear, cannot detach himself from a male-centred, literary and very English way of judging life.

An inability to break free from old ways of looking is at the very heart of Graham Swift's *Waterland* (1983). A middle-aged history teacher is facing redundancy; history is not going to be taught any more. He tells the story of his life, telling it in the same way that he has told stories about the past to his audience of school children. In a history lesson, as in his own life, he deals with violence, suffering and tragedy, but a story imposes coherence, and, as such, a sense of comfort, on chance events. The teacher knows, however, that he is a middle-aged Englishman, and that there is, therefore, something that belongs to the past and that is too insular about the narratives he constructs. But what alternative is there? How can an English author break free from old ways of seeing, and, more generally, how can English fiction break free from received ways of telling a story?

It is a problem that Martin Amis engages with in his novels. In works such as *Money* (1984) and *London Fields* (1989), Amis paints a picture of Britain during the Thatcher years, with characters cynically pursuing their own interests in a society where both culture and compassion are redundant concepts. But what really distinguishes Amis's novels is that he narrates in the voice of this society, reproducing, albeit in a stylised manner, the discourses of contemporary English and American life. The effect is that modern life appears to be looked at from the perspective of the present rather than through the lens of an inherited style. Amis's detractors, however, question his originality, arguing that the word-play in his novels cannot conceal a curmudgeonly contempt for modern life that echoes the stance in the novels of his father, Kingsley Amis. As a member of the literary establishment, Martin Amis, they would argue, can offer nothing more than the mannerisms of something new.

A different level of inventiveness is found in the works of a long list of writers who are outsiders in one way or another. The first evidence of this is found in working-class novels of the post-war period, such as Alan Sillitoe's *Saturday Night and Sunday Morning* (1958), which tells the story of a factory worker, Arthur Seaton, whose aspirations do not rise above the pursuit of drink and women. The attraction of Sillitoe's novel is that it offers a different perspective on English life; the fact that it deploys, very convincingly, a working-class Nottingham voice brings to life the point that there are many voices present within Britain, and that a different voice sees the world in a different way. Doris Lessing, as a woman from Southern Africa, is an outsider in a similar way. Indeed, it can be argued that, whereas a mainstream of white, middle-class, male-authored works have in recent times struggled to add anything new to the tradition of fiction, outsiders have found new ways of looking and in doing so have reformed the English novel.

Novels by women writers who have absorbed and been shaped by the emergence of a feminist discourse over the past thirty years provide the clearest examples of genuinely new voices in fiction. Angela Carter, before her premature death in 1992, wrote novels, short stories, film scripts, polemic and journalism. Her novels include *The Passion of New Eve* (1977) and *Wise Children* (1987), but in all her work there is a subversive playfulness and theatricality. *Nights at the Circus* (1984), her eighth novel, concerns Fevvers, a circus artist, and Walser, a journalist who hopes to debunk the improbable stories about her life. In the inventive manner that characterises her novels, Carter plays with fantasy and narrative points of view. The effect is that, rather than Walser debunking Fevvers, traditional patriarchal ways of telling a story and ordering the world are debunked. It is a tactic that extends into Carter's treatment of sexuality, the behaviour and motives of her characters eluding received categorisations. There is a rather similar quality in the novels of Jeanette Winterson, such as *Oranges are Not the Only Fruit* (1985), an account of a girl's upbringing by her Evangelical adopted mother and her decision in her teens to come out as a lesbian. Interestingly, this is more than a case of male religious authority being set against the girl's emotional instinct; on the contrary, the eccentricity of the cult members seems to fuel the girl's unconventionality.

Other outsiders who are, at the same time, also heirs to the English tradition in the novel are Scottish, Welsh and Irish authors; these are writers who seem to speak the same language as everyone else but who actually have a distinctive voice, and stance, of their own. This can be seen in James Kelman's *How Late It Was, How Late* (1995). Kelman, a Scottish nationalist, relies upon an aggressive Glasgow voice. Perhaps the biggest impression in recent years, however, has been made by writers whose roots are elsewhere or who, as residents of other countries, continue to be affected by the legacy of British colonial rule. V. S. Naipaul is the author of works such as *The Mystic Masseur* (1957) and *A House for Mr Biswas* (1961). His novels illustrate a constant theme in postcolonial fiction, which is finding an appropriate tradition in which to write. This is also a central issue in the novels of Salman Rushdie (discussed in the Postscript). The postcolonial novelist, reflecting on the nature of the authority implicit in European narrative forms, puts himself or herself in a position where, in establishing a distance from the received tradition, observations, implicit or explicit, can be made both upon the nature of English fiction and upon the nature of English thought and behaviour. We can see this in Kazuo Ishiguro's *The Remains of the Day* (1989), a postcolonial novel of manners that dissects the structure and meaning of Englishness in a way that is only possible for a writer looking in from outside.

Poetry

The point has sometimes been made that English literature in the second half of the twentieth century lacks major figures. It is, perhaps, easy to see why. The story of English literature, particularly from the sixteenth through to the nineteenth century, is a story that coincides with the rise of Britain as the dominant world power. In the twentieth century, with that rule ceded to the USA, Britain became a significant but second-rate power. It is, though, unfair, and certainly too glib a generalisation, to describe British literature in the second half of the twentieth century as significant but just a little second-rate. If we turn now to consider poets in this period, what we repeatedly witness is the arrival of outsiders with new voices who have enlivened and redirected English poetry.

This is not entirely a recent phenomenon. In the era of modernism, the two most significant poets, Eliot and Yeats, were both outsiders injecting something new into British culture. Alongside their originality and ambition, the poems of, perhaps the most distinctively English poet in the post-war period, Philip Larkin, appear modest and unassuming. His poems, in collections including *The Less Deceived* (1955), *The Whitsun Weddings* (1964) and *High Windows* (1974), characteristically touch on the pathos and humour of everyday experience; ordinary lives are described in a fairly direct style. It is easy to be dismissive of Larkin, but his carefully constructed poems, with layer upon layer of complexity in their depiction of contemporary English life, represent a subtle expression of the changing mood of Britain in the decades following the end of the Second World War. Larkin's near-contemporary Ted Hughes, particularly in *Crow* (1970), is a different kind of poet, with a consistent strain of violence in his work; in particular, he sets the savagery of nature against the pretensions of civilisation.

Hughes was married to Sylvia Plath, whose real place is in a history of American literature, but who, as a more radical and disturbing poet than her husband, stands as a good example of how an outsider can manage to speak in a new voice. In the case of Plath, this was a matter of being both an American and a woman. Stevie Smith, whose *Collected Poems* were published in 1975, was a woman writer who could produce poems with a discomforting emphasis on sexual anxiety, something that combines uneasily in her work with an ambivalence towards Christianity. Smith can, in fact, be located in a tradition in poetry by women in which private, suppressed, and in a sense unsanctioned, feelings are allowed to intrude into what looks like a well-mannered poem; there is a break of decorum, but a break of decorum with fascinating implications.

We can see this today in the poems of Carol Ann Duffy (see *Selected Poems*, 1994), particularly in her disturbing dramatic monologues. These lines are from 'Warming Her Pearls', a poem about a maid who has to wear her mistress's pearls to warm them before they are put on:

> Next to my own skin, her pearls. My mistress
> bids me wear them, warm them, until evening
> when I'll brush her hair. At six, I place them
> round her cool, white throat. All day I think of her,
>
> resting in the Yellow Room, contemplating silk
> or taffeta, which gown tonight? She fans herself
> whilst I work willingly, my slow heat entering
> each pearl. Slack on my neck, her rope.

(ll. 1–8)

Duffy's skill lies in the way she manages to invest simple, mundane details and words with both a sensuality and a kind of erotic menace. The 'slow heat' that enters each pearl infuses it with an impregnating life, while the 'rope' suggests an uneasy link between the voyeuristic love of the maid and death. The poem seems to encourage this sort of over-reading through its careful pacing of the speaking voice in hushed tones. It is a voice that mimics the burning desire of the Petrarchan lover as in, for example, Wyatt's sonnet 'Whoso List to Hunt', but in this case the desire is not simply illicit but arousing.

Dylan Thomas was another writer who breached poetic decorum. Thomas (Collected Poems, 1953) adopts an elaborate, rhetorical style for poems that celebrate natural energy and the emotions. The critical disparagement Thomas has received over the years is interesting; he has often been slated for adopting an exaggerated Celtic pose, but this metropolitan dismissiveness is a way of overlooking the fact that, like a postcolonial writer, Thomas, as a Welshman writing in English, must not only negotiate a relationship with the English tradition but also be true to his sense of the feelings he recognises in his own culture (which might be unlike the natural reserve of the English). There is a similar dimension in the poems of R. S. Thomas, a clergyman, writing in North Wales, who died in 2000. Superficially, Thomas's poems (Selected Poems, 1946–1968, 1973, and Later Poems: A Selection, 1983) might appear to be inconsequential descriptions of Welsh farm life, but implicit in the poems is an awareness of a huge cultural distance between Wales and England, the danger being that Englishness will consume another culture, another way of life and even another language within the British Isles.

Scottish poetry has always been characterised by figures who, like R. S. Thomas in Wales, wish to register and maintain their distance from the English. A notable example is Hugh MacDiarmid (1892–1978), who in a long career focused on the use of the Scots vernacular as a modern literary language. Black writers, both in Britain or in a post-colonial setting, can also present a distinctive sense of the relationship between a dominant culture and those who are outside the cultural consensus. This is evident in the poems of Derek Walcott, in a volume such as The Castaway (1965), and, more recently in the poems of Linton Kwesi Johnson. Born in Jamaica, but coming to Britain at the age of nine, Johnson writes what is essentially performance poetry, dealing with issues of race and social problems, but relying for its effectiveness on the use of a voice that seems close to a disaffected London street-voice.

Perhaps the most interesting British poetry of the last quarter of a century, however, has originated from Northern Ireland, with three quite outstanding poets, Seamus Heaney (discussed in the Postscript to this book), Derek Mahon and Paul Muldoon. The vitality of poetry from Northern Ireland is more than a matter of chance. Poetry, more than any other art form, has always reflected on adversity and suffering. The 'Troubles' that have affected Northern Ireland since the 1960s are, in fact, not often dealt with directly in poetry, but a Northern Ireland poet cannot avoid being aware that it is a country that is, at the same time, a part of the United Kingdom and not part of the United Kingdom. A Northern Ireland poet, as such, is interestingly placed as an outsider; to a certain extent, whatever a poet in Northern Ireland writes about, he or she is also writing about how the province relates to Britain yet also relates to the Irish Republic.

Consequently, although a writer such as Paul Muldoon may have little to say directly in his poetry about local political issues, a certain tension is always present. One of Muldoon's finest poems is 'Cuba':

> My eldest sister arrived home that morning
> In her white muslin evening dress.
> 'Who the hell do you think you are,
> Running out to dances in next to nothing?
> As though we hadn't enough bother
> With the world at war, if not at an end.'
> My father was pounding the breakfast-table.
>
> 'Those Yankees were touch and go as it was –
> If you'd heard Patton at Armagh –
> But this Kennedy's nearly an Irishman
> So he's not much better than ourselves.
> And him only to say the word.
> If you've got anything on your mind
> Maybe you should make your peace with God.'
>
> I could hear Mary from beyond the curtain.
> 'Bless me, Father, for I have sinned.
> I told a lie once, I was disobedient once.
> And, Father, a boy touched me once.'
> 'Tell me, child. Was this touch immodest?
> Did he touch your breast, for example?'
> 'He brushed against me, Father. Very gently.'

The poem reflects on the hold of the church, the family, the father and her brother over the young woman. As is the case with so much modern writing, it examines how, in an age when individuals seem to have more freedom, old structures of authority, and power, including the legacy of colonialism and, as we look to the future, American colonialism, still affect and constrain people's lives. There is a sense of how the past manages to maintain its hold over the present, frustrating a movement forward.

16 *Postscript*

The Twenty-First Century

It is far too early to write about the literature of the present century. It is possible, however, to forecast directions and concerns. When we look at the texts produced at the end of the nineteenth century, we can see how they are beginning to explore the issues and to adopt the formal approaches that will become central in the modernist era. In a similar way, books produced at the end of the twentieth century have laid trails that writers are likely to pursue in the opening decades of the twenty-first century.

The first point it is necessary to come to terms with is that the United States, rather than Britain, is, and will continue to be, the centre for books written in English. Indeed, these days it is essential to register the difference between English Literature and Literature in English. This book has focused on English Literature, but in the future it might become the standard approach to focus on the tremendous variety of works from many countries that happen to be written in English. Against this broader background, we suggest – although we might be proved totally wrong – that it is unlikely that a major English novelist, poet or playwright will emerge in the course of the next twenty years. If a major writer does emerge in Britain, this will be an outsider in some way, a writer with a far from straightforward connection with the dominant literary tradition (for example, it could be a Welsh, Scottish or Irish author). Writers such as Peter Ackroyd, Julian Barnes and Will Self are interesting, but it is difficult to see them providing a fresh direction for the novel in the same way that, for example, Joyce changed it in 1922 with the publication of *Ulysses*; they are essentially extending the tradition rather than changing it. This, however, is a state of affairs that we have grown used to in Britain, just as we have grown used to the fact that the vacuum at the centre of British literary culture creates all kinds of opportunities for writers on the margins. For example, a work such as *Trainspotting* (1993), by Irvine Welsh, who is Scottish, dealing with an Edinburgh-based drug culture, confronts us with the diversity of modern Britain. This kind of novel, however, although important and popular, is usually a fairly modest project.

In this respect, Welsh's novels can be contrasted with the novels of Salman Rushdie. When *Midnight's Children* (1981) appeared, there was an immediate realisation that this was a major text and, in an ambitious way, quite unlike anything published before. *Midnight's Children* is a history of India since independence, this story coinciding with the narrator's personal history: Saleem Sinai was born on 15 August 1947, in the first hour that an independent India came into existence. When the novel, a Western European genre, usually focusing on the relationship between individuals and society, is relocated in a different geographical and cultural context, it either lamely echoes the original model, or, as is the case with *Midnight's Children*, mutates into something different. Rushdie does not offer a linear, realistic history of modern India. On the contrary, employing an approach that might be referred to as fabulation or magic realism, he presents a bizarre, disconcerting tale, with strange characters, odd events, and plot developments that defy any conventional logic. Rushdie's approach to narration establishes a distance from the conventions of Western story-telling, an approach that is relevant to his subject matter as a history of India inevitably must dwell on the continuing ramifications of the relationship between the coloniser and the colonised. A central aspect of this is linguistic, *Midnight's Children* exploring the divergence between Western and Indian forms of the English language.

The result is a book that belongs in two traditions. *Midnight's Children* belongs in the history of Indian literature, but it also belongs in the history of English literature. It does justice to Indian history, but also, both in terms of its formal and structural qualities and in its subject matter, reflects back on the West. In the East, the political implications of Rushdie's work have received most attention, something that certainly proved to be the case with *The Satanic Verses*

(1988), a novel about modern-day Pakistan that led to demands for the book to be banned and to death threats to Rushdie that forced him to go into hiding for a number of years. In the West, the response to *Midnight's Children* and *The Satanic Verses* is rather different. The Western reader is interested in the representations of the societies depicted, but is also conscious of how the structure of the novels reflects on how we order experience; this is echoed in the way that Rushdie's analysis of Asian society alerts us to the nature of the values and codes we construct in our own society. There is a similar effect of dealing primarily with Indian life but also, in the process, offering an oblique commentary on British life and the English novel, in the works of two more outstanding Indian novelists, albeit that Vikram Seth, in *A Suitable Boy* (1993) and Arundhati Roy, in *The God of Small Things* (1997), employ a rather more traditional manner of narration than Rushdie.

A fuller account of current literature would also demand consideration of a number of Black-British and Asian-British writers. Caryl Phillips, born in St Kitts, but who has lived in Britain since childhood, has produced novels focusing on colonialism and the legacy of colonialism. These include *The Final Passage* (1985), *A State of Independence* (1986), *Cambridge* (1991) and *The Nature of Blood* (1997). While Phillips's works move back and forth between Britain and the West Indies, Hanif Kureishi, with an English mother and a Pakistani father, who has written plays, the screenplay of *My Beautiful Laundrette* (filmed 1985), and novels including *The Buddha of Suburbia* (1990), *The Black Album* (1995) and *Intimacy* (1998), focuses more on cross-generational differences in multicultural Britain. These can take a surprising form. Kureishi's screenplay *My Son the Fanatic* (1998) deals with the conflict between a liberal-minded immigrant and his son, who is a fundamentalist convert. Buchi Emecheta, born in Nigeria, moved to London at the age of twenty. Her novels include *In the Ditch* (1972), *The Bride Price* (1976), and *Gwendolen* (1989). *The Joys of Motherhood* (1979) deals with the struggles of Nnu Ego to raise a family; in looking at her as the mother of nine children, the novel amounts to an account of her long martyrdom. As with Emecheta's other novels, also set in West Africa, there is both compassion and anger in her advocacy of women's rights. There are, obviously, enormous differences between

Phillips, Kureishi and Emecheta (differences that are to some extent
defined by where they choose to locate the events that take place in
their works), but in the case of all three we can see the complexity of
the relationship when one social and cultural tradition encounters
another social and cultural tradition.

If one element in current English literature is the kind of tangential
perspective encountered in the works of these Asian and Black novelists, another is looking back. The British have never been as obsessed
with history as they are at the start of the twenty-first century. If, in
1947, Britain began to lose its identity as a colonial power, for some
years it has, often reluctantly, been trying to adjust to or work out a
new sense of itself as a nation state within Europe. If, at the moment,
the British are uncertain about quite who they are and where they
stand (particularly following devolution and the continuing debate
about Europe), it is the past that can help give some meaning to the
present. In literature, a central aspect of this has been the emergence
of a certain kind of historical novel that finds parallels between the
past and present, but also reflects on the differences between the past
and present. A typical example is Rose Tremain's *Restoration* (1989),
a novel set at the court of Charles II, following the rise and fall in
the fortunes of Robert Merivel. Banished from the court, he
embarks upon a painful journey of self-discovery. The novel is, to
some extent, a mirror held up to the excesses of the 1980s, contrast-
ing materialism and cynicism with a quest for a more substantial
direction in life.

A. S. Byatt's *Possession: A Romance* (1990) returns to the Victorian
period in order to consider, indirectly, Britain at the end of the twentieth century. In particular, it explores how Victorian ideas about
gender relations correspond with but also differ from our own per-
ceptions. But there is also, in a novel that focuses on twentieth-century academics researching the relationship between a Victorian poet
and his mistress, a consideration of the values and codes of conduct
that are encountered in two different historical contexts. Peter
Ackroyd, in novels including *Hawksmoor* (1985), *Chatterton* (1987), *The
House of Doctor Dee* (1993), and *Milton in America* (1990), is another
writer whose interest in the past is really motivated by his interest in
the present. Significantly, Ackroyd is also a literary biographer, with

subjects including Dickens (1990), William Blake (1995) and Thomas More (1998), and, curiously but very interestingly, a biography of London (2000). These are always mould-breaking biographies, in which, alongside meticulous research, Ackroyd does not hesitate to employ the imaginative approach of a novelist. The result, to a greater extent than in a conventional biography, is an active sense of how the past connects with, yet is different from, the present. Among other novelists who look at the past in the manner outlined here are Barry Unsworth (*Sacred Hunger*, 1993), Sebastian Faulks (*Birdsong*, 1993), Pat Barker (*The Regeneration Trilogy*, 1996), and Michael Ondaatje (*The English Patient*, 1993).

If there is one period that is returned to more than any other it is the four years of the First World War. That is the moment when Britain was still a great power but also started to lose its status as a world power. The novel in Western Europe is a genre whose ascendance corresponds entirely with the emergence and consolidation of the nation state within the continent. The present condition of the English novel, it can be argued, is both a reflection of and a comment upon current uncertainties in Britain, including uncertainties about the country's status as a nation state. In short, we have a national literature that reflects confusion and a lack of direction. Given this state of affairs, it is those works that look back and those works that offer a tangential perspective that seem to deliver most. It is with these ideas in mind that we can turn to the poetry of Seamus Heaney. Heaney, from Northern Ireland, but who sees himself as Irish, writes from the margin, and in all his works, but most clearly in his recent translation of *Beowulf* (1999), is always drawn to looking back.

By general assent the outstanding poet of his generation, Heaney has published numerous collections of work, including *Death of a Naturalist* (1966), *Field Work* (1979), *The Haw Lantern* (1987), *The Spirit Level* (1996) and *Electric Light* (2001). He was awarded the Nobel Prize for Literature in 1995. There is a double quality to Heaney, who can be accommodated in an English tradition but also needs to be seen in an Irish tradition. His work is often a consideration of his native soil, his own complicated relationship to it, and the conflicts that have been fought on and over that soil. His translation of *Beowulf* is a means, albeit an indirect means, of writing about conflict between close neighbours. At the same time, at the start of a new millennium, it looks back across more than a thousand years of English literature, calling upon the past; the past will not illuminate or solve the problems of the present, but has to be considered. As we start the twenty-first century, English literature, including works by authors such as Rushdie and Heaney, which, with more than a touch of colonial arrogance, we continue to appropriate into English literature, seems fixated with self-analysis and self-dissection, as we continue to strive towards an understanding of who we are and where we stand now.

Periods of English Literature and Language

When discussing the English language, linguists usually distinguish just three periods:

Old English	450–1100
Middle English	1100–1500
Modern English	1500–

When discussing the periods of English literature, the following terms are generally used:

Old English literature	450–1066
Middle English literature	1066–1485
Renaissance literature	1485–1660
Restoration literature	1660–1700
Augustan/Eighteenth-century literature	1700–1789
Romantic literature	1789–1837
Victorian literature	1837–1880
Late Victorian literature	1880–1900
Twentieth-century literature	1900–1999

We can subdivide this last:

Edwardian literature	1900–1914
Modernism	1914–1930
The thirties	1930–1939
The forties	1940–1949
Post-war literature	1945–

Some critics prefer to emphasise literary events over historical events when describing periods. For example, the Romantic period might be said to begin in 1798, with the publication of the *Lyrical Ballads* by

Wordsworth and Coleridge, or in 1789, the date of the French Revolution. Similarly, different events can be chosen, so that the Victorian period might be said to begin in 1832 with the Reform Bill rather than in 1837 with the coming of Victoria to the throne. Generally, however, there is agreement about the terms and approximate dates used.

Chronology

Dates for texts from earlier periods are often only approximate, as, for example, with Chaucer's poems and Shakespeare's plays. There is also the problem that many texts circulated in manuscript. In the outline below, first names of authors are given for their first but not subsequent entries (not every work by every author is listed). Unless stated otherwise, the date is that of publication. In the case of serial publication, the date used is that of the first instalment.

407	Romans withdraw their forces from Britain to protect Rome
410	Sacking of Rome by Goths
c.425	Raids by Angles, Saxons and Jutes (northern Germanic tribes)
449	Jutes settle in Kent
450	The coming of the Saxons to England to settle in Wessex
597	St Augustine's mission to convert England to Christianity arrives in Kent
664	Synod of Whitby accepts Roman Catholicism as the established religion
c.670	**Caedmon's** *Hymn* (earliest surviving record of oral Anglo-Saxon poetry)
c.700	Seven kingdoms established in England: Northumbria, Mercia, East Anglia, Essex, Kent, Sussex, Wessex
c.720	Lindisfarne Gospels in Latin (Anglo-Saxon gloss added in tenth century)

731	**Bede**, *Ecclesiastical History of the English People (Historia Ecclesiastica Gentis Anglorum)*
735	Death of Bede
c.750	*Beowulf* composed
779	Offa becomes king of all of England
793	Viking raids begin; sacking of Lindisfarne
796	Death of Offa of Mercia
871	Alfred becomes King of Wessex
871	*Anglo-Saxon Chronicle* (history) begun
899	Death of Alfred
960	Dunstan becomes Archbishop of Canterbury
991	The Battle of Maldon
992	**Aelfric**, *Catholic Homilies* (sermons translated from Latin)
1000	Date of the four major surviving manuscript copies of Anglo-Saxon poetry: Exeter (c.970), Vercelli (c.975), Cædmon, and *Beowulf* manuscripts
1042	Accession of Edward the Confessor
1066	Death of Edward the Confessor; accession of Harold; defeats Harold Hardrada (King of Norway) at Stamford Bridge but is defeated at Battle of Hastings; William of Normandy becomes King of England
1070	Lanfranc becomes Archbishop of Canterbury
1086	Domesday Book (survey of England) compiled
1087	Accession of William II
1096	First Crusade (following appeal by the Pope to Christian nations to free the 'Holy Places' from the Muslims); crusades end 1291
1099	Crusaders capture Jerusalem
1100	Death of William II; accession of Henry I
1135	Death of Henry I; accession of Stephen
1138	**Geoffrey of Monmouth**, *History of the Kings of Britain (Historia Regum Britanniae)*

1147	Second Crusade
1152	Future Henry II marries Eleanor of Aquitaine
1154	Death of Stephen; accession of Henry II (start of the House of Plantagenet)
1154	**Wace**, *Roman de Brut* (history of Britain); End of the *Peterborough Chronicle*, last branch of the *Anglo-Saxon Chronicle*
1169	Invasion of Ireland by Norman barons
1170	Murder of Thomas à Becket (St Thomas)
c.1184	**Andreas Capellanus**, *De Amore* (on courtly love)
1187	Saracens recapture Jerusalem
c.1188	**Gervase**, *History of Canterbury*
1189	Death of Henry II; accession of Richard I
1189	Third Crusade
1199	Death of Richard I; accession of John
c.1200	*The Owl and the Nightingale*; **Laȝamon**, *Brut* (history of Britain); **Jocelin de Brakelond**, *Chronicle*
1202	Fourth Crusade
1204	Loss of Normandy by English crown; Crusaders sack Constantinople (Byzantium)
1215	Magna Carta signed (defines limitations on royal power: a freeman may not be imprisoned or punished except by law)
1216	Death of John; accession of Henry III
1217	Fifth Crusade
c.1220	*Ancrene Riwle* (devotional manual)
1221–4	Dominican and Franciscan friars arrive in England
c.1225	*King Horn* (English verse romance)
1228	Sixth Crusade (Jerusalem recaptured)
1244	Egyptians capture Jerusalem from Christians
1272	Death of Henry III; accession of Edward I
c.1275	**Guillaume de Lorris**, *Roman de la Rose* (dream-vision: poem, allegory of love affair)
1291	Saracens recapture Acre: end of Crusades
1307?	**Dante Alighieri**, *Divina Commedia* (*Divine Comedy*) (1307?–1321)

1314	Battle of Bannockburn (Robert the Bruce defeats the English)
1327	Accession of Edward III
1327	Petrarch sees Laura in church; inspiration behind his sonnets (the *Canzoniere* or *Rime sparse* published in 1470–1)
1337	Edward II declares himself king of France following attacks on his French territories: beginning of Hundred Years War between England and France (ends 1451)
c.1343	Birth of Geoffrey Chaucer
c.1344	Founding of Order of Garter
1346	Defeat of French by English at Battle of Crecy
1349	The Black Death (bubonic plague) in England; wipes out one-third of population in Europe
1349	Giovanni **Boccaccio**, *The Decameron* (1349–51)
1360	Edward III gives up his claim to the French throne
1362	English displaces French as the language of the law courts and Parliament
1367	William **Langland**, *Piers Plowman* (A Text)
c.1369	**Chaucer**, *Book of the Duchess*
c.1373	**Julian of Norwich**, *Sixteen Revelations of Divine Love* (revised 1393?)
c.1375	*Sir Gawain and the Green Knight*
1376	Earliest reference to the York cycle of mystery plays
1377	Death of Edward III; accession of Richard II
c.1377	**Langland**, *Piers Plowman* (B Text)
c.1380	(Wycliffe's?) English translation of the Bible
1381	The Peasants' Revolt (led by Wat Tyler) against serfdom (people tied to the land as part of the property of a lord)
1384	Death of John Wycliffe
c.1385	**Chaucer**, *Troilus and Criseyde*
c.1385–6	**Langland**, *Piers Plowman* (C Text)
c.1387	**Chaucer** begins *The Canterbury Tales*
1390	John **Gower**, *Confessio Amantis*
1394	Birth of Charles d'Orleans and James I of Scotland
1399	Richard II deposed; accession of Henry IV (House of Lancaster)

1400	Death of Chaucer; murder of Richard II
c.1400	Only surviving manuscript of the four alliterative poems *Sir Gawain*, *Pearl*, *Cleanness*, and *Patience*
1408	Death of Gower
1411–12	Thomas **Hoccleve**, *The Regiment of Princes*
1413	Death of Henry IV; accession of Henry V
1415	Henry V revives claim to French throne; defeats French at Battle of Agincourt
1422	Death of Henry V; accession of Henry VI
1422	Earliest reference to the Chester cycle of mystery plays
1426	Death of Hoccleve
1429	Joan of Arc raises Siege of Orleans
1439	Joan of Arc burnt as a witch at Rouen, Normandy
1431–8	John **Lydgate**, *The Fall of Princes*
1432–8	Margery **Kempe**, *Book of Margery Kempe*
c.1435	**James Stewart**, *The Kingis Quair*
1440	Johann Gutenberg invents printing with movable type
1449	Death of Lydgate
1451	End of Hundred Years war between England and France
1453	Battle of Castillon; loss of last English territory in France; Fall of Constantinople to the Turks
1455	Wars of the Roses begin (end 1485)
1461	Henry VI deposed; Edward IV becomes king (House of York)
1470–1	Henry VI restored to throne
1470–1	**Petrarch**, *Canzoniere*, *Trionfi* (both written 1327–74)
1471	Henry VI murdered; Edward IV regains throne
1471	Death of Sir Thomas Malory
1473–4	William Caxton, *Recuyell of the Historyes of Troye* (*History of Troy*), the first book printed in English
1483	Death of Edward IV; accession and presumed murder of Edward V; accession of Richard III
1484	Witchcraft declared a heresy
1485	Richard III defeated at Battle of Bosworth (end of Wars of the Roses); accession of Henry VII (start of the Tudors)

1485	Caxton prints **Malory**'s *Le Morte D'Arthur*
*c.*1490	Date of manuscript of Towneley (Wakefield) mystery plays
1492–1504	Christopher Columbus discovers America
*c.*1500	John **Skelton**, *Bouge of Court*
*c.*1500	Date of manuscript of N-Town mystery plays
1504	Colet becomes Dean of St Paul's
*c.*1504	**Skelton**, *Philip Sparrow*
1508	Michelangelo begins painting ceiling of Sistine Chapel in the Vatican (completed 1512)
1509	Death of Henry VII; accession of Henry VIII
*c.*1510	*Everyman* printed
1513	Battle of Flodden (defeat of Scots by Henry VIII)
1513	Gavin Douglas, translation of Virgil's *Aeneid*; Niccolò **Machiavelli**, *Il Principe* (*The Prince*) (English translation 1640)
1516	Sir Thomas **More**, *Utopia* (Latin version; political/philosophical treatise); **Skelton**, *Magnyfycence*
1517	Martin Luther publishes 95 theses at Wittenberg challenging sale of indulgences (pardons for sins); start of Reformation (reform of church) leading to Protestantism
1520	Field of the Cloth of Gold (meeting of Henry VIII and Francis I in France to arrange an alliance in a setting of splendour); Henry VIII proclaimed 'Defender of the Faith' by Pope Leo X
1521	Luther condemned as a heretic by the Pope; publishes a Protestant translation of the New Testament
1523	**Skelton**, *Garlande of Laurell*
1526	William Tyndale prints the first Protestant New Testament in English
1528	Baldassare **Castiglione**, *Il Cortegiano* (*The Courtier*: prose dialogues discussing the ideal qualities of the courtier)
1529	Fall of Thomas Wolsey, Archbishop of York; Thomas Cromwell becomes Chief Minister; More becomes Lord Chancellor

1531	Sir Thomas **Elyot**, *Boke named the Governour* (treatise on education and politics)
1533	Cranmer becomes Archbishop of Canterbury; Henry VIII divorces Catherine of Aragon, marries Anne Boleyn, and is excommunicated.
1534	Final break with Rome; Henry makes himself 'Supreme Head of the Church' in England
1535	Execution of Thomas More for refusing to recognise Henry VIII's divorce
1535	Thomas **Coverdale**'s translation of the Bible
1536	Execution of Anne Boleyn; William Tyndale burned to death in the Netherlands; Union of England and Wales; John Calvin leads Protestants in Geneva (beginning of Calvinism, a strict form of Protestantism); Thomas Cromwell supervises Dissolution of the Monasteries in England
1540	Institution of the Society of Jesus (Jesuits); Thomas Cromwell executed
1542	Accession of Mary Queen of Scots on death of James V of Scotland
1542	First edition of Edward **Hall**'s chronicle history, *The Union of the Two Noble and Ilustre Families of Lancaster and York* (traces rise of the Tudors as if a matter of divine providence)
1543	Copernicus's theory of the sun as centre of the solar system
1545	(Catholic) Council of Trent (start of the Counter-Reformation to reform the Catholic Church and counter the growth of Protestantism)
1547	Death of Henry VIII; accession of Edward VI
1549	Act of Uniformity, imposing uniform religious practices
1549	Thomas Cranmer, (Protestant) Book of Common Prayer
1552	Birth of Edmund Spenser
1553	Death of Edward VI; accession of Mary I (Catholic)
1554	Roman Catholicism re-established in England by Parliament

1555–6	Executions of Cranmer, Ridley, and Hugh Latimer (Protestant reformer)
1556	Stationers' Company gains monopoly of English printing
1557	Richard **Tottel**'s edition of *Songes and Sonettes* ('Tottel's Miscellany'), includes poems by Sir Thomas **Wyatt**; Earl of **Surrey**'s translation of *Aeneid*, II and IV
1558	Crown loses control of Calais; death of Mary I; accession of Elizabeth I
1558–9	Martin Marprelate pamphlets (attacking bishops)
1559	Religious reform in Scotland (Calvinism); Religious Settlement in England (Protestantism re-established)
1560	'Geneva' Bible (favoured by Puritans)
1561	Sir William Hoby's translation of Castiglione's *The Courtyer*; Thomas **Sackville** and Thomas **Norton**, *Gorboduc*
1563	Plague in London kills many
1563	John **Foxe**, *Actes and Monuments* (about Protestant martyrdom)
1564	William Shakespeare born; Christopher Marlowe born
1567	Red Lion playhouse opens
1568	Bishops' Bible (Anglican)
1570	Excommunication of Elizabeth I by the Pope
1570	Roger **Ascham**, *The Scholemaster* (education manual)
1571	Battle of Lepanto (Turkish fleet destroyed)
1572	St Bartholomew's Day massacre of Protestants in Paris; Birth of John Donne
1576	The Theatre opens
1577	Francis Drake sets out on circumnavigation of world
1577	Raphael **Holinshed**, *Chronicles Of England Scotland and Ireland* (history); Sir Philip **Sidney**, 'Old' *Arcadia* (1577–81)
1578	John **Lyly**, *Euphues: The Anatomy of Wit*; second part *Euphues and his England* published 1580
1579	**Spenser**, *The Shepheardes Calender*
1579–80	**Sidney**, *Defence of Poesie* (published 1595; also under the title *An Apologie for Poetrie*)
1580	Performance of plays on Sundays forbidden
1582	**Sidney**, *Astrophil and Stella* (published 1591)

1583–4	**Sidney**, 'New' *Arcadia* (published 1590)
1585	Sir Walter Ralegh establishes first colony in Virginia
1586	Death of Sidney at Zutphen
1587	Execution of Mary Queen of Scots; opening of Rose Theatre
1587	Christopher **Marlowe** *Tamburlaine* Part I acted (published 1590); William **Camden**, *Britannia* (description of Britain)
c.1587	Thomas **Kyd**, *The Spanish Tragedy* (published 1592)
1588	Defeat of Spanish Armada
1589	George **Puttenham**, *Arte of English Poesie* (treatise on criticism); Thomas **Hakluyt**, *The Principal Navigations, Voyages, Traffiques and Discoveries of the English Nation*; Thomas **Lodge**, *Rosalynde*.
1590	**Spenser**, *The Faerie Queene* (I–III)
1590–1	**Shakespeare**, 2, 3 *Henry VI*,
1591–2	**Shakespeare**, 1 *Henry VI*,
1592?	**Marlowe**, *Doctor Faustus* (published 1604, with additions 1616)
1592	Plague closes theatres for two years
1592	Thomas **Kyd**, *The Spanish Tragedy*; Samuel **Daniel**, *Delia*; **Shakespeare**, *Richard III*, *Comedy of Errors*
1593	Death of Marlowe
1593	**Marlowe**, *Hero and Leander* (published 1598); **Shakespeare**, *Venus and Adonis*; Michael **Drayton**, *Idea's Mirror*; Richard **Hooker**, *Laws of Ecclesiastical Polity* (I–IV) (defence of Church of England); **Sidney**, *Arcadia* (Old and New combined)
1593–4	**Shakespeare**, *Titus Andronicus*, *Taming of the Shrew*, *Two Gentlemen of Verona*
1594	Death of Kyd; Lord Chamberlain's men established (Shakespeare's acting company)
1594	Thomas **Nashe**, *The Unfortunate Traveller*
1594–5	**Shakespeare**, *Love's Labours Lost*, *Romeo and Juliet*
1595	Samuel **Daniel**, *Civil Wars* (I–IV); Sir John **Davies**, *Orchestra*; **Shakespeare**, *Sonnets* (published 1609); **Spenser**, *Amoretti*, *Epithalamion*
1595–6	**Shakespeare**, *A Midsummer Night's Dream*

1596	Blackfriars Theatre opens
1596	**Spenser**, *Faerie Queene* (IV–VI)
1596–7	**Shakespeare**, *King John, The Merchant of Venice*
1597	Francis **Bacon**, *Essays*
1597	**Shakespeare**, *Richard II*
1597–8	**Shakespeare** 1, 2 *Henry IV*
1598	George **Chapman**–Christopher **Marlowe**, *Hero and Leander*; John **Stow**, *Survey of London*; Ben **Jonson**, *Everyman in His Humour* (first version); **Daniel**, *Poetical Essays*, Thomas **Nashe**, *Lenten Stuffe*
1598–9	**Shakespeare**, *Much Ado About Nothing, Henry V*
1599	Globe Theatre opens
1599	Oliver Cromwell born
1599–1600	**Shakespeare**, *Julius Caesar, The Merry Wives of Windsor, As You Like It*
1600–1	**Shakespeare**, *Hamlet, Measure for Measure, Twelfth Night*
1601	Rebellion of Earl of Essex against Elizabeth (and his execution)
1601–2	**Shakespeare**, *Troilus and Cressida*
1602–3	**Shakespeare**, *All's Well That Ends Well*
1603	Death of Elizabeth; accession of James VI of Scotland as James I of England (start of the Stuarts); union of the crowns of England and Scotland
1603	**Jonson**, *Sejanus*
1604	Peace between England and Spain (at war since 1587)
1604	**Shakespeare**, *Othello*
1605	Gunpowder plot; Jonson's first court masque with Inigo Jones
1605	**Jonson,** *Volpone* acted (published 1607); **Bacon**, *The Advancement of Learning*; Saavedra **Cervantes**, *Don Quixote* (1605, 1615); **Shakespeare**, *King Lear*
1605–6	**Shakespeare**, *Macbeth*
1606	Virginia Company granted charter
1606–7	**Shakespeare**, *Antony and Cleopatra*
1607	Thomas **Middleton** (or Cyril Tourneur), *The Revenger's Tragedy*

1583–4	**Sidney**, 'New' *Arcadia* (published 1590)
1585	Sir Walter Ralegh establishes first colony in Virginia
1586	Death of Sidney at Zutphen
1587	Execution of Mary Queen of Scots; opening of Rose Theatre
1587	Christopher **Marlowe** *Tamburlaine* Part I acted (published 1590); William **Camden**, *Britannia* (description of Britain)
c.1587	Thomas **Kyd**, *The Spanish Tragedy* (published 1592)
1588	Defeat of Spanish Armada
1589	George **Puttenham**, *Arte of English Poesie* (treatise on criticism); Thomas **Hakluyt**, *The Principal Navigations, Voyages, Traffiques and Discoveries of the English Nation*; Thomas **Lodge**, *Rosalynde*.
1590	**Spenser**, *The Faerie Queene* (I–III)
1590–1	**Shakespeare**, *2, 3 Henry VI*,
1591–2	**Shakespeare**, *1 Henry VI*,
1592?	**Marlowe**, *Doctor Faustus* (published 1604, with additions 1616)
1592	Plague closes theatres for two years
1592	Thomas **Kyd**, *The Spanish Tragedy*; Samuel **Daniel**, *Delia*; **Shakespeare**, *Richard III, Comedy of Errors*
1593	Death of Marlowe
1593	**Marlowe**, *Hero and Leander* (published 1598); **Shakespeare**, *Venus and Adonis*; Michael **Drayton**, *Idea's Mirror*; Richard **Hooker**, *Laws of Ecclesiastical Polity* (I–IV) (defence of Church of England); **Sidney**, *Arcadia* (Old and New combined)
1593–4	**Shakespeare**, *Titus Andronicus, Taming of the Shrew, Two Gentlemen of Verona*
1594	Death of Kyd; Lord Chamberlain's men established (Shakespeare's acting company)
1594	Thomas **Nashe**, *The Unfortunate Traveller*
1594–5	**Shakespeare**, *Love's Labours Lost, Romeo and Juliet*
1595	Samuel **Daniel**, *Civil Wars* (I–IV); Sir John **Davies**, *Orchestra*; **Shakespeare**, *Sonnets* (published 1609); **Spenser**, *Amoretti, Epithalamion*
1595–6	**Shakespeare**, *A Midsummer Night's Dream*

1607–8	**Shakespeare**, *Coriolanus, Timon of Athens*
1608	Birth of John Milton; **Shakespeare**, *Pericles*
1609	**Jonson**, *Epicene*; **Shakespeare**'s sonnets published; **Spenser**, *The Faerie Queene*; **Jonson**, *The Masque of Queens*
1610	**Shakespeare**, *Cymbeline*; **Donne**, *Pseudo-Martyr* (attack on Catholic martyrs); **Jonson**, *The Alchemist*
1610–11	**Shakespeare**, *The Winter's Tale*
1611	Colonisation of Ulster
1611	Authorised Version of Bible (King James Bible)
1611	**Shakespeare**, *The Tempest*; Cyril **Tourneur**, *The Atheist's Tragedy*; George **Chapman**, *The Revenge of Bussy D'Ambois*; Aemilia **Lanier**, *Salve Deus Rex Iudaeorum*
1612	Last recorded burning of heretics in England
1612	John **Webster**, *The White Devil*
1612–13	**Shakespeare**, *Henry VIII, The Two Noble Kinsmen*
1613	Globe Theatre burned down
1614	Sir Walter **Ralegh**, *The History of the World*; **Jonson**, *Bartholomew Fair*
1616	Death of Shakespeare; Ben **Jonson**, *Works*
1617	**Webster**, *The Duchess of Malfi*
1618	Execution of Ralegh; Beginning of Thirty Years War in Europe between Catholics and Protestants
1620	Puritan Pilgrim Fathers reach America
1621	John Donne becomes Dean of St Paul's
1621	Robert **Burton**, *Anatomy of Melancholy* (wide-ranging enquiry into the melancholic mind); Mary **Wroth**, *Urania*; Thomas **Middleton**, *Women Beware Women*
1622	**Middleton**, *The Changeling*
1623	First Folio of **Shakespeare**'s *Complete Works*
1625	Death of James I; accession of Charles I
1625	Samuel **Purchas**, *Purchas his Pilgrimes*
1629	Charles I dissolves Parliament; assumes personal rule until 1640
1631	**Milton**, 'L'Allegro', 'Il Penseroso'
1633	William Laud becomes Archbishop of Canterbury
1633	John **Donne**, *Poems*; John **Ford**, *'Tis Pity She's a Whore*; George **Herbert**, *The Temple*

1634	**Milton**'s *Comus* performed
1635	Francis **Quarles**, *Emblems* (moral poems with engravings)
1637	**Milton**, *Lycidas*
1640	Long Parliament called (lasted until 1653)
1642	Charles I attempts to arrest five Puritan Members of Parliament opposed to his powers; beginning of English Civil War; theatres closed by Parliament
1642	**Milton**, *The Reason of Church Government* (pamphlet on role of church)
1644	Battle of Marston Moor; victory of Parliamentary Army (turning point in Civil War)
1644	**Milton**, *Areopagitica* (pamphlet on the subject of the freedom of the press)
1645	Execution of Laud; Cromwell's Model Army defeats Charles I at Naseby
1646	Charles surrenders to Scots
1646	William **Crashaw**, *Steps to the Temple*
1647	Charles escapes and makes deal with Scots; Scots hand over Charles to Parliament
1647	Abraham **Cowley**, *The Mistress*
1648	Rump Parliament (consisting of those MPs still opposed to the King); Scots invade England; defeated at Preston
1648	Robert **Herrick**, *Hesperides*
1649	Trial and execution of Charles I; England a Commonwealth; Church of England no longer recognised as the state religion
1649	Richard **Lovelace**, *Lucasta*
1649–52	Cromwell's military campaigns in Ireland and Scotland
1649	Andrew **Marvell**, 'An Horation Ode'; Henry **Vaughan**, *Silex Scintillans*
1650	Thomas **Hobbes** (political philosopher), *Leviathan* (treatise on political philosophy)
1653	Cromwell becomes Lord Protector (in place of a king)
1653	Ann **Collins**, *Divine Songs and Meditations*
1656	James **Harrington**, *The Commonwealth of Oceana* (analysis of a utopian republic)

1658	Death of Cromwell; Richard Cromwell succeeds his father but forced to resign by army; recall of Rump Parliament
1660	End of Civil War; Charles II restored to throne by Parliament; reopening of theatres
1660	John **Dryden**, *Astraea Redux*; Samuel **Pepys** starts his diary
1662	Restoration of Church of England; final revision of Book of Common Prayer; Royal Society for Science founded
1664	War between Britain and Holland
1664	Katherine **Philips**, *Poems*
1665	Great Plague in London
1666	Great Fire of London destroys the City
1667	**Dryden**, *Annus Mirabilis*; **Milton**, *Paradise Lost*
1670	Aphra **Behn**, *The Forced Marriage*
1671	**Milton**, *Paradise Regained*, *Samson Agonistes*
1675	John Wilmot, Earl of **Rochester**, 'A Satyre against Mankind'; William **Wycherley**, *The Country Wife*
1677	**Dryden**, *All for Love*
1677	**Behn**, *The Rover* (1677–81)
1678	John **Bunyan**, *The Pilgrim's Progress* (Part 1)
1679	Habeas Corpus Act against arbitrary imprisonment of citizens
1680	**Rochester**, *Poems*
1681	Lord Shaftesbury tried for treason: acquitted
1681	**Marvell**'s *Miscellaneous Poems* posthumously published; **Dryden**, *Absolom and Achitophel*
1682	**Dryden**, *MacFlecknoe*
1685	Death of Charles II; accession of James II (brother of Charles and fanatical Catholic); Duke of Monmouth's (illegitimate son of Charles II, Protestant) rebellion crushed at Sedgemoor; last recorded burning of a witch in England
1687	Sir Isaac **Newton**, *Philosophiae Naturalis Principia Mathematica* (scientific treatise on gravity and the solar system)

1688	'Glorious Revolution' in England; William III of the Netherlands invited to become king to save country from Catholicism; James II flees to France; William III and Mary II succeed
*c.*1688	**Behn**, *Oroonoko*
1690	John **Locke**, *Essay Concerning Human Understanding*
1690	Battle of the Boyne in Ireland – defeat of exiled James II by William III
1694	Death of Mary II
1695	William **Congreve**, *Love for Love*
1698	Jeremy **Collier**, *A Short View of the Immorality and Profaneness of the English Stage* (attack on Restoration comedy for indecency)
1700	**Congreve**, *The Way of the World*
1701	War of Spanish Succession; Great Britain allied with Holland against France
1701	Act of Settlement, that all future monarchs belong to the Church of England
1702	Death of William III; accession of Anne (James I's grand-daughter)
1702	Edward Hyde, Earl of **Clarendon**, *The True Historical Narrative of the Rebellion and Civil Wars in England* (1702–3)
1704	Duke of Marlborough's victory at Blenheim against the French
1704	Jonathan **Swift**, *The Battle of the Books* and *A Tale of a Tub*
1706	George **Farquhar**, *The Recruiting Officer*
1707	Act of Union between England and Scotland
1707	**Farquhar**, *The Beaux Stratagem*
1709	Richard **Steele** (and others), *The Tatler* (periodical)
1710	St Paul's Cathedral (Wren) completed
1710	Earl of **Shaftesbury**, *Characteristicks of Men, Manners, Opinions, Times* (prose writings on morals)
1711–12	Joseph **Addison** and Richard **Steele**, *The Spectator* (periodical)
1711	Alexander **Pope**, *Essay on Criticism*
1712	**Pope**, *The Rape of the Lock*

1713	Peace of Utrecht ends War of Spanish Succession
1713	Anne **Finch**, *Miscellany Poems*; **Congreve**, *Incognita*
1714	Death of Anne; accession of George I, Elector of Hanover (start of house of Hanover)
1715	Jacobite Rebellion in favour of James Edward (the 'Old Pretender', son of James II)
1716–18	Lady Mary Wortley **Montagu**, *Letters* (published 1763)
1717	**Pope**, *Works*
1719	Daniel **Defoe**, *Robinson Crusoe*
1720	South Sea Bubble – thousands of investors lose money
1720	**Pope**, translation of *The Iliad*
1721	Sir Robert Walpole, first British prime minister
1722	**Defoe**, *Moll Flanders* and *Journal of the Plague Year*
1726	**Swift**, *Gulliver's Travels*; James **Thomson**, *Winter* (first of *The Seasons*, 1726–30)
1727	Death of George I; accession of George II; Walpole remains in power; death of Isaac Newton
1728	John **Gay**, *Beggar's Opera*; **Pope**, *Dunciad* (first version)
1729	**Swift**, A. *Modest Proposal*
1733–4	**Pope**, *Essay on Man*
1735	**Pope**, 'An Epistle from Mr Pope, to Dr Arbuthnot'
1736	Repeal of witchcraft laws
1738	Dr Samuel **Johnson**, *London*
1739	War against Spain
1739	Charles **Wesley** (Methodist leader), first collection of hymns; Lady Mary Wortley **Montagu**, *Letters* (published 1763–7)
1740	War of Austrian Succession begins (Britain sides against France)
1740	Samuel **Richardson**, *Pamela*; **Thomson**, 'Rule Britannia'
1741	Henry **Fielding**, *Shamela*
1742	Fall of Walpole
1742	**Fielding**, *Joseph Andrews*
1742–5	Edward **Young**, *Night Thoughts*
1743	**Pope**, *The Dunciad* (final version)
1744	Sarah **Fielding**, *David Simple*

1745	Second Jacobite Rebellion led by Charles Edward (the 'Young Pretender', Bonnie Prince Charlie, grandson of James II) beaten at Culloden (1746)
1747	**Richardson**, *Clarissa* (1747–8)
1748	Peace of Aix-la-Chapelle ends War of Austrian Succession
1748	Tobias **Smollett**, *Roderick Random*
1749	**Fielding**, *Tom Jones*
1750–2	**Johnson**, *The Rambler* (periodical)
1751	**Smollett**, *Peregrine Pickle*; **Fielding**, *Amelia*; Thomas **Gray**, *Elegy Written in a Country Churchyard*
1752	Charlotte **Lennox**, *The Female Quixote*
1753	**Richardson**, *Sir Charles Grandison* (1753–4)
1755	**Johnson**, *Dictionary*
1756	Beginning of Seven Years War against France
1757	General Clive captures Calcutta and begins British rule in India
1757	Edmund **Burke**, *A Philosophical Enquiry into the Origin of our Ideas of the Sublime and Beautiful* (prose treatise)
1759	British capture Quebec from French
1759	**Johnson**, *Rasselas*
1759	Laurence **Sterne**, *Trstram Shandy* (1759–67)
1760	Death of George II; accession of George III
1763	Peace of Paris ends Seven Years War; British territorial gains in India and North America
1764	Horace **Walpole**, *The Castle of Otranto*
1765	Thomas **Percy**, *Reliques of Ancient English Poetry* (collection of ballads)
1766	Oliver **Goldsmith**, *The Vicar of Wakefield*
1767	Manchester–Liverpool canal
1768	**Sterne**, *A Sentimental Journey*; *Encyclopaedia Britannica* (1768–71)
1769	James Watt's steam engine
1770	James Hargreaves's spinning jenny; Lord North, prime minister; suicide of Thomas Chatterton at 17
1770	**Goldsmith**, *The Deserted Village*
1771	Tobias **Smollett**, *The Expedition of Humphrey Clinker*; Henry **Mackenzie**, *The Man of Feeling*

1773	**Goldsmith**, *She Stoops to Conquer*
1775	First shots of American War of Independence
1775	Birth of Jane Austen; Richard Brinsley **Sheridan**, *The Rivals*
1776	American Declaration of Independence
1776	Edward **Gibbon**, *The History of the Decline and Fall of the Roman Empire* (1776–88)
1777	**Sheridan**, *School for Scandal*; **Reeve**, *The Old English Baron*
1778	Frances (Fanny) **Burney**, *Evelina*
1779	**Johnson**, *The Lives of the Poets* (critical essays) (1779–81)
1780	Gordon Riots (popular riots led by Lord George Gordon against 1778 law to relieve condition of Catholics)
1781	British defeated by Americans at Yorktown
1781	**Sheridan**, *The Critic*; **Burney**, *Cecilia*
1783	Treaty of Paris recognises independence of American Colonies
1785	Edmund Cartwright invents the power loom
1785	*The Times* newspaper begins; William **Cowper**, *The Task*
1786	William **Beckford**, *Vathek*; Robert **Burns**, *Poems, Chiefly in the Scottish Dialect*
1787	Foundation of the Association for the Abolition of the Slave Trade
1788	Mary **Wollstonecraft**, *Mary*; Charlotte **Smith**, *Emmeline*
1789	French Revolution; Fall of Bastille; Declaration of the Rights of Man
1789	William **Blake**, *Songs of Innocence*
1790	Edmund **Burke**, *Reflections on the Revolution in France* (political prose); **Blake**, *The Marriage of Heaven and Hell* (1790–3); **Wollstonecraft**, *A Vindication of the Rights of Men* (political treatise)
1791	Flight of Louis XVI of France
1791	James **Boswell**, *Life of Samuel Johnson*; Thomas **Paine**, *The Rights of Man* (Part I) (political treatise)
1792	Siege of Tuileries (French royal palace); September Massacres of the imprisoned nobility in France; Beginning of Napoleonic Wars

1792	**Wollstonecraft**, *A Vindication of the Rights of Woman* (political treatise); Thomas **Holcroft**, *Anna St Ives*
1793	Execution of Louis XVI; Reign of Terror led by Maximilien de Robespierre; Britain and France at war
1793	**Blake**, *America* (political prose work); William **Godwin**, *Inquiry Concerning Political Justice* (political treatise); Charlotte **Smith**, *The Old Manor House*
1794	Executions of Jean Jacques Danton and Robespierre (ends Reign of Terror in France); suspension of Habeas Corpus Act in Britain; Thomas Holcroft (ardent supporter of French Revolution) found not guilty of treason; French invade Dutch republic and occupy the Netherlands
1794	**Blake**, *Songs of Experience*; **Godwin**, *Caleb Williams*; Ann **Radcliffe**, *The Mysteries of Udolpho*; **Holcroft**, *Hugh Trevor*
1795	5-man Directory rules in France; 'Speenhamland' sytem of poor relief to supplement wages of labouring classes
1795	Birth of John Keats
1796	Napoleon Bonaparte leads French army to conquer Italy; Jenner introduces vaccination against small pox
1796	**Burney**, *Camilla*; Robert **Bage**, *Hermsprong*; Matthew Gregory **Lewis**, *The Monk*
1798	French occupy Rome; rebellion in Ireland by United Irishmen seeking separation from Britain; Battle of the Nile – Nelson defeats French fleet
1798	William **Wordsworth** and Samuel Taylor **Coleridge**, *Lyrical Ballads*; **Wollstonecraft**, *The Wrongs of Woman* (political prose work); **Mary Robinson**, *Thoughts on the Condition of Women, and on the Injustice of Mental Insubordination* (political analysis)
1799	Napoleon Bonaparte becomes First Consul in France
1800	Act of Union with Ireland
1800	Maria **Edgeworth**, *Castle Rackrent*
1801	Union of British and Irish Parliaments; Habeas Corpus Act again suspended

1801	Amelia **Opie**, *The Father and Daughter*
1802	Treaty of Amiens ends war between Britain and France
1802	Sir Walter **Scott**, *Minstrelsy of the Scottish Border* (collection of ballads); the *Edinburgh Review* (periodical) begins; William **Cobbett** starts his *Political Register*; **Opie**, *Poems*
1803	Renewal of war against France
1804	Bonaparte overthrows government and becomes Emperor Napoleon I of France
1804	**Blake**, *Milton* (1804–8)
1805	Battle of Trafalgar – British fleet under Nelson defeats French/Spanish fleet
1805	**Scott**, *The Lay of the Last Minstrel*; **Wordsworth** begins *The Prelude*
1807	Abolition of slave trade in the British empire
1807	**Wordsworth**, *Poems*
1808	Peninsular War in Spain (Britain against France) begins (ends 1814)
1808	**Scott**, *Marmion*; Leigh **Hunt**, *The Examiner* (periodical)
1809	Lord (George Gordon) **Byron**, *English Bards and Scotch Reviewers*; foundation of the *Quarterly Review*
1810	John Dalton (chemist) explains atomic theory and table of atomic weights
1810	George **Crabbe**, *The Borough*; **Scott**, *The Lady of the Lake*
1811	George III declared insane; Prince of Wales becomes Regent; Luddite riots against mechanisation of textile industry
1811	Jane **Austen**, *Sense and Sensibility*
1812	Napoleon invades Russia but is forced to retreat from Moscow; birth of Charles Dickens
1812	George **Crabbe**, *Tales*; **Byron**, *Childe Harold's Pilgrimage*; **Edgeworth**, *The Absentee*; Felicia **Hemans**, *Domestic Affections*
1813	French driven from Spain by Wellington
1813	**Austen**, *Pride and Prejudice*; Percy Bysshe **Shelley**, *Queen Mab*

1814   Napoleon abdicates and is exiled to Elba; restoration of
        Louis XVIII; Robert George Stephenson invents steam
        locomotive

1814   **Wordsworth**, *The Excursion*; **Byron**, *The Corsair*;
        Austen, *Mansfield Park*; **Scott**, *Waverley*; **Burney**, *The
        Wanderer*

1815   Wellington defeats Napoleon at Battle of Waterloo;
        English Corn Laws against cheap imports

1815   **Wordsworth**, *Poems*; **Scott**, *Guy Mannering*

1816   **Coleridge**, *Christabel* and *Kubla Khan*; **Shelley**, *Alastor*;
        Austen, *Emma*; Scott, *The Antiquary* and *Old Mortality*;
        Peacock, *Headlong Hall*

1817   Habeas Corpus Act suspended; death of Jane Austen

1817   **Coleridge**, *Biographia Literaria* (critical writings); **Byron**,
        Manfred; **Keats**, *Poems*; **Hazlitt**, *The Characters of
        Shakespeare's Plays* (prose criticism); foundation of
        Blackwood's Edinburgh Magazine

1818   Habeas Corpus Act restored

1818   **Austen**, *Northanger Abbey* and *Persuasion*; **Keats**,
        Endymion; **Scott**, *Rob Roy* and *The Heart of Midlothian*;
        Mary **Shelley**, *Frankenstein*; William **Hazlitt**, *Lectures on
        the English Poets*; Susan Edmonstone **Ferrier**, *Marriage*

1819   Peterloo massacre at Manchester (soldiers fire on politi-
        cal meeting)

1819   **Crabbe**, *Tales of the Hall*; Byron, *Don Juan* (1819–24);
        Scott, *The Bride of Lammermoor, Ivanhoe*

1820   Death of George III; accession of George IV

1820   **Shelley**, *Prometheus Unbound*; **Keats**, *Lamia, Isabella, The
        Eve of St Agnes and Other Poems*; John **Clare**, *Poems
        Descriptive of Rural Life*; Charles **Lamb**, *Essays of Elia*;
        Cobbett, *Rural Rides* (essays); Charles Robert **Maturin**,
        Melmoth the Wanderer

1821   Greeks rise against Turks and begin War of
        Independence

1821   **Byron**, *Cain*; **Shelley**, *Adonais*; **Clare**, *The Village
        Minstrel*; Thomas De **Quincey**, *Confessions of an English
        Opium Eater*; John **Galt**, *Annals of the Parish*

1821	**Wordsworth**, *Ecclesiastical Sketches*; **Byron**, *The Vision of Judgement*; **Galt**, *The Entail*
1824	National Gallery opened
1824	Death of Byron in Greece; **Scott**, *Redgauntlet*; James **Hogg**, *Private Memoirs and Confessions of a Justified Sinner*; The *Westminster Review* (periodical) begins
1825	Financial crisis; Trade Unions legalised; opening of Stockton and Darlington Railway (first passenger line)
1825	**Hazlitt**, *The Spirit of the Age* (essays); publication of **Pepys**'s diary
1826	**Opie**, *The Black Man's Lament*
1827	**Clare**, *The Shepherd's Calendar*; John **Keble**, *The Christian Year* (sacred verse)
1828	Test and Corporation Acts repealed (required all crown officers to conform to Anglican Church)
1829	Catholic Emancipation Act in Britain (granting civil rights to Catholics); beginning of police force under Sir Robert Peel
1830	Death of George IV; accession of William IV; opening of Manchester and Liverpool railway
1830	Alfred Lord **Tennyson**, *Poems, Chiefly Lyrical*
1831	Unsuccessful introduction of Reform Bills (to distribute MPs to the centres of population rather than the country); riots in Bristol and elsewhere
1832	Reform Act extends vote to middle classes
1832	Death of Scott; **Tennyson**, *Poems*
1833	Slavery abolished throughout British empire; Keble's Assize sermon (start of the 'Oxford Movement', a Catholic revival within the Church of England); Factory Act in Britain – children under nine not to be employed
1833	Thomas **Carlyle**, *Sartor Resartus* ('the tailor repatched') (1833–4)
1834	Tolpuddle Martyrs – six labourers transported for trying to form a trade union; New Poor Law (workhouse system established); Houses of Parliament destroyed by fire

1835	Municipal Reform Act; photography developed by William Fox Talbot
1835	Robert **Browning**, *Paracelsus*
1836	Beginning of Chartist movement demanding vote for all adult males
1836	Charles **Dickens**, *Sketches by 'Boz'* and the first number of *Pickwick Papers* (1836–7)
1837	Death of William IV; accession of Queen Victoria (subsequently married to Prince Albert of Saxe-Coburg-Gotha); Chartist Movement advocating political rights for working classes excluded from Reform Bill of 1832
1837	**Carlyle**, *History of the French Revolution*; **Dickens**, *Oliver Twist* (1837–8)
1838	'People's Charter' published by William Lovett and Francis Place; London–Birmingham Railway opened
1838	**Dickens**, *Nicholas Nickleby*
1839	Introduction of Penny Post in Britain
1839	**Carlyle**, *Chartism* (political prose work dealing with the 'Condition of England')
1840	Opium War with China; new Houses of Parliament built; People's Charter presented to Parliament
1840	**Dickens**, *The Old Curiosity Shop* and *Barnaby Rudge* (1840–1); **Browning**, *Sordello*
1841	Miners' Association formed
1841	**Carlyle**, *On Heroes and Hero Worship* (lectures); John Henry **Newman**, *Tract XC* (analysis of religious issues); foundation of *Punch*
1842	Chartist riots; second presentation of People's Charter to Parliament; Copyright Act; first use of general anaesthetics for an operation
1842	**Tennyson**, *Poems*; **Browning**, *Dramatic Lyrics*
1843	Theatre monopoly removed from Covent Garden and Drury Lane theatres
1843	Thomas Babington **Macaulay**, *Essays*; **Carlyle**, *Past and Present* (political prose); John **Ruskin**, *Modern Painters* (criticism); **Dickens**, *A Christmas Carol*

1844	Royal Commission on Health in Towns; Morse telegraph used for first time
1844	Benjamin **Disraeli**, *Coningsby*; William Makepeace **Thackeray**, *The Luck of Barry Lyndon*
1845	Famine follows failure of Irish potato crop
1845	**Disraeli**, *Sybil*; **Browning**, *Dramatic Romances and Lyrics*
1846	Repeal of Corn Laws (had protected high price of home-grown corn)
1846	**Dickens**, *Dombey and Son* (1846–8)
1847	Ten Hours Bill limits working hours of women and young people
1847	**Tennyson**, *The Princess*; Charlotte **Brontë**, *Jane Eyre*; Emily **Brontë**, *Wuthering Heights*; Anne **Brontë**, *Agnes Grey*; **Thackeray**, *Vanity Fair* (1847–8)
1848	Chartist demonstration in London; New Public Health Act; foundation of Pre-Raphaelite Brotherhood; Year of Revolutions, with revolutions in France, Germany, Poland, Hungary, and Italy; Second Republic proclaimed in France; Republic in Rome
1848	Karl **Marx** and Friedrich **Engels**, *The Communist Manifesto*; Elizabeth **Gaskell**, *Mary Barton*; Anne **Brontë**, *The Tenant of Wildfell Hall*; **Thackeray**, *Pendennis* (1848–50)
1849	Charlotte **Brontë**, *Shirley*; John **Ruskin**, *The Seven Lamps of Architecture* (criticism); **Macaulay**, *History of England* (1849–50)
1850	'Papal Aggression' (following re-establishment of Roman Catholic hierarchy in England)
1850	**Tennyson**, *In Memoriam AHH*; Thomas **Carlyle**, *Latter-Day Pamphlets*; Elizabeth Barrett **Browning**, *Sonnets from the Portuguese*; Charles **Kingsley**, *Alton Locke*; **Dickens**, *David Copperfield* (1849–50); death of Wordsworth
1851	Great Exhibition; Louis Napoleon overthrows the government in France and makes himself Emperor Napoleon III; Amalgamated Society of Engineers formed
1851	**Gaskell**, *Cranford*; **Ruskin**, *The Stones of Venice* (1851–3) (architectural study)
1852	Death of the Duke of Wellington

1852	**Thackeray**, *The History of Henry Esmond*; Matthew **Arnold**, *Empedocles on Etna*; **Dickens**, *Bleak House* (1852–3)
1853	Charlotte **Brontë**, *Villette*; **Gaskell**, *Ruth*; **Arnold**, *Poems*; **Thackeray**, *The Newcomes* (1853–5)
1854	Crimean War (Britain and allies against Russia); Russia defeated at battles of Alma, Inkerman, and Balaclava (Charge of the Light Brigade); strike of Preston cotton spinners; opening of Working Man's College
1854	**Dickens**, *Hard Times*; **Gaskell**, *North and South* (1854–5)
1855	Fall of Sebastopol; Metropolitan Board of Works established; Stamp Duty on newspapers abolished; Florence Nightingale reforms Army nursing care
1855	**Tennyson**, *Maud*; **Kingsley**, *Westward Ho!*; Robert **Browning**, *Men and Women*; **Trollope**, *The Warden*; **Dickens**, *Little Dorritt* (1855–7)
1856	Treaty of Paris ends Crimean War; Pasteur begins study of bacteriology
1857	Indian Mutiny (local soldiers rebel in Bengal army)
1857	Elizabeth Barrett Browning, *Aurora Leigh*; **Trollope**, *Barchester Towers*; **Gaskell**, *The Life of Charlotte Brontë*; George **Eliot**, *Scenes of Clerical Life*; **Thackeray**, *The Virginians* (1857–9)
1858	End of Indian Mutiny; India transferred from East India Company to British Crown
1858	Arthur Hugh **Clough**, *Amours de Voyage*; **Carlyle**, *Frederick the Great* (biography, 1858–65)
1859	Construction of Suez Canal
1859	**Dickens**, *A Tale of Two Cities*; **Eliot**, *Adam Bede*; George **Meredith**, *The Ordeal of Richard Feverel*; John Stuart **Mill**, *On Liberty* (political treatise); Charles **Darwin**, *The Origin of Species*; **Tennyson**, *The Idylls of the King* (1859–72); Samuel **Smiles**, *Self Help* (political prose on work ethic)
1860	Giuseppe Garibaldi's campaign in Sicily and Naples to free Italy from Austrian control
1860	**Eliot**, *The Mill on the Floss*; Wilkie **Collins**, *The Woman in White*; John **Ruskin**, *Unto This Last*; **Dickens**, *Great Expectations* (1860–1)

1861	Victor Emanuel, King of United Italy; Abraham Lincoln becomes President; start of American Civil War; death of Prince Consort; Post Office bank established
1861	**Eliot**, *Silas Marner*; Anthony **Trollope**, *Framley Parsonage*
1862	Gatling machine gun invented
1862	Henry **Mayhew**, *London Labour and the London Poor* (letters); Christina **Rossetti**, *Goblin Market*; **Meredith**, *Modern Love*; **Eliot**, *Romola* (1862–3); Mary Elizabeth **Braddon**, *Lady Audley's Secret*
1863	'Cotton Famine' in Lancashire; Battle of Gettysburg – Confederate defeat; construction of London Underground begins
1863	**Gaskell**, *Sylvia's Lovers*
1864	Geneva Convention
1864	**Gaskell**, *Wives and Daughters* (1864–6); John Henry **Newman**, *Apologia pro Vita Sua* ('Apologies for his life' – prose defence of spiritual life); **Dickens**, *Our Mutual Friend* (1864–5)
1865	Jamaican rebellion suppressed by Governor Eyre; Lincoln assassinated
1865	**Arnold**, *Essays in Criticism*; Algernon Charles **Swinburne**, *Atalanta in Calydon*; **Carroll**, *Alice in Wonderland*
1866	John Stuart Mill presents first female suffrage petition to Parliament; Austro-Prussian War begins and ends; dynamite invented by Alfred Nobel
1866	**Eliot**, *Felix Holt*; **Swinburne**, *Poems and Ballads*
1867	Second Reform Bill: extends vote to all working-class men in towns; USA buys Alaska from Russia
1867	**Arnold**, *New Poems*; **Trollope**, *The Last Chronicle of Barset*; **Marx**, *Das Kapital* ('Capital': political analysis); Émile **Zola**, *Thérèse Raquin*
1868	**Collins**, *The Moonstone*; **Browning**, *The Ring and the Book* (1868–9); William **Morris**, *The Earthly Paradise* (1868–70)
1869	First Vatican Council; first Trades Union Congress
1869	**Trollope**, *Phineas Finn*; **Mill**, *The Subjection of Women* (political tract); **Arnold**, *Culture and Anarchy* (collection of critical essays)

1870   Married Woman's Property Act; Franco-Prussian War; Education Act sets up school boards to compel attendance at school until thirteen; Kingdom of Italy incorporates Papal States; death of Dickens

1870   **Dickens**, _Edwin Drood_; Dante Gabriel **Rossetti**, _Poems_

1871   Paris Commune set up in opposition to the national government; Britain legalises trade unions; unification of Germany

1871   Edward **Lear**, _The Owl and the Pussy Cat_; **Eliot**, _Middlemarch_ (1871–2); **Zola**, _Les Rougon-Macquart_ (1871–93) (series of naturalistic novels about the Rougon and Macquart families)

1872   Lewis **Carroll**, _Through the Looking-Glass_; Samuel **Butler**, _Erewhon_; Thomas **Hardy**, _Under the Greenwood Tree_

1873   **Arnold**, _Literature and Dogma_ (study of the Bible); **Mill**, _Autobiography_; **Pater**, _Studies in the History of the Renaissance_ (criticism); **Trollope**, _The Way We Live Now_ (1873–4)

1874   **Hardy**, _Far From the Madding Crowd_; **Butler**, _The Way of All Flesh_ (published 1903); **Eliot**, _Daniel Deronda_ (1874–6)

1875   Agricultural Depression

1876   Gerard Manley **Hopkins**, 'The Wreck of the _Deutschland_' (published 1918)

1876   Telephone invented by Alexander Graham Bell

1877   Victoria proclaimed Empress of India by British prime minister Disraeli

1877   **Hopkins**, 'The Windhover' (published 1918)

1878   Congress of Berlin

1878   **Hardy**, _The Return of the Native_

1879   Irish Land League formed by Stewart Parnell

1879   **Meredith**, _The Egoist_

1880   Gladstone, prime minister

1880   **Hardy**, _The Trumpet Major_; George **Gissing**, _Workers in the Dawn_

1881   Death of Disraeli

1881   William Hale **White**, _The Autobiography of Mark Rutherford, Dissenting Minister_; Henry **James**, _The Portrait of a Lady_

1882	Phoenix Park murders in Dublin of government officials
1882	**Hardy**, *Two on a Tower*; Walter **Besant**, *All Sorts and Conditions of Men*
1883	Robert Louis **Stevenson**, *Treasure Island*; George **Moore**, *A Modern Lover*
1884	Reform Bill extends vote to males in rural areas
1884	**Gissing**, *The Unclassed*
1885	Radio waves discovered; fall of Khartoum and death of General Gordon; first successful petrol-driven car invented by Karl Benz
1885	Walter **Pater**, *Marius the Epicurean*; **Meredith**, *Diana of the Crossways*; Rider **Haggard**, *King Solomon's Mines*; **Moore**, *A Mummer's Wife*; **Hopkins**, 'Dark Sonnets' (published 1918)
1886	Home Rule Bill for Ireland defeated; gold discovered in South Africa; Coca-Cola invented
1886	**Moore**, *A Drama in Muslin*; Robert Louis **Stevenson**, *Kidnapped* and *Dr Jekyll and Mr Hyde*; **Gissing**, *Demos*; **James**, *The Bostonians*; **Hardy**, *The Mayor of Casterbridge*
1887	Golden Jubilee of Queen Victoria
1887	**White**, *Revolution in Tanner's Lane*; Conan **Doyle**, first Sherlock Holmes story (in the *Strand Magazine*); **Hardy**, *The Woodlanders*; **Haggard**, *Allan Quatermain*
1888	Rudyard **Kipling**, *Plain Tales from the Hills*; Mrs Humphry **Ward**, *Robert Elsmere*
1889	William Butler **Yeats**, *The Wanderings of Oisin*; **Stevenson**, *The Master of Ballantrae*
1890	Fall of Parnell as leader of Irish Home Rule Party after being named in a divorce case
1890	Oscar **Wilde**, *The Picture of Dorian Gray*; **Kipling**, *Barrack Room Ballads*
1891	**Hardy**, *Tess of the D'Urbervilles*; **Gissing**, *New Grub Street*; **Kipling**, *The Light That Failed*
1892	George Bernard **Shaw**, *Widowers' Houses*; **Yeats**, *The Countess Kathleen*; **Wilde**, *Lady Windermere's Fan*
1893	House of Lords rejects Second Home Rule Bill; Independent Labour Party founded by Keir Hardy

1893	Sir Arthur Wing **Pinero**, *The Second Mrs Tanqueray*; **Shaw**, *Mrs Warren's Profession*; **Gissing**, *The Odd Women*; **Kipling**, *Many Inventions*; **Wilde**, *A Woman of No Importance*
1894	**Ward**, *Marcella*; George **Moore**, *Esther Waters*; **Shaw**, *Arms and the Man*
1895	X-rays discovered by William Roentgen; Sigmund **Freud** publishes first work on psychoanalysis; first public film show by Lumière in Paris
1895	**Wilde**, *The Importance of Being Earnest* and *An Ideal Husband*; Herbert George **Wells**, *The Time Machine*; **Hardy**, *Jude the Obscure*
1896	Wireless telegraphy invented by Marconi
1896	Alfred Edward **Housman**, *A Shropshire Lad*; **Shaw**, *You Never Can Tell*
1897	Victoria's Diamond Jubilee (60 years of rule)
1897	Bram **Stoker**, *Dracula*; **James**, *What Maisie Knew*; **Shaw**, *Candida*; **Wells**, *The Invisible Man*
1898	**Hardy**, *Wessex Poems*; **Bennett**, *A Man from The North*; **Wells**, *The War of the Worlds*
1899	**James**, *The Awkward Age*; **Yeats**, *The Wind Among the Reeds*
1899–1902	Boer War
1900	Relief of Mafeking; Kodak 'Brownie' camera with removable film
1900	**Freud**, *The Interpretation of Dreams*; Joseph **Conrad**, *Lord Jim*
1901	Death of Victoria; accession of Edward VII
1901	**Kipling**, *Kim*
1902	**Bennett**, *Anna of the Five Towns*; **James**, *The Wings of the Dove*; **Conrad**, *Heart of Darkness*; **Yeats**, *Cathleen Ni Houlihan*
1903	Wright brothers make first aeroplane flight; foundation of Women's Social and Political Union (Suffragettes) by Mrs Emmeline Pankhurst
1903	**Butler**, *The Way of All Flesh*; **Gissing**, *The Private Papers of Henry Ryecroft*

1904	Entente cordiale between Britain and France
1904	**Conrad**, *Nostromo*; **Hardy**, *The Dynasts* (1904–8); **James**, *The Golden Bowl*
1905	**Shaw**, *Major Barbara* and *Man and Superman*; **Wells**, *Kipps*; Edward Morgan **Forster**, *Where Angels Fear to Tread*
1906	Election of Liberal government; launch of HMS *Dreadnought* (revolutionary battleship)
1907	Anglo-Russian Entente; Cubist exhibition in Paris
1907	John Millington **Synge**, *The Playboy of the Western World*; **Conrad**, *The Secret Agent*
1908	Old age pensions introduced in Britain; Elgar's first symphony
1908	**Bennett**, *The Old Wives Tale*; **Forster**, *A Room with a View*; Gilbert Keith **Chesterton**, *The Man Who Was Thursday*; **Wells**, *Tono-Bungay*
1909	'People's Budget'; English Channel flown
1909	**Wells**, *Anne Veronica*
1910	Death of Edward VII; accession of George V; first exhibition of Post-Impressionist art in London
1910	**Bennett**, *Clayhanger*; **Forster**, *Howards End*; **Wells**, *The History of Mr Polly*
1911	National Insurance Act; Amundsen reaches South Pole
1911	**Conrad**, *Under Western Eyes*; **Wells**, *The New Machiavelli*; David Herbert **Lawrence**, *The White Peacock*
1912	Second Post-Impressionist Exhibition; Lords reject Home Rule (for Ireland) Bill; sinking of SS *Titanic*; death of Scott in the Antarctic
1913	Second rejection of Home Rule Bill by Lords; Ford introduce the moving assembly line for car production; Stravinsky's *The Rite of Spring* performed in Paris
1913	**Lawrence**, *Sons and Lovers*
1914	Parliament passes Home Rule Bill; Britain declares war on Central Powers (Germany, Austria, Hungary, Turkey)
1914	Percy Wyndham **Lewis**, *Blast*; James **Joyce**, *Dubliners*; **Yeats**, *Responsibilities*; **Hardy**, *Satires of Circumstances*

1915	Second battle of Ypres (Germans use poison gas for first time); sinking by U-Boat of SS *Lusitania* (passenger ship)
1915	Ford Madox **Ford**, *The Good Soldier*; Virginia **Woolf**, *The Voyage Out*; **Lawrence**, *The Rainbow*; Rupert **Brooke**, *1914 and Other Poems*; Dorothy **Richardson**, *Pointed Roofs*
1916	Battle of the Somme; Gallipoli Campaign (in Turkey); Easter Rising in Dublin (April 24)
1916	**Joyce**, *Portrait of the Artist as a Young Man*
1917	Third Battle of Ypres (Passchendaele); T.E. Lawrence's campaigns in Arabia; Revolution in Russia led by Lenin and Trotsky; royal family changes name from House of Saxe-Coburg-Gotha to House of Windsor
1917	Thomas Sterns **Eliot**, *Prufrock and Other Observations*; Wilfred **Owen**, *Poems* (1917–18; published 1920); Siegfried **Sassoon**, war poems published in *The Old Huntsman*
1918	Second battle of the Somme; last major German offensive collapses; Armistice with Germany (11 November); women over 30 get the vote; death of Owen
1918	**Lewis**, *Tarr*; **Hopkins**, *Poems* (written 1876–89, published by Robert Bridges); Lytton **Strachey**, *Eminent Victorians* (biographical essays)
1919	Treaty of Versailles signed by Germans; Atlantic flown; rebellion in Ireland led by Sinn Féin party
1919	Mary **Sinclair**, *Mary Olivier*; **Conrad**, *The Shadow Line*; **Yeats**, *The Wild Swans at Coole*; **Woolf**, *Night and Day*
1920	Civil War in Ireland
1920	**Owen**, *Poems*; **Shaw**, *Heartbreak House*; Roger Eliot **Fry**, *Vision and Design* (collected essays on painting)
1921	Establishment of Irish Free State
1921	Aldous **Huxley**, *Crome Yellow*; **Lawrence**, *Women in Love*; **Yeats**, *Michael Robartes and the Dancer*
1922	Fascist government in Italy, led by Mussolini; USSR established; BBC makes first regular broadcast
1922	**Eliot**, *The Waste Land*; **Joyce**, *Ulysses*; **Lawrence**, *Fantasia of the Unconscious*; **Woolf**, *Jacob's Room*

1923	**Huxley**, *Antic Hay*; **Shaw**, *St Joan*; **Bennett**, *Riceyman Steps*
1924	J. Ramsay MacDonald leads first Labour Government
1924	**Forster**, *A Passage to India*; Sean **O'Casey**, *Juno and the Paycock*; Noël **Coward**, *The Vortex*
1925	**Woolf**, *Mrs Dalloway*; William Alexander **Gerhardie**, *The Polyglots*
1926	General Strike in Britain
1926	Hugh **MacDiarmid**, *A Drunk Man Looks at the Thistle*
1927	First solo flight across the Atlantic
1927	**Woolf**, *To the Lighthouse*
1928	Death of Hardy; **Yeats**, *The Tower*; **Lawrence**, *Lady Chatterley's Lover*; Evelyn **Waugh**, *Decline and Fall*; R. C. **Sherriff**, *Journey's End*; **Woolf**, *Orlando*; **Sassoon**, *Memoirs of a Fox-Hunting Man*
1929	US stock market collapses (Wall Street Crash)
1929	Richard **Aldington**, *Death of a Hero*; Richard Henry **Green**, *Living*; **Woolf**, *A Room of One's Own*; Richard **Hughes**, *A High Wind in Jamaica*
1930	World economic depression
1930	Wystan Hugh **Auden**, *Poems*; **Eliot**, *Ash Wednesday*; **Waugh**, *Vile Bodies*; **Coward**, *Private Lives*
1931	National Government formed; Commonwealth of Nations replaces British Empire
1931	**Woolf**, *The Waves*
1932	**Huxley**, *Brave New World*; Lewis Grassic **Gibbon**, *Sunset Song* (first part of *A Scots Quair*)
1933	Hitler becomes Chancellor of Germany
1933	George **Orwell**, *Down and Out in Paris and London*
1934	**Eliot**, 'Burnt Norton'; **Waugh**, *A Handful of Dust*; Robert **Graves**, *I, Claudius*; Samuel **Beckett**, *More Pricks than Kicks*
1935	George V's Silver Jubilee; persecution of Jews begins in Germany
1935	Christopher **Isherwood**, *Mr Norris Changes Trains* and *Lions and Shadows*; **Auden** and **Isherwood**, *The Dog Beneath the Skin*; **Eliot**, *Murder in the Cathedral*

1936	Death of George V; accession of Edward VIII; abdicates to marry Mrs Wallis Simpson (abdication crisis); accession of George VI; Civil War breaks out in Spain; Keynes publishes economic theory of employment, interest and money
1936	**Auden**, *Look Stranger!*; Terence **Rattigan**, *French Without Tears* (published 1937)
1937	**Auden** and Louis **MacNeice**, *Letters from Iceland*; David **Jones**, *In Parenthesis*; **Orwell**, *The Road to Wigan Pier*; J. R. R. **Tolkien**, *The Hobbit*
1938	Germany annexes Austria Munich agreement; Germany gains part of Czechoslovakia
1938	**Beckett**, *Murphy*; Elizabeth **Bowen**, *The Death of the Heart*; **Orwell**, *Homage to Catalonia*; Graham **Greene**, *Brighton Rock*
1939	End of Civil War in Spain; Russo-German pact; Germany annexes Czechoslovakia and invades Poland; Britain and France declare war on Germany
1939	**MacNeice**, *Autumn Journal*; **Green**, *Party Going*; **Isherwood**, *Goodbye to Berlin*; **Eliot**, *The Family Reunion*; **Joyce**, *Finnegans Wake*
1940	Germany invades Denmark and Norway; fall of France; evacuation of British troops at Dunkirk; beginning of the 'blitz' on London
1940	**Auden**, *New Year Letter*; **Eliot**, 'East Coker'; **Greene**, *The Power and the Glory*; Arthur **Koestler**, *Darkness at Noon*
1941	Germany invades Russia; Japanese attack American Fleet at Pearl Harbor
1941	**Eliot**, 'The Dry Salvages'; **Woolf**, *Between the Acts*; **Coward**, *Blithe Spirit*
1942	Japanese take Singapore; British victory in North Africa at El Alamein; beginning of extermination in concentration camps of Jews, Gypsies and homosexuals by Germany
1942	**Eliot**, 'Little Gidding'

1943	Allied invasion of Italy; Russians defeat German army at Stalingrad
1943	**Eliot**, *Four Quartets*; **Greene**, *The Ministry of Fear*
1944	Allied landings in Normandy ('D Day'); Allies liberate Paris
1944	Joyce **Cary**, *The Horse's Mouth*
1945	Germany surrenders, 7 May; first atomic bomb dropped on Hiroshima, second on Nagasaki; Labour Party wins election
1945	**Green**, *Loving*; **Orwell**, *Animal Farm*; **Waugh**, *Brideshead Revisited*; Philip **Larkin**, *The North Ship*
1946	Nuremberg Trials of Nazi leaders; nationalisation of coal industry; start of National Health Service; War in Indochina
1946	**Larkin**, *Jill*; **Rattigan**, *The Winslow Boy*; Dylan **Thomas**, *Deaths and Entrances*
1947	Independence of India and Pakistan
1947	Ivy **Compton-Burnett**, *Manservant and Maidservant*
1948	USSR blockades Berlin and airlift begins (the 'cold war'); transistors invented
1948	**Greene**, *The Heart of the Matter*; Christopher **Fry**, *The Lady's Not For Burning*; **Rattigan**, *The Browning Version*
1949	NATO formed
1949	Elizabeth **Bowen**, *The Heat of the Day*; **Orwell**, *Nineteen Eighty-Four*; **Eliot**, *The Cocktail Party*
1950	Labour re-elected; Suez Canal crisis; Korean War
1950	**Auden**, *Collected Shorter Poems*; D.J. **Enright**, *Poets of the 1950s* (the 'Movement'); Derek **Walcott**, *Henri Christophe*
1951	Conservatives win General Election; Festival of Britain
1951	Keith **Douglas**, *Collected Poems*; Anthony **Powell**, *A Question of Upbringing* (first volume of *A Dance to the Music of Time*); Doris **Lessing**, *The Grass is Singing*; **Beckett**, *Molloy*; **Walcott**, *Henri Denier*
1952	Death of George VI; accession of Elizabeth II
1952	**Jones**, *Anathemata*; **Rattigan**, *The Deep Blue Sea*; **Beckett**, *Waiting for Godot*; Angus **Wilson**, *Hemlock and After*; **Lessing**, *Martha Quest*; **Waugh**, *Men at Arms*

1953	Dylan **Thomas**, *Collected Poems*
1954	Beginning of Vietnam wars; beginning of Algerian War of Independence
1954	**Rattigan**, *Separate Tables*; **Golding**, *Lord of the Flies*; Kingsley **Amis**, *Lucky Jim*; **Lessing**, *A Proper Marriage*
1955	**Larkin**, *The Less Deceived*; **Golding**, *The Inheritors*; **Beckett**, *Waiting for Godot* (first British performance); **Waugh**, *Officers and Gentlemen*; Patrick **White**, *The Tree of Man*
1956	Egypt nationalises Suez Canal; Britain and France intervene and are obliged to withdraw; Soviet invasion of Hungary
1956	**Golding**, *Pincher Martin*; **Wilson**, *Anglo-Saxon Attitudes*; John **Osborne**, *Look Back in Anger*
1957	CND formed; Treaty of the European Economic Community (EEC)
1957	Ted **Hughes**, *The Hawk in the Rain*; Muriel **Spark**, *The Comforters*; Lawrence **Durrell**, *Justine*; **Osborne**, *The Entertainer*; **Beckett**, *Endgame*; Harold **Pinter**, *The Room*; **White**, *Voss*
1958	USSR launches Sputnik I (start of space race)
1958	Barbara **Pym**, *A Glass of Blessings*; John **Betjeman**, *Collected Poems*; **Pinter**, *The Birthday Party*; Iris **Murdoch**, *The Bell*; Alan **Sillitoe**, *Saturday Night and Sunday Morning*; **Lessing**, *A Ripple From the Storm*; Chinua **Achebe**, *Things Fall Apart*
1959	**Spark**, *Memento Mori*; Arnold **Wesker**, *Roots*; **Golding**, *Free Fall*; John **Arden**, *Serjeant Musgrave's Dance*; T.M. **Aluko**, *One Man, One Wife*
1960	Unexpurgated text of *Lady Chatterley's Lover* published after obscenity trial
1960	**Hughes**, *Lupercal*; **Pinter**, *The Caretaker*; **Beckett**, *Krapp's Last Tape*; **Spark**, *The Ballad of Peckham Rye*; Sylvia **Plath**, *The Colossus*; R.K. **Narayan**, *The Guide*
1961	Yuri Gagarin first person in space
1961	**Beckett**, *Happy Days*; **Osborne**, *Luther*; **Spark**, *The Prime of Miss Jean Brodie*; V.S. **Naipaul**, *A House for Mr Biswas*

1962	National Theatre established; Algeria becomes independent; satellite communications begin
1962	**Wilson**, *Late Call*; **Lessing**, *The Golden Notebook*; Anthony **Burgess**, *A Clockwork Orange*; **Walcott**, *In a Green Night*
1963	John F. Kennedy (US president) assassinated; death of Plath
1963	**Amis**, *One Fat Englishman*; John **Fowles**, *The Collector*; Wole **Soyinka**, *The Lion and the Jewel*
1964	**Orton**, *Entertaining Mr Sloane*; **Larkin**, *The Whitsun Weddings*; **Golding**, *The Spire*; **Osborne**, *Inadmissible Evidence*; **Achebe**, *Arrow of God*
1965	Rhodesia (Zimbabwe) declares independence from Britain
1965	**Rhys**, *Wide Sargasso Sea*; **Orton**, *Loot*; **Pinter**, *The Homecoming*; **West**, *The Birds Fall Down*; Paul **Scott**, *The Jewel in the Crown*; Edward **Bond**, *Saved*; **Walcott**, *The Castaway*; **Lessing**, *Landlocked*; **Plath**, *Ariel*; **Soyinka**, *The Interpreters*
1966	Legalisation of homosexuality and abortion
1966	Tom **Stoppard**, *Rosencrantz and Guildenstern are Dead*; **Achebe**, *A Man of the People*; Elechi **Amadi**, *The Concubine*
1967	First heart transplant operation; Arab–Israeli Six Day War
1967	**Orton**, *The Erpingham Camp*; **Hughes**, *Wodwo*
1968	Assassination of Martin Luther King; assassination of Robert Kennedy (presidential candidate and brother of John F. Kennedy)
1968	Student unrest in Paris; Soviet invasion of Czechoslovakia; the 'Troubles' begin in Northern Ireland
1968	**Stoppard**, *The Real Inspector Hound*; Geoffrey **Hill**, *King Log*
1969	Neil Armstrong first person to walk on moon; abolition of capital punishment; Britain sends troops to Northern Ireland

1969	**Heaney**, *Door into the Dark*; **Orton**, *What the Butler Saw*; **Fowles**, *The French Lieutenant's Woman*; **Lessing**, *The Four-Gated City*; **Amadi**, *The Great Ponds*
1970	Age of majority reduced from 21 to 18; US begins war in Cambodia
1970	**Hughes**, *Crow*; Germaine **Greer**, *The Female Eunuch*; **Walcott**, *The Gulf*
1971	Bangladesh breaks away from Pakistan
1971	**Hill**, *Mercian Hymns*; **Bond**, *Lear*; **Pinter**, *Old Times*; **Spark**, *Not to Disturb*
1972	Britain assumes direct rule in Ulster
1972	Buchi **Emecheta**, *In the Ditch*
1973	United Kingdom joins European Economic Community; US withdraws troops from Vietnam
1973	**Beckett**, *Not I*; **Murdoch**, *The Black Prince*; Howard **Brenton**, *Magnificence*; R. S. **Thomas**, *Selected Poems*; **Walcott**, *Another Life*
1974	Watergate scandal – Richard Nixon forced to resign as US president
1974	**Beckett**, *That Time*; **Spark**, *The Abbess of Crewe*; **Larkin**, *High Windows*; **Stoppard**, *Travesties*
1975	End of Vietnam War; first International Women's Year
1975	**Heaney**, *North*; **Pinter**, *No Man's Land*; Trevor **Griffiths**, *Comedians*; Malcolm **Bradbury**, *The History Man*; Stevie **Smith**, *Collected Poems*; Ruth Prawer **Jhabvala**, *Heat and Dust*
1976	Race riots in South Africa
1976	**Walcott**, *Sea Grapes*; **Emecheta**, *The Bride Price*
1977	**Stoppard**, *Professional Foul*; Margaret **Drabble**, *The Ice Age*; **Pym**, *Quartet in Autumn*
1978	First test-tube baby born
1978	**Pinter**, *Betrayal*; **Murdoch**, *The Sea, The Sea*; Antonia Susan **Byatt**, *The Virgin in the Garden*; **Hill**, *Tenebrae*; **Brenton**, *Romans in Britain*; David **Hare**, *Plenty*; **Amadi**, *The Slave*
1979	Election of Conservative government led by Margaret Thatcher, first woman prime minister; Polish Solidarity

movement heralds end of Communism; first direct elections to European Parliament; John Lennon murdered in New York

1979   **Golding**, *Darkness Visible*; **Heaney**, *Field Work*

1980   Iran–Iraq war begins

1980   **Golding**, *Rites of Passage*; **Burgess**, *Earthly Powers*; Brian **Friel**, *Translations*

1981   Inner-city riots (Bristol, Liverpool)

1981   Salman **Rushdie**, *Midnight's Children*

1982   Falklands war against Argentina

1982   Caryl **Churchill**, *Top Girls*

1983   Thatcher government re-elected

1983   Graham **Swift**, *Waterland*

1984   Brighton bombing – IRA attempts mass assassination of government ministers; miners' strike

1984   **Heaney**, *Station Island*; Angela **Carter**, *Nights at the Circus*; Martin **Amis**, *Money*

1985   Famine in Africa: Live Aid concert across the world

1985   **Hare** and **Brenton**, *Pravda*; Peter **Ackroyd**, *Hawksmoor*; Jeanette **Winterson**, *Oranges Are Not the Only Fruit*; Caryl **Phillips**, *The Final Passage*

1986   IRA attacks multiply; nuclear disaster at Chernobyl

1986   **Walcott**, *Collected Poems*; **Phillips**, *Independence*; Festus **Iyayi**, *Heroes*

1987   Thatcher government elected for third term of office; Gorbachev in Russia extends policy of glasnost (openness)

1987   **Ackroyd**, *Chatterton*; **Churchill**, *Serious Money*; David **Edgar**, *That Summer*

1988   Lockerbie bomb jet disaster; Iran–Iraq war ends

1988   **Pinter**, *Mountain Language*; **Stoppard**, *Hapgood*; **Rushdie**, *The Satanic Verses*

1989   Overthrow of Communist regimes in Eastern Europe; fall of the Berlin Wall

1989   Martin **Amis**, *London Fields*; Kazuo **Ishiguro**, *Remains of the Day*; **Walcott**, *Omeros*

1990   Anti-poll tax riots in London; fall of Margaret Thatcher; Mary Robinson first female president in Ireland

1990	**Friel**, *Dancing at Lughnasa*; **Byatt**, *Possession*; Hanif **Kureishi**, *Buddha of Suburbia*
1991	USSR dissolved
1991	**Carter**, *Wise Children*
1992	Conservative government re-elected under John Major; Czechoslovakia partitioned
1992	Michael **Ondaatje**, *The English Patient*; **Phillips**, *Crossing the River*
1993	IRA bomb at Warrington; EEC becomes the European Union (EU); genetic cloning of a sheep
1993	Vikram **Seth**, *A Suitable Boy*; Barry **Unsworth**, *Sacred Hunger*
1994	Nelson Mandela becomes president of South Africa; IRA cease-fire declared
1994	Carol Ann **Duffy**, *Selected Poems*
1995	Microsoft launches global operating system
1995	James **Kelman**, *How Late It Was, How Late*
1996	BSE scandal; Prince Charles and Princess Diana divorce
1997	Princess Diana killed in car crash in Paris; death of Mother Teresa; Labour win landslide victory
1997	Arundhati **Roy**, *The God of Small Things*
1998	General Pinochet arrested in London
1999	Armed strife in Albania; Euro currency introduced; parliaments for Scotland and Wales
1999	Seamus **Heaney**, *Beowulf*
2000	Millennium celebrations world-wide; petrol tax strike in Britain; widespread flooding as a result of global warming; age of homosexual consent lowered to 16; Stock Exchange collapse of dot.com companies
2000	Peter **Ackroyd**, *London*; **Heaney**, *The Midnight Verdict*
2001	Labour re-elected for second term; terrorist attacks on World Trade Centre in New York and the Pentagon in Washington provoke US-led military action in Afghanistan.

Further Reading

In compiling this list we have sought to include books which are likely to appeal to readers interested in the interaction of literature, history and criticism. The list is deliberately brief. The intention is to point in the direction of works that seem particularly helpful or thought-provoking; the books themselves will, of course, provide ideas about where to turn next.

Aers, David, *Chaucer, Langland and the Creative Imagination* (London: Routledge, 1979).

Ashcroft, Bill, Griffiths, Gareth and Tiffin, Helen, *The Empire Writes Back: Theory and Practice in Post-Colonial Literature* (London: Routledge, 1989).

Barrell, John, *Poetry, Language and Politics* (Manchester: Manchester University Press, 1988).

Beer, Gillian, *Darwin's Plots: Evolutionary Narrative in Darwin, George Eliot and Nineteenth-Century Fiction* (London: Routledge and Kegan Paul, 1983).

Belsey, Catherine, *Critical Practice* (London and New York: Routledge, 1980).

Bennett, Andrew and Royle, Nicholas, *Introduction to Literature, Criticism and Theory* (London: Prentice Hall, 1999).

Boehmer, Elleke, *Colonial and Postcolonial Literature* (Oxford: Oxford University Press, 1995).

Brown, Peter (ed.), *A Companion to Chaucer* (Oxford: Blackwell, 2000).

Butler, Marilyn, *Romantics, Rebels and Reactionaries* (Oxford: Oxford University Press, 1981).

Callaghan, Dympna (ed.), *A Feminist Companion to Shakespeare* (Oxford: Blackwell, 2000).

Connor, Steven, *Postmodernist Culture* (Oxford: Blackwell, 1996).

Corcoran, Neil, *English Poetry since 1940* (London: Longman, 1993).

Cox, John D. and Kastan, David Scott (eds), *A New History of English Drama* (New York: Columbia University Press, 1997).

Culler, Jonathan, *Literary Theory: A Very Short Introduction* (Oxford: Oxford University Press, 1997).

Eagleton, Terry, *Myths of Power: A Marxist Study of the Brontës* (Basingstoke: Macmillan, 1975, 2nd edn, 1987).

Fussell, Paul, *The Great War and Modern Memory* (Oxford: Oxford University Press, 1975).

Gilbert, Sandra M. and Gubar, Susan, *The Madwoman in the Attic: The Woman Writer and the Nineteenth-Century Imagination* (New Haven, CT: Yale University Press, 1979).

Greenblatt, Stephen, *Renaissance Self-Fashioning* (Chicago: Chicago University Press, 1980).

Richetti, John (ed.), *The Columbia History of the British Novel* (New York: Columbia University Press, 1994).

Rogers, Pat, *Literature and Popular Culture in Eighteenth-Century England* (Brighton: Harvester, 1985).

Ryan, Kiernan, *Shakespeare*, 3rd edn (Basingstoke: Palgrave, 2001).

Rylance, Rick, and Simons, Judy (eds), *Literature in Context* (Basingstoke: Palgrave, 2001).

Showalter, Elaine, *A Literature of their Own: British Women Writers from Brontë to Lessing* (Princeton, NJ: Princeton University Press, 1977).

Sinfield, Alan, *Faultlines: Cultural Materialism and the Politics of Dissident Reading* (Oxford: Oxford University Press, 1992).

Trotter, David, *The English Novel in History, 1895–1920* (London: Routledge, 1993).

Waugh, Patricia (ed.), *Revolutions of the Word: Intellectual Contexts for the Study of Modern Literature* (London: Arnold, 1997).

Widdowson, Peter, *Hardy in History: A Study in Literary Sociology* (London: Routledge, 1989).

Williams, Raymond, *The English Novel from Dickens to Lawrence* (London: Chatto & Windus, 1970).

Index